WISE Guide
for Spelling

W	ords,
I	nstructions, &
S	pelling
E	nrichments

by Wanda Sanseri

Published by

Back Home Industries
P.O. Box 22495
Milwaukie, OR 97269

Published in the United States of America

Library of Congress Catalog Card Number: 99-97631

old ISBN 1-880045-21-4
new ISBN 978-1880045-21-3

Dedication

The Wise Guide is dedicated to my only brother, Denny Wise, who gave me a love for language. His fascination with words was contagious. I am pleased not only to honor him but also to acknowledge the special heritage in my maiden name, Wanda Wise.

Appreciation

Without my husband, Gary, and my home-educated sons, Samuel, Daniel, and Michael, this project would have never been completed. My motherly love for my sons led me to seek a better way to teach language arts. My husband's support kept me going when I might have given up. I appreciate their patience when supper was late or the furniture undusted because I needed to finish my train of thought in writing this book. Without the many students attending my seminars I would not have continued to develop these materials after my now-adult sons moved on to other things. Teaching is a wonderful stimulation to mastering a subject.

Two students planted early seeds of the vision for this book. Years ago Karen Davidson spent hours showing me the value of computer work in sorting files like word lists. She encouraged me to number the words. Gloria Milmont shared the N-Abel's list developed by the Nebraska State Department of Education. This planted the seed idea for me to upgrade the Ayres List with additional, more modern research.

I am indebted to my team of *Spell to Write and Read* trainers as well as program users who gave me practical support, editorial help, and creative suggestions. Lois Dillman, Jean Evans, Elizabeth FitzGerald, Jeannean Kintner, and Mary Tanksley have been especially helpful. I value the artwork by Kelly Cracksberger. I also appreciate the editing help from Rhonda Bedee, Sherine Forest, LaNeal Miller, Samuel Sanseri, Lori Ann Sparks, Lori Sekol, and Jennifer Tarantello. I particularly want to thank the students in the Extended seminar hosted by Jean Evans in Pennsylvania years ago as I started this project and the Extended seminar in Oregon and Texas in 1999 when I field-tested it.

I am grateful for the students from Veritas Christian School in Newberg and the Tuesday School co-op scholars at Berean Bible Fellowship in Portland which included: Anna Alcala, Kelly Arnich, Nathan and Jonathan Barton, Thad Donaghue, Rachel Farrand, Paul and Marilee Janzen, Jonathan Johnson, Karina Casperian, Heather Peters, Katherine Peters, and Jarrett and Marith Williams.

Monica Beebe, Claudia Cordray, and the teachers at the Oakbrook Elementary School in Charleston, South Carolina, helped guide and stimulate me as we joined hands to help create a stronger product for both public and private school use.

My prayer for this work was expressed well by Frank Irish a century ago when he wrote the following in the preface to his book, *Fundamentals of the English Language:*

> *Humbly believing that the cheerful toil and sacrifice given to the preparation of this book*
> *may lead many to a greater love and a more perfect mastery of the English language,*
> *the author trustfully commits it to a citizenship in the great commonwealth of letters.*

Materials Required to Teach this Language Arts Program

Spell to Write and Read (the replacement for *Teaching Reading at Home & School*)
    -- the teacher's overall guide to the entire program

Wise Guide for Spelling -- spelling words and reinforcement activities

70 Basic Phonogram Cards

Phonogram CD

Spelling Rule Cards

Student Spelling Notebooks (select type below)
    Black Log -- regular lined notebook paper (3rd grade+)
    Primary Learning Log -- paper approximately 9/16" lines with dotted half lines for K-2nd
        Blank reference pages are formatted in the back of the Primary Log.

Optional Materials that Will Be Helpful

ABC's and All Their Tricks -- A reference guide for answering questions about phonics.
13.81 Amazon

Alpha List -- An alphabetical listing of the Wise List (the words in *Wise Guide*). Each word is marked with spelling markings and cross-referenced by word number to *Wise Guide,* with special notes, possible derivatives, and rules.

Beginning Readers -- *Play by the Sea, Let's Play, "I See."*

Clock Stamp -- A rubber stamp to help teach penmanship strokes as well as telling time.

Grammar Readers -- *I Can Run!, Up, Over and Out.*

McCall-Crabb Test Lessons in Reading Books A-E (with original copyright date of 1926).
$10.95 Amazon

The New England Primer of 1777 -- A classic beginning reader used by the founders of our country.

Suggested Book List -- A list of suggested books the Sanseri family enjoyed.

SWR Companion CDs (set of six) *for Review and Mastery.*

Other items -- Check catalog for grammar helps, aids for teaching composition, plus reading books for all ages.

All these products are available from BHI. To check current prices or make on line orders visit our web site *http://www.BHIbooks.net.*

Introduction

What does The Wise Guide Contain?

WORDS. We use 2000 core words (plus derivatives) to teach the foundational principles of English. The Wise List expands the Ayres List (1915) to include later research such as the N-Ables List, and the American Heritage Word Frequency List. We draw from the scientific work of Margaret Bishop, Dr. Edward Fry, Dr. Paul Hanna, Dr. Samuel Orton, Edward Thorndike, and my personal teacher, Romalda Spalding. The Wise List includes the 1000 most frequently used words and many commonly misspelled words. This guide divides the words into lots of twenty, organized by spelling difficulty levels labeled as Section A to Section Z. Every twenty spelling words has two pages of lesson plan ideas.

INSTRUCTIONS. Information is given for teaching each set of twenty spelling words.

<u>Preliminaries</u>. Warmup activities and teasers for introducing the lesson are at the top of the two pages. A fast-paced review of specific phonograms and spelling rules may be suggested. Notes to teach or review specific spelling reference pages are provided with links to *Spell to Write and Read* for the instructions.

<u>Sentences</u>. The left-hand page illustrates each word in a sample sentence. Selections come from literature (R. L. Stevenson, Shakespeare), history (Washington, Lincoln, Churchill), or instructive comments *(Doing is better than saying)*. You can substitute your own sentence instead.

<u>Spelling Rules</u>. The right-hand page repeats the word, divides it into syllables and marks it with our special spelling markings. All rules that apply are listed by rule number for teacher convenience. Helpful hints are given for learning to spell the word. The format is as follows:

---

1. When a letter or a word is given between two slashes // as in /ph/, it means to think it by sound /f/, not letter names (P-H).

2. A long vowel is indicated by a capital letter as in /A/. A short vowel sound is indicated by a lower case letter as in /a/.

3. Foreign language derivations are indicated in the following format:
Example: **accuse** [<L ad- (to) + causa (cause)].

[ ]	sets off foreign language information
<	means derived from
L	an abbreviation for Latin
ad-, causa	Latin words or word parts
( )	sets off English meaning
+	added to

Abbreviations for Foreign Languages:

<F -- French	<Gk -- Greek	<OE -- Old English
<G -- German	<L -- Latin	<OF -- Old French
<GB -- Great Britain	<ME -- Middle English	<Sp -- Spanish

SPELLING **E**NRICHMENTS. At the bottom of the page, a number of spelling reinforcement activities are recommended.   With traditional spelling, the student writes each word five or ten times. Such a passive activity is boring busy work. Why not encourage the student to write the words in a way that not only helps practice spelling the word correctly, but teaches something else at the same time? Our reinforcement activities help cement the spelling words in the child's mind while simultaneously enriching other facets of language arts. A number of activities are listed so the teacher can pick and choose.

Spelling is the backbone to all writing and reading but is often neglected in beginning language arts instruction. We use spelling to teach penmanship, composition, grammar, literature, creativity and vocabulary enrichment.   This time-efficient method unifies language arts and adds interest to spelling instruction.

Why is Spelling so Important?

If you can phonetically spell well, you will be a good reader; however, you may learn to read without ever learning to spell well. Spelling is the more precise skill. To spell you must produce a word from your head to paper. Reading requires merely recognizing what is already on the paper. The difference between spelling and reading is analogus to taking a fill-in-the-blank test in contrast to a multiple choice test.

Strong spelling skill is desirable for a number of reasons. It helps:

1. **Improve communication**. Misspelled words jump off a page and distract the reader from following the writer's train of thought. Words spelled incorrectly may make your message hazy or unclear. I read once about a man with "aints in his paints." What did the writer intend to say? Was he trying to say the the man was unclothed (He ain't in his pants), that he had insects in his paints, or ants in his pants? Accuracy in spelling enhances communication.

2. **Increase credibility**.   When you cannot express ideas clearly and accurately, your knowledge of those ideas comes into question. Is your viewpoint reliable?   Poor spellers lose respect.

3. **Aid accurate speech**.   When you can think to spell a word, you can more likely say it correctly. For example, you are less likely to say "liberry" for "library." Correct, phonetically-based spelling helps eliminate confusion with pronunciation.

4. **Encourage precise thought**. A student's intellectual development can be linked to a student's ability to spell. A good written vocabulary facilitates logical, accurate thinking. A weak spelling vocabulary hinders sequential reasoning.

5. **Guard against learning disabilities**. We dictate words which the student builds by sound as he moves from left to right through the word. Words taught as a visual whole can be more easily scrambled in a student's brain.   Learning disabilities have escalated since teachers changed to focus on reading first with spelling presented as an afterthought.   The National Advisory Council on Adult Literacy reviewed over 124 different studies which all demonstrated the superiority of phonics-first instruction as a way of assuring success for all students.

6. **Stimulate faster, more accurate comprehension**. In the early days of this country when we had high literacy, the student learned to spell his way into reading.   The student learned to analyze letters in words on the spelling level so the mind would be freed up for comprehension of sentences in reading.   A strong speller tends to read faster with higher understanding.

7. **Build a foundation to all academic subjects.** The ideal beginning place for formal instruction in written language is with an understanding of the sound/symbol system as used in spelling. We first train students to sound out spelling words and to reproduce them on paper from their heads (without copying). Reading naturally develops in a child who has been trained to sound out words rapidly. An effective reader can decipher words at a glance and comprehend thoughts in sentences. By training students in spelling before expecting reading skills, we tend to help our students be more proficient in both reading and writing. The most important book for a person to read and study is the Holy Bible, a book that consistently points to Christ, "in whom are hid **all the treasures of wisdom and knowledge**" (Col. 2:3).

Written language is a gift God gave to humans. No other life form can write or read thoughts.

Throughout the Bible one can find many references to writing and reading.

Deuteronomy 17:18-19. *And it shall be, when he sitteth upon the throne... that he shall **write** him a copy of this law in a book... and he shall **read** therein all the days of his life.*

Nehemiah 8:8. S*o they **read** in the book in the law of God distinctly, and gave the sense, and caused them to understand the reading.*

Acts 8:30. *And Philip ran thither to him, and heard him **read** the prophet Isaiah, and said, 'Understandest thou what thou readest?'*

Acts 17:11. *These were more noble than those in Thessalonica, in that they received the word with all readiness of mind, and **searched the Scriptures** daily, whether those things were so.*

Jesus presupposed that people learn to read the Scriptures.

Matthew 12:3, 5; 19:4 *...have ye not **read**....*

Matthew 21:16. *...have ye never **read,** 'Out of the mouth of babes and sucklings thou hast perfected praise'* (Psalm 8:2).

Matthew 21:42. *Jesus saith unto them, 'Did ye never **read** in the Scriptures...?'*

Luke 10:26. *He said unto him, 'What is written in the law? ... How **readest** thou?'*

John 5:39. **Search the scriptures;** *for in them ye think ye have eternal life: and they are they which testify of me.*

8. **Free the mind for higher order thinking skills**. A good speller does not need to interrupt his train of thought when transcribing thoughts. He can write as naturally and fluidly as he can speak. Instead of teaching true spelling, many educators today use "inventive spelling." In personal journals or rough drafts students write words any way they can quickly.

Unfortunately, early disregard for correct spelling produces long-term problems. Wouldn't it be better to give a student strong spelling skills as a foundation to other learning? A strong speller can focus energy on the message he wants to communicate. Careful training at a young age produces long term dividends.

9. **Help a dyslexic student overcome this handicap**. Research by Berninger, Nielsen, and others reports in the <u>Journal of School Psychology</u> 46 (2008) that, "writing problems in developmental dyslexia is under-recognized and under-treated." They conclude, "An appropriate education for students with dyslexia includes explicit, systematic instruction for both writing and reading.... Such instruction should focus on spelling."

10. **Provide what a spell-checker can never do**. Contrary to popular opinions, computer spell-checkers cannot substitute for good spelling skills. They help someone with good general spelling skills to self-monitor typos in his work. Spell-checkers do not generate proper spelling for someone who cannot produce a close proximity to the desired written word or recognize that it is indeed the intended word.

The following poem by an unknown author demonstrates why "wee joust can knot real eye two much on spell Czech."

Spell Checker

Eye halve a spelling checker,
It came with my pea sea.
It plainly marks four my revue
Miss steaks eye kin knot sea.

Eye strike a key and type a word
And weight four it two say
Weather eye am wrong oar write
It shows me strait a weigh.

As soon as a mist ache is maid
It nose bee fore two long
And eye can put the error rite
Its rare lea ever wrong.

Eye have run this poem threw it,
I am shore your pleased two no,
Its letter perfect awl the weigh,
My checker tolled me sew.
                    --sauce unknown

<u>Why Does a Teacher Need the *SWR Manual*</u>?

Wise Guide **is not designed as a stand-alone book!** It provides an actual spelling list and specific suggestions for teaching the individual words. Call it the nuts and bolts of the program. *Spell to Write and Read*, the general teacher's guide, provides the global view. *SWR* explains why we do what we do. It sets the stage for teaching, provides the diagnostic tools for placing students in the program and monitoring their success, gives a detailed explanation of our spelling dictation techniques, relays how to introduce each specific reference page, and shows how to adapt a reference page to increasingly difficult levels.

New teachers to the program want to combine these two books. The beauty of keeping the general overall guide separate becomes apparent as you progress. It provides one compact set of materials for teaching a span of spelling levels from K-12. The steps that keep repeating at the various levels can be discussed in one central place. The teacher can see the full scope of a rule. Advanced considerations generally omitted at the beginner level are easy to find if your beginner asks hard questions.

How Can We Build Long-Term Spelling Memory?

1. **Introduce new words in a way that promotes better retention**. Spelling is primarily an auditory skill, but several obstacles make it challenging to just sound out words. First, we have more than one way to spell many sounds. To address this issue, we teach students the 70 basic phonograms and the rules that govern them. Next, in the natural flow of speech some sounds are not distinct. We exaggerate the sound to match the standard spelling. The teacher says each new word normally and then the way we need to "think-to-spell" it for accurate spelling.   See a dictation guide on the inside back cover.

Simultaneous multi-sensory dictation is explained in Step 12 of SWR. The student hears a new word, repeats it, and with teacher guidance writes it correctly BEFORE seeing it. Then together they analyze the word and mark it to highlight specific spelling rules. Learners remember best what they not only hear, say, write, and see, but also what they can logically explain.

2. **Establish long-term memory with repetition and use**. Many students can memorize words for a spelling test, but our goal is long-term mastery which comes with time and practice. Retention of proper spelling is enhanced if the student uses the spelling words to write original sentences or uses the words in various other ways. The goal is to make the process more enjoyable and profitable than a boring activity like copying a word over and over. Instead the student practices using the spelling words while at the same time learning something else of value.

Generic ways to reinforce words are described in *Spell to Write and Read* Step 13 and on *Wise Guide* pages 8, 16, 52, and 146. Specific activities tailored to each lesson are included with each list of twenty words. These *Spelling Enrichments* combine spelling with other language arts activities. The student may make words plural, add derivatives, practice grammar concepts, alphabetize the words, study word analogies, draw and label words, and practice creative writing tips. One happy teacher wrote, "For the first time in years I enjoy teaching spelling. The *SWR* program is effective and helpful."

How Does SWR Spelling Dictation Process Work?

SWR covers spelling dictation extensively in Step 12. Some educators make the grave mistake of buying only *Wise Guide*. They can tell that it holds an exceptional list of words. They proceed to teach it following the unsuccessful methods that their teachers used on them. To get the full dynamic of the program, you need to follow the spelling dictation pattern carefully. The goal is to actively involve the student in the whole mental process. You want to teach him for a lifetime.

CLARIFYING THE PROCESS

1. **Train students to think.   Dictation should not be copied**.   The student does not just copy a word that the teacher shows him! The student should write the word from HEARING guided dictation. The student does not see the word until AFTER he has written it. This is a crucial part of our procedure, especially for dyslexic students. It trains the brain in multi-faceted ways. Copying does not engage the mind in a way that matches the spelling process. Spelling in real life is not a sight-first activity. It needs to come from the head to the paper. If a student just copies, the visual student is not stretched in a way that strengthens the other language learning centers of the brain. A significant number of students have a weakness in visual learning activities. They may learn best by hearing, saying, or writing.   If we teach in a manner that employs these four senses together, we will teach to every student's strength. At the same time we will remediate each student's weakness.

2. **Elicit the sounds one by one from the student**. The goal is to have the student learn to hear a word and break it into the correct parts. The teacher may need to help initially with the ungluing aspect of dictation. With young beginners or with potentially troublesome words, she may need to break a word apart. Once a child has captured how to segment sounds, it is best for the student to do so with as little help as possible. Irregular words may need extra guidance.

3. **Focus on the sound each phonogram uses in the word**. When teaching spelling, the teacher does not just dictate a list of phonograms with all their sounds. To spell "man" the student needs to think the three sounds that build that word: /m-a-n/. He does not think the word as /m/-/a-A-ah/-/n/.

4. **Establish the foundation for good legible penmanship as early as possible**. Use big motor skills for the preschool learner or someone with motor delays. Physically shaping a phonogram while repeating the sound or sounds is a more dynamic activity than moving around letter magnets or tiles.

5. **Expect accountability only for something you have taught**. When you dictate a new word that has more than one way to spell a sound, indicate which phonogram to use in the following ways.

    a. Show by Fingergrams. We have a number of ways to spell the sound /O/. If I dictate "no," the student will sound out /n/, I will hold up one finger, meaning that it takes one letter to make that sound. The student will say /O/ and I will hold up another finger. The single finger for /O/ clarifies the spelling. We have only one single letter that spells /O/.

    b. Clarify with Phonogram Language. If I am dictating "snow," when the student says /O/, I will hold up two fingers held together. It takes two letters to represent that sound. I will clarify which 2-letter phonogram to use since more than one 2-letter phonogram can spell that sound. I will use the same language we use when we practice that phonogram. "Use /ow-O/." The student then sounds out the word to write it: /s-n-ow/. We put a 2 over the /O/ because it is the second sound.

6. **Streamline teacher dialog**. When possible, replace verbal clues with action clues. For example, when ready for the student to dictate a word back, a teacher can put her chalk to the board in a ready position and look at the child expectantly. This can be her signal for the child to start dictating the word to her. If she does this action consistently, she can eliminate saying repeatedly, "Dictate the word back to me."

7. **Add markings only after the student has written the whole word and double-checked his spelling against the teacher's**. Spelling markings are discussed only after the student has dictated the word to the teacher and double-checked his spelling.

8. **Coach the student to analyze the new word and explain how to mark it and why**. When a type of marking is new, the teacher will explain it. When a student forgets a marking, she will help him. In time she wants him to be able to see a new word and explain how and why to mark it without any help on her part. The goal is for the student to identify patterns in a word independently.

9. **Wean yourself as much as possible from routine verbiage and prompts**. If he is wrong, this gives the chance to correct his thinking before he writes in his book. The teacher points to each syllable when analyzing the word. The student either says "no," (meaning "no marking") or he will give directions on what and how to mark.

SAMPLE DICTATION WITH A ONE-SYLLABLE WORD

Student, with pencil down, looks and listens attentively to the teacher.

Teacher: "School -- I go to school at home -- school."

"How many syllables?" (Have the student figure this out for himself. Beginning readers may need some help initially, but wean them as quickly as possible.)

Teacher: "Think-to-spell /s-k-OO-l/. Help me sound it out."

Student says /s/. Teacher holds up right pinky finger (palm facing student).
Student says /k/. Teacher puts up 2 fingers (ring and middle fingers together).
Student says /OO/. Teacher puts up 2 fingers (pointer and thumb together).
Student says /l/. Teacher brings over her left thumb. (This is a six-letter syllable. We need to "borrow" a finger from the other hand to complete the syllable.)

Teacher: Points to the 2 fingers representing /k/ and uses the phonogram language for CH. "Use /ch-k-sh/." Then she points to the next 2 fingers, and says, "Use /OO-oo-O/."

Repeat the word the way we think it.

Student: "We think /s-k-OO-l/." He picks up his pencil and softly says to himself the sounds in the word as he writes it. (When he writes /k/, he only says /k/, not /ch-k-sh/.)

When he sees the teacher at the board with chalk ready, he dictates to the teacher. He says the word, "school." Then he dictates it sound by sound. "/s-k-OO-l/". She writes on the board each sound as he says it and gives him time to check his word. When he has finished proofreading, she puts her chalk at the beginning of the word and waits for him to tell her how to mark the word. She helps him only if necessary.

The correct student response would be to say, "Underline /k/ and put a 2 over it. It is a two-letter phonogram that makes the 2nd sound. Underline /OO/. It is a 2-letter phonogram." In the training process, prompts from the teacher may be needed.

SAMPLE DICTATION WITH A MULTI-SYLLABLE WORD

Teacher: "*Elephant* – We saw the *elephant* in the zoo. -- *elephant*. How many syllables?"

Student: "Three."

Teacher: "Think /el-E-fant/." (Over emphasize the unstressed vowel sound. Student needs to hear /a/ in /fant/.) "Sound it out." (Encourage the student to do this on his own as much as possible. His voice will drive the teacher's fingers.)

Student: (Says first syllable.) "/el/". (Then he says each sound.) "/e-l/."
(This syllable has two sounds and two single letters.)

(Says the second syllable.) "/E/." (The teacher demonstrates the syllable shift in some way. I prefer switching hands. Some teachers, with my blessing, use the same hand the whole time, but bring the fist over to the chest between syllables.)

(Says third syllable.) "/fant/." (When the student says /f/, the teacher holds up 2 fingers stuck together. This helps alert the student to use "two-letter /f/.")

Repeat the word.

Student: "Elephant" (as in normal speech); "/el-E-fant/" (as we think-to-spell.)

The student picks up his pencil and writes, "elephant." He should whisper the sounds softly to himself as he writes. He skips a space between the syllables.

Student: (Reads the word he has written.) "elephant." (Dictates it for the teacher to write on the board. He says each syllable first. Then he gives the sounds that make up the syllable. "El (e-l), E (E), fant (f-a-n-t)."

The student double-checks to see if he spelled the word correctly. If not, he erases the entire word and rebuilds it correctly, whispering the sounds as he goes.

Teacher: "Markings?" (The markings should be done sequentially in the word.)

Student: "Underline the phonogram that said /E/. E said /E/ at the end of a syllable."

Teacher: (Nods approval. Both mark their word.) Teacher may say, "Prove it to me." The student can recite the full spelling rule. "A, E, O, U usually say /A-E-O-U/ at the end of a syllable."

Review the word together. "Think /el-E-fant/." (The vowel in the unstressed syllable is muffled. Exaggerate it to match the actual spelling.) "Say, *elephant*."

SPELLING SECTIONS
A through C

Students should build their own "text book." *Wise Guide* is the teacher's reference aid for overseeing the process. The spelling words in this program should be dictated for students to write sight unseen into a Primary Learning Log (a book designed for student use by BHI), or a Black Log (a blank nonspiral notebook that can be purchased from some office supply stores or from BHI).

Notice the way the words are organized. Each set of twenty words should be taught ten words per column. In *Wise Guide* a horizontal line is drawn between the first ten and the second ten words as a reminder to start a new column in the student notebook. The words have been organized so that when a student reads his spelling book, often the words across from each other are related in some way. Seeing these connections adds interest to the practice of reading the words and helps spark the composition of original sentences.

The teacher must make her own Learning Log for optimum success in teaching *Wise Guide.* The instructor needs a general idea of the entire program before she specializes in the year she is teaching. The act of building a teacher's master book will help familiarize the educator with the overall program. Don't just pick up *Wise Guide* cold turkey in class and start teaching. Be prepared!

Follow these steps in planning for each lesson.

    1. Review the preliminary activities and gather any necessary material.

    2. Read all the information about the twenty words and build a model page in your master book. Flag any of the sample sentences you particularly like. Compose alternative sentences if you prefer.

    3. Practice pronunciation of the spelling words. Exaggerate each syllable for "thinking to spell" and then in the natural rhythm of speech. Step 12 in SWR explains this concept in depth including detailed dictation of all the words in Section A.

    4. Check your understanding of the rules or concepts to be taught. Be prepared to answer questions. Rule numbers are given in *Wise Guide,* but each [R#] notation is intended for the teacher. The students should learn the concept rather than the rule number. If need be, refer to the the summary of spelling markings (p. 238), the list of the spelling rules (p.239), or the list of phonograms and their sounds (p. 240).

    5. Select reinforcement activities or design original ones. Enjoy!

Preliminaries. Before teaching these words, cover steps 1-11 in *Spell to Write and Read*.
Phonograms: Introduce *sh, th, oo, ee, er*. Reference Page: Add all except *er* to the **Multi-letter Phonogram Page** (SWR Step 10). Advance exposure to phonograms will help prepare the student for future sections.

Words for Section A (See SWR Step 12 for clarification of spelling dictation process.)

1	top	Start from the *top* and count the words.
2	but	You can do that *but* be careful.
3	and	Christ is all, *and* in all. -- Colossians 3:11
4	cat	A *cat* can eat a rat. --Webster's *Bluebacked Speller*
5	red	The sky is *red*.
6	six	Abraham Lincoln read the Bible through *six* times during his youth.
7	all	God is with me at *all* times. *--McGuffey Primer*
8	my	*My* mother teaches me good things.
9	not	Do *not* withhold good. --Proverbs 3:27
10	ten	A dime is worth *ten* cents. A shilling is worth *ten* pence.
11	hat	Abraham Lincoln removed his top *hat* to pray.
12	be	If you walk with wise men you will *be* wise. --Proverbs 13:20
13	am	He is ten and I *am* six.
14	is	The cat *is* purring.
15	bed	My *bed* is a little boat. --Robert Louis Stevenson. See SWR Step 14, p. 96.
16	run	All rivers *run* into the sea, and yet the sea is not full. --Ecclesiastes 1:7
17	ran	All six boys *ran* up a hill.
18	go	You can *go* play after lunch.
19	do	I cannot what I will not *do*. -- Shakespeare
20	did	Today, I do; yesterday, I *did*.

Spelling Enrichments (focus on exercises with * for non-readers)

*NUMBER PAGE. Start building the Number Page in the Log (available from BHI) or number a blank notebook sheet of paper from 1 to 12 down the left side of the margin line. Beside 6 have the student write *six* and *sixth*. Beside 10 write *ten* and *tenth*. Add additional numbers to the Number Page as they are taught in spelling or needed. See sample completed chart on page 200 of *Wise Guide* and Step 15 in SWR.

*REINFORCE SHORT-TERM MEMORY. Cut 3x5 cards in half to make two 3 x 2 1/2 cards. After the student has written the spelling words in his log, have him close his book and write from dictation the same words on a card, one card per word. Keep an ongoing set of cards for practice drills. Practice reading quickly through the cards as a timed drill. Move them around to form sentences or phrases. Have the student read them out loud. *My hat [bed, top] is [not] red. All six [ten] did go. My cat ran.* Learn these words!

Spelling Dictation. The student writes each word from dictation (not copying), reads the word he just wrote, and sounds it out for the teacher to write on the board.   The student checks his spelling by the teacher's work. See SWR pages 71-75 for the dictation pattern illustrated with these twenty words.

Instructions		**Rules**
top		
⌈ but		
⌊ and	Bracket *but, and.* These words connect ideas. (We call them conjunctions.)	
cat	C usually spells /k/ at the beginning of a word, but it can't before E, I, or Y.	[R2]
red		
six		
all³	Add a silent L. We often double L after a single vowel at the end of a base word.	[R17]
m<u>y</u>	Underline Y. It said /I/ at the end of a syllable.	[R5,6]
not		
ten		
hat		

⌈ b<u>e</u>	Underline E. E said /E/ at the end of a syllable.	[R4]
	am	
⌊ i²s	Put a 2 over /z/. We cannot SEE it is the 2nd phonogram sound. Bracket related verbs.	
bed		
⌈ run		
⌊ ran	Bracket related verbs.	
g<u>o</u>	Underline O. O said /O/ at the end of a syllable.	[R4]
⌈ d³o	Put a 3 over /OO/. It's the 3rd sound of the phonogram.	
⌊ did	Bracket related verbs.	

OPPOSITES. Call out a word while the student writes the spelling word that means the opposite: *Enrichment guide pg 20.*

none/*all*	walk/*run*	come/*go*	bottom/ *top*	undo/ *do*
is not/ *is*	am not/ *am*	your/ *my*	did not/ *did*	

*SENTENCES.

    <u>Original Oral</u>: Student reads words he has written going across the page then composes an original sentence using the words. Example: *top hat. Abraham Lincoln had a top hat.*

    <u>Written from Dictation</u>: Dictate simple sentences using these words such as: *All six did go. Ten did not run.* Have student capitalize the first word and put a period at the end.

CONTRACTIONS. Teach students to make contractions: *do not / don't; is not / isn't; did not / didn't.*

Preliminaries. Phonograms: Review the phonograms taught so far. Practice seeing, saying, hearing, writing them. Hide the cards and try hearing, saying, writing, seeing. Introduce: *oy, oi, ch, ow, ou*. Reference Page: Add new phonograms to the **Multi-letter Phonogram Page**. See SWR Step 10.

Words for Section B

21	tan 1	In Oregon it rains so much that we do not *tan,* we rust.
22	can 2	I *can* do it!
23	so 3	I am *so* glad you want to learn to read.
24	no 4	*No* cat is the mother to puppies.
25	pet 5	The maple is a dainty maid, the *pet* of all the wood.
26	a 6	*A* bad boy has woe. *--McGuffey Primer*
27	an 7	The cat sees *an* old dog.
28	the 8	Do not walk in *the* way of evil. *--Proverbs 4:14b*
29	good 9	*Good* children must fear God all day. *--New England Primer*
30	last 10	Christians never see each other for the *last* time.
31	bag 11	Give me the tan paper *bag.*
32	beg 12	My teacher says I should not *beg.*
33	big 13	The little hills were so *big* to me.
34	bog 14	No, I must not let them *bog* me down with too much work.
35	bug 15	My pet is as snug as a *bug* in a rug.
36	fish 16	I see a *fish.*
37	odd 17	An unusual fish can be called an *odd* fish.
38	hill 18	I ran to the top of the *hill.*
39	hit 19	That was a good base *hit.*
40	step 20	The first *step* is harder than the last *step.*

Spelling Enrichments (focus on exercises with * for non-readers)

ANTONYMS. Call out the first word and have the student write the spelling word that is the opposite.
   bad / *good*   valley / *hill*   little / *big*   pale skin / *tan*   help / *bug*   yes / *no*   first / *last*
   demand / *beg*   can't / *can*   desert / *bog*   normal / *odd*   out (as in baseball) /*hit*

COMPOUND WORDS. Spelling words sometimes are joined together to make compound words. If you can spell the words separately, you can easily spell the new word and guess the meaning. Have the student write the following compound words: bedbug, cannot, hilltop, catfish.

* READING PRACTICE. Read spelling words out of the student notebook or Learning Log moving across the page to help develop the left-to-right orientation. Example: *tan bag.* Have student make an oral original sentence using sets of adjoining words. *The **tan bag** is odd. Can the pet beg? The pet is so **big**. The hill is **no bog**. My **pet** is not a **bug**. A **fish** is good. An **odd** bug is red. The hill is tan. My **good hit** did go to the top of the hill. Go to the **last step**.* Select a sentence for the student to write on practice paper and then carefully in the *Learning Log*.

Spelling Dictation

Learn to follow the spelling dictation pattern described in detail in Step 12 of SWR and the summary of the procedure outlined on page 76. Although we refer to rule numbers in *Wise Guide*, our interest is in teaching a student to know the rule concepts, not the numbers.

---

tan		
can	C usually spells /k/ at the beginning of a word, but it can't before E, I, or Y.	[R2]
s<u>o</u>	Underline O. O said /O/ at the end of a syllable. A- E -O-U usually say ... A E O + U	[R4]
n<u>o</u>	Underline O. O said /O/ at the end of a syllable. A- E -O-U usually say ...	[R4]
pet		
<u>a</u>	For spelling think /A/. A usually says /A/ at the end of a syllable.	[R4]
an		
th<u>e</u>²	For spelling think /E/. See SWR p. 79. Bracket the articles: a, an, the.	[R4]
g<u>oo</u>d²	Underline /oo/. It's a 2-letter phonogram. Put a 2 over it. It's the 2nd sound of phonogram.	
last	We cannot use C here. Why? It would say /lakt/.	[R2]
bag	Listen carefully for the changing vowel sound in the next five words.	
beg		
big		
bog		
bug	Bracket from *bag* to *bug* to show how changing one letter can change a word completely.	
fi<u>sh</u>	Underline /sh/. It's a 2-letter phonogram. SH can spell /sh/ at the end of a syllable.	[R10]
odd	Occasionally we double D after a single vowel at the end of a base word.	[R17]
hill	We often double L after a single vowel at the end of a base word.	[R17]
hit		
step		

PRACTICE SPELLING WORDS. Work for long-term memory. After the student writes five or ten new words in his notebook, immediately close the book and dictate the same words for the student to write and mark independently on 3x5 cards. Check work. This activity strengthens spelling retention and helps build cards for later activities. These early words are essential ones we use over and over. Teach these words well!

SENTENCE FORMATION. Try to organize the cut 3x5 cards into sentences or dictate sentences for the student to write. Teach them to capitalize the first word and end the last word with closing punctuation. The following examples use only words taught so far: *A cat hit the big bed. My pet can run. No fish can beg. My good hat is so big. The red bag did not last. Did the top hit the step? My last fish is so good. A bog is odd. The last hill is tan. The big tan cat cannot run.*

VOWEL SOUND DRILL. Have a student pick one of the words *bag, beg, big, bog,* or *bug* and dictate it for someone else to write on the board. This will help test the student's pronunciation. Take turns to test both listening and speaking discrimination. For more practice try: *dad, did, dud. sap, sip, sop, sup. pat, pet, pit, pot [putt]. bat, bet, bit, but.*

Preliminaries

Phonograms: Introduce *ay, ai, ea, or, ui*. Note: EW was once taught here but is moved to Section I-1.

Reference Page: Add new phonograms to **Multi-letter Phonogram Page**. Drill all the phonograms taught so far. Use a stuffed dog, a box, and the sentences with the first ten words below to illustrate prepositions.

Words for Section C

41	in	11)	The dog is *in* the kennel.	
42	by	2)	The dog is *by* the kennel.	[English words do not end in I. Use the stand-in vowel.]
43	out	5)	The dog comes *out* the door of the kennel.	
44	to	6)	He goes back *to* the kennel.	
45	in to	12	He crawls *into* it.	[Think to spell syllable by syllable.]
46	up	3	He climbs *up* the kennel.	
47	on	7)	He is *on* the kennel.	
48	o ver	1)	He jumps *over* it.	[Think to spell syllable by syllable.]
49	at	13)	The dog is *at* the kennel.	
50	of	14)	This is the kennel *of* the dog.	[Think to spell /o/-/f/. We say /o/-/v/.]

51	I	26)	Use the word *I* if it is something you do.	(*I* dropped a book.)
52	me	4	Use the word *me* if it is something you receive.	(Give the book to *me*.)
53	you	8	*You* refers to the person you are talking to directly.	(*You* dropped a book.)
54	he	9)	*He* refers to a male who does something.	(*He* dropped a book.)
55	him	10)	*Him* refers a male who receives something.	(Give the book to *him*.)
56	she	15)	*She* refers to a female who does something.	(*She* dropped a book.)
57	her	19	*Her* refers a female who receives something.	(Give the book to *her*.)
58	it	16)	*It* refers to a thing that is not a person.	(*It* dropped the book.)
59	we	18)	*We* refers to you and I doing the action.	(*We* dropped the book.)
60	us	17)	*Us* refers to you and I receiving the action.	(Give the book to *us*.)

Spelling Enrichments (focus on exercises with * for non-readers)

* TIMED READING. Time a student reading from his own spelling notebook starting with Section A. Record the time it takes to read the page and periodically have the student compete with his own record until he can read the page smoothly at a normal talking speed. It takes awhile before many students get the magic of blending words. Be patient and keep plodding! You will see success!

SUBJECT/OBJECT PRONOUNS. As you read across this page some combinations sound right. Say "OUCH" when one hurts our ears, then substitute the correct combination. [*in I* (ouch) *in me; to he* (ouch) *to him* ; *up she* (ouch) *up her; at we* (ouch); *at us*. Only an object pronoun can be the object of a preposition.

COMPOUND WORDS. Two words often combine to make a new word [air +plane= airplane]. Write on the board: *all, bed, bug, do, hill, in, on, out, over, run, set, step, to, top, up*. Match with words taught to date: *bedbug, hilltop, instep, onto, outdo, outset, overall, overalls, overdo, overrun, overstep, uphill, upon, upset*.

* DICTATION: I can do it! Also select sentences from Webster's *Blue-backed Speller*: Am I to go? I am to go. Can he go? He is to go. We go to it. Is it by us? It is by me. Is she by you? She is by him.

Bonus Grammar Instruction with Spelling Words

Although it is not necessary, some grammar can be taught with these spelling words. The first ten words are **prepositions**. See SWR Step 16 for more ideas on prepositions. The last ten words are **personal pronouns**. The sample sentences on the facing page can help students anticipate the correct pronoun.

---

in

b<u>y</u>   Underline /I/. Y said /I/ at the end of a syllable.   [R5,6]

<u>out</u>   Underline /ow/. It's a 2-letter phonogram.

t$\overset{3}{o}$ Put a 3 over /oo/. Third sound of the phonogram.

in t$\overset{3}{o}$ Put a 3 over /oo/. Violate R4? No. O <u>usually</u> says /O/ at end of a syllable, but not always.

up

on

<u>o</u> v<u>er</u>   Underline /O/. O said /O/ at the end of a syllable. Underline /er/. It's a 2-letter phonogram.   [R4]

at   <u>Abbreviation: @</u>   [R12]
$\overset{x}{of}$ <u>An X shows an eXception. Only word in 20,000 where f = /v/.   See SWR p. 80.</u>

⎡<u>I</u>   I said /I/ at the end of a syllable. A rare spelling at the end of a word. See SWR p. 61.   [R5]
⎣m<u>e</u>   E said E at the end of a syllable.   [R4]

y$\underset{3}{\underline{ou}}$ A rare spelling at the end of a word. English words do not end with U. See SWR p. 61.

⎡h<u>e</u>   E said E at the end of a syllable.   [R4]
⎣him

⎡<u>she</u>   E said E at the end of a syllable.   [R4,10]
⎣<u>her</u>

it

⎡w<u>e</u>   E said E at the end of a syllable.   [R4]
⎣us

Spelling Enrichments

PREPOSITION GAME. A preposition shows the relationship between two things. Use sentences for the first ten words to show the relationship between a stuffed dog and his house. (*The dog is in his house*, etc.) Choose a different pair of objects such as a student and a desk. Have the student read each preposition one at a time out of his notebook, compose an oral sentence using that preposition, and act out the sentence. For example: This is the desk *of* the student.   He goes *to* the desk.   The student is *at* this desk; etc.

PRONOUNS. The last ten words can be used to teach personal pronouns. Divide paper into 3 columns. In the first list: 1st, 2nd, 3rd. Beside "1st," write the words describing yourself or yourself and others. Beside "2nd," write the word describing the person to whom you are talking. Beside "3rd," write the words describing a person or thing about which you are talking. Advanced option: Include *they* and *them*.

	Subject		Object	
	singular	plural	singular	plural
1st	I	we	me	us
2nd	you	you	you	you
3rd	he, she, it	___(they)	him, her, it	___(them)

7

Build a Booklet that Illustrates the Phonograms in Spelling Words

Some children love this optional activity. Use loose-leaf notebook paper folded into three or four columns to assemble a booklet. Head each column with a phonogram representing one of its sounds. Organize in alphabetical order. Have the students independently place his spelling words in the appropriate columns.

a	a²	a³		b	c	c²		d	e	e²		f	g	g²	h
and	a	all		but	cat			and	red	be		fish	go		hat
cat				be	can			red	ten	the		of	good		hill
hat				bed				bed	bed	me			bag		hit
am				bag				do	pet	he			beg		he
ran				beg				did	beg	she			big		him
tan				big				good	step	we			bog		her
can				bog				odd					bug		
an				bug											
last				by											
bag															
at															

i	i²	j		k	l	m	n			o	o²	o³	
six	I				all	my	and	into		top	go	do	
is					last	am	not	on		not	so	to	
did					hill	me	ten			bog	no	into	
big						him	run			odd	over		
fish							ran			on			
hill							tan			of			
hit							can						
in							no						
into							an						
him							in						
it													

p	qu	r		s	s²	t			u	u²	u³	
top		red		six	is	top	pet	at	but			
pet		run		so		but	last	it	run			
step		ran		last		cat	hit		bug			
up				step		not	step		up			
				us		ten	to		us			
						hat	out					
						tan	into					

			consonant	vowel			
v	w	x	y	y	y²	z	
over	we	six	you		my		
					by		

Notice that although we teach from the beginning all the basic sounds that our single alphabet letters make, some of the sounds may not be used for awhile. Don't be worried about blank spaces.

SPELLING SECTIONS
D through F

Long-term mastery of the work covered is an important goal. This list includes the 1000 most frequently used words in the language. **The first 80 words in this program (A through D) include more than 30% of all we read and write.** The students need to have these internalized for automatic retrieval in writing and reading.

✿ Future spelling tests should include random words taught to date, not just ones taught that week.

✿ Future writing assignments should seek to have all of these words spelled correctly.

✿ The student(s) should practice reading these words out loud from the Learning Log until reading is fluid without stumbling. Have student(s) read across the page to practice left-to-right orientation. This can be done as a group in unison or individually.

Time reading with an eventual target goal of 40 words a minute. Be patient. Mastery speed comes faster for some than others. Not all children start walking at the same time. Likewise, the magic of blending words quickly into reading "clicks" at different times for different students. Don't be discouraged by delay. All learning types can learn from this method! Some require more time and practice before they get it. Just keep exposing the students to the phonograms and spelling words, the pieces needed for the process to work. Some of the quicker students who grasp how the written language works would have learned to read if no one had taught them at all. In a similar way, some people can sit down at a piano and start playing by ear. All types, those with an inner sense of a subject and those without, benefit from a systematic presentation of complex skills like playing the piano and learning to read.

The two biggest mistakes teachers make with this program are moving too slowly and not providing enough reinforcement. Strive for proficiency, but don't get bogged down here! Balance a goal of mastery and the need to give a broad-base exposure to as many words as possible, as quickly as possible. Keep moving in the program, but maintain constant review.

Preliminaries Phonograms: Introduce *ng, ar, wh, aw, au*. Quiz especially *ay, ch, ee, er, oo, oy, th*.
    1. Pronounce phonograms and say any clarifying language necessary in order for a student to write each one sight unseen. eg. Say *E double E always says /E/* as a signal for the student to write *ee*.
    2. "Read" them. Show a card and have a student say the sound(s) the phonogram can make (/E/).
    Reference Pages: Add new phonograms to the **Multi-letter Phonogram Page**. Start a new column. See page 62 in SWR. Teach **Silent Final E Page**. Follow instructions in SWR Step 17.

Words for Section D (Remember to follow special spelling dialogue taught in SWR Step 12.)

61	man ⑪	In a calm sea every *man* is a pilot. --John Ray, 1705
62	boy ②	When does a *boy* become a man?
63	book ③	This *Book* will keep you from sin or sin will keep you from this Book. --D. L. Moody
64	dog ⑤	A barking *dog* seldom bites.
65	home ④	What is a *home* without a Bible? --Charles Meigs
66	school ⑭	*School* at home is good. *--New England Primer*
67	street ①	An old unpainted fence staggered down the winding *street*.
68	moth er ②	No man is poor who has had a godly *mother*. --Abraham Lincoln
69	time ⑫	You may delay, but *time* will not. *--Poor Richard's Almanack*
70	hand ⑮	The *hand* that rocks the cradle rules the world.
71	make ⑯	I did not *make* the world out of nothing, but God did.
72	jump ㉙	May we *jump* rope this sunny day?
73	say ⑥	The deeds we do, the words we *say*, are all reserved for Judgment Day.
74	play ⑦	You must *play* quietly when the baby is sleeping.
75	are ⑧	What we *are* is more important than what we do. --Hudson Taylor
76	must ⑰	Boys and girls *mus*t not be rude in play. *--McGuffey Primer*
77	was ⑨	Long ago the man *was* a little boy.
78	has ⑩	The boy *has* no time to play.
79	have ⑱	Words *have* more power than atom bombs.
80	had ⑲	I have *had* more trouble with myself than with any other man. --D. L. Moody

---

Spelling Enrichments (focus on exercises with * for non-readers)

* ORAL SENTENCES. Oral sentence work will pave the way for written sentences later. The student should continue reading spelling words from his own handwritten notebook. Have him read the two words across the column *(man/make)* and orally make up his own original sentence. *(The man makes his son a toy plane.)* Explain how we sometimes have to add an -s or -es to the verb. (I make; you make; he, she, it make**s**. I fish; you fish; he, she, it fish**es**.) If the student reads *home are* and *time have* say OUCH. These verbs only go with a plural subject. Have student make the corrections: *homes are, home is, time has*.

* SUBJECT/ VERB. All sentences need a subject and a verb. Scramble and rearrange the words to make different combinations.   Use at least one noun in the first column (#61-70) as the subject and one verb from the second column (# 71-80). Have student write a simple subject/ verb on the board *(boy plays/ mother makes/ man says/ dog jumps/ street has/ time must/ hand was)*. Then give an oral sentence *(The boy plays ball)*.

·Bonus Grammar Instruction with Spelling Words

Some grammar can be taught along with these spelling words. The first ten words can be used as **nouns**. A noun can name a person, place, thing, or idea. The last ten words can be used as verbs. Every sentence must have a subject (a noun or pronoun) and a verb. Draw a chart on the board to illustrate nouns. Make four columns. Draw a picture in each to illustrate.

a person   place   thing   and an idea.

As the nouns are taught ask the students which type of thing is named. Example: boy is a person.

---

man

boy   *Which /oy/ should we use?* /OY/ that we may use at the end of English words.

book

dog

home   O said /O/ because of the E.   [R7]

school   *How many letters in this word?* (six) *How many phonograms?* (four)

street   Teacher tells students to use the 2-letter E. <u>Abbreviations</u>: St. or ST   [R12]

moth er   Using the overtone for /o/ helps make speech more precise. See SWR p. 82.

time   I said /I/ because of the E.   [R7]

hand

---

make   A said /A/ because of the E. *Why can't we use C?* It would say /mace/.   [R7,2]

jump

say   A-Y usually says /A/ at the end of a base word.   [R18]

play   A-Y usually says /A/ at the end of a base word.   [R18]

are   A silent E not covered by the first four reasons is an odd job E.   [R7]

must

was

has

have   English words do not end with V. Without the E the V would fall over.   [R7]

had

Spelling Enrichments

COMPOUND WORDS. Dictate review words: *bag, bed, out, over, step, up.* Combine these words with the current spelling words to make as many compound words as possible. *(bedtime, handbag, handbook, handout, homeschool, makeover, makeup, outplay, overhand, overtime, stepmother)*

CONTRACTIONS. A contraction replaces a letter or letters with an apostrophe to contract (or shorten) a phrase [R13]. Teach the idea of contractions using review words. See SWR Step 28.

   did not/didn't   *is not*/isn't   *are not*/aren't   I am/I'm   he is/he's   she is/she's

Student writes last six words on separate paper and makes contractions with words plus *not, I, you, we.*

are -- you *are*/you're; we *are*/we're; *are* not/aren't	*must* -- *must* not/mustn't
had -- *had* not/hadn't; I *had*/I'd; you *had*/you'd; we *had*/we'd	*was* -- *was* not/wasn't
have -- *have* not/haven't; I *have*/I've; you *have*/you've; we *have*/we've	*has* -- *has* not/hasn't

Preliminaries

Phonograms: Quiz:*ay, ar, ee, ng, oo, or, ou, oy, sh, th.* Introduce *ck, oe, oa, ed.*

Reference Page: Add new phonograms to the **Multi-letter Phonogram Page**. (Teach OE as 2-letter /O/ that we may and OA as 2-letter /O/ that we may NOT use at the end of English words.) Start **SH Page** with review words *she, fish.* After Section E add new words *short, wash.*

Words for Section E

81	thick	He likes a *thick* rug.
82	look	Father, I am weak, but You *look* into my heart and be my help. --H. C. Andersen
83	see	Christians may not *see* eye to eye, but they can walk arm in arm.
84	may	You *may* not play with bad boys. [Teacher tells student: Use the 2-letter /A/.]
85	this	Do you understand *this*?
86	your	Trust in the Lord with all *your* heart. --Proverbs 3:5
87	bad	After my *bad* fall she comforted me.
88	love	*Love* of self may lead us to pray, but love of God leads us to praise.
89	short	I am tall to a grasshopper and *short* to a giant.
90	wave	Please *wave* to us on the hill.
91	ring	She lost her diamond *ring* down the drain.
92	kill	Thou shall not *kill*. [Tell student to add an L.]
93	toy	Get the soft *toy* for the baby.
94	like	The child's tear flows *like* the dew-drop on the rose.
95	will	To *will* is not enough; we must do. --J. Goethe [Tell student to add an L.]
96	fun	We had *fun* with the baby.
97	trade	Can we make a *trade?*
98	robe	Please send my red and green *robe*.
99	wash	*Wash* your hands before you eat.
100	ba by	The cold *baby* needs a blanket. [Teacher: We think to spell "bA-bi."]

Spelling Enrichments (focus on exercises with * for non-readers)

VERBS. In a column going down dictate: *I; you; he, she, it.* Beside "I" dictate: *look, see, love, wave, kill, like, trade.* Have the student add the correct verb forms to go with *you* and *he, she, it.*

I	look	see	love	wave	kill	like	trade
you	look	see	love	wave	kill	like	trade
he, she, it	looks	sees	loves	waves	kills	likes	trades

OPPOSITES. Call out the first word for each set below and have the student write the matching opposite using a spelling word. You may or may not do this as an open book activity depending on the student's ability level. For example: Teacher: The opposite of good. Student: *bad.*

can't / *may*	overlook / *see*	long / *short*	dislike / *like*	thin / *thick*
hate / *love*	that / *this*	misery / *fun*	adult / *baby*	sell /*trade*
heal / *kill*	dry / *wash*	won't / *will*	tool / *toy*	my / *your*

* SENTENCES. Compose original oral sentences using all the spelling words.

Standard Spelling Dictation (SWR p. 76)

Do you pronounce the word, say it in a sentence, and pronounce the word again? Do you ask the student to say the word in syllables, then sound it out phonogram by phonogram as he writes? If needed do you clarify which phonogram to use? Do you have the student dictate the word back to you as you write it on the board? After he checks his spelling, do you ask him how to mark the word and why?

thick	Why can we use the two-letter /k/? It follows a single vowel saying /i/.	[R25]
look²	Why can't we use the 2-letter /k/? The vowel is not a single vowel.	[R25]
see	Teacher tells student to use E double E.	
may	What would the word say without Y? (ma) If a word ends with A it says /ah/.	[R18]
this²	Touch your throat and feel the vibration for the voiced sound of /TH/.	
your³	Underline /OO/. It's a 2-letter phonogram. Put a 3 over it. It's the 3rd sound.	
bad		
love₂	English words do not end with V.	[R7]
short	We need the /sh/ that we use at the beginning of a word.	[R10]
wave	What are the 2 reasons for the silent E? We mark the first one that works.	[R7]
ring		
kill	Why can't we use /k-s/ here? C says /s/ before E, I, or Y.	[R2,17]
toy	We must use OY because English words do not end with I.	[R6]
like	I said /I/ because of the E. Why can't we use C here? The word would be "lice."	[R7]
will	We often double L after a single vowel at the end of a base word.	[R17]
fun		
trade	A said /A/ because of the E.	[R7]
robe	O said /O/ because of the E.	[R7]
wash³	Often A says /ah/ after a W. Add to the **SH Page**: *short, wash.* Step 18.	[R10]
ba by	Y in an unaccented syllable is a cross between /E/ and /i/. If we exaggerate it as /E/, students tend to write "babe" or use one of the other ways to spell /E/. Y in this word is logically linked to I. In Middle English it was spelled "babi." Today, English words do not end with I [R5]. Y stands in for I in *baby* but switches back to I in *babies, babied.* Even though it sounds silly, exaggerate the Y as /i/ for spelling *baby*, then say the word as we do in normal speech. See SWR pages 82-85.	

Spelling Enrichments

* PANTOMIMING WORDS. Students should select a spelling word from Section A- E words to act out. When the word is guessed everyone writes down that word on a sheet of loose-leaf paper so that it may not be used again. Did anyone select: *was, are, has, have, or had?* Why not? These words do not give us a mental picture. Our message will be better understood if we write or speak with more vivid words.

COMPOUND WORDS. Pull from the past list of 3x5 cards: *a, child, home, man, out, over* and any problem words the students needs to reinforce. Use these along with the current spelling words to make as many compound words as possible. Examples: *alike, childlike, homelike, tradesman, oversee, washout.*

CONTRACTIONS. Dictate *I, you, he, she, it, we.* Have student add *will* to each and then form a contraction for the two words. *I will* / I'll; *you will* / you'll; *he will* / he'll; *she will* / she'll; *it will* / it'll; *we will* / we'll.

Preliminaries

    Reference Pages: Add the new phonograms to **Multi-letter Phonogram Page**.
    Teach the **A-E-I-O-U Page**. See instructions in *Spell to Write and Read*, Step 19.
    Phonograms: Teach the five ERs *(er, ur, ir, wor, ear)*. Review *ai, ay, ar, ch, ea, ee, ng, oo, sh*.
    Review Rules: 7,8,10,17,18,19,25. See SWR Step 20. Students learn by concepts not numbers.

Words for Section F

101	old	Do not grow *old* before your time.	[O may say /O/ before 2 consonants --R19].
102	lit tle	Great oaks from *little* acorns grow.	[Every syllable must have a vowel --R7].
103	hot	*Hot* words make cool friends.	
104	cold	Will we fish if it is *cold*?	
105	green	A hedge between keeps friendship *green*.	
106	ice	Steam, *ice*, and water; these three are one.	
107	long	Old sins cast *long* shadows.	
108	wild	Who set the *wild* donkey free? --Job 39:5	
109	sea	He that cannot pray, let him go to *sea*, and there he will learn.	
110	flat	His bike has a *flat* tire.	
111	bread	Man shall not live by *bread* alone.	
112	child	Even a *child* is known by his doings. --Prov. 20:11	
113	star	Twinkle, twinkle, little *star*, God has placed you where you are.	
114	day	My joy is in God all the *day*. --Thomas Dilworth	
115	wall	No *wall* is high enough, no army strong enough to prevent God's judgment.	
116	milk	You can't hide a piece of broccoli in a glass of *milk*.	
117	hair	If your Mom is mad at your Dad, don't let her brush your *hair*.	
118	shot	As the boy ran, Jonathan *shot* an arrow behind him.	
119	floor	The boy can sit on the *floor*.	
120	land	Woe to the *land* that is governed by a child! --William Shakespeare, *Richard III*	

Spelling Enrichments (focus on exercises with * for non-readers)

* VOWEL SOUNDS. Divide paper into four columns labeled : 1st, 2nd, 3rd, 2X.
    Under "1st" student lists spelling words that use the first sound of a single letter phonogram
        (land, hot, milk, little, flat, shot, long).
    Under "2nd" words using the second sound...*(old, cold, ice, wild, child)*.
    Under "3rd" words using the third sound...*(wall)* .
    Under "2x" two-letter phonograms...*(green, long, sea, bread, child, star, day, hair, shot, floor)*.

*DICTATION. Dictate sentence starters for students to finish using new spelling words.   Make sure they use the correct punctuation.

I am _ (a child).	*You are _.*	*She was _.*
Is it _?	*Is he _?*	*It is so _.*
He is _.	*Was she _?*	*Is it so _?*

    Dictate the sentence: *The little child with wild hair had old bread on a cold day.*

A Note on Spelling Markings

"I and O may say /I/ and /O/ before 2 consonants." Words illustrating Rule 19 sometimes create a question regarding markings. Should we put a 2 over the vowel since it is the second phonogram sound? No. We only put a 2 over phonograms making a second sound at unpredictable places. We put a 2 over the /z/ in *is*. No rule tells us to expect the second sound. We do not put a 2 over the /j/ in *gym*. The Y serves as an internal marking because of the rule, "G may say /j/ before Y" [R3]. The two consonants after an I or an O are internal markings for words below like *old, cold, wild,* and *child*. See **A-E-I-O-U Page.**

---

old	We can SEE why the 2nd sound (the 2 consonants). No special markings needed. [R19]	
lit tle₌₄	Think /t/ in both syllables for spelling but not for normal speech.	[R29,7]
hot		
cold	O may say /O/ before 2 consonants.	[R19]
green	The word uses four phonograms but five letters.	
ice	I said /I/ because of the E. The C saying /s/ because of the E is secondary.	[R7,2]
long		
wild	I may say /I/ before 2 consonants.	[R19]
sea	<u>Homophone</u>: *see.* SWR Step 30.	
flat		
bread		

---

child	I may say /I/ before 2 consonants.	[R19]
star	This word uses three phonograms but four letters.	
day	A-Y usually says /A/ at the end of a base word.	[R18]
wall	We often double L after a single vowel at the end of a base word.	[R17]
milk	I may or may not say /I/ before 2 consonants. Use CK only after a single vowel.	[R19,25]
hair	A one-syllable word which some say it like it is two.	
shot	Use the /sh/ that we use at the beginning of a word. Add to **SH Page.**	[R10]
floor	Floor and door are the only words in this list where /OO-oo-O/ says /O/.	
land		

ADJECTIVES. Match first column words with as many words as possible in the second column.

old   +   *bread, star, wall, milk, floor*   **little** +   *child, star, wall, milk, hair, land*
hot   +   *bread, child, star, day, milk, shot*   **cold** +   *bread, child, day, wall, milk, floor, land*
green +   *wall, hair, floor, land*   **ice**   +   *milk*

OPPOSITES.   Dictate the first word in each pair below. Student writes the spelling word opposite.
young / *old*   night / *day*   hot / *cold*   adult / *child*   steam / *ice*   bumpy / *flat*
sea / *land*   tame / *wild*   big / *little*   short / *long*   ceiling / *floor*

SENSE WORDS.   Organize words by things we can
    SEE   *old, little, green, long, flat*   FEEL   *hot, cold, ice, flat, long*
    TASTE   *flat, hot, old*   HEAR   *long, wild, flat*

COMPOUND WORDS.   Dictate review words: *bed, cat, do, fish, home, in, like, mother, over, up.* Student combines with current words to make compound words.
    hot -- hotbed, hotshot;   **wild** -- wildcat;   **sea** -- seabed;   **child** -- childlike;   **star** -- starfish;
    hair -- hairdo;   **shot** -- overshot, upshot;   **land** -- homeland, inland, motherland, overland

---

Optional Reinforcement Activities

PRACTICE SPELLING WORDS IN A VARIETY OF WAYS. Please don't get carried away feeling you must do all these activities. Some students need extra reinforcement and it is enjoyable to add variety when possible. These are some possible ways to provide that change of pace when needed.

    a. <u>Spelling tic-tac-toe</u>. Student earn a right to go in the game for every word spelled correctly.

    b. <u>Finger paint spelling</u>. Sneak in spelling review of several challenge words with an art assignment. Students design colorful backgrounds of swirls and swiggles. Then, with their fingers they can write in spelling words needing reinforcement. After the teacher checks for correct spelling, the student can wipe the word away and repeat the activity with another word.

    c. <u>Daily Quizzes</u>. Quiz at least some of the new words daily as well as testing the words at the end of the week. You can often integrate this quizzing with reinforcement activities. Instead of calling out spelling words as individual words, dictate sentences using the words.

    d. <u>Dictate simple sentences</u>. Compose sentences made from spelling words taught to date and dictate them. Students often misspell words in sentences that they may get right when doing a list of words in isolation as on a typical spelling test. Correct spelling executed in the flow of ideas demonstrates more clearly that a student has a solid mastery of the words.

REINFORCE PHONOGRAMS IN A VARIETY OF WAYS. All phonograms that have been introduced should be drilled two times a day. After mastery, review once a day, but do not drop on going drill.

    a. <u>Phonics Bingo</u>. Make a simple grid with five lines down and across. Student writes a phonogram in each box. Scramble the cards taught so far and call them out one at a time. If he has that one, he places a marker on it. The winner is the first to get a full line down, across, or diagonally. Check for accuracy.

    b. <u>Phonogram Search</u>. Spread selected phonograms cards out across the table. Make sure the cards are facing the student right side up. Have the student as quickly as possible touch the one you call out.

    c. <u>Giant Game Board</u>. Spread the phonograms you have taught so far in snake fashion on the floor. Have the student roll a die. Count forward the corresponding number of cards and point with a stick to the one in question. If the student can say the phonogram sound(s) correctly, he can walk ahead to stand by that card. The first to finish is the winner. To make things more interesting you can insert between phonogram cards, various instructions. For example: Step back one. Say the last four phonograms. Return to the beginning of the game. You may also insert spelling rule cards covered by Section F which include: rules 1, 2, 3, 4, 5, 6, 7, 8, 10, 12, 13, 17, 18, 19, 25.

    d. <u>Speed Drill</u>. "Reading" the phonograms as a timed activity helps keep motivation high. Teacher holds up phonograms one at a time and as quickly as possible the student calls out the sounds it could make in a word. (Do not use extra dialogue here. For example with EIGH simply say /A/, not four-letter /A/.) Keep a record of the time. Have student try to break his personal record.

    e. <u>Sign Letters of Alphabet Using Deaf Sign</u>. See p. 82 for instructions. Teach as phonograms.

    f. <u>Treasure Hunt</u>. Hide phonograms. When children find one they run to the chalkboard, say the sound and write from memory the phonogram letter(s) on the board.

SPELLING SECTIONS
G through H

After Section G, the spelling sections vary in length. Never again will any sections have only twenty words. Most sections have a hundred or more words.

Move ahead with confidence. Your work has great value. One of the highest professions in any age is teaching language to children.

The first 140 words in this program (Sections A through G) are vital. They include more than 40% of all we read and write.

We do not officially ask a child to read from books until we have taught all 70 phonograms. See I-1 for the first reading assignment. Many children are unnecessarily harmed when prematurely pushed into reading. If a child has to labor over every sound, reading will seem like a tortue to avoid. We prefer teaching the subskills for reading through spelling until the student can smoothly recognize individual words well enough to capture the meaning of series of words in the flow of thought.

What about that student who starts reading without outside pressure? Some children pick up reading rapidly on their own using the tools we have taught by this point. We don't force a child to read before he is ready, but if a student is already reading independently we do not try to stop him. An excellent beginning reader for such a student is *Play by the Sea*. This book published by BHI includes all the spelling words taught in Sections A-F. This tender story with both conflict and humor is an ideal resource for such a student. *Play by the Sea* will also be a valuable resource for any student any time after Section I-1.

Preliminaries. Phonograms: Start teaching capital letters by sounds. Drill: *ea, ee, ng, oo, or, ow, th*.
 Reference Page: Introduce *igh, ie, dge, wr*. Add to **Multi-letter Phonogram Page**.
 Rule Cards: Review 1,2,3,4,5,6,7,8,10,12,13,17,18,19,20,25. Teach R20.
 Sentences: Students begin to write original sentences using spelling words. See Step 21 in SWR.

Words for Section G

121	ask	*Ask* God's blessing on your work, but don't *ask* Him to do it for you. --F. Robson
122	let	Gravity will *let* you down.
123	then	Pride comes, *then* comes shame. --Proverbs 11:2
124	gas	We will get *gas* for the car today.
125	read	*Read* the Bible, and you will live and die a better man. --A. Lincoln
126	for	Obey your parents in the Lord *for* this is right. --Ephesians 6:1
127	yes	*Yes*, you may go, but not yet.
128	door	When one *door* shuts, another opens.
129	now	Eternity is an everlasting *now*.
130	lot	A friend is a *lot* of things, but a critic he isn't. --Bern Williams
131	ba con	We had *bacon* and eggs for breakfast.
132	live	I have a *live* baby chicken.
133	live	In God we *live*, and move, and have our being. --Acts 17:28
134	heat	*Heat* not a furnace for your foe so hot that it does singe yourself. --Shakespeare
135	box	I put the pin on my tin *box*. --Webster's *Bluebacked Speller*
136	three	Fish and visitors smell after *three* days. --Benjamin Franklin
137	if	*If* God loved you as much as you love Him, where would you be?
138	stand	The path that causes the godly to *stand* will cause the wicked to stumble.
139	come	When he has tested me I will *come* forth as gold. --Job 23:10
140	wing	Every bird that upward swings bears the cross upon its *wing*. --J. Neale

Spelling Enrichments (Focus on exercises with * for non-readers)

COMPOUND WORDS. Pull from the past list of 3x5 cards: *a, ice, in, man, over, out, & steps* plus any trouble words. Use these words along with the current spelling words and have students make into as many compound words as possible. Examples: *alive, icebox, indoors, inlet, income, doorman, overheat, overcome, outdoors, outlive, outstanding, doorsteps.*

ASSOCIATED WORDS. Say the first word; student writes associated spelling word. eg.: sink OR swim; pen AND ink. Have students verbalize how the words are related.

| die / *live* | write / *read* | now / *then* | sit / *stand* | eggs / *bacon* |
| window / *door* | no / *yes* | against / *for* | answer / *ask* | dead / *live* |

MAKING CONDITIONAL SENTENCES. Use "if...then" with as many spelling words as possible. For example: *If you ask mother for bacon and milk, then ask for a box.*

A Reminder for the Teacher

Make sure all students actively participate. Each one should say out loud the sounds he hears in the word as he writes it. Also the class should in unison respond to questions on spelling highlights. Likewise, when spelling rules are repeated, make sure all participate vocally. When the student says something out loud, a pattern is left on his brain that helps that idea stick. Vocalizing is an important part of learning.

---

ask	Pronounce carefully.	
let	Contraction: *let* + *us* = *let's*. SWR Step 28.	[R13]
then	Touch your throat and feel the vibration for the voiced sound of /TH/.	
gas		
read	These same letters can also spell rẻad. Today I read a book. *Yesterday I read it.*	
for		
yes		
door	*Door* and *floor* are the only words in this list where OO says /O/.	
now	Could we use OU here? No. Why? English words do not end with U.	
lot		

---

ba con	A said /A/ at the end of a syllable. See SWR p. 87.	[R4]
live	I said /I/ because of the E. You may also teach the word *a-live*.	[R7]
live	No V at the end. *Live & live* look the same/sound different; context is the clue.	[R7]
heat		
box	X and S don't go together. To make plural, add -es.	[R20]
three	Add to the **Number Page**. See SWR Step 15.	
if		
stand		
come	This E is the ghost of a sound no longer said. One reason for an odd job E.	[R7]
wing	This word uses three phonograms but four letters.	

Spelling Enrichments

VOCABULARY. Some words are homographs. They can be pronounced two different ways. Example: A *tear* slid down my face when I saw a *tear* in my skirt. Find two spelling words like this (live/read).

STUDENT DICTATION. Have student read her troublesome spelling words onto a cassette tape. The next day or so have the student play back the tape and take a spelling quiz from her own dictation.

* ORIGINAL SENTENCES. Student can now write original sentences. See SWR Step 21. As a warm-up activity, have student first make up some oral sentences. You may want to use adjoining words. Example: ask / bacon. I will *ask* for *bacon* with breakfast. let / live. He *let* the *live* snake in the house.

GRAMMAR. Students read through the words in Sections E-G looking for nouns to categorize. **Person**: baby, child. **Place**: land, star, flat (as in apartment), wall, sea, floor. **Thing**: wash (as in *hang up the wash*), wave (as in *sea wave*), ring, toy, robe, milk, hair, gas, wing, bacon, bread, stand (as in *popcorn stand*), heat (as in *turn up the heat*), door, floor, box. **Idea**: fun, trade (as in *making a trade*).

Preliminaries. Phonograms: Review especially *ay, aw, ch, ea, ng, oo, ou, th*.

      Reference Page: Introduce *ti, ci, si, tch*.   Add to the **Multi-letter Phonogram Page**.

      Diagnostic Scale: Test at least the first ten words on Diagnostic Test 1 or 2 in Appendix B of SWR. A student who misses any of the first six words lacks mastery of the words covered to this point. Continue to review those words but press on! Test monthly from this point forward.

Words for Section H-1

141	his	God is always true to *His* Word and *His* Name. [We capitalize pronouns for God.]
142	just	*Just* because you can does not mean you should.
143	a bout	He who goes *about* as a talebearer reveals secrets.
144	much	He who is thankful for little things enjoys *much*.
145	ball	Can we play *ball* today?
146	law	A *law* is better unmade than unkept. --Henry Smith
147	lay	I will both *lay* me down in peace and sleep.
148	soft	A *soft* answer turns away wrath, but harsh words stir up anger.--Proverbs 15:1
149	path	God doesn't always smooth the *path*, but sometimes he puts springs in the wagons.
150	as	What looks dark in the distance may brighten *as* I draw near. --Mary G. Brainard
151	lone	A *lone* bird flew over the beach.
152	a lone	'Tis better to be *alone* than in bad company. --George Washington
153	one	Saying is *one* thing, and doing is another. --Aesop. [Think to spell /O-n/; say /won/.]
154	food	*Food*, water, clothes -- everything that Midas touched turned to gold.
155	five	*Five* pennies are worth one nickel.
156	led	The boy *led* the cat home.
157	year	Nobody outgrows Scripture; the Book widens and deepens with each *year*. --Spurgeon
158	house	Every wise woman builds her *house*. --Proverbs 14:1
159	way	The Lord knows the *way* that I take. --Job 23:10
160	some	Read *some* to me today.

Spelling Enrichments

WORD ANALOGIES. This optional activity requires higher level thinking. Many students will need help in working through the process. Discussion is necessary for some in learning to see the relationships. Examples: Night is to dark as day is to __ (light). [How is night different from day?]   Green is to go as red is to __(stop). [The green light means our car can go; the red light means we must what?]   Shirt is to cloth as window is to __ (glass). [A shirt is made from cloth. From what is a window made?]

      Students are to complete the following oral statements by writing a Section H spelling word:

Poor is to rich as little is to __ *(much)*.	Day is to week as month is to _ *(year)*.
Fans are to the football team as most are to _ *(some)*.	Car is to garage as family is to _*(house)*.
Glass is to smooth as towel is to _ *(soft)*.	Lady is to man as hers is to__ *(his)*.
Contestants are to the winner as many is to _ *(one)*.	Thirst is to water as hunger is to _*(food)*.
Here is to there as this is to ___ *(that)*.	Dime is to ten as nickel is to ___ *(five)*.

Language on the Move

Math is composed of absolutes. Two plus two always makes four. Language, however, changes with time. In this lesson we will learn a word that was once pronounced differently. In the past we spelled the word just as we say it. Then people started saying it another way. What we think to spell and what we say don't always match. The amazing thing is not that we have some rule-breaker words; the surprising thing is that we have so few. With our phonograms and spelling rules only 1% of common words are rule-breakers. What word is a rule-breaker in this list of words?

his	3rd person, singular, masculine, possessive pronoun.	
just	The phonogram /g/-/j/ cannot be used here. It would say *gust*.	[R3]
a bout	Think to spell /A-bout/; say /a-bout/. Exaggerate A to remember for spelling.	[R4]
much		
ball	We often double L after a single vowel at the end of a base word.	[R17]
law	Why don't we use AU in this word? English words do not end with U.	[R6]
lay	A-Y usually spells /A/ at the end of a base word. Without Y it would say /lah/.	[R18]
soft	Oxymoron: *soft rock*. An oxymoron is a combination of contradictory words.	
path	This word uses three phonograms but four letters.	
as		
lone	A lone bird means how many? (one)	[R7]
a lone	If someone is by himself how many people are there? (one)	[R4,7]
one	Think to spell *one* as *lone* and *alone* even though we say as /won/. SWR p. 81.	
food		
five	Two reasons for this E. Mark the first that applies (I said /I/ because of the E).	[R7]
led	Do not underline ED here; -ed is not an ending in this word.	
year	Abbreviation: yr.	[R12]
house₅	A Silent E not covered by the first four reasons is an odd job E.	[R7]
way	A-Y usually spells /A/ at the end of a base word.	[R18]
some₅	A Silent E not covered by the first four reasons is an odd job E.	[R7]

Spelling Enrichments

CREATIVE WRITING. Read *King Midas' Touch*. Orally compose sentences on the theme, "Some wishes cannot give happiness." Use as many spelling words as possible. See SWR p. 161.

COMPOUND WORDS. Quiz spelling words and review words: *a, as, by, day, door, hand, in, out, over, book, play, sea, three, top.* Beside current words have students list compound word derivatives (***much** --inasmuch, overmuch;* ***ball**-- handball, softball;* ***law**-- bylaw, outlaw;* ***lay**-- inlay, layover, layout, outlay, overlay;* ***soft**-- softball;* ***path**-- pathway;* ***lone**-- lonesome;* ***food**-- seafood;* ***year**-- yearbook;* ***house** --out-house, housetop, playhouse;* ***way**--away, byway, doorway, layaway;* ***some**-- someday, someway, threesome*).

NUMBERS. Add to the **Number Page** *one, five.* See SWR Step 15.

DICTATION: The year I was five I saw a boy alone on a path by my house with one big soft ball. I wished I had his ball just about as much as I wanted food.

Preliminaries.   Spelling Rules: Warm up by reviewing cards 3, 4, 7, 12, 13, 17, 18, 22, 28.
Phonograms: Do a fast-paced review "reading" all the phonograms learned so far.
Quiz at least: *ar, er, ng, oa, ow, th*. Include others that need practice.
Introduce: *eigh, ei, ey, ph*. Add to the **Multi-letter Phonogram Page**.
Reference Page: **ED Page**. See SWR Step 22 and Verbs in Spelling Enrichment on facing page.

Words for Section H-2

161	call	He who pays the piper can *call* the tune.
162	row	Pray to God, but *row* for the shore. --Russian proverb
163	salt	The *salt* shaker is empty.
164	be long	Little ones to Him *belong*. They are weak, but He is strong. --Anna Warner
165	bring	I will *bring* a salad to the picnic.
166	bite	Don't *bite* the hand that feeds you. --Aesop
167	get	The best way to *get* even is to forget.
168	send	Can you *send* the child over the hill?
169	coat	The old, red *coat* belongs to me.
170	tell	Be wiser than other people, if you can, but do not *tell* them so. --Philip
171	how	To know *how* to use knowledge is to have wisdom. --Spurgeon
172	yard	Shut the gate and keep the hogs out of the *yard*. --Webster's *Bluebacked Speller*
173	low	Be it high or be it *low*, there is no place I can go where God can never find me.
174	oth er	Children rarely play at being *other* children. --David Holloway
175	men	The best *men* are at best only *men*.
176	ap ple	Good things to eat are berries, nuts, and an *apple* so sweet.
177	well	It shall be *well* with them that fear God.
178	late	The boy was *late* today.
179	that	Taste and see *that* the LORD is good! --Psalm 34:8
180	them	You took good things for granted; now you must earn *them* again. --G. Washington

Spelling Enrichments

DICTATION. Dictate some of the following sentences made up of current or previously taught spelling words: *The lone house led to a row of five apple trees. How much are the soft apples that lay in the yard? Ask the men on the path by the well. Tell them how you need to get food for the others at home. Low salt and apples can help them get well. I can sit in the yard and eat an apple. I can read a good book. I can run on the path. I can play ball, but it is late. I will go home and give mother a hand. I will tell her I love her.*

ORIGINAL SENTENCES. Ask students to **write** original sentences using the spelling words. They can ask for help to spell words they do not know, but try to guide them to think for themselves rather than just spelling a word for them. Always proofread the student's work to avoid letting errors go uncorrected.

INTERJECTIONS. Review words: No! Yes! What new spelling word can be an interjection? *Well!*

Vocabulary Development

Some words carry two or more different unrelated meanings. Earlier spelling words that demonstrate this characteristic include: **ball** (a round object, a party), **play** (drama or fun activity) and **ring** (jewelry or a sound). Listen for words in this section that have multiple meanings. [**row** (a fight; line of seats; to move boat with oars); **yard** (land; 36-inch-long measurement); **low** (short; sound of a cow); **well** (a hole for water; something good)]

---

call³	We often double L after a single vowel at the end of a base word.	[R17]
row²		
salt³	Often the A says /ah/ before an L. This is not an official rule, just an observation.	
be long	E said /E/ at the end of a syllable. Does E usually say /E/ at the end of a syllable?	[R4]
bring	Past tense: brought.	
bite	I said /I/ because of the E. Past tense: bit.	[R7]
get	G may say /j/ before E but it doesn't always. Past tense: got.	[R3]
send	Past tense: sent.	
coat		
tell	Often double L after a single vowel at the end of a base word. Past tense: told	[R17]
how		
yard	Abbreviation: yd.	[R12]
low²		
oth² er		
men	The plural form of man. Instead of adding -s the word changes internally.	[R22]
ap ple₄	Think /p/ in both syllables for spelling but not for normal speech.	[R29,7]
well	We often double L after a single vowel at the end of a base word.	[R17]
late	A said /A/ because of the E.	[R7]
that²	Contraction: *that is = that's*. See SWR Step 28.	[R13]
them²	Touch your throat to feel the vibration for voiced sound of /TH/ in *that, them*.	

Spelling Enrichments

NOUNS. Students identify the new words that could be used as nouns and list them under one of the categories for nouns: **person** *(men)*, **place** *(yard, path, well)*, **thing** *(apple, salt, ball, coat, oil, row)*, or **idea** *(bite, yard -- a measurement)*. A noun has two distinct characteristics. 1. A noun can change from singular to plural *(boy, boys)*. 2. Nouns may be preceded by an article *(a, an, the)*. Note: the part of speech is determined in context. For example: *Row* is a noun in "a row of chairs" but a verb in "row the boat."

VERBS. Verbs are the only part of speech that can change to indicate time: present, past, future. Usually to make a word past tense, we just add -ed [R28]. Sometimes the verb changes in an irregular way. We must memorize these. Together make some review words past tense: *land*--landed; *heat*--heated; *play*--played: *jump*--jumped; *run*--ran; *do*--did; *hit*--hit; *have*--had: *let*--let. Assign students to independently make the first ten words above past tense: *call*--called; *row*--rowed; *salt*- salted; *belong* --belonged; *bring*--brought; *bite*--bit; *get*--got; *send*--sent; *coat*--coated; *tell*--told; *box*--boxed. See SWR pages 122-123.

An Extra Way to Reinforce Spelling or Phonograms

WORD MAGNETICS. Photocopy and attach the following list of review words and phonograms on 4 x 6 inch peel'n' stick magnetic sheets. [One company that manufactures these magnets is MC Enterprises, Inc. in Owing Mills, MD 21117.] Cut out the individual words with scissors. Place these word or letter magnetics on some metal surface and encourage students to manipulate them to organize words or original sentences.

top but and cat red six my not flat alone is bed run ran shot
did tan can so now odd the good last bag beg big Mom bug fish
pet am an hit step in by out into up on time of I me you he
him she we us man short book dog home school street wing hill
mother Dad make jump say play are must was has her thick all
look see may this your bad love tell ring kill toy like will fun
trade robe wash old little hot cold green ice long wild sea bread
child star day wall milk hair floor land ask let then be gas ten
read for yes door bacon live heat box three if stand come to at
his just about much ball law lay soft path have one food five it
no led year house way some row salt belong bring bite get send
coat a yard low as other men well late that them Jesus apple is
do over bog boy hand had hat baby wave lot lone call how go

a a a a a a a a e e e e e e e
e e e e i i i i i i i i o o o o o
o o o o o u u u u u u y y y y
b b b b b c c c c d d d d f f g g
g h h h h h j k k l l l l m m m m
n n n n p p qu r r r r r r s s s
s s s s t t t t t v w w w x z
ai ar au aw ay ch ci ck dge ea ear
ed ee ei eigh er ew ey gn ie igh ir
kn ng oa oe oi oo or ou ough ow oy
ph sh si tch th ti ui ur wh wor wr

SPELLING
SECTION I

Don't feel compelled to complete all the spelling reinforcement activities any one year! Save some activities for a subsequent year. The best way to ensure long-term mastery of this vital list of words is for all the words in this program to be taught two different years. For example, with a beginning first grader you may go from Section A through L or M the first year, at least doing twenty words a week. The following year dictate into a new spelling notebook or Primary Learning Log words possibly starting back at the beginning with Section A but move quickly by covering forty words a week. Continue teaching perhaps through Section Q. For a third year then you may move back to Section M (or where indicated by the diagnostic test) and teach to Section T or U. For a fourth year move back to Section R and teach through Section Z. See SWR Step 11, especially page 64.

Modify the placement in the Spelling List and the specific number of words taught a week to your teaching situation. Student needs differ. Guard against the common mistake of going too slowly. Don't get bogged down if you don't think the student is "getting it all." Some students need the bigger picture before they can see the smaller parts. Keep up an ambitious pace with the confidence that at a later time you will go through these words a second time.

The first 260 words (A through I) include over 50% of all words we read and write. Long term mastery of these words is important!

Preliminaries.

Phonograms: Quiz at least *ck, dge, ee, er, ie, igh, ng, oo, ow, sh, th, wh, wr.* Introduce *kn, gn, ough, ew.* (Celebration! We've covered all 70.)   Reference Page: Add final ones to **Multi-letter Phonogram Pg.**
Spelling Rules: Use cards for a quick warm-up review of rules *2, 3, 4, 7, 10, 11, 12, 13, 17, 19, 25.*
Reading: Assign an easy book of your choice for the student to read aloud. See SWR Step 23.

Words for Section I-1

181	white	The United States flag is red, *white*, and blue.
182	pa per	Could you help me *paper* my bedroom wall?
183	cut	Better be pruned to grow than *cut* up to burn. --J. Trapp
184	its	His dish, her dish, and *its* dish are all dirty.
185	it's = it is	*It's* a little bit the fiddle, but lots more who holds the bow. --Wilburn Wilson
186	sick	He that eats until he is *sick* must fast until he is well. --Hebrew proverb
187	gave	Job did not say, "The Lord *gave*, and the devil took away." --T. Watson
188	give	*Give* me liberty or *give* me death. --Patrick Henry
189	free	You shall know the truth, and the truth shall make you *free*. --John 8:32
190	back	I do not pray for a lighter load, but for a stronger *back*. --P. Brooks
191	thing	It is one *thing* to be tempted, another *thing* to fall. --William Shakespeare
192	roll	*Roll* on, thou deep and dark blue ocean, *roll*! -- the English poet, Byron
193	stone	A *stone* is heavy... but a fool's wrath is heavier. --Proverbs 27:3
194	foot	If you don't place your *foot* on the rope, you'll never cross the chasm. --L. Smith
195	dance	Come *dance* as you go on light fantastic toe.
196	lift	God asked Job, "Can you *lift* your voice to the clouds and demand that they rain?"
197	page	The world is a great book and those who never leave home read only a *page*. --Augustine
198	af ter	You shall not go *after* other gods. --Deut. 6:14
199	show	Outside *show* is a poor substitute for inner worth. --Aesop
200	thank	It is good to *thank* the LORD. --Psalm 92:1

Spelling Enrichments

BEGIN READING. An optional first reader is *The New England Primer of 1777* published by BHI. The students begin reading the *Basic Introductory Words* on pages 16-17. The list contains 99 of the first 200 spelling words we have studied at this point.   Students can read across the page the same words written in their spelling book, but now in a different order and typed in book face. If they can read these words at a comfortable speed, then they are ready for their first official reading assignment on page 20 of the *Primer.* The nine *I Can Read a Book* stories are composed of the words in the *Basic Introductory Words* List. Each story has a moral theme and a Bible verse to illustrate the moral. The Bible verses have a broader based vocabulary, but many students read these passages as well.

ORIGINAL STORY COMPOSITION. Let one person read a word plus the word across from it and then make a sentence using both words. The next person will use the second pair of words in a sentence that links in some way to the beginning sentence. Continue through the whole list of words in this way. Example: **white thing** -- What is the *white thing* on your desk? **paper roll** -- It is a *paper roll*. **stone cut** --The paper is rough like *stone* and hard to *cut*. **its foot** -- *Its* measurement is a *foot* long.

Possession

When we make singular nouns show ownership we add an apostrophe and an S. For example: baby's or child's. Possessive pronouns, however, do not use an apostrophe: boy's (his), mother's (hers), pet's (its), class's (theirs). *It's* does not mean "belonging to it," rather *it's* is a contraction for *it + is*. SWR Step 28 deals with contractions.

white	I said /I/ because of the E.	[R7]
pa per	A said /A/ at the end of a syllable.	[R4]
cut		
its	Pronouns do not use an apostrophe to show possession.	
it's = it is	The apostrophe here stands for the letter left out in the contraction for *it is*.	[R13]
sick	2 letter /k/ is used after a single vowel that says /i/.	[R25]
gave	A said /A/ because of the E. English words do not end with V is secondary.	[R7]
give	G may or may not say /j/ before I. English words do not end with V.	[R3,7]
free		
back	2-letter /k/ is used after a single vowel that says /a/.	[R25]
thing	This word uses five letters but only three phonograms.	
roll	O may say /O/ before 2 consonants. We often double L after . . .	[R19,17]
stone	O said /O/ because of the E.	[R7]
foot	Abbreviation: ft.	[R12]
dance	C said /s/ because of the E.	[R7]
lift		
page	A said /A/ because of the E. G said /j/ because of the E . Mark primary reason.	[R7]
af ter		
show	The /sh/ we use at the beginning of a word. . . **SH Page.** See SWR Step 18.	[R10]
thank	In speech /a/ and /n/ sound like /A/ and /ng/ in preparation to say /k/ which is made in the back of the mouth. We think to spell th-a-n-k. We say /th-a-ng-k/.	

Spelling Enrichments

COMPOUND WORDS. Dictate review words: *ball, bed, boy, bread, hand, home, man, no, out, some, step, wall, wash, way, yard*. Combine with current words to create as many compound words as possible. (*backhand, backyard, bedroll, freehand, freeman, freeway, football, footstep, handbook, handout, homesick, nothing, pageboy, paperback, showbread, sickbed, something, stonewall, whitewash*)

ASSOCIATED WORDS. Say the first word and have the student write the spelling word that is related.

hide / *show*	hand / *foot*	before / *after*	enslaved / *free*	glue / *cut*
black / *white*	took / *gave*	healthy / *sick*	front / *back*	drop / *lift*

CORRESPONDENCE. Write a thank-you note using as many spelling words as possible.

GRAMMAR. Review -ED Rule [R. 28]. Make past tense: *paper, lift, thank, show, roll, cut, give* (papered, lifted, thanked, showed, rolled, cut, gave). Bonus: *stone, page, dance* (stoned, paged, danced-- Rule 16). See SWR Step 22.

Preliminaries.

Phonograms: Review *ai, ay, ch, dge, ear, ee, er, ie, igh, ir, ng, oa, oo, or, ow, ou, th, ur, wh, wor, wr.*
Spelling Rules: Give a warm-up review of rules 7, 12, 13, 17.
Derivatives: See Step 24 of *SWR.*

Words for Section I-2

201	what	He is no fool who gives *what* he cannot keep to gain *what* he cannot lose. -J. Elliot
202	spring	Nightingales sing in time of *spring.* *--New England Primer*
203	sum mer	It will not always be *summer.* Build barns. --Hesiod
204	fall	Autumn is sometimes called *fall.*
205	win ter	No one thinks of *winter* when the grass is green. --R. Kipling
206	or	My favorite season is either spring *or* fall.
207	yet	Though he slay me, *yet* will I trust in him. --Job 13:15
208	moon	I have seen the full *moon.* --N. Webster
209	than	Doing is better *than* saying.
210	take	Time can *take* nothing from the Bible. --Richard Cecil
211	sea son	After the autumn *season,* people long for spring.
212	storm	The *storm* roared like an angry parent.
213	corn	The farmer sowed the *corn* that fed the cock that crowed in the morn.
214	tree	Few things grow well in the shade of a big *tree.*
215	blow	It feels colder in the winter when the winds *blow.*
216	a like	God sends the sun and the shower; *alike* they're needful to the flower. --Sam Adams
217	put	Who has *put* wisdom in the mind? --Job 38:36
218	riv er	On goes the *river* and out past the mill, away down the valley, away down the hill. - Stevenson
219	each	*Each* of our tasks will be reviewed and rewarded by God. --Bill Gothard
220	din ner	The sun falls asleep before *dinner.* --B. Tuason

Spelling Enrichments

ORIGINAL SENTENCES. Have student write original sentences related to the topic of seasons and/ or dictate: *What season* do you like? *Each spring* the *trees put* out buds. In *summer* we can have *dinner* under the *moon* by the *river.* *Each fall* we *thank* God for *corn.* In *winter* an ice *storm* may *blow.*

ART, SCIENCE, & MUSIC. Divide unlined paper into quarters. Students title the page, "What Season?" and draw the trunk of a tree in each of the squares. Label each with a different season of the year. Complete the page to illustrate the appropriate season. Popcorn can stand for spring flowers, green paper leaves for summer, yellow and red leaves for fall, and pieces of cotton for winter snow. While students work, play as background music Antonio Vivaldi's *The Four Seasons* or selections of George Winston's piano works: *Spring, Summer, Autumn, Winter.* See if the students can identify the season represented by the music.

COMPOUND WORDS. Dictate the following previously taught words: *less, like, in, out, over, time.* Combine review words with current words to make new words. Possibilities include: *blowout, input, intake, moonless, moonlike, output, overtake, springtime, treeless, wintertime.* **Contraction.** *what is = what's*

Help Students Develop Observational Skills

Seasons give us a sense of time passing. They provide important landmarks. We can give thanks for the different seasons and the benefits of each. Let's discuss how seasons compare and contrast with one another. What season did native Americans describe as: *time of new leaves, time of many flowers, time of falling leaves, time of great snow?*

what	Hold your hand in front of your mouth and compare "**what**" with "**watt**."	
spring		
sum mer	Think both M's for spelling but not for normal speech.	[R29]
fall	We often double F,L,S after a single vowel at the end of a base word.	[R17]
win ter	Bracket these words to show they all can be used as names for seasons.	
or		
yet		
moon		
than	Hold throat to feel the inner vibrations ("motor on") when saying /TH/.	
take	A said /A/ because of the E. *Like what word on the silent final E chart? (dime).*	[R7]
sea son		
storm		
corn		
tree		
blow		
a like	Think to spell A saying /A/ at the end of a syllable. I said /I/ because of the E.	[R4,7]
put		
riv er		
each	Abbreviation: ea.	[R12]
din ner	Think /n/ twice for spelling but not for normal speech.	[R29]

Spelling Enrichments

ADD WORD PARTS. Some words can be enlarged by adding prefixes and suffixes. See SWR Step 24.

Mid- can be added to the beginning of a word (midday, midland, and midway). Mid- means *in the middle*. Do you see any new spelling words that can use this prefix? *midsummer, midwinter, midseason.* Why do you think only two of the four seasons use this prefix? Is it because on very hot or very cold days we long for the relief that the next season will bring?

-Y can be added to the end of a word (hilly, jumpy, milky). What new spelling words can take this suffix? *moony, springy, summery, wintry, stormy.*

PUNCTUATION. A colon is used before a series of items. Commas separate different things.
Dictate examples. *For dinner I will cook three foods: fish, corn, and apples.*

LITERATURE. Read R L. Stevenson's poem, "Where Go the Boats," from *A Child's Garden of Verses.*
See the quote for "river" on p. 28.

Preliminaries.

Phonograms: "Read" all 70 phonograms. Quiz at least *ay, ci, ee, ng, oo, si, ti.*
Spelling Rules: Review cards for rules *2, 3, 4, 7, 12, 17, 18, 19, 22, 26, 27, 28.*
Reference Pages: On separate sheets of loose-leaf paper or using photocopies of SWR Chart Masters start collecting abbreviations (SWR Step 25) and be prepared to build ED Page (SWR p. 123).

Words for Section I-3

221	sing	I will *sing* to the Lord, because Jesus has been good to me.
222	sang	The man *sang* each Sunday for my church.
223	sung	My sister has *sung* songs for our grandmother.
224	song	Would you praise Christ with a *song?*
225	doll	A girl's loss of a *doll* and a king's loss of a crown are events of the same size. --M.Twain
226	feet	The lamps glitter down the street. Faintly sound the falling *feet. --R. L. Stevenson*
227	zoo	God made all of the animals in the *zoo.*
228	miss	*Miss* Jane will *miss* all the money she spent on the dress.
229	add	My church will not *add* to or subtract from God's Word.
230	lace	The lady helped my aunt select *lace* for the dress.
231	Mr.	*Mr.* George Muller trusted God to answer prayer.
232	finds	Happy is the man who *finds* wisdom. --Proverbs 3:13
233	nice	Grandmother is very *nice* to my family.
234	plant	The man learned a new way to *plant* corn.
235	got	Our church *got* new song books for the song leader.
236	a way	When the cat is *away,* the mice will play.
237	came	Men overlooked the baby's birth when love unnoticed *came* to earth. --Tatlow
238	west	Men risked their lives to move *west* in covered wagons.
239	went	Sue *went* north last fall to meet her uncle.
240	lake	Our families like the camp with a *lake.*

Spelling Enrichments

SUBJECT/ OBJECT PRONOUNS. Read aloud these sentences: *Mother got up. Mother read the Bible and prayed. Give Mother a hug.* We get tired of saying *mother* over and over, so we use a pronoun instead. Sometimes we will say *she* and sometimes we will say *her.* We say *she* if mother is the one doing it. *She got up. She read the Bible and prayed.* We say *her* if she is receiving it. *Give her a hug.*

Students should write each spelling word in a column going down on a sheet of paper. The teacher will read the above sentences for each word. Beside the appropriate word, the student should write the two pronouns that can replace the underlined nouns of the sentence (the words underlined above). Example: I will *sing* to the Lord because Jesus has been good to me. **sing**--Him/ He.

sang-- He/ us --->	**sung**-- She/ her	**song**-- Him/ it	**doll**-- Her/his	**feet**-- They/it
zoo-- He/them	**miss**-- She/it	**add**-- We/it	**lace**--She/her	**Mr.**--He/Him
finds-- he/it	**nice**-- She/us	**plant**--He/it	**got**-- We/ him	**away**--she/they
came--They/ His	**west**-- They/ them	**went**-- She/him	**lake**--We/it	

Capitalization and Abbreviations: *Capitalize proper names of persons, places, or things* [R 26]. A word is misspelled if it is capitalized when it should not be. *Miss Lake* found a *nice lake* in *Nice*, Italy.

Abbreviations use a few letters to represent a larger word [R12]. Students sound out as you write on the board the review word *street*. Sometimes instead of writing the whole word we write *ST*, as in the new two-letter all-cap postal code, or *St.* as in traditional abbreviations. What other abbreviations have we learned? (@/at; yr./year.; yd./yard /; ft./foot) Watch for words in this list that are commonly abbreviated (feet, Mister, west).

sing		
sang	Irregular past tense of "sing." Why not just add -ed to "sing?"	[R3]
sung		
song	Bracket to show these words are related in meaning.	
doll	We often double L after a single vowel at the end of a base word.	[R17]
feet	Abbreviation: ft. Plural of "foot."	[R12,22]
zoo	Z, never S, says /z/ at the beginning of a base word.	[R27]
miss *or* Miss	We often double S after... Capitalize if used as a title for a lady.	[R17,26]
add	We often double F, L, S... Occasionally we double other letters...	[R17]
lace	A said /A/ because of the E. C said /s/ because of the E.	[R7]
Mr. = Mis ter	Abbreviation for *Mister*. Capitalize a person's title.	[R12,26]
finds	I may say /I/ before two consonants.	[R19]
nice	I said /I/ because of the E. C said /s/ because of the E.	[R7]
plant		
got		
a way	A said /A/ at the end of a syllable. AY usually spells /A/ at the end of a word.	[R4,18]
came	The vowel sound changed because of the E.	[R7]
west	Abbreviation: W	[R12]
went	Irregular past tense of "go."	
lake	Can we use C here? No. C would say /s/. A said /A/ because of the E.	[R2,7]

ORIGINAL SENTENCES. Use the spelling words to write sentences that relate to the Oregon Trail. They *came west*. What did they want to *find*? From what did they try to get *away*? What *songs* did they *sing* on the way? Why did the girls have handkerchief *dolls*? The best dolls had *lace added*.

VERBS. "What is the past tense of these verbs?" sing (sang); miss (missed); add (added); lace (laced); plant (planted); find (found); get (got); come (came); go (went). See SWR step 22, p.123. Conjugate these verbs using first person singular. Fold the paper into thirds for: present--past--future.

I sing, I sang, I will sing	*I miss, I missed, I will miss*	*I add, I added, I will add*
I lace, I laced [R. 16], I will lace	*I find, I found, I will find*	*I plant, I planted, I will plant*
I get, I got, I will get	*I come, I came, I will come*	*I go, I went, I will go*

DICTATION. (Advanced) Watch for correct capitalization and abbreviations. Job *got* a job by the *lake*. Herb *went away* to the *west* to *plant* herbs at a *zoo*. *Mr. Lace finds nice dolls' feet* in Nice.

Preliminaries.

<u>Phonograms</u>: "Read" all the phonograms. See how quickly you can do it correctly.
Quiz at least *ar, ch, ck, dge, ea, ed, er, ew, ie, igh, oo, or, ow, wr.*
<u>Reference Page</u>: Teach or review **A-E-I-O-U Page**.

<u>Spelling Rules</u>: Use cards for a warm-up review of rules 2, 7, 19, 25, 27, 28.

Words for Section I-4

241	bow	It's a little bit the fiddle, but lots more who holds the *bow*. --Woodrow Wilson
242	let ter	In the midst of great anger, do not answer anyone's *letter*. --Chinese proverb
243	soon	A fool and his money will *soon* part.
244	ver y	Little faith will get great mercies, but *very* great faith still greater. --C. Spurgeon
245	rich	The generous soul will be made *rich*. --Proverbs 11:25
246	best	A good laugh and a long sleep are the *best* cures in the doctor's book.
247	zip	The girl needs to *zip* her suitcase.
248	brave	Any fool can be *brave* when it's be brave or be killed. --Margaret Mitchell
249	face	You can lean backward so far that you fall flat on your *face*. --B. Bagdikian
250	far	God said to the sea, "This *far* you may come, and here your proud waves must stop!"
251	sold	Judas *sold* Jesus for 30 pieces of silver.
252	told	Don't listen to things *told* by a gossip.
253	nine	A stitch in time saves *nine*.
254	new	There is nothing *new* under the sun.
255	spent	Mary *spent* all Jane's money.
256	block	One of the secrets of life is to make a stepping stone out of a stumbling *block*.
257	down	You can't hold a man *down* without staying down with him. --Booker T. Washington
258	dear	Die, my *dear* doctor, that's the last thing I will do! --Lord Palmerston
259	formed	God *formed* the creatures with His Word and then pronounced them good.--Watts
260	end	The chief *end* of man is to glorify God.

Spelling Enrichments

GRAPHIC DESIGN. Have student lightly (in pencil on a blank sheet of typing paper) trace a sketch of a girl with a big bow taking a bow. Outline the perimeter of the bow with the spelling words reading them across the page rather than just down the column.

Homophones (same sound) and Homographs (same spelling).

Some words are spelled the same and pronounced the same, but have very different meanings. Example: bat (stick for hitting a ball) and bat (animal). Other words are spelled the same but have a different sound and a different meaning. Example: *live* (I saw a live bear at the zoo.) *live* (Where do you live?) The context is the clue to the meaning of the word. Watch for words like this in the following spelling words.

bow	Different sound & meaning: *bow* (tied ribbon), *bow* (bend). A girl with a *bow* took a *bow*.	
let ter		[R29]
soon		
ver y	The 1 over the E means think E-R separately, NOT /er/. See SWR pages 87-88.	[R5,6]
rich		
best		
zip	Z, never S, says /z/ at the beginning of a base word.	[R27]
brave	2 reasons for E. Mark first. Homographs: brave (an Indian), brave (courageous).	[R7]
face	A said /A/ because of the E. C says /s/ because of the E. Mark primary reason.	[R7]
far		
sold	O may say /O/ before 2 consonants. Irregular past tense of "sell."	[R19]
told	O may say /O/ before 2 consonants. Irregular past tense of "tell."	[R19]
nine	I said /I/ because of the E. Add *nine* to **Number Page**. See SWR Step 15.	[R7]
new	Alternative marking: You can treat EW as the second sound. Dictionaries vary.	
spent	Irregular past tense of "spend."	
block	Does CK follow the rule? Yes, it's used after a single vowel that says /o/.	[R25]
down		
dear		
formed	ED forms another syllable if the base word ends with D or T. If not, ED says /d/ or /t/.	[R28]
end		

Spelling Enrichments

PREFIXES. Add UN- to as many spelling words as possible: *untold, unzip, unspent, unsold, unformed.* Several words can take UN- if we make additional changes: unending, unblocked.

DEGREES OF COMPARISON. Complete the following phrases by writing the missing word.

rich, richer, ___ (richest)   soon, sooner, ___ (soonest)   dear, dearer, ___ (dearest)
new, newer, ___ (newest)   far, farther, _____ (farthest)   good, better, ___ (best)

DICTATION.

a. Good, better, best/ I will never rest/ 'til my good is better/ and my better best.

b. A *dear* lady with a nice *face formed the very best new bows*. A bad man from *far down* west got her *bows, sold* them, and *soon* became *rich*. A *brave* man *spent nine* days helping her *zip* out a *letter* to *block* the sale of her *bows*. He *told* me it came to a good *end*. (All spelling words are included in this little paragraph.)

Combine Optional Typing Instruction with Phonogram and Spelling Review

Physical involvement enhances learning. Keyboard work is an excellent variation to the kinesthetic re-inforcement of pencil and paper work. A computer-age student needs to know proper typing form. The recommended general flow of instruction is as follows.

Lesson 1: Show finger placement for the home keys on the key board. Practice a little each day.

Student should say the phonogram sound(s) out loud as he pushes the correct key. First teach the right and left forefingers of the home keys: **fff jjj**. Then the second fingers: **ddd kkk**. Next third fingers: **sss lll**. Then fourth fingers: **aaa ;;;** Have student repeat phonograms sounds as he types: **fjdksla;**. Scramble the order in different ways. Do not allow the student to watch his fingers. He must learn to do this by feel! Dictate spelling words we have learned using these keys: *a; as; ask; all; fall; sad; dad; lad; fad; add*. When typing individual phonograms say all possible sounds. When typing words, say only the sound a phonogram makes in the word.

Lesson 2: Teach **h** (J finger), **e** (D finger), **o** (L finger). Dictate: *oo; ee; ea; ed; oe; oa; sh;* she; he; had; do; doll; so; odd; old; sold; hold; sea; see; food; led; lake; look

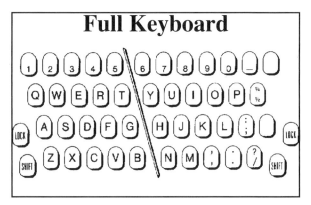

Lesson 3: Teach **m, r, i.** Dictate: *er; ear; ir; ar; or; ei; oi; ai; ie; si;* am; is; it, its, if; mad; red; me; did; him; her; hill; his; home; make; are; has; kill; like; ice; child; milk; hair; for; floor; door; moon; come; some; free; roll; miss; came; letter; far; dear; formed; fish; read

Lesson 4: Teach **t, n.** Dictate: *th; ti; kn;* tell; the; time; then; trade; this; soon; that; three; an; ran; tan; men; ten; last; hat; hit; it; in; to; into; on; at; flat; and; land; hand; no; not; lot; hot; school; street; other; man; mother; moon; little; late; letter; short; star; shot; then; heat; stand; soft; lone; alone; one; salt; send; them; stone; foot; feet; after; lift; thank; than; take; season; storm; tree; alike; dinner; find; told; nine; end; let; man; moon; letter

Lesson 5: Teach **c, v.** Dictate: *ch; ck; ci; tch;* cad; call; can; cat; cad; coat; cold; come; corn; dance; thick; sick; ice; child; each; nice; rich; lace; face; five; live; river

Lesson 6: Teach **w, g.** Dictate: *wh; ew; ng; ow; aw; igh; wr; dge; eigh; gn; wor;* go; got; good; give; gave; thing; ring; show; what; wing; sing; sang; long; song; over; dog; we; will; have; love; wave; wash; west; was; now; wild; white; winter; wall; gas; green; law; new; down

Lesson 7: Teach **b, u.** Dictate: *au; ou; ough; eu; ur; ui;* bad; bacon; bag; be; bed; beg; big; bog; bug; but; book; robe; run; just; about; much; out; house; sung; best; brave; bow; blow

Lesson 8: Teach **p, qu, z.** Dictate: *ph;* put; plant; path; pet; top; jump; step; spring, up; spent; zoo; zip.

Lesson 9: Teach **y, x.** Dictate: *oy; ay; ey;* by; my; boy; toy; six; very; you; your; yes; yet; year; baby; box; day; say; play; may; lay; way; away

SPELLING
SECTION J

Teachers use this program with a large variety of ages and ability levels. Daily lesson plans by necessity will vary. An average kindergartner will do ten words a week, a first grader twenty or more, and later grades forty. Most instructors teach the new words for the week early in the week and do reinforcement activities the balance of the week.

Some highly successful teachers give DAILY spelling quizzes on at least some of the words for the week. Even on the day(s) new words are introduced, the teacher can have the students close their spelling notebooks and take a quiz on the words just taught. On all quizzes except the final one for the week the students may self-correct their work. They read back the words, one at a time, sounding them out as the teacher writes them correctly on the board. The student corrects any misspelled words. The teacher should spot-check for errors. If a student misses a word, she should erase the whole word and rebuild it correctly.

On Friday a regular test is given on all the words for the week, plus some of the phonograms and five or ten review words from earlier in the year. The teacher doesn't say which specific review words will be added to the Friday test. Students should learn to be accountable for any word taught that year, not just the words for the week.

The first 360 words (A through J) and their derivatives include over 60% of all words we read and write.

Preliminaries.

      Phonograms: Review all 70 phonograms.
      Spelling Rules: Use cards for a warm-up review of rules 3, 5, 6, 7, 8, 12, 26.
      Reference Pages: Introduce **ER Page**. See Step 26 in SWR. Introduce or review the **Consonant/ Vowel, Multi-letter Phonogram,** and **Silent Final E Pages**.   See Steps 9, 10, 17 in SWR.

Words for Section J-1

261	why	For every *why* he had a wherefore. --Samuel Butler
262	ev er y	The eyes of the Lord are in *every* place. --Proverbs 15:3
263	proud	A humble man has this advantage over a *proud* man, for he cannot fall.
264	hap py	The only truly *happy* men I have ever known were Christians. --J. Randolph
265	son	A wise *son* makes a glad father. --Proverbs 10:1.
266	with	He who walks *with* wise men will be wise.--Proverbs 13:20
267	our	In what or in whom do we put *our* faith?
268	same	The future is made of the *same* stuff as the present. --Simmeweil
269	fine	The seven girls were *fine* in the hayloft.
270	name	Multitude does not argue the goodness of a thing. The Devil's *name* is Legion.
271	read	What is the best book you have ever *read?*
272	word	The Christian is bred by the *Word,* and he must be fed by it. --William Gurnall
273	dad dy	We affectionately call our father *"Daddy."*
274	girl	A trick that everyone abhors in a *girl* is slamming doors. --Hilaire Belloc
275	nev er	A kindness is *never* wasted. --Aesop, *The Lion and the Mouse*
276	for get	O what a wonderful, wonderful day, Day I will never *forget.* --hymn by J. Peterson
277	think	*Think* first and speak afterwards.
278	life	The most important things in *life* aren't things.
279	un der	*Under* the shadow of Thy throne still may we dwell secure. --Isaac Watts
280	lord	He lived as a *lord* in the days of King Arthur.

Spelling Enrichments

DEAF SIGNING. After first teaching the words normally, have students pretend to be deaf. Teach them to "say" and "hear" their spelling words using deaf signing. (See pages 38-39 for instructions.)

SENTENCE DICTATION. Dictate sentences as a variation to traditional spelling test.   For example: *Why* does *every girl* not *think* the *same?*   *Every girl* can have a *fine life*. *Read* the *word under our name.* *Why* did *Daddy read to* his *sons* about the *Lord?*

AESOP'S FABLE "The Lion and the Mouse." Story summary: A mouse pleads for mercy from a lion that has him in his claws. The mouse squeals, "The day may come when I can repay your kindness." The lion, amused that a creature so small could ever help the king of beasts, let him go. Later the mouse nibbled with his sharp teeth and freed the lion from a hunter's tangled nest. Dictate the moral: A kindness is *never* wasted.

CORRESPONDENCE. Use spelling words to write a letter. Example: *Dear Daddy,*
                                           I will never forget.....

Introduce the ER Page

So far we have learned a number of ER words. Which ER's have we used? *(her, over, mother, other, paper, after, summer, winter, river, dinner, letter).* Add these from dictation to the ER page (See Step 26 in *Spell to Write and Read.*) Which of the five ER's do we use the most often? We use the first ER ten times more often than all the others combined. From now on we will start using the other ER's as well. After the lesson we will add all the new ER words we learned to the ER page.

why	Y may say /I/ at the end of a syllable. English words do not end with I.	[R5,6]
ev er y.		[R5,6]
proud		
hap py	Double consonants both sounded for spelling. Y usually says /i/ at the end of...	[R29,5,6]
son	Think to spell exaggerating the vowel as /o/. Add *sonship* to the **SH Page**.	
with	Alternative marking: with. Abbreviation: w/	[R12]
our	First person, possessive, plural pronoun.	
same	A said /A/ because of the E.	[R7]
fine	I said /I/ because of the E.	[R7]
name	A said /A/ because of the E.	[R7]
read	Same spelling, different sounds & meanings: *read* (present tense), *read* (past tense).	
word	O-R usually says /er/ when W comes before O-R. Add to **ER Page**.	[R8]
dad dy	English words do not end with I. Use the stand-in vowel.	[R29,5,6]
girl	G may say /j/ before I, but not always. Add to **ER Page**.	[R3]
nev er	[<OE ne- (not) + aefre (ever)].	
for get		
think	See note for "thank" on p. 27.	
life	I said /I/ because of the E.	[R7]
un der		
lord	Add *lordship* to **SH Page**. See SWR Step 18.	

Spelling Enrichments

COMPOUND WORDS. Quiz the following review spelling words: *after, by, cut, dog, foot, go, hand, lay, like, long, one, over, shot, stand, step, take, thing, time, went.* Correct paper. Use together with current spelling words to make as many compound words as possible.

after -- afterlife	lay -- underlay	step -- stepson, stepdaddy
by -- byword	like -- lifelike	take -- undertake
cut -- undercut	long -- lifelong	thing --everything
dog -- underdog	one -- everyone	time -- lifetime
foot -- underfoot	over -- overlord	went -- underwent
go -- undergo	shot -- undershot	
hand -- underhand	stand -- withstand, understand	

ER PAGE. We will start collecting ER words for the ER page. Once the first ER column is filled, concentrate on the other four. What ER words can we add to our reference page from these spelling words? *(every, word, girl, never, under)*

"A" Hand 	**why**  Flick middle "sensitive" finger off forehead--*the seat of reason.*	**every** Rub knuckles of right "A" hand several times on thumb of left "A" hand. Right thumb *pointing to individuals.*
proud Draw tip of thumb of right "A" hand up the chest. *Face shows swelling with pride.*	**happy**  Pat chest several times with right hand to show *bubbling emotion inside*	**son**  Grab imaginary bill of boy's cap and then cradle right arm in left arm for baby. Combine sign for boy and sign for baby.
with 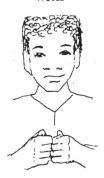 Bring both "A" hands together with thumbs upward. Both hands together.	**our**  Move right vertical palm from right shoulder out and around to left shoulder. *Yours and mine.*	**same**  Put index fingers side by side; from right to left. *Fingers look alike and move alike.*
fine  Touch thumb of right hand, palm leftward, below right shoulder. *Fancy ruffles once worn by gentlemen.*	**"H" Hand** 	**name**  Make an X with right "H" hand on the left "H" hand. *Making mark like someone who can't write their name.*

Art work by Kelly Cracksberger

"B" Hand	"L" Hand	"V" Hand	"5" Hand	**read**

Move right "V" hand across the left prone hand from the tips of the fingers to the heel of the hand. *Eyes scan the page.*

word

Measure first joint of left index finger with thumb and index fingertip of right hand. *One separate part of a sentence.*

daddy

Place "five" hand on forehead. Male sign on forehead.

girl

Draw "A" hand along lower jaw as if straightening the tie to a bonnet. *Show bonnet string.*

never

Move open right hand, with palm leftward, back and forth in a waving motion. *Head shaking "no."*

forget

Move horizontal "B" hand from in front of forehead to the right and change to "A" hand. Thought washed out of mind.

think

Bore tip of right index finger into forehead. *Boring into brain.*

life

Make "L" sign with each hand and pass up the sides of the chest. *Blood rising in body.*

under

Place right "A" hand, thumb upward, under left prone hand. *One hand under other.*

lord

Lift "L" right hand from left shoulder to right hip. *Shows royalty.* (Use same actions with the "K" hand for KING.)

Faces above are students from Mr. Cracksberger's class at school for deaf in Portland, OR.   39

Preliminaries.

Phonograms: Quiz phonograms *ar, er, ng, oi, oo, ou, oy, sh*. A student often misses ones he previously got right. Time and repetition help build long-term memory. Spelling Rules: 7, 10, 13,19. Reference Page: If you have not already this year, teach **A-E-I-O-U Page** (SWR Step 19) and the **SH Page** (SWR Step 18).

Words for Section J-2

281	side	Christians not only move the world, we turn it right *side* up.
282	out side	Happiness lies *outside* yourself. --V. Solanas
283	in side	He likes running but he cannot run *inside* the house.
284	oil	His words were softer than *oil*, yet were they drawn swords. --Psalms 55:21
285	hard	It is easy to tell a lie, but *hard* to tell only one.
286	from	A wise man fears and departs *from* evil. --Proverbs 14:16
287	noon	The moon gives light in time of night, the sun at *noon*.
288	most	They who forgive *most*, shall be most forgiven. --J. Bailey
289	hang	We must *hang* together or most assuredly we shall *hang* separately. --B. Franklin
290	cast	*Cast* all your cares on the Lord, for He cares for you. -- 1 Peter 5:7
291	line	Lightning tore a dotted *line* down the sky.
292	post	He went to buy a *post* for the fence.
293	arm	Have you an *arm* like God? Or can you thunder with a voice like His? --Job 40:9
294	skin	After my *skin* has been destroyed, yet in my flesh I will see God. --Job 19:26
295	ship	It was as idle as a painted *ship* upon a painted ocean. --Samuel Taylor Coleridge
296	here	The frost is *here* and fuel is dear. --Tennyson
297	sun	The *sun* looks like it rises and sets each day. --Noah Webster
298	age	A tart temper never mellows with *age*. --Washington Irving
299	cov er	You can't tell a book by its *cover*.
300	mine	Thank you, Lord Jesus, for my kitty's food and *mine*. --*Christian Mother Goose*

Spelling Enrichments

PREPOSITIONS. Define: A preposition shows the relationship to an object. Demonstrate: Ask the student to put his pencil on the table. What is the preposition? (on) What is the object? (table). Put the pencil in your hand (in/ hand). Put the pencil into a box (into/ box). Put the pencil over your head (over /head). Dictate the prepositions taught as spelling words so far: *in, by, out, to, into, up, on, onto, over, at, of, like, for, about, after, down, with*. See SWR p. 104. Find new prepositions in Section J-2 (*from, outside, inside*). The Grammar Reader *Up, Over, and Out* published by BHI teaches prepositions.

SENTENCES. Write original sentences using the new spelling words. Include a prepositional phrase in each sentence. Dictate one or more of the following examples:

I get *in the covers* to get warm.   She sat *on the sideline*.   He stood *outside the post*.
At my age I find that *hard*.   He came *from the ship*.   He came *inside the line*.

SH PAGE. If you have not done so already this year, start building the SH Page in the Learning Log. Look through the Wise List to get examples of SH at the beginning, at the end, and with the ending *-ship*. *-Ship* words can include derivatives such as: *sonship, lordship, hardship*. Add more SH words as they occur.

This System Works!

Note the amazing regularity of spelling words based on the 70 phonograms and the 29 spelling rules. At this point we have taught the 300 easiest-to- spell words out of the 1000 most frequently used words in the English language. In only two of the 300 words does the phonogram sound not agree with the written form of the word: *one, of.*

---

side	I said /I/ because of the E.	[R7]
out side		[R7]
in side	Bracket the root word *side* with examples of compound words built from it.	[R7]
oil		
hard	Add *hardship* to **SH Page** (the "except for the ending -ship" portion).	[R10]
from		
noon	[<L nones (ninth hour-- 3 p.m.). Now 12:00 o'clock.]	
most	The reason for the O (the 2 consonants) is readily seen without special markings.	[R19]
hang	Past tense varies. A man is *hanged.* A picture is *hung.*	
cast		

---

line	I said /I/ because of the E.	[R7]
post	O may say /O/ before two consonants.	[R19]
arm		
skin		
ship	Use the /sh/ that we use at the beginning of a word. Add to the **SH Page**.	[R10]
here	E said /E/ because of the E. Contraction: here is = here's. SWR Step 28.	[R7,13]
sun	Homophone: son	
age	A said /A/ because of the E.	[R7]
cov er		
mine	I said /I/ because of the E.	[R7]
	Same spelling, different meanings: mine (belongs to me), mine (place for ore).	

COMPOUND WORDS. Make 36 or so new compound words by combining current words or one of the following review words: *after, away, bed, by, down, fish, hill, life, man, out, over, set, tan, under, up.* Bonus extras: *fire, head, pig, room, teen.*

side -- bedside, hillside, sideline [fireside]
oil -- oilskin
hard -- hardship
noon --afternoon
most -- upmost [headmost]
hang --hangover, hangout
cast -- outcast, downcast, castaway
line -- lifeline, underline [headline]

post -- outpost
arm -- overarm, underarm [firearm]
skin -- oilskin [pigskin]
ship -- hardship [headship]
here -- hereafter, hereby, herein
sun -- sundown, sunfish, sunset, suntan [sunroom]
age -- overage, underage ·[teenage]
cover -- undercover
mine -- undermine

Preliminaries.   Rules: Review rule cards 2, 4, 7, 17, 18, 19, 23.

Phonograms: Review the phonograms needed in this lesson: *er, ch, aw, ar, ou, dge, or, sh, ay*. For a stimulating change you may want to play the Phonogram Guessing Game on p. 146. Students try to identify each phonogram by asking elimination questions: *Does it have more than two letters? Three? Does it have more than one phonogram sound? Two? Three? Five? Does it say /A/?*

Words for Section J-3

301	wind	The ungodly... are like the chaff which the *wind* drives away. --Psalm 1:4
302	race	Slow and steady wins the *race*. --Robert Lloyd
303	perch	My bird sat on the *perch* and sang.
304	saw	I never *saw* a dog nor a cat learn to read. --McGuffey
305	left	Virtuous Ruth *left* all for truth. *--New England Primer*
306	fill	Sign on cement-mixer truck: "We find a need and *fill* it."
307	part	A fool and his money will soon *part*.
308	group	Be careful not to be entangled with the wrong *group*.
309	place	A sleeping pill will never take the *place* of a clear conscience. --E. Cantor
310	fudge	Make *fudge* to eat at the edge of the bridge.
311	force	Faith is the *force* of life. --L. Tolstoy
312	bank	"I cried all the way to the *bank*." --(Liberace, after he was criticized.)
313	dust	The devil is not afraid of the Bible with *dust* on it.
314	shape	There is a divinity that will *shape* our ends. --Wm. Shakespeare
315	print	It is exciting reading something you've written in *print*.
316	re port	Whatsoever things are of good *report*...think on these things. --Philippians 4:8
317	pay	Those who *pay* are masters of those who are paid. --James Madison
318	band	He played in the church *band*.
319	hope	I only *hope* to be forgiven by trusting in the blood of Christ. --Otto Bismark
320	bill	The *bill* from the doctor for your sprained wrist was over five hundred dollars!

Spelling Enrichments

LITERATURE. Read one of the classic Amelia Bedelia books by Peggy Parish. Have the student identify the possible double meanings of terms that cause miscommunication.

ART FOR DEMONSTRATING GRAMMAR. Each of these spelling words can be used either as a noun (a word naming something) or a verb (a word showing action). Pick at least half of the words and draw a sketch that demonstrates both meanings.

Words with Multiple Meanings. Listen for a new word that can be pronounced two ways like *read* and *live*.

WIND uses a short /i/ when it names an object that moves and flows like air [< OE *wind*].

WIND uses the long /I/ sound when it identifies the action of twisting and turning [< OE *win-dan*].

Listen for words that sound the same but come from different origins and have very different meanings.

LINE meaning "piece of rope" [< L linea (thread)]. LINE meaning "fill." *Line the box*. [< OE lin (flax)].

wind	I may say /I/ before 2 consonants but often doesn't. Either way can apply here.	[R19]
race	A said /A/ because of the E. C also says /s/ because of the E. Mark the 1st reason.	[R7]
perch	Multiple meanings: *a pole* or *a type of fish*.	
saw	Use the /aw/ that we may use at the end. English words do not end with U.	
left	Multiple meanings: *past tense of leave* or *opposite of right*.	
fill	We often double L after a single vowel at the end of a base word.	[R17]
part		
group 3		
place	A said /A/ because of the E. C says /s/ because of the E. Mark the 1st reason.	[R7]
fudge	Three letter /j/ is used only after a single vowel that says /a-e-i-o-u/.	[R23]
force 3	C says /s/ because of the E.	[R7]
bank	Multiple meanings: *a place to keep money, side of a river, a mound*.	
dust	Could we use the letter C here to say /s/? No. It is not before an E, I, or Y.	[R2]
shape	Add to **SH Page**. A said /A/ because of the E.	[R10,7]
print		
re port	[<L re- (back) + portare (carry)]. E said /E/ at the end of the syllable.	[R4]
pay	A-Y usually spells /A/ at the end of a base word. If a word ends with A it says /ah/.	[R18]
band	Multiple meanings: *group of people* or *something that ties*.	
hope	O said /O/ because of the E.	[R7]
bill	We often double L after a single vowel at the end of a base word.	[R17]

Spelling Enrichments

VOCABULARY ENRICHMENT.

Compound Words. Add *hand* or *over* to current spelling words to make new words:
handsaw, handbill, handprint, leftover, overfill, overpay.

Derivatives. Add the suffixes *-less* (without), *-ful* (full of), *-ment* (act or state of):
forceful, hopeless, hopeful, placement, payment, shapeless.

HELPING VERBS. Dictate the following review words: *can, may, will, must*. These words can be added to the verb to help express the meaning more exactly. *I can race* (I am able to race). *I may race* (I have permission to race). *I will race.* (I am determined to race). *I must race.* (I am required to race). Make sentences using the new spelling words. Let each sentence include one of these helping verbs.

Examples: I can *perch* on the *swing* by the *farm*. I may *place* the *report* on your desk. I will *saw* the wood with my *left* hand. I must *fill* the dishwasher for Mom.

Preliminaries.   Spelling Rules: Review cards 4, 5, 6, 7, 12, 19, 22.
Phonograms: Have student(s) "read" all seventy phonograms. (Omit spelling dialogue distinctions such as "four letter A.") Time your students. Can the class "read" all seventy in less than seventy-five seconds? Keep working during the weeks to come to reach top speed.
Reference Page: Introduce **Plural Page**. See SWR Step 27.

Words for Section J-4

321	sev en	*Seven* days without prayer makes one weak. --Allen E. Bartlett
322	fun ny	Everything is *funny* as long as it's happening to someone else. --Will Rogers
323	blue	*Blue* are the hills far away.
324	e lev en	One added to ten makes *eleven.*
325	found	Lost time is never *found* again. --*Poor Richard's Almanack*
326	gal lon	Did you know a "10-*gallon* hat" holds only about three quarts?
327	gold	Fools kneel before *gold,* the greater to the lesser.
328	lost	Nothing is really *lost.* It's just where it doesn't belong. --S. Mueller
329	grand	I sat by the *grand* piano.
330	for got	I *forgot* my list at the store.
331	sis ters	The *sisters,* wives, and mothers keep the world sweet and beautiful. --C. Brink
332	card	Write your verse on a three-by-five *card.*
333	bird	If God made a *bird,* it is worth painting. --Francis A. Schaeffer
334	fools	*Fools* mock at sin. --Proverbs 14:9
335	inch	He grew an *inch* this year.
336	sup per	You can't trust a dog to watch your *supper*, especially the dessert.
337	grain	Without Thy sunshine and Thy rain, we could not have the golden *grain.*
338	game	Please step over my *game,* not on it.
339	spur	These studies are a *spur* to the young. --Cicero
340	role	Men and women each have a valuable *role* to play.

Spelling Enrichments

PLURALS. Write the singular and plural form of the last ten words: sister/ sisters; card/ cards; bird/ birds; fool/ fools; inch/ inches (when the word ending hisses, add -es); supper/ suppers; grain/ grains; game/ games; spur/ spurs; role/ roles.

NUMBERS. Add to **Number Page** (SWR Step 15) *seven, seventh, eleven, eleventh.*

ALLITERATION. Group together the spelling words that begin with the same first sound *(band bill).*
        seven, sisters, supper, spur   *blue, bird*
        funny, found, forgot, fools   *gallon, gold, grand, grain, game*
Write original sentences, using alliteration. Example: *Fools forgot where they found funny* fudge.

DICTATION. Grandma had a role as good as gold. She cooked grain for supper, shined the spurs, fed the birds, found the game I lost, and made a funny card saying, "How many gallons in an inch? How many sisters in a pinch? How much wisdom in seven fools? Can you name eleven rules? I forgot but don't be blue. Always know that I love you."

Forming Plurals

To make a word plural we usually just add an **-s**. Since it is hard to say two hissing sounds in a row, after words that end with *ch (1st,3rd sound), s, sh, x, and z* we add **-es**. (Some words do not change and are spelled the same way whether they are singular or plural.) In the spelling words for this lesson the last ten words can be made into plural words. These words illustrate both situations. Several other conditions exist in forming plurals but do not need to be taught at this point. See the rule for forming plurals [R22].

sev en	Add to **Number Page.**	
fun ny	Sound /n/ twice for spelling but not speech. Y stands-in for I at the end of English words.	[R29,5,6]
blue	English words do not end with U.	[R7]
e lev en	E said /E/ at the end of a syllable. Add to **Number Page.**	[R4]
found		
gal lon	Sound /l/ twice for spelling but not normal speech. <u>Abbreviation</u>: gal.	[R29,12]
gold	O may say /O/ before two consonants.	[R19]
lost	O may say /O/ before two consonants but it doesn't have to!	[R19]
grand		
for got	_____	
sis ters	Add to **ER Page** and **Plural Page.**	[R22]
card		
bird	Add to **ER Page.**	
fools	<u>Oxymoron</u>: a wise fool. Add to **Plural Page.**	[R22]
inch	[<L uncia (the twelfth part)]. <u>Abbreviation</u>: in.	[R12]
sup per	Meaning varies: night meal (America); a late snack (Australia).	[R29]
grain		
game	A said /A/ because of the E.	[R7]
spur	Add to **ER Page**.	
role	[<F role (roll of paper on which a part was written)]. O said /O/ because of the E.	[R7]

Spelling Enrichments

ADJECTIVES. An adjective modifies (restricts or changes) the meaning of a noun or pronoun. Example: *sad son, glad son, funny son, fine son.* Use the adjectives from this list *(seven, funny, blue, eleven, gold, lost, grand)* to change the meanings of any five of the last ten words.

sisters	lost sisters, funny sisters, seven sisters, eleven sisters
card	gold card, blue card, lost card, funny card, grand card, seven cards, eleven cards
bird	gold bird, blue bird, lost bird, funny bird, grand bird, seven birds, eleven birds
fools	lost fools, funny fools, seven fools, eleven fools
inch	lost inch, seven inches, eleven inches
spurs	gold spurs, blue spurs, lost spurs, funny spurs, grand spurs, seven spurs, eleven spurs

COMPOUND WORDS. Dictate review words: *red, son, dog, fish, child, daddy, mother, step.* Use with spelling words to make compound words: redbird, grandchild, grandson, granddaddy, grandmother, stepsister, birddog, goldfish, bluefish.

Preliminaries. <u>Spelling Rules</u>: Review cards 4, 7, 12, 13, 17, 19, 28.

<u>Reference Page</u>: Build **-ED Page** and collect contractions. See Steps 22, 28 in SWR.

<u>Phonograms</u>: Play the Phonogram Guessing Game. Hints help students name mystery phonogram. This 2-letter phonogram sounds like one consonant (*ck, gn, kn, ph, wh, wr*). This 2-letter phonogram sounds like one vowel (*ai, ay, oe, ee, oa*). This 2-letter phonogram represents 3 sounds (ea, ei, ie, ey, oo). This 2-letter phonogram always says the same thing (*ee, sh, ck, ay, ai, ng, or, oy, oi, oe, oa, ar, ng, wr, ph*).

Words for Section J-5

341	can not	God, who *cannot* lie, promised eternal life to all who believe.
342	said	What's *said* is *said* and goes upon its way, like it or not, repent it as you may. --Chaucer
343	a long	Come then, my friend, my genius, come *along*. --Alexander Pope
344	east	*East* is *east* and west is west and never the twain shall meet. --Rudyard Kipling
345	strike	A soft tongue may *strike* hard. *--Poor Richard's Almanack*
346	made	God *made* the cows and God made us. --McGuffey Primer
347	deep	The snow lay round about, *deep* and crisp and even. -Good King Wenselas, an ancient carol
348	still	Be *still* and know that I am God. --Psalm 46
349	want	Many things are lost for *want* of asking. --English proverb
350	glad	Folded hands are ever weary; selfish hearts are never *glad*.
351	for give	A sin too great to forsake is too great to *forgive*.
352	won	What is evil *won* is evil lost. --Aesop
353	rest	Seek home for *rest* for home is best. --Thomas Tusser
354	room	Shall I think of death as doom, or stepping to a bigger, brighter *room?* --Freeman
355	toe	I felt pain when the rock fell on my *toe*.
356	meat	I like what I EAT with m*EAT*.
357	air	How do you like to go up in a swing, up in the *air* so blue? --Robert L. Stevenson
358	kind	I love thee for a heart that's *kind,* not for the knowledge in thy mind. --W. Davies
359	joy	Let it be your *joy* to do the will of God. *--McGuffey Primer*
360	when	It's *when* you run away that you're most liable to stumble. --C. Robinson

Spelling Enrichments

GRAMMAR. Dictate the following sentences made up of past and current spelling words.

✻ What did he <u>want</u> the *most?* --how much		Will he *never* <u>forgive</u>?	--how long
✻The <u>room</u> will be done *soon.* --how long,when		✻Go <u>*east*</u> then turn at the <u>rest</u> stop.	--where, when
Now we <u>won</u>. --when		I am *so* <u>glad</u> you like <u>meat</u>.	--how much
✻ <u>*When*</u> will you be <u>kind</u>? --when		Do *not* <u>strike</u> your sister.	--how
✻Are you <u>*still*</u> <u>glad</u>? --how long		<u>*When*</u> did he cover my <u>toe</u>?	--when

Adverbs may be added to verbs and adjectives to answer the questions: *how?, when?, where?, how much?, how long?* Can you find the adverb in each sentence? (The adverbs above are italicized.) What question does the adverb answer? Adverbs are often made by adding LY (kindly, gladly, deeply, joyfully).

History of the Language

Specific spelling for specific words developed for specific reasons, some of which are now lost to us. Sometimes spelling reflects the ghost of lost sounds. One of the words taught in this lesson illustrates this well. To the American speaker of English the spelling for the present and past tense of *say* is irregular. We say /sed/ but spell s-ai-d. To the speaker from Scotland the word may be spelled just like it sounds.

---

can not	Compound word. Contraction: can't. Add to **Contraction Page**.	[R13]
said	Think to spell the Scottish way, /s-A-d/. Americans say /sed/. Root = say.	
a long	Exaggerate unaccented syllable for spelling. A said /A/ at the end of a syllable.	[R4]
east	Abbreviation: E	[R12]
strike	I said /I/ because of the E.	[R7]
made	A said /A/ because of the E.	[R7]
deep		
still	We often double L after a single vowel at the end of a base word.	[R17]
want	After a W an A usually says /ah/.	
glad		
for give	English words do not end with V.	[R7]
won	[<OE winnan (struggle for)]. Root = win. Homophone: one.	
rest		
room		
toe		
meat	The word *meet* will be taught later. Stick to teaching this one alone here.	
air	[GB aero- (air) as in aerobics].	
kind	I may say /I/ before two consonants. Oxymoron: cruel kindness.	[R19]
joy		
when	Pronounce /wh/ carefully.	

CONTRACTIONS. Contractions replace a letter or letters with an apostrophe to contract (or shorten) a phrase [Rule 13]. Dictate the following phrases and have the students form their contractions.

cannot -- *can't*	was not -- *wasn't*	has not -- *hasn't*	have not -- *haven't*
it is -- *it's*	what is -- *what's*	you are -- *you're*	here is -- *here's*
that is -- *that's*	he is -- *he's*	she is -- *she's*	one is -- *one's*

DERIVATIVES. Add *un-, -er, -ern, -est, -ful, -less, -ly, -ness, -y* to as many words as possible.

said -- unsaid	*glad* -- gladness, gladder, gladdest*	*air* -- airy
east -- eastern	*forgive* -- forgiveness	*kind* -- un-, -er, -est, -ly
made -- unmade	*rest* -- restless, restful	*joy* -- joyless, joyful
deep -- deeper, -est, -ly	*room* -- roomy	_____
still -- stillness	*meat* -- meatless, meaty	* See Rule 14

SENTENCES. When writing original sentences using these words, include at least one contraction, one adverb, and one of the derivatives listed above.

Preliminaries. Phonograms: Review especially *ai, ay, ar, ch, ck, ea, ee, oa, oo, ow, wor.*   For an active variation have the student stand up and hop as he says each different phonogram sound. Three hops will be needed for the letter EA but only one for AI. Spelling rules: Review 7, 8, 12, 17, 18, 25.

Words for Section J-6

361	more	Lord, help me be *more* laid back and help me do it exactly right.
362	town	The nuts are getting brown; the berry's cheek is plump, the rose is out of *town.* -- E. Dickinson
363	car	Webster in 1828 defined *car* as a small vehicle on wheels, usually drawn by one horse.
364	train	The wind is like a whistling *train* or sometimes a roaring hurricane. --Cheaney
365	boat	We trust in Thee, whatever befall; Thy sea is great, our *boat* is small. --Henry van Dyke
366	cook	The *cook* was a good cook, as cooks go; and as cooks go, she went. --Saki
367	brown	Dark *brown* is the river; Golden is the sand. --Robert L. Stevenson
368	egg	The rotten *egg,* though underneath the hen, if cracked, stinks. --John Bunyan
369	eat	*Eat* to live; live not to *eat. --Poor Richard's Almanack*
370	farm	*Farm* work looks easy when your plow is a pencil and you're miles from a cornfield. --Eisenhower
371	help	Sincerity does not *help* if you are sincerely wrong.
372	work	*Work* as if you will live a hundred years; pray as if you will die tomorrow. --Ben Franklin
373	large	Heaven is *large* but the way to heaven is narrow.
374	rock	A cliff is a high steep *rock.*
375	stay	Come again when you cannot *stay* so long. --Walter Sickert
376	dark	Heed the Word of God as "light that shines in a *dark* place." --2 Pet. 1:19
377	sleep	Earth wakes like a young maiden from her *sleep* and smiles. --McGuffey
378	near	While youths do cheer, death may be *near. --New England Primer*
379	fire	The fool sticks his fingers in the *fire.*
380	chair	Inspiration is the act of drawing up a *chair* to the desk.

Spelling Enrichments

DEAF SIGNING. Teach these spelling words normally, then teach the deaf sign for each word. (See p. 50.) Students whisper the word using their lips carefully forming the shape of the word as they sign it.

COMPOSITION. Dictate: *Different people enjoy different forms of transportation.*   Student can write four or five related sentences using as many words as possible from all of Section J.

DIRECT QUOTES. Use one or two quotes as a part of the discussion on transportation suggested above. Punctuate the direct quotes correctly. For example: My grandmother said, "I will never forget my trip to America by *boat.* The *cook* fried *brown farm eggs* to *eat.*"

PLURALS. Find the nouns in this lesson and write their singluar/ plural forms (town/towns, car/ cars, train/ trains, boat/ boats, egg/ eggs, farm/ farms, work/works, rock/ rocks, fire/ fires, chair/ chairs.)

COMPOSE A STORY. A story needs characters (cook, farm help). A story needs a setting (town, train, boat, chair). A story needs a conflict (sleep, fire, rock). A story needs a resolution to the problem (stay).

INTERJECTIONS. Two words in J-6 can be used as interjections. *Help! Fire!*

Literature

One of the new spelling words can form a compound word with *box* to become part of the title to a popular series of children's books. Who can identify the books in question? (Boxcar Children)

---

more	1st silent E makes a better "sound picture for spelling" than <u>OR</u> and an odd job E. [R7]
town	
car	Popular book series: *Boxcar Children*.
train	
boat	
cook	
brown	
egg	Occasionally we double G after a single vowel at the end of a base word. [R17]
eat	Irregular past tense: ate
farm	

---

help	
work	O-R may say /ER/ when W comes before O-R. Add to **ER Page**. [R8]
large	G says /j/ because of the E. <u>Abbreviation</u>: lg. [R7,12]
rock	CK is used after a single vowel at the end of a base word. [R25]
stay	A-Y usually spells /A/ at the end of a base word. When a word ends with A it says /ah/. [R18]
dark	
sleep	Irregular past tense: slept
near	[<OE neah (nigh)]
fire	One syllable. Think to spell /f/-/I/-/r/. See SWR p. 88.
chair	

DRAWING ADJECTIVES. An adjective modifies a noun or pronoun. Illustrate artistically the difference the change of adjectives makes in the following situations.

brown egg   large egg   more eggs   cooked eggs

Illustrate and label: large fire, train fire, cook fire, boat fire, more fires, town fire.

COMPOUND WORDS. Dictate: *arm, back, box, day, down, foot, hand, house, life, never, over, plant, ship, side, stone, up.* Combine those review words and current spelling words to make new words.

more --	moreover, nevermore	*egg* --	eggplant
town --	downtown, uptown, township	*farm* --	farmhouse
car --	boxcar	*work* --	foot-, hand-, house-, over-, -day, -out
boat --	houseboat, boathouse, lifeboat	*stay* --	overstay
cook --	overcook	*sleep* --	oversleep
brown --	brownstone	*fire* --	-arm, back-, firehouse, fireside, fireworks

Note: *Cargo* is not a compound word made up of car + go. *Cargo* comes from Spanish *cargar* (to load).

"And" Hand

"B" Hand

"H" Hand

more

Repeatedly touch tips of fingers of both "and" hands. *Adding a little at a time.*

town

Repeatedly make the shape of housetops while moving hands from right to left. *Many housetops.*

car

Grasp an imaginary steering wheel with both hands and turn it from side to side. *Steering an automobile.*

train

Move right "H" fingers back and forth on left "H" fingers; both palms down. *Train on tracks.*

boat

Form the shape of a boat with hands. Move hands forward to show motion over the waves. *Boat tossing in waves.*

cook

Put right hand palm down on left hand palm up, then lift and turn over; repeat several times. *Turning the pancakes.*

brown

Draw right "B" hand down cheek near hair. *Long brown hair.*

egg

Hit right "H" hand with left "H" hand, then separate hands with a downward semi-circle movement. *Breaking eggs.*

eat

Place right "and" fingertips at the lips repeatedly at the lips. *Putting food in the mouth.*

farm

Move tip of thumb of right "five" hand across the chin from left to right. *Plowing the field.*

"A" Hand	"S" Hand	"L" Hand	"V" Hand	**help**

Lift right "A" hand with left prone hand.
Giving a lift.

work

Hit right "S" hand against back of
of wrist of left "S" hand several times.
Hammering to show work effort.

large

Move "L" hands apart. *Shows
largeness.*

rock

Strike right "A" hand against wrist of left "S"
hand several times. *Hard, can't be broken.*

stay

Thumb of right "A" hand holds down
thumb of left "A" hand. *Keep in place.*

dark

Pass vertical hands, palms inward, in
front of the face until hands are crossed
at wrists. *Shades pulled over eyes.*

sleep

Place "five" hands in front of eyes; close hands
to become "and" hands. *Eyes closed as in sleep.*

near

Place left palm near body with fingers
pointing to the right; bring the palm of
right hand to the back of left hand.
One hand near other hand.

fire

Wiggle all fingers to show the
flames of fire flickering

chair

Left "H" fingers represent the seat of a chair.
Hang "V" fingers of right hand over left "H"
fingers. *Legs hanging down.*

More Reinforcement Activities

USE READING COMPREHENSION AIDS. To improve reading comprehension and speed, use the McCall-Harby and the McCall-Crabb series. These books can be ordered from BHI. Sample pages can be seen in Step 31 of SWR.

QUIZ SPELLING WORDS FREQUENTLY. As a worthy goal, try to teach 40 words a week for second grade and up. You might present 20 on Monday. Test immediately after teaching words. On Tuesday do reinforcement activities, correct, and test. Repeat this procedure Wednesday and Thursday with the next 20 words. Test again on 45 words on Friday (40 new words plus 5 review) plus 5 phonograms. The students should not be told what review words or phonograms will be on the test. Hold students accountable the rest of the year for all words taught. The goal is long-term mastery.

COMBINE LITERATURE AND ART WITH SPELLING REVIEW. The morals to many of *Aesop's Fables* use spelling words. See SWR pages 98-99 for an index of the ones that apply to particular lessons. Tell or read the stories. Dictate the morals for the students to write. Have the student sketch an illustration of the story. Many different versions of *Aesop's Fables* are available, some quite attractively illustrated.

The Lion and the Mouse. A mouse begs a lion to spare him and promises to repay the kindness. The lion was amused by such a funny idea but generously decided to let the mouse go. Later the lion is caught in a hunter's net and the mouse, finding him trapped, gnawed the ropes and set the lion free. The mouse reminded the lion that he had laughed earlier, but even a mouse can help a lion.
Moral: A kindness is never wasted.

The Wolf and the Lion. A lion takes a lamb from a wolf. The wolf from a safe distance away complains, "You have no right to steal my property." The lion scoffs, "Your property? How did you get it? Did the shepherd give it to you? Did you buy it?"
Moral: What is evil won is evil lost.

PLAY SPELLING TIC-TAC-TOE. Draw the lines for standard tic-tac-toe (#). In each square write a spelling word or phonogram that has been troublesome for the student(s). Each player takes turns selecting a square and reading the word or phonogram written there. If she does so correctly, she can place her marker in that square. The first student to get three in a row horizontally, vertically, or diagonally wins the match.

PLAY HAPPY MAN. The teacher prepares a list of review words needing extra review. On the board or a piece of paper she draws a line for each phonogram in the word. A word with three phonograms may have a varying number of letters.

Example: ___ ___ ___

The opponent gets at least twelve chances to guess the word. Each time a phonogram guessed is used in a word, the challenger must write the phonogram in its appropriate spot. Each time the opponent guesses incorrectly, the challenger must draw one part of a man with a happy face starting with the big circle for the head, a stick body, stick arms (one at a time), stick legs (one at a time), ears (one at a time), eyes (one at a time), a curl of hair, a nose, and finally a happy smile for stumping the opponent. A completed man should look something like this.

SPELLING
SECTION K

I hear, I forget. I see, I remember. I do, I understand. --Chinese Proverb

One reason this program of unified language arts is so effective is that it employs multisensory learning. A student HEARS the phonogram or word spoken by his teacher. As the student SAYS it, he FEELS the way the sound is made in his throat, on his lips, in his mouth. He MOVES the appropriate large and small muscles as he WRITES the phonogram or word. Lastly, he SEES what he has written and READS it. We add doing to hearing and seeing.

Many intensive phonics programs teach students to see, to say, and to read printed language. *Wise Guide* goes a step further by linking together reading and writing. *Wise Guide* synthesizes two distinct skills: reading (decoding) and writing (encoding). A student who has been carefully taught this program not only becomes a better reader, but also becomes a more proficient speller.   When he reads he can focus his energy on the thought the author wants to communicate rather than struggling to identify the words themselves. When he writes compositions, he can focus on the thoughts he wants to convey, rather than agonizing over how to spell certain words. The goal is for written communication to become as fluent as spoken communication.

The W in *two* is the ghost of a forgotten sound. This graphic can help reinforce the silent letter in "two" by connecting it with another related word where we can still hear the /w/.

Tw͟o Twins

How many are there if we have **twins**?

tw͟o

Don't forget..."two" starts like "twin" !

This sheet can be photocopied for use with Section K-1 spelling.

Preliminaries. Phonograms: Review *ai, ay, ea, ee, igh, ou, ow, th.* Rules: Review 4, 5, 6, 7, 12.
Reference Pages: Introduce or review **Consonant/Vowel, Multi-letter Phonogram,** and **Silent Final E Pages**. See SWR Steps 9, 10, 17.

Words for Section K-1

381	twin	*Twin* boys were born on the same day to the same mother.
382	be tween	The difference *between* a hero and a coward is one step sideways. --G. Hackman
383	twen ty	*Twenty* is two tens.
384	twice	Think *twice* before you act. --Aesop
385	twelve	*Twelve* months makes one year. --Webster's *Bluebacked Speller*
386	twelfth	The *twelfth* one is ten and two more.
387	two	One sin becomes *two* sins when it is denied.
388	seem	True worth is to be and not just to *seem* like.
389	may be	*Maybe* means perhaps, possibly.
390	with out	'Tis hard to behold our own gifts *without* pride, and the gifts of others *without* envy. --V. Powell
391	male	God created *male* and female after His own image.
392	fe male	The woman is called *female* because she came from the male.
393	round	"Twas midnight on the mountain brown; the cold *round* moon shone brightly down. --Lord Byron
394	a round	When there's a lot of it *around,* you never want it very much. --Peg Bracken
395	seen	No man has *seen* God at any time. --1 John 4:12
396	sum ma ry	Can you give a *summary* of the book you read?
397	to night	Let the wind stay up *tonight,* but in your bed may you sleep tight.
398	clean	A leper said, "Lord, if You are willing, You can make me *clean.*" --Matt. 8:2
399	cleanse	Who can understand his errors? *Cleanse* thou me from secret faults. --Psalm 19:12
400	some one	God never asks you to be something or *someone* you cannot be.

Spelling Enrichments

NUMBERS AND MONTHS. Step 15 in SWR describes a **Number Page** for collecting the proper spelling of numbers, months of the year, and days of the week. See page 200 of this book for a sample of the information. On this Reference Page students add, beside the appropriate number, the spelling words *one, two, twelve.* (If you have not done so already add the other numbers taught as spelling words by this point: *three, five, six, seven, nine, ten, eleven.*) On the same line with *twelve,* beside *12th,* write *twelfth.* Find the number of the current month and on the corresponding line, under the month column, spell the name for the month, dividing the word into syllables and marking it. Under the days of the week column, on the same line with one, write the name for the first day of the week, etc.

DERIVATIVE FROM THE BIBLE. Which root word and derivative in this lesson can be traced to the story of creation in Genesis? (male and female). God made *man.* He took a rib from man to shape a helper for him and called her *woman* because she was taken from man. *Man* is a base word for *woman.* A *derivative* is taken or derived from something else. The woman was derived or taken from the man.

SUFFIXES. Make cards with each of the suffixes *-ly, -er, -est, -ing.* See how many you can add to *seem, round, clean* (seemly, seeming, roundly, rounder, roundest, rounding, cleanly, cleaner, cleanest, cleaning).

Root Words and Derivatives. Just as we combine phonograms to make words, we combine words and word parts to make additional words. Example: We can make the base word *do* into more words by combining two words together: *outdo, overdo*. We can add a word part to the front of the word: *redo, undo*. We can add a word part to the end of a word: *doer, doing*. If you know the meaning of root words you can often identify or better understand many words. In this spelling list see how many root words you can find.

twin	See SWR p. 86.	
be tween	[<OE be- (by) + twa (two)].	[R4]
twen ty	-ty means ten; twenty means 2 tens.	[R5,6]
twice	I says /I/ because of the E. C said /s/ because of the E. Mark the 1st type of E.	[R7]
twelve	English words do not end with V.	[R7]
twelfth	V is a voiced version of /f/. The changed spelling matches the changed sound.	
two	[<OE twa (two)]. W once made a sound as it still does in *twin, twelve, twenty*.	
seem	[<G ziemen (suitable)].	
may be	E said /E/ at the end of a syllable.	[R4]
with out	If you voice TH, put a 2 over it. Abbreviation: w/o	[R12]
male	A said /A/ because of the E.	[R7]
fe male	E said /E/ at the end of a syllable. A said /A/ because of the E.	[R4,7]
round		
a round	A said /A/ at the end of a syllable. In the rhythm of speech this unaccented vowel is softened.	[R4]
seen		
sum ma ry		[R29,4,5,6]
to night		
clean		
cleanse	Odd job E. See the reason on SWR page 108.	[R7]
some one	For spelling "one" think to spell like "lone." See SWR p. 81.	[R7]

Spelling Enrichments

IDENTIFYING DERIVATIVES. Dictate the following words in a column going down the page of a loose-leaf sheet of paper: *two, see, may, with, male, round, sum, night, clean, some*. Have the student write beside each of these words all spelling words built from them: *two* (twin, between, twenty, twice, twelve, twelfth), *see* (seem, seen), *may* (maybe), *with* (without), *male* (female), *round* (around), *sum* (summary), *night* (tonight), *clean* (cleanse), *some* (someone).

ANTONYMS. Have the student write the spelling words that are the opposite of the following words: female *(male)*; dirty *(clean)*; today *(tonight)*; within *(without)*; no one *(someone)*; flat *(round)*.

SENTENCE DICTATION. In place of an ordinary spelling quiz, where you call out individual words one at a time, dictate sentences that include as many spelling words as possible. For example:
    Maybe tonight someone between twelve and *twenty* can *clean twice around* the room.
    In *summary*, have you *seen* a *male* with a *female twin?*

Preliminaries. Phonograms: Quiz at least *ar, ea, ear, er, ir, ou, oo, oa, sh, ui, ur, wh, wor.*
Rules: 2, 4, 5, 6, 7, 8, 10, 12. Reference: Introduce or review **ER** and **SH Pages**. See SWR Steps 18, 26.

Words for Section K-2

401	sto ry	A preacher promised to speak on the marvelous *story* of the loaves and fishes.
402	shore	For Bible truths our fathers abandoned their native *shore* for the wilderness. -- Pres. Z. Taylor
403	oak	God made each tree and herb, the tall *oak,* and the low bush. *--McGuffey Primer*
404	hour	The darkest *hour* is just before dawn.
405	bet ter	The narrow way is the far *better* road that leads to life.
406	cent	A penny is called one *cent.*
407	wheat	We like whole *wheat* for cooking.
408	bone	The hungry dog chewed a bare *bone.*
409	camp	Family *camp* was the better *camp.*
410	fly	A buzzing *fly* always seems to know when I have a *fly* swatter.
411	la dy	The elm, a lovely *lady,* is in shimmering robes of gold. --author unknown
412	drive	We took the baby for her first *drive* in the country.
413	wood	The green *wood* laughs with the voice of joy. --William Blake
414	drink	I enjoy a special blender *drink.*
415	start	He had a slow *start* but he won the race.
416	head	A still tongue makes a wise *head.*
417	fruit	In some countries trees bear no *fruit* because there is no winter there. --J. Bunyan
418	pole	He broke the fishing *pole.*
419	plane	A huge *plane* flew overhead.
420	tone	Drawing from his pocket a well-worn Testament, President Garfield read with a soft, rich *tone.*

Spelling Enrichments

ADJECTIVE/ NOUNS. An adjective modifies (limits the meaning of) a noun or pronoun. Adjectives are like paintbrushes that reveal vivid details about a subject (What kind? Which one? How many?, Whose?). Look through Section K for words to modify *man* (*better, head, super, young, twelfth, clean*).

Dictate the spelling words again as a quiz for the students to write in a column going down on a loose-leaf sheet of paper. Next, read each of the sentences above written next to the new spelling words. Have the students orally identify the adjective describing the spelling word. Ask questions ("What kind of ...?).

401.	story	*marvelous*	408.	bone	*bare*	415.	start	*slow*
402.	shore	*native*	409.	camp	*family*	416.	head	*wise*
403.	oak	*tall*	410.	fly	*buzzing*	417.	fruit	*no*
404.	hour	*darkest*	411.	lady	*lovely*	418.	pole	*fishing*
405.	better	*far*	412.	drive	*first*	419.	plane	*huge*
406.	cent	*one*	413.	wood	*green*	420.	tone	*rich*
407.	wheat	*whole*	414.	drink	*blender*			

ORIGINAL SENTENCES. Include adjective/noun combinations in original student sentences. Draw an arrow from the adjective to the noun it modifies.

Example: *I like to hear the story lady read the better book.*

Abbreviations. *Abbreviations use a few letters to represent a word.* What is the abbrev. for *street?* (St. or ST) Mister? (Mr.) In this lesson we have two words that we commonly abbreviate. One can be used for two different words, but you can easily tell which it means by the context. (Dr. may mean *drive* or *doctor.*) See if you can recognize in this lesson the words we commonly abbreviate.

sto ry	O said /O/ at the end of a syllable. Y stands in for I at the end of a word.	[R4,5,6]
shore	Use SH at the beginning... Add to **SH Page**. O said /O/ because of the E.	[R10,7]
oak	[<OE ac (related to acorn)].	
hour	[<G hora (time)]. Think /h-ou-r/; say /our/. <u>Homophone</u>: our. <u>Abbrev.</u>: hr.	[R12]
bet ter	Both T's are sounded for spelling but not for normal speech. **ER Page**.	[R29]
cent	[<L centum (hundred)]. C says /s/ because of the E.	[R2]
wheat		
bone	O said /O/ because of the E.	[R7]
camp	[<L campus (field)]	
fly	Y stands in for I at the end of a word. Y may say /I/ at the end of a syllable.	[R5,6]
la dy	A said /A/ at the end of a syllable. Y usually says /i/ at the end of a syllable.	[R4,5,6]
drive	2 reasons for silent E; mark first. <u>Abbreviation</u>: Dr. (I live on Oak *Drive*.)	[R7,12]
wood		
drink	Irregular past tense: drank.	
start		
head	Add *headship* to **SH Page** (except for the ending -ship).	[R10]
fruit		
pole	O said /O/ because of the E.	[R7]
plane	A said /A/ because of the E.	[R7]
tone	O said /O/ because of the E.	[R7]

CREATIVE WRITING: Use the last forty spelling words to write a little story, or dictate the following.

The <u>lady</u> told a <u>story</u> in a sad <u>tone</u>. Her <u>twin</u> sat by the <u>shore</u> <u>hour</u> after <u>hour</u>. He sat <u>between</u> <u>oaks</u> and fished with a <u>wooden</u> <u>pole</u>. He would not move even after he had <u>seen</u> ants on his <u>fruit</u>. His <u>bones</u> hurt. He needed <u>twenty</u> dollars for <u>camp</u>. He had <u>two</u> dollars and <u>twelve</u> <u>cents</u>. After he saw a <u>plane</u> <u>fly</u> over-<u>head</u>, he plucked a <u>head</u> of <u>wheat</u>, took a <u>drink</u> of water, and <u>started</u> on the <u>drive</u> for home. He had failed to reach his goal, but he <u>better</u> not delay <u>tonight</u>.

COMPOUND WORDS. Compound words are two words put together like cow + boy = cowboy. Identify the four compound words in Section K: *some + one, to + night, with + out, may + be.*

Use review spelling words to make compound words with current spelling: *after, air, back, book, bug, fire, letter, line, over, red, ship, teller, under, up, way, work.* Bonus: *beach, cake, flag, grape, horse.*

story-- storybook, storyteller	bone-- backbone	wood-- red-, backwoods, -work
shore-- shoreline	camp-- campfire	start-- upstart
fly-- firefly [horsefly]	hour-- storyhour, afterhours	lady-- -bug
fruit-- [fruitcake, grapefruit]	drive-- overdrive, driveway	wheat-- [wheatcake]
plane-- airplane [GB aeroplane]	drink-- (no compound)	tone-- over-, under-
pole-- [flagpole]		
head-- -ship, -line, letter-, over-, red- [beach-]		

Preliminaries. Phonograms: Review phonograms, especially *ay, ai, ch, dge, ea, ew, sh, ou, ph, ur.*
Spelling Rules: Review Spelling Rule Cards for rules 4, 7, 10, 13, 17, 18.
Reference Page: Teach **E's Dropping Page**. See Step 29 in *Spell to Write and Read.*

Words for Section K-3

421	shall ·	Because the LORD is at my right hand I *shall* not be moved. --Psalm 16:8
422	should	You cannot help permanently by doing for men what they could and *should* do for themselves. -A. Lincoln
423	would	Only a fool *would* say to himself, "There is no God." --Psalm 53:1
424	could	But for the Bible we *could* not know right from wrong. --Abraham Lincoln
425	fin ish	Give us the tools and we will *finish* the job. --Winston Churchill
426	clear	Repentance is the heart's sorrow, and a *clear* life ensuing. --William Shakespeare
427	reach	You *reach* a distant goal by many small steps.
428	sent	He *sent* from above, he took me, he drew me out of many waters. --Psalm 18:16
429	de lay	Children, make no *delay* in doing good. *--New England Primer*
430	hurt	The wicked are *hurt* by the best things; the godly are bettered by the worst. - -W. Jenkyn
431	move	Trying to outsmart God has never been a wise *move.*
432	test	Do you want the Lord to *test* your heart? See Proverbs 17:3.
433	care	Take *care* that no one hate you justly. --P. Syrus
434	spell	Reading is easy when you can *spell* well.
435	state	Keep the church and the *state* forever separate. --Ulysses S. Grant
436	price	No *price* can recompense the pangs of vice. *--Poor Richard's Almanack*
437	base	*Base* means the foundation or key part that supports something.
438	bake	We *bake* with honey and whole wheat flour.
439	burn	Did not our hearts *burn* within us while He talked with us on the road? --Luke 24:32
440	fail	How did Moses *fail* when he hit the rock instead of speaking to it?

Spelling Enrichments

SUFFIXES.   Starting with *finish,* write each word on a separate sheet of paper and build as many new words as possible using suffixes *-ed, -er, -ing, -less*, *-ly*.   Watch for the **E's Dropping** words!

finish -- finished, finisher, finishing
clear -- cleared, clearing, clearly
reach -- reached, reaching
sent* -- (irregular verb, no suffix applies)
delay -- delayed, delayer, delaying
hurt* -- hurter, hurting, hurtless
move -- moved, mover, moving, movingly
test --   tested, tester, testing

care --   cared, caring, careless, carelessly
spell -- spelled*, speller, spelling
state -- stated, stating, stately
price -- priced, pricing, priceless
base -- based, basing, baseless
bake-- baked, baker, baking
burn -- burned, burner, burning
fail --   failed, failing, failingly

* Usually we make a verb past tense by adding -ed. In some cases the word makes no change (hurt), has an irregular form (send / sent), or varies with British spelling (spell / spelt). See SWR Step 22.

Rule-Breaker Words.
With our spelling rules and phonograms the English language is amazingly consistent. This lesson has three rule-breaker words; fortunately, they all look alike and sound alike. We can learn them at the same time. Can you identify this troublesome threesome?

shall	SH spells /sh/ at the beginning of a word. We often double L ...	[R10,17]
should	Silent L from root word *shall*. OU is an eXception. Add *should, shall* to **SH Pg**.	[R10]
would	Silent L from root word *will*. OU is an eXception.	
could	L not in *can*. Looks like and rhymes with *would, should*. OU is an eXception.	
fin ish	SH can be used to spell /sh/ at the end of a syllable. Add to **SH Page**.	[R10]
clear		
reach		
sent	The meaning determines spelling. Homophone: cent, sent, scent.	
de lay	E said /E/ at the end of a syllable. A-Y usually spells /A/ at the end of a word.	[R4,18]
hurt	Add to the **ER Page**.	
move	English words do not end with V.	[R7]
test		
care	A said /A/ because of the E. AR does not say /ar/ as in car here.	[R7]
spell	We often double L after a single vowel at the end of a base word.	[R17]
state	A said /A/ because of the E.	[R7]
price	2 reasons for the E. Mark the first one. I said /I/ because of the E.	[R2,7]
base	A said /A/ because of the E.	[R7]
bake	A said /A/ because of the E. Why can't we use C here?	[R7,2]
burn	Add to the **ER Page**.	
fail		

Spelling Enrichments

HELPING VERBS. A verb can consist of one word (I set the table.) or can include helping verbs (I should set the table; I should have set the table.)

    Match each of the spelling words with one of the four helping verbs: **shall, should, would, could.** Examples: shall finish, should clear, would base, could spell, shall burn, should reach, would move, could test, should have sent, should price, would state, could care, shall hurt, should bake, would delay, could fail. Have students make complete oral sentences using these sets of verbs.

PREFIXES. Add **un-** which means *not* or *the opposite of* to as many words in this section of 20 words as possible. You may use derivative forms of the spelling words. For example, we don't say unmove, but we do say unmoved (*unfinished, unclear, unreached, unsent, undelayed, unhurt, unmoved, untested, uncareful, uncaring, unstated, unpriced, unbased, unbaked, unburned, unfailing*). Bonus: **mis-** means *wrong*. What words can take this prefix? (*misstate, misspell, misspelled*).

CONTRACTIONS. Make contractions with would, could, and should. Examples: should not (shouldn't), would not (wouldn't), could not (couldn't), I would (I'd), you would (you'd), he would (he'd), she would (she'd), we would (we'd), they would (they'd). See SWR Step 28.

Preliminaries.

Phonograms: Especially quiz phonograms: *ea, ed, er, igh, ir, ng, oe, ou, ow, sh, tch, th, wh, wr.*
Spelling Rules: Especially review rules: 2, 4, 5, 6, 7, 10, 12, 16, 19.
Reference Page: If you haven't done so already this year, teach **A-E-I-O-U Page**. SWR Step19.

Words for Section K-4

441	an y	Be never proud by *any* means, build not your house too high. --*New England Primer*
442	man y	The lips of the righteous feed *many,* but fools die for lack of wisdom. --Prov. 10:21
443	on ly	The *only* objection to the Bible is a bad life. --John Wilmot's last words
444	these	Whoever hears and obeys *these* sayings is a wise man.
445	o pen	There is more power in the *open* hand than in the clenched fist. --*Hardware News*
446	cit y	Unless the LORD guards the *city,* the watchman stays awake in vain. --Ps. 127:1
447	bare	Birds sing on a *bare* bough; O believer, canst not thou? --C. Spurgeon
448	high	I wandered lonely as a cloud that floats on *high* o'er vales and hills. --Wordsworth
449	com ing	Sing a bright and happy tune that Jesus is *coming* back real soon.
450	shut	Who *shut* in the sea with doors? --Job 38:8
451	ant	Consider the ways of the hardworking *ant* and be wise.
452	mouth	Every time you open your *mouth* your mind is on parade.
453	first	If at *first* you don't succeed, sky diving is not for you.
454	weak	You cannot strengthen the *weak* by weakening the strong. --A. Lincoln
455	win dow	You may see if you will look through the *window* of this book. --Robert L. Stevenson
456	where	Think of whence you came, *where* you are going, and to whom you must give account. --Franklin
457	grave	There is no repentance in the *grave.* --Isaac Watts
458	light	*Light* candles rather than curse the darkness.
459	ease	True *ease* in writing comes from art, not chance. --Alexander Pope
460	eas y	The way down to hell is *easy.* --Virgil

Spelling Enrichments

SUFFIXES. Try to add either the suffix **-ly** or **-ness** to as many spelling words as possible.

open -- openly, openness   *grave* -- gravely, graveness
bare -- barely, bareness   *light* -- lightly, lightness
high -- highly, highness   *easy* -- easily, easiness [R 24]
weak -- weakly, weakness

PREFIXES. Add **un-** which means *not* or *the opposite of* to as many new words or their derivatives as possible. We don't say unmove, but we do say unmovable, or unmoved *(unopened, unshut, uneasy).*

COMPOUND WORDS. Make compound words by combining new words with review words: *body, place, way, foot, thread, in, over, eat, land, head, yard, house.*

any -- anybody, anyplace, anyway   ant -- anteater
bare -- barefoot, threadbare   first -- firsthand, headfirst
high -- highlight, highland, highway   grave -- graveyard
coming -- incoming, overcoming   light -- -house, head-, high-, moon-, sun-

Variations in Speech: Shakespeare once said, "Though this be madness, yet there is method in it!" So, too, we find the English language. While we marvel at the general regularity of most words using our system, occasionally we find an unexpected twist. We have two common words in today's list that sound like /e/ but are spelled with the first sound of A. (I don't know why. If you find out, write to BHI and tell me.) We learn these words by saying, "We think to spell____; We say _____."

an y	Think to spell /an/; in the rhythm of speech say /en/. X over the A is optional.	[R5,6]
man y	Think to spell /an/; in the rhythm of speech say /en/. X over the A is optional.	[R5,6]
on ly	Root = one. O may say /O/ before 2 consonants. Y stands in for I	[R19,5,6]
these	E said /E/ because of the silent E.	[R7]
o pen	O said /O/ at the end of a syllable.	[R4]
cit y	C says /s/ because of the I. Y stands in for I at the end of English words	[R2,5,6]
bare	A said /A/ because of the E.	[R7]
high	The homophone "hi" is slang and does not follow the English rule.	[R6]
com ing	Silent final E words may lose the need for the E when adding a vowel suffix.	[R16]
shut	SH can be used to spell /sh/ at the beginning of a word. Add to **SH Page**.	[R10]
ant		
mouth		
first	Add to **ER Page** and **Number Page**. See sample on p. 200 of the Wise Guide.	
weak	Listen carefully for the meaning.	
win dow	root = wind	
where 5	The 1 over the first E shows we think /e/-/r/ and not /er/. Add an odd job E	[R7]
grave	A said /A/ because of the E. English words do not end with V. Mark 1st of 2 reasons.	[R7]
light	American past tense *lit;* British *lighted.* Abbreviation: lgt.	[R12]
ease 5	Odd job E. We need an E but not for any of the other four reasons.	[R7]
eas y	Silent final E words may lose... Add to **E's Page**. Y usually says /i/ at the end.	[R16,5,6]

DRAW AND LABEL WORDS. Examples are by BBF Homeschool Co-op students: Anna Alcala, Rachel Farrand, Kalen and Krista Tse, Katie Peters, Jarrett Williams, and Jonathan Johnson.

Preliminaries.

Phonograms: Especially quiz *ai, ay, ar, ea, ear, ee, ei, eigh, er, ey, igh, ir, ng, ou, qu, th.*
Spelling Rules: Review 1, 2, 3, 4, 5, 6, 7, 10.
Reference Page: Start collecting homophones. See Step 30 in SWR.

Words for Section K-5

461	sin gle	The journey of a thousand miles must begin with a *single* step. --Chinese proverb
462	earth	*Earth* with her thousand voices praises God. --Samuel Taylor Coleridge
463	gar den	A cow is a good animal in the field, but we turn her out of a *garden.* --Sam Johnson
464	bear	Never sell the *bear* skin before one has killed the beast. --Jean de La Fountaine
465	cot ton	George Washington Carver showed the benefit of growing peanuts instead of only *cotton.*
466	rain	God sends *rain* and sun then, one by one, flowers pop up in a row. *--Christian Mother Goose*
467	fear	The *fear* of the Lord is to hate evil. --Proverbs 8:13
468	e vil	What is *evil* won is *evil* lost.
469	mail	Grandmother loves to receive *mail* from her family.
470	night	Every *night* my prayers I say. --Robert L. Stevenson
471	king	He is the happiest, be he *king* or peasant, who finds peace at home. --Goethe
472	queen	The *queen* is the most powerful piece in chess, but the king is the most essential.
473	par ty	Did you have a birthday *party?*
474	dan ger	*Danger* is sauce for prayers. *--Poor Richard's Almanack*
475	bas ket	She gathered the fruit in a *basket.*
476	cloud	A *cloud* cover makes the difference on a dark day, not the sun.
477	thirst	I am dying of *thirst* by the side of the fountain. --Charles d'Orleans
478	eye	For the ways of man are before the *eye* of the LORD, and He ponders all his paths. --Prov. 5:21
479	wag on	God doesn't always smooth the path, but sometimes he puts springs in the *wagon.*
480	crime	The root cause of *crime* is moral, not economic.

Spelling Enrichments

COMPOUND WORDS. Dictate (or pull 3x5 cards made earlier of) these review words: *over, bow, fall, some, doer, box, man, fall, time, ship, like, house, ball, less, glass, let, load.* Have students use the review words together with current spelling words to form new compound words: *overbearing, rainbow, rainfall, fearsome, evildoer, mailbox, mailman, nightfall, nighttime, overnight, kingship, queenlike, houseparty, basketball, cloudless, eyeball, eyeglass, eyelet, wagonload.* As a bonus give these new words that can be used for making compounds: *worm, cup, seed, drop (earthworm, cupbearer, cottonseed, raindrop).*

SUFFIXES. Add **-ly** to as many as possible of the K words taught so far. What will we do with an E's Dropping Word? Will we drop the E? (No.) Why not? (The ending -ly is not a vowel suffix.)

seemly	*hourly*	*basely*	*firstly*	*lightly*	*earthly*	*kingly*
roundly	*clearly*	*openly*	*weakly*	*easily*	*evilly*	*queenly*
cleanly	*stately*	*highly*	*gravely*	*singly*	*nightly*	**thirstily*

Note: *Bearly* is not a word. *Barely* is. **Thirst* does not take -ly but its derivative *thirsty* can [R24].

Tricky Sound Alike or Look Alike Words. Illustrate homophones with examples: *Would* you please chop the *wood?* My *aunt* had an *ant* farm.   He shouted "*Hi*" from *high* in the tree. Watch for homophones in this lesson: *bear/ bare; rain/ rein; mail/ male; night/ knight; eye/I.* Some words are pronounced differently when capitalized. Ex.: A *Po-lish* man will *pol-ish* the car. *Herb* planted an *herb* garden.   Watch for a derivative of a new spelling word that works this way. (**r<u>ai</u>n-i-<u>er</u>/ Rai-n<u>ie</u>r**)

sin gl<u>e</u> ₌₄	Every syllable must have a vowel.	[R7]
<u>ear</u>th	At the end of the lesson, add to **ER Page**.	
<u>gar</u> den		
b<u>ea</u>r ³	A big *bear* had *bare* feet.	
cot ton	Think both t's for spelling, but not for normal speech.	[R29]
r<u>ai</u>n	*You think this is rainy! It it <u>rainier</u> at Mt. <u>Rainier</u>.*	
f<u>ea</u>r		
e vil	E said /E/ at the end of a syllable.	[R4]
m<u>ai</u>l	[<OF male (wallet)].	
n<u>igh</u>t		
ki<u>ng</u>	We cannot use C to say /k/ here. Add *kingship* to **SH Page**.	[R2,10]
q<u>ue</u>en	Q always needs a U. U is not a vowel here.	[R1]
<u>par</u> ty ²	Y usually says /i/ at the end of a syllable. English words do not end with I.	[R5,6]
dan <u>ger</u> ²	A says /A/ unexpectedly. The 2 indicates that we cannot see why. G says /j/ before E.	[R3]
bas ket	Why do we use the K to spell /k/?	[R2]
cl<u>ou</u>d		
th<u>ir</u>st	At the end of the lesson, add to **ER Page**.	
eye (eye)	Unusual marking. See SWR p. 82. <u>Homophone</u>: I.	
wag on		
crim͡e .	I said /I/ because of the E.	[R7]

DICTATION. *A <u>single</u> <u>crime</u> happened to the <u>earth</u> <u>queen</u> the <u>night</u> after her <u>garden</u> <u>party</u>. <u>Rain</u> fell from the <u>cloudy</u> sky and she felt a <u>fear</u> of <u>evil</u>. She saw the <u>eyes</u> of a <u>thirsty</u> <u>bear</u>. He took her <u>cotton</u> <u>basket</u>. She ran for her <u>wagon</u> where the <u>king</u>, unaware of <u>danger</u>, sat quietly reading his <u>mail</u>.*

COMPOSITION. Have the student(s) write original sentences using the adjective/noun combinations made from these words plus other words in this list or in the previous list.

     only single -- My brother was the *only single* in the room.

     bare earth -- I like to feel the *bare earth* between my toes.

     any garden -- My garden is not just *any garden*.

LITERATURE. Read aloud stories about King Arthur and his adventures. Have one student at a time read a spelling word, starting at the top of the list, and then compose a sentence using that word in a way that relates to the days of the knights of the round table.

single	The *single* knight wanted a fair maiden to protect.
earth	He searched over all the *earth* for her.
garden	He spotted her one day in a *garden*. (etc.)

Preliminaries. Reference Page: Introduce or review **Plural Page**. See SWR Step 27.
> Phonograms: Quiz especially *ci, ck, ea, ee, er, kn, oa, oe, oo, or, ou, ough, ow, ti, th, si*.
> Spelling Rule Cards: 3, 4, 5, 7, 12, 17, 22, 25. Students learn rules but not the rule numbers!

Words for Section K-6

481	free dom	*Freedom* is not free. --Michael New
482	pound	"Penny wise and *pound* foolish" refers to British paper money called a pound.
483	stick	Mary Jones picked up *stick* after *stick* to earn money to buy a Bible.
484	gift	Advice is an uncertain *gift*.
485	class	You cannot further brotherhood of men by inciting *class* hatred. --A. Lincoln
486	af ter noon	*Afternoon* is the part of the day which follows noon. --Dryden
487	horse	Have you given the *horse* strength? Have you clothed his neck with thunder? --Job 39:19
488	he ro	Being a *hero* is about the shortest lived profession on earth. --Will Rogers
489	broth er	You can't spell "*brother*" without spelling "other."
490	wife	A prudent *wife* commands her husband by obeying him. --John Trapp
491	club	I don't want to belong to any *club* that will accept me as a member. --Groucho Marx
492	goose	Hus means *goose* in the Czech language, as in John Huss the Christian martyr.
493	loaf	How is a *loaf* of bread related to a person who likes to *loaf*?
494	knife	A gossip is someone who's the *knife* of the party. --M. Bender
495	ear	God made the *ear* and He can hear. --Noah Webster's *Bluebacked Speller*
496	week	Safely through another *week* God has brought us on our way. --John Newton
497	ti tle	John Wycliffe is given the *title* "Morning Star of the Reformation."
498	stamp	I will pay for the *stamp* for my letter.
499	glass	The word *glass* comes from the Danish word for blue. --Webster, 1828
500	set	To *set* up self is to deny Christ. --Henry Sandham

Spelling Enrichments

ALLITERATION. Dictate down the page, skipping five lines after each: c, g, h, s, w. Have students find spelling words in Section K that begin with the same FIRST SOUND. Write original sentences using alliteration and as many new spelling words as possible. For example: The hero hurt the head of his horse.

> c -- clean, cleanse, camp, could, clear, care, coming, cotton, cloud, crime, class, club
> g -- grave, garden, gift, goose, glass
> h -- head, hurt, high, horse, hero (Not hour; The H is silent)
> s-- seem, seen, summary, someone, story, start, sent, spell, state, single, stick, stamp, set
> > Also C saying /s/: cent, city. Not SH words: shore, shall, should, shut
> w --without, wood, would, weak, window, wagon, wife, week (not WH words: wheat, where)

COMPOUND WORDS. Build derivatives with new words plus review words: drum, yard, room, out, saw, back, fly, step, house, some, shot, end, day, eye, hour.

drumstick	*yardstick*	*classroom*	*outclass*	*sawhorse*	*horseback*
horsefly	*stepbrother*	*housewife*	*eardrum*	*earshot*	*weekend*
weekday	*eyeglass*	*hourglass*			

* *Gooseberry* is not a compound word since there is no known link between *berries* and *geese!*

Abbreviation. *Abbreviations use a few letters to represent a larger word.* What abbreviations have we learned so far? (See SWR Step 25). Some abbreviations take the letters from the foreign spelling of the word or concept. "And so forth" is abbreviated as *etc.* from the Latin words *et cetera*. Watch for 3 abbreviations in this lesson including one that abbreviates the Latin word with the same meaning.

fr<u>ee</u> dom	Root = free.	
p<u>ou</u>nd	[< L libra pondo (pound by weight)]. <u>Abbreviation</u>: lb.	[R12]
sti<u>ck</u>	CK is used after a single vowel which says /i/.	[R25]
gift	G may say /j/ before I, but not always.	[R3]
class	We often double S after a single vowel at the end of a base word.	[R17]
af ter n<u>oo</u>n	Compound word: after + noon.	
h<u>orse</u>,	Odd job E.	[R7]
he r<u>o</u>	E said /E/ at the end of a syllable. O said /O/ at the end of a syllable.	[R4]
bro<u>th</u> er	Think to spell first vowel with a French overtone. See SWR p. 82. <u>Abbreviation</u>: bro.	[R12]
wif<u>e</u>	Voice added to the sound of /f/ = /v/. The plural of wife becomes wives.	[R22]
club		
g<u>oose</u>,	Odd job E lets us know the word is not the plural of *goo*.	[R7]
l<u>oaf</u>	[<OE hlaf (loaf, a lump or mass)].	
knif<u>e</u>	I said /I/ because of the E.	[R7]
<u>ear</u>		
w<u>ee</u>k	<u>Homophone</u>: weak. <u>Abbreviation</u>: wk.	[R12]
ti tl<u>e</u>,	I may say /I/ at the end of a syllable. Every syllable must have a vowel.	[R5,7]
stamp		
glass	We often double S for a nonplural base word.	[R17]
set		

PLURALS. Apply the principles of the **Plural Page** in the Log to the new words just taught. Divide a piece of notebook paper into three columns and label as *-s, -es, other*. Under *-es* make three categories with three lines saved under each. *(hisses, f to v, o)*. Make current spelling words plural and organize them in the category that best describes them.

-s	-es	other
freedom -- freedoms	**hisses**	goose -- geese
pound -- pounds	class -- classes	
stick -- sticks	horse -- horses*	
gift -- gifts	glass -- glasses	
afternoon -- afternoons		
brother --brothers	**f to v**	*Note: *Horse* ends with a hissing sound followed by an odd job E so that the word will not be confused as a plural form. We drop the silent E when adding the suffix -es which has a voiced vowel. It is okay if a student wants to classify "horse" as a word where we just add -S.
club -- clubs	wife -- wives	
ear -- ears	loaf -- loaves	
week -- weeks	knife -- knives	
title -- titles		
stamp -- stamps	**o**	
set -- sets	hero -- heroes	

Preliminaries. Spelling Rules: Review 4, 5, 7, 12, 13, 17, 19, 27. Phonograms: Quiz all 70.
Comprehension: For students ready to do so, begin lessons in the McCall series. See SWR Step 31.

Words for Section K-7

501	draw	I must obey and love and fear him. By faith in Christ I must *draw* near him. *-New England Primer*
502	felt	I *felt* sad over my sin and repented.
503	up on	When God lays men *upon* their backs, then they look up to heaven. -Thomas Watson
504	poor	You cannot help the *poor* man by destroying the rich. --A. Lincoln
505	owe	I *owe* to Christ anything and everything in my life that may be of any worth. --Robert B. Fulton
506	herd	The cowboy rode beside a *herd* of cattle.
507	li on	One may die just as well choking on a small fly as devoured by a huge *lion*.
508	keep	Blessed are those who *keep* my ways. --Proverbs 8:32
509	join	Though they *join* forces, the wicked will not go unpunished. --Proverbs 11:21
510	they	*They* lose nothing who gain Christ. --Samuel Rutherford
511	wa ter	Wealth is like sea *water;* the more we drink the thirstier we become. --Arthur Schopenhauer
512	e ven	*Even* a child is known by his doings. --Proverbs 20:11
513	mile	*Mile* comes from the Latin "mille passus" meaning a thousand paces.
514	sir	*Sir*, a title of honor, was given to loin of beef by an English king in a fit of good humor.
515	ze ro	Good without God becomes *zero*.
516	grow	I should like to rise and go where the golden apples *grow*. --Robert L. Stevenson
517	rung	When he had *rung* the bell, the shock made me slip from the ladder *rung*.
518	a cross	The grass must bend when the wind blows *across* it. --Confucius
519	be hind	Blow the dust off the clock. Your watches are *behind* the times. --Solzhenitsyn
520	cost	Salvation is free but it will *cost* your life.

Spelling Enrichments

HOMOPHONES. *Homo* means same and *phone* means sound. Different words with the same sound (like *sea* and *see*) are called *homophones*. Give students one word in each pair and have them search for the matching homophone in Spelling Section K words.

aunt (ant)	seam (seem)	mail (male)	our (hour)	I (eye)
wood (would)	cent (sent)	bare (bear)	heard (herd)	to (two)
hi (high)	weak (week)	knight (night)	poll (pole)	oh (owe)
plain (plane)	hoarse (horse)	bass (base)		

Students can draw a picture or write a sentence for each pair. Bonus sentences includes both forms of the homophone. Example: My *aunt* stepped on an *ant*. I *heard* the sound of the *herd*.

SENTENCES. Instead of a regular spelling test, dictate sentences with Section K new and review words.

> *Sir, can you draw clean water for the poor twins?*
> *He stepped upon a ladder rung, felt danger, and ran a mile.*
> *The herd will grow if we can keep the lions across the woods.*
> *By lowering the cost, they are even now. They owe zero.*

GRAMMAR. See SWR p.124 for ways to practice changing verbs from present to past tense.

Numbers. One word today is a very valuable number to mathematicians but not large enough to satisfy most people. What is it? (zero). Add to the **Number Page**. If you haven't done so already this year also spell the first twelve numbers except *four* and *eight*. See page 200 in this book or Step 15 in SWR.

dr<u>aw</u>		
felt	2 meanings: (verb) past tense of feel; (noun) type of cloth.	
up on	Compound word: up + on	
p<u>oo</u>r		
ǒwe₅	Odd job E. Significant words need at least three letters. See SWR p. 108.	[R7]
h<u>er</u>d	Add to **ER Page**.	
li on	I may say /I/ at the end of a syllable.	[R5]
k<u>ee</u>p		
j<u>oi</u>n		
thěy	This is a first person plural nominative pronoun.	
wa ter	After W the A commonly says /ah/.	
e ven	E said /E/ at the end of a syllable.	[R4]
mile	I said /I/ because of the E. **Abbreviation:** mi.	[R7,12]
s<u>ir</u>	[<F sieur (monsieur) <Norm. sire (lord) <Heb. shur (to rule)]. Add to **ER Page**.	
ze ro	Z, never S, says /z/ at the beginning of a word. O said /O/ at the end of a syllable.	[R27,4]
gr<u>ow</u>		
rung	2 meanings: (verb) past tense of ring; (noun) slat on a ladder	
a cross	A said /A/ at the end of a syllable. We often double S after a single vowel ...	[R4,17]
be hind	E said /E/ at the end of a syllable. I may say /I/ before 2 consonants	[R4,19]
cost		

ALPHABETIZE. Dictate for the student to write going down the page on a loose-leaf sheet of paper the single letter phonograms in alphabetical order. Say each by phonogram sound. Explain that we call the /a/- /A/- /ah/, the letter A, etc. Ask the student to write the spelling word that begins with an A beside the letter A, etc. We call lining up the words in this way *alphabetizing*.

a -- across	f -- felt	l -- lion	t -- they
b -- behind	g -- grow	m -- mile	u -- upon
c -- cost	h -- herd	o -- owe	w -- water
d-- draw	j -- join	p -- poor	z -- zero
e -- even	k -- keep	r -- rung	

CONTRACTIONS. See SWR Step 28. Have students form at least four contractions with *they*.

COMPOUND WORDS. Have students make compound words with spelling words plus the review words: *back, book, fall, here, house, line, out, over, post, stone, there, time, under, way, with.* As an alternative, dictate these compound words: *overdraw, withdraw, hereupon, thereupon, housekeeper, bookkeeper, timekeeper, backwater, waterfall, waterline, waterway, underwater, milepost, milestone, outgrow.*

PREPOSITIONS. Build a chart of prepositions taught to this point. See SWR page 104. Have students write original sentences with the new spelling words including a prepositional phrase in each sentence.

Can you set the table?
Remember the alphabet and you'll know where to put the fork, knife, and spoon.

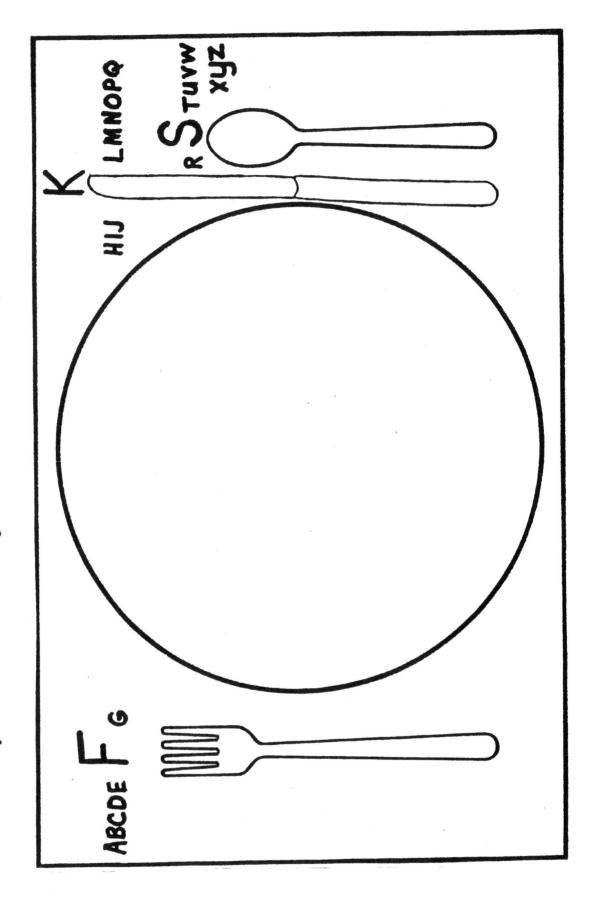

Permission granted to photo copy this aid for teaching alphabet skills, designed by Jeannean Kintner.   © 2003, Wanda Sanseri

SPELLING
SECTION L

"Reading maketh a full man, conference a ready man, and writing an exact man."
--Francis Bacon

From this point on, students will not only write original sentences using spelling words, but they can practice writing related sentences to form paragraphs. Many students fear facing a blank piece of paper and writing anything. It often helps to ease this anxiety if they practice thinking orally with you before they are required to write. Take turns making up sentences or in some way guide the student until his own sparks of creativity are ignited, and then let his ideas flow naturally from there.

Look through the spelling list and find a key word that could inspire a theme. In Section L-2 the word "honey" brings to mind the proverb: *Honey catches more flies than vinegar.* The word "lesson" can fit with a sentence like, "I learned a lesson on what that means." We can see words like "push, fence, neck, groans, mad" and imagine a conflict. Words like "stop, leave" give hints of avoiding unnecessary confrontation. Stimulate a student with such observations and set him free to mold his own paper. Challenge him to incorporate all the spelling words in a logical way. Additional helps for composition are discussed in *Spell to Write and Read* Steps 21, 33.

The first 640 words in this program (A-L) and their derivatives include more than 70% of all the words we read and write!

This boy is all al**one**.

Is he l**one**ly?

How many boys are here?

Write the numeral.

Spell the number.

Spell the L-2 word meaning " one time only."

This sheet can be photocopied for use with Section L-2 spelling.

Preliminaries   Phonograms: Quiz at least *ch, ck, ea, ee, er, ew, ng, oa, ou, ow, qu, sh, th, ui, ur, wh.*
  Rules: Review 1, 4, 5, 6, 7, 10, 12,16, 25. Reading: Introduce McCall lessons. See SWR Step 31.
  Reference Pgs: Teach or review **Consonant, Silent E, E's Dropping, M. Phonogram Pages**.

Words for Section L-1

521	talk	A spelling bee is smarter than a dog that can *talk*.
522	walk	He who will *walk* with wise men will be wise.
523	coun try	Don't criticize your government when out of the *country;* never cease to do so at home. -Churchill
524	half	*Half* a loaf is better than none.
525	done	What's *done* cannot be undone.
526	gone	The sun has *gone* to rest, the bee forsakes the flower, and the bird hurries to its nest. --McGuffey
527	soap	Though you wash with lye, and use much *soap*, yet your iniquity is marked before me. --Jer. 2:22
528	black	"Any color so long as it's *black*," said Henry Ford about the Model-T car.
529	clothe	I *clothe* my naked villainy with Holy Writ and seem a saint when most I play the devil. -Shakespeare
530	cloth ing	Beware of false prophets who come to you in sheep's *clothing*. --Matt. 7:15
531	pow er	Christianity is the greatest civilizing, moulding, uplifting *power* on this globe. --M. Hopkins
532	road	What is the use of running when we are not on the right *road?* --German proverb
533	stream	His *stream* of mercies never ceasing calls for songs of loudest praise. --Robinson
534	church	Three kinds of people go to *church:* believers, unbelievers, and make-believers.
535	dash	*Dash* may mean the same as splash (dash paint on paper) or smash (dash the boat to pieces).
536	feed	Others may *feed* our ego, but it is up to us to constrain it. --Aesop
537	news	The best *news* of all time came from a graveyard: He is risen!
538	suit	Prayer is putting promises into *suit*, or in other words, putting on promises.
539	ta ble	Home is a lighthouse with the lamp of God on the *table*. --Henry Rische
540	dead	Three may keep a secret if two of them are *dead*.

Spelling Enrichments

COMPOUND WORDS. Dictate the review words in italics. Check spelling. Have student combine these review words with current spelling to make as many new words as possible.

back	backtalk	backhalf		*ball*	blackball	
bed	bedclothes	roadbed		*bird*	blackbird	
board	blackboard	dashboard	boardwalk	*box*	soapbox	
in	inroad	walkin		*law*	lawsuit	
line	streamline	clothesline	deadline	*mail*	blackmail	
man	countryman	walkman		*news*	newsstand	
out	blackout	walkout	outtalk	*sleep*	sleepwalk	
over	overpower	overdone	overfeed	*time*	halftime	
side	countryside	sidewalk	roadside	*top*	blacktop	
under	undergone	underclothes	underclothing	*turn*	turntable	
	underdone	underfeed		*yard*	churchyard	
way	roadway	walkway	halfway			

ORIGINAL SENTENCES. Write sentences about a church located near a stream in the country. Try to use all the spelling words. You could dictate this beginning sentence: *We had a talk about power over sin as we took a walk down the road.*

Teach E's Dropping Rule. *Silent Final E words commonly lose the need for the E when adding a vowel suffix.* Illustrate the rule with the following words: *owe, bare, fine.* Add endings such as: *-ed, -er, -est, -ing, -ly* to build words such as: *owed, owing, bared, barely, finer, finest.* In the spelling reinforcement activity with this lesson you will need to watch for E's Dropping Words.

talk	A often says /ah/ before /l/.	
walk	A often says /ah/ before /l/.	
coun try	I usually says /i/ at the end of a syllable. English words do not end with I.	[R5,6]
half	[<OE healf (half)].	
done	Think to spell /o/. Odd job E.	[R7]
gone	Odd job E.	[R7]
soap		
black	CK may be used only after a single vowel that says /a-e-i-o-u/.	[R25]
clothe	O said /O/ because of the E. See SWR top of p.106.	[R7]
cloth ing	Silent final E words are written without the E when ...We can see the O still says /O/.	[R16,19]
pow er		
road	Abbreviation: rd. or RD	[R12]
stream		
church	Add to **ER Page**.	
dash	SH can spell /sh/ at the end of a syllable. Add to **SH/TI Page**.	[R10]
feed		
news	Alternative marking: put a 2 over the EW.	
suit	In some regions ui = /U/.	
ta ble	A said /A/ at the end of a syllable. Every syllable must have a vowel.	[R4,7]
dead		

Spelling Enrichments

PAST TENSE VERBS. At least eleven of these twenty words are or can be made into past tense verbs. Students on a blank sheet of notebook paper can write the present and past tense of each verb. Tell them that while most use -ed, some verbs form irregular past tense endings. For example: sing/ sang.

talk -- talked -->	walk -- walked	soap -- soaped	clothe -- clothed
power -- powered	stream -- streamed	dash -- dashed	church -- churched
feed -- fed	suit -- suited	table -- tabled	half -- halved

DICTATION. Dictate a modified version of Aesop's "The Fox and the Crow."

A fox on the <u>road</u> by a <u>stream</u> saw a crow. He wanted the food in her beak so he <u>walked</u> to the tree and <u>talked</u> to the bird. "You are lovely <u>clothed</u> in your <u>black</u> <u>suit</u>," he cooed. "Before long <u>news</u> of your splendor will have <u>gone</u> far and wide in the <u>country</u>. If you can sing <u>half</u> as well as you look, you must be better than the <u>church</u> soloist." The crow opened her mouth to sing. Down fell the food. The fox grabbed it and <u>dashed</u> away. Moral: Others may <u>feed</u> our ego, but it's up to us to constrain it.

Preliminaries. Reference Pages: If you haven't yet this year, teach **SH, Number, and AEIOU** Pages.
Rules: 2, 4, 5, 6, 7, 10, 17,19, 22, 25, 27. Phonograms: *ck, ea, ed, ee, ei, eigh, ey, oa, oe, sh, th, tch.*

Words for Section L-2

541	ride	If wishes were horses, beggars might *ride*. --John Ray
542	push	If you never budge, don't expect a *push*. --Malcolm Forbes
543	with in	By God's power, matter holds together *within* the atom and *within* the universe.
544	a bove	The price of a virtuous woman is far *above* rubies. --Proverbs 31:10
545	stop	A good snapshot can *stop* a moment from running away.
546	pick	Wherever you fall, *pick* up something. --Oswald Avery
547	leave	Be careful not to *leave* leaves littered on the ground.
548	bu y	Never argue with people who *buy* ink by the barrel. --Anonymous
549	mind	If you don't *mind* your manners, someone else will for you.
550	four	One bee, two bees, three bees, *four*. Hurry up and shut the door!
551	once	The head that *once* was crowned with thorns is crowned with glory now. --T. Kelley
552	track	I saw the Congo . . . cutting through the forest with a golden *track*. --Vachel Lindsay
553	fenc es	Good *fences* make good neighbors. --Robert Frost
554	mad	We must bind our passions in chains, lest like *mad* folks, they break their locks. --Taylor
555	groans	The best prayers have often more *groans* than words. --John Bunyan
556	neck	Have you given the horse strength? Have you clothed his *neck* with thunder? --Job 39:19
557	les son	Life is a long *lesson* in humility.
558	hon ey	The bee, though it finds every rose has a thorn, comes back with *honey*. --T. Halliburton
559	un less	Christ is not valued at all *unless* He be valued above all. --St. Augustine
560	catch	If your brother hits you, don't hit him back. They always *catch* the second one.

Spelling Enrichments

PARAGRAPH DICTATION using all the spelling words.

> *Once* on a *riding lesson* I had a *mad* horse. He would not *mind* or stay *within* the pen. He ran off the *track* and jumped *above four fences*. I *groaned*. *Unless* someone could *catch* us, I felt doomed. I held on to his *neck* like *honey* to a jar and prayed. Then he came to a *stop* and *pushed* his nose in some *leaves*. You may *buy* that horse if you like. I will *pick* a slower one.

COMPOUND WORDS. Quiz review words: *back, hand, hay, here, high, house, lace, light, man, moon, over, side, tie, up, word.* Have students combine with new word to form compound words.

back --backstop, backtrack	**hand** --handpick	**hay** --hayride	**here** --herewithin
high --highminded	**house** --madhouse	**lace** --necklace	**light** -- stoplight
man --madman	**moon** --honeymoon	**over** --override	**side** --sidetrack
tie --necktie	**up** --pickup	**word** --catchword	

ORIGINAL SENTENCES. Students can write sentences using adjoining words. A sentence can include more than one word pair. Example: I will *ride once* if you do not *push* me on the *track within* the *fences*.

Review a Non-phonetic Word Needed for This Lesson. Write *lone* and *alone* on the board. Say, "Who can tell us the base word for these words?" That's right -- one. Historically we used to say /O-n/; we now say /wŏn/. Watch in this lesson for another word based on one. Photocopy and use graphic on p. 69.

---

word	note	rule
rīde	I said /I/ because of the E.	[R7]
pu<u>sh</u>	SH can spell /sh/ at the end of a syllable. Add to **SH/TI Page**.	[R10]
wi<u>th</u> in	Alternative marking: put a 2 over the TH if you used the voiced version.	
a bo<u>ve</u>₂	With unstressed, neutral vowels, think as spelled. See SWR p. 79.	[R4,6,7]
stop		
pi<u>ck</u>	CK may be used only after a single vowel that says /a-e-i-o-u/.	[R25]
lea<u>ve</u>₂	English words do not end with V.	[R7]
bu y	Think to spell /bu-I/ and say /bI/. See SWR p. 88. <u>Homophone</u>: by.	[R5,6]
mind	I may say /I/ before two consonants.	[R19]
f<u>ou</u>r	Add to **Number Page**. See Step 15 in SWR. <u>Homophone: for.</u>	
on<u>ce</u>₃	As in the base word "one," we say /w/ but no W is there. See SWR p. 81.	[R2,7]
tra<u>ck</u>	CK may be used only after a single vowel that says /a-e-i-o-u/.	[R25]
fenc es	The base word's silent E is heard in a new syllable.	[R2,22]
mad		
gr<u>oa</u>ns	To make a word plural we usually just add -S.	[R22]
ne<u>ck</u>	CK may be used only after a single vowel that says /a-e-i-o-u/.	[R25]
les son	Think both S's for spelling but not for normal speech.	[R29]
hon <u>ey</u>	ey = /i/ in an unaccented syllable.	
un less	We often double S after a single vowel at the end of a base word.	[R17]
ca<u>tch</u>		

Spelling Enrichments

ANALOGIES. Call out the first part of the analogy and have the student on a clean piece of notebook paper write the spelling word that completes the thought.

<u>Under</u> is to <u>over</u> as <u>below</u> is to _____ (above).   <u>Feet</u> are to <u>walk</u> as <u>car</u> is to _____ (ride).

<u>Smile</u> is to <u>frown</u> as <u>happy</u> is to _____ (mad).   <u>Hand</u> is to <u>wrist</u> as <u>head</u> is to _____ (neck).

<u>Ship</u> is to <u>water</u> as <u>train</u> is to _____ (track).   <u>All</u> is to <u>one</u> as <u>every</u> is to _____ (each).

<u>Door</u> is to <u>wall</u> as <u>gate</u> is to _____ (fence).   <u>Give</u> is to <u>get</u> as <u>throw</u> is to _____ (catch).

<u>Sour</u> is to <u>sweet</u> as <u>vinegar</u> is to _____(honey)   <u>Weeds</u> are to <u>pull</u> as <u>flowers</u> are to __(pick).

<u>Give</u> is to <u>get</u> as <u>sell</u> is to _____ (buy).   <u>Drag</u> is to <u>shove</u> as <u>pull</u> is to _____ (push).

PUNCTUATION. Write sentences using the spelling words. Make every other sentence a question. These are called interrogative sentences. Be sure to use the correct end punctuation. Examples:

Did you <u>catch</u> a fish?   May I have a <u>ride</u> home?   Did you <u>push</u> her?

May I <u>buy</u> some <u>honey</u>?   Will you <u>stop</u> and <u>pick</u> up <u>leaves</u>?   <u>Honey</u>, are you <u>mad</u> at me?

Preliminaries.

Phonograms: Quiz *ar, ch, ci, ck, ear, ee, er, gn, igh, ir, oi, oo, or, ow, oy, sh, si, tch, ti, ui, ur, wor.*
Rules: Review spelling rule cards 7, 8, 10, 11, 14, 16, 22, 24, 25.
Reference Page: Teach the **1-1-1 Page**. See SWR Step 32.

Words for Section L-3

561	save	'Twas to *save* thee from dying, bitter groans and endless crying, that thy blest Redeemer came.-Watts
562	list	Making a grocery *list* can help you to save money.
563	date	December 7, 1941 [Pearl Harbor Day] is "a *date* that shall live in infamy." --FDR
564	grant	*Grant* us, O Lord, a spirit of contentment.
565	fight	God has battles for you to *fight* and win in His strength.
566	rise	If Shakespeare came in this room, we would *rise*; but if Jesus Christ came, we would kneel. -Lamb
567	hop	My arms start to swing as I *hop* in the spring.
568	war	If you want peace, you must prepare for *war*.
569	own	Be not wise in your *own* eyes; fear the Lord and depart from evil. --Proverbs 3:7
570	warm	*Warm* summer sun shine kindly here. --Mark Twain
571	turn	The man who is waiting for something to *turn* up might start on his shirt sleeves.--Garth Henrichs
572	point	When you *point* a finger at someone else, three fingers point at you.
573	watch	I don't make jokes. I just *watch* the government and report the facts. --Will Rogers
574	wish	*Wish* not to live long, as to live well. --*Poor Richard's Almanack*
575	bat tle	A leader who doesn't hesitate before sending his nation into *battle* is not fit to lead. -Golda Meir
576	march	Truth is on the *march;* nothing can stop it now. --Emile Zola
577	root	The very heart and *root* of sin is an independent spirit. --Richard Cecil
578	meet	No one graduates from Bible study until he can *meet* the Author face to face. --E. Harris
579	shoe	You cannot put the same *shoe* on every foot. --Publilius Syrus--1st Century BC
580	pock et	There is no *pocket* in a shroud (the burial garment for the dead).

Spelling Enrichments

APPLY **1-1-1** RULE. Dictate the following review words. Ask the process of elimination questions to determine if the consonant should be doubled when we add -ing to any of these words? If not, why?

dash	(no, 2 consonants)	dashing		*shut*	(yes)	shutting
set	(yes)	setting		*feed*	(no, 2 vowels)	feeding
stream	(no, 2 vowels)	streaming		*club*	(yes)	clubbing
hop	(yes)	hopping		*walk*	(no, 2 consonants)	walking
soap	(no, 2 vowels)	soaping		*war*	(yes)	warring

COMPOUND WORDS. Make compound words from these spelling words.

save -- lifesaver	*warm* -- housewarming	*root* -- uproot
date -- outdate, update	*turn* -- turnout, turnover, upturn	*meet* -- meetinghouse
fight -- bullfight	*point* -- pinpoint, standpoint	*shoe* -- horse-, over-
rise -- sunrise	*watch* -- over-,-word, -dog	snow-, -lace
war -- wartime, warhead	*wish* -- wishbone	shoestring
own -- landowner	*battle* -- battleship	*pocket* -- -book, pick-

LITERATURE. "Marching Song" in *A Child's Garden of Verse* by R.L. Stevenson. See SWR p. 96.

Analyze Part of the 1-1-1 Rule. We need to determine if we see and hear one vowel then one consonant. One tricky place is with the R-influenced phonograms: *ar, er, ir, or, ur.* The vowel sound is affected by the R but it is still a vowel sound. We double the consonant in words like *jar/ jarring; stir/ stirring; blur/ blurring.* ER and OR will be doubled for 2-1-1-accent words: *re-fer/ re-fer'-ring; ab-hor/ ab-hor'-ring.*

sāve	A said /A/ because of the E. English words do not end with V. Mark 1st reason.	[R7]
list		
dāte	A said /A/ because of the E.	[R7]
grant		
fight		
rĭse	I said /I/ because of the E.	[R7]
hop	Hop is a 1-1-1 word!	[R14]
war	Think to spell /w-ar/; some say /w-or/ or whatever you say.	
ŏwn		
warm	[<OE wearm]. We think to spell /w-ar-m/; some say /w-or-m/.	
turn	Add to **ER Page**. If you haven't built the ER Page yet this year, wait until L-5.	
point		
wătch	A commonly says /ah/ after W.	
wi**sh**	SH can spell /sh/ at the end of a syllable. Add to **SH/TI Page**.	[R10]
bat tle	Sound /t/ twice for spelling but not normal speech. Every syllable must have a vowel.	[R29,7]
march	[<F marcher (to trample) <L marcis (hammer)]	
root		
meet	Homophones: meet, meat. To mEEt we see EyE to EyE. We EAT mEAT.	
shoe	SH can spell /sh/ at the beginning... Add to **SH/TI Page**. Odd job E.	[R10,7]
poc**k** et	[<F poque (little poke)]. CK is used after a single vowel that says /o/.	[R25]

ART. Draw and label as many spelling words as possible and label.

DERIVATIVES. Quiz spelling words for the student to write in a column going down the page. As homework, beside each word the student should write the word adding -ing. Watch for E's Dropping and 1-1-1 words. Bonus: Make words past tense, watching for irregular verbs. Make words plural nouns.

save	saving, saved	*war*	warring, wars	*battle*	battling, battled, battles	
list	listing, listed, lists	*own*	owning, owned	*meet*	meeting, **met,** meets	
date	dating, dated, dates	*warm*	warming, warmed	*root*	rooting, rooted, roots	
grant	granting, granted, grants	*turn*	turning, turned, turns	*shoe*	shoeing	
rise	rising, **rose**	*point*	pointing, pointed, points		(Retain E for meaning)	
watch	watching, watched, watches	*fight*	fighting, **fought,** fights		**shod,** shoes	
hop	hopping, hopped, hops	*wish*	wishing, wished, wishes			
pocket	pocketing, pocketed, pockets	*march*	marching, marched, marches			

Preliminaries

Phonograms: Review especially *ai, ay, ar, dge, ei, er, ew, ey, ie, kn, ng, ou, ow, ph, tch, th, wr.*
Spelling Rules: 5, 6, 7, 9, 13, 17, 18, 23. Composition: See Step 33 in SWR.

Words for Section L-4

581	held	The mother *held* her baby in her arms.
582	know	Many men *know* a great deal and are the greater fools for it. --C. Spurgeon
583	noth ing	*Nothing* can cut a diamond but a diamond; *nothing* can interpret Scripture but Scripture. -Watson
584	were	We *were* praising the Lord for all He has done.
585	bod y	Your *body* is your baggage through life; the more baggage, the shorter the trip. --Glasow
586	rode	She *rode* with me on a bicycle built for two.
587	butch er	The *butcher* knows how to cut meat.
588	rose	He *rose* from the **clods** and He's coming again from the **clouds**.
589	kitch en	Our *kitchen* needs cleaning.
590	edge	The finest *edge* is made with the blunt whetstone. --John Lyly
591	close	We *close* our eyes to the faults of close friends.
592	cli mate	The *climate* makes people move more slowly in warmer areas.
593	flew	The birds *flew* high in the sky.
594	ground	The *ground* drank the raindrops like a thirsty man.
595	fell	The unclean spirits *fell* down before Him and cried out, "You are the Son of God." --Mark 3:11
596	trip	The *trip* ended much too soon.
597	drew	The artist *drew* the landscape.
598	flow er	A lovely *flower* is the smile of God's goodness. --William Wilberforce
599	flour	OUR *flOUR* spilled on OUR kitchen floor.
600	stair	The *stair* slants steeply.

Spelling Enrichments

SUBJECT/ VERB. A *sentence* is a group of words that gives a sense of completeness. Every sentence needs a subject and a verb. The *subject* names what we are talking about and the *verb* tells us something about it. Example: A dog barks. Who barks? (dog -- subject). The dog does what? (barks -- verb).

Read the sample sentences above and have the students write from dictation the simple subject/verb for each.

held	mother held	*rose*	He rose	*fell*	spirits fell
know	men know	*kitchen*	kitchen needs	*trip*	trip ended
nothing	nothing can cut	*edge*	edge is made	*drew*	artist drew
were	we were praising	*close*	we close	*flower*	flower is
body	body is	*climate*	climate makes	*flour*	flour spilled
rode	she rode	*flew*	birds flew	*stair*	stair slants
butcher	butcher knows	*ground*	ground drank		

COMPOUND WORDS. Quiz review words in bold. Combine with new words for compound words.

any --anybody	**back** --background	**bush** --rosebush	**down** --downstairs
every --everybody	**may** --Mayflower	**no** --nobody	**over** --overdrew
play --playground	**some** --somebody	**sun** --sunflower	**up** --upstairs
way --stairway	**under** --underground	**with** --withdrew, withheld	**work** --groundwork

Word Variations. In this lesson we will see four kinds of word variations. Look for examples of each.
  a. Words that look exactly alike may not sound alike: *do* (act), *do* (first note on musical scale).
  b. Words may sound exactly alike but not look alike: *meat* (food), *meet* (get together).
  c. Words that sound and look alike but mean something very different: *bat* (animal), *bat* (club).
  d. Words with different meanings but so close in sound they are often confused: *finally, finely.*

---

held	Irregular past tense of "hold."	
know	Homophone: know/ no. See b. above.	
noth ing	Compound: no + thing.	
were	Contraction: were not = weren't. See SWR Step 28.	[R13]
bod y	For spelling think of the unstressed Y as /i/. English words do not end with I.	[R5,6]
rode	O said /O/ because of the E. Homophone: rode/ road. See b. above.	[R7]
butch er		
rose	Homograph: *rose* (got up) or (flower). See c. above. Homophone: *rows/rose.* See b. above.	
kitch en		
edge	DGE is used only after a single vowel that says /a-e-i-o-u/.	[R23]
close	O said /O/ because of the E. Heteronym: close (shut), close (near). See a. above.	[R7]
cli mate	I may say /I/ at the end of a syllable. A said /A/ because of the E.	[R5,7]
flew	Homophone: flew (to fly), flu (short for *influenza*), flue (chimney). See b. above.	
ground	Homograph: ground (earth) or (past tense of *grind*). See c. above.	
fell	We often double L after a single vowel at the end of a base word.	[R17]
trip	Homograph: trip (fall) or (vacation). See c. above.	
drew	Past tense of *draw*.	
flow er	2-syllable word. Don't confuse with the one-syllable word *flour.* See d. above.	
flour	Last sound is /r/, not /er/. Think f-l-ou-r.	
stair	Homophone: stare (gaze). See b. above.	

ANTONYMS. For a spelling quiz, call out the first word in each set below and have the student(s) write the spelling word that is the opposite or alternative. Not included are: *flour, trip, climate, butcher, kitchen.*

climbed/*fell*	sky/*ground*	open /*close*	unsure/*know*	thorn/*rose*
something/*nothing*	walked/*rode*	landed/*flew*	dropped/*held*	spirit/ *body*
elevator/*stairs*	center/*edge*	weren't/*were*	erased/*drew*	weed/*flower*

ALPHABETIZE. Show how to alphabetize words that begin with the same first letter, or same first and second or third letter *(body, butcher, climate, close, drew, edge, fell, flew, flour, flower, ground, held, kitchen, know, nothing, rode, rose, stair, trip, were)*.

SENTENCES. Brainstorm to establish links between spelling words.
  Food: *butcher, kitchen, ground, flour.* (A butcher dropped flour and ground beef in the kitchen.)
  Art: *drew, held, rose, close.* (She drew close the rose she held.)
  A vacation: *trip, rode, climate, flew.* (On a trip they flew to a better climate and rode a horse.)

Can you build a connection between them all? What about a paragraph about a vacation to Paris, the land of French cooks and beautiful art?

Preliminaries: Spelling Rules: Review 3, 4, 5, 7, 8, 10, 17, 22, 28.
Phonograms: Quiz *au, aw, ch, ci, ea, ear, ee, er, igh, ir, ng, oa, or, ough, sh, si, ti, th, ur, wor.*
Reference Page: Add the **ER Page** if you have not done so already this year.

Words for Section L-5

601	be gin	Heaven will *begin* where sin ends. --Thomas Adams
602	be gan	Praise shall conclude that work which prayer *began.* --William Jenkyn
603	be gun	A nation has *begun* to get back on its feet when it gets down on its knees.
604	ex press	The law may *express* sin but cannot suppress sin. --Thomas Adams
605	false	Good children must no *false* thing say. --*New England Primer*
606	earn	You cannot lift those who *earn* the wage by pulling down those who pay the wage. --Lincoln
607	an oth er	One falsehood leads to *another.* --Aesop
608	a ble	Who is *able* to stand before jealousy? --Proverbs 27:4
609	leaf	God bids the tree to put forth its *leaf,* and at His word it fades and falls. --McGuffey
610	feath er	Mammals are clothed in fur, but a *feather* comes from a bird.
611	right	Two wrongs don't make a *right.*
612	an y thing	*Anything* one imagines of God apart from Christ is useless thinking. --Martin Luther
613	be cause	Sin is not hurtful *because* it's forbidden; it is forbidden because it's hurtful. --Ben Franklin
614	her self	A woman is a great way from God when she is always talking about *herself.* --D. L. Moody
615	glo ry	Not only the splendor of the sun, but the glimmering light of the glowworm proclaims God's *glory.* -Newton
616	cheese	What happens to the hole when the Swiss *cheese* is gone? --B. Brecht
617	coal	After the Mt. St. Helens volcano, *coal* formed in ten years, not ten million years.
618	lead	The clue will *lead* the detective to Colonel Mustard with the lead pipe in the kitchen.
619	worms	After *worms* destroy this body, yet in my flesh shall I see God. --Job 19:26
620	fash ion	Troubles are often the tools God uses to *fashion* us for better things. --Henry Beecher

Spelling Enrichments

COMPOSITION. Read Aesop's "The Monkey and the Dolphins" and/ or the following student sentences building on this theme. Ask students to write original sentences using as many spelling words as possible.

One falsehood leads to another. For self-glory a monkey began to express anything false that might impress the dolphin. When the monkey said Piraeus was an intimate friend, the dolphin knew that wasn't right because Piraeus was a harbor. The dolphin began what the monkey earned by dipping him in the water. --Jonathan Johnson

To begin with, express the truth because one falsehood leads to another. Trying to cover up fashions sin. The can of worms will be opened. People who don't do right earn a bad name. Don't say anything untrue and give glory to God. --Paul Janzen

One falsehood leads to another. Mother found feathers near my Barbie fashions. I had picked them off Dad's stuffed pheasant. I said the feathers came from the beach. She expressed disbelief. I lost my glory and honor in her sight. I decided to do right and turn over a new leaf. I want to be able to do good and not lie about anything. --Merilee Janzen

One falsehood can lead to another. Lying is not right. A girl who lies hurts herself and others. Lying is wrong because God expresses it in his commandment. To tell another lie to cover the first is even a greater sin. A lie is a false saying to cover up anything. A Christian should bring glory to God. --Anna Alcala

ER Words. Dig up and write on the board /er/ words taught so far in Section L including derivatives. Answers may include *talker, walker, goner, power, church, feeder, deader, rider, pusher, stopper, picker, buyer, tracker, madder, groaner, catcher, saver, fighter, riser, hopper, owner, warmer, turner, pointer, watcher, marcher, rooter, were, butcher, edger, closer, grounder, flower*. After teaching L-5 add new ER words to **ER Page.**

be gin		Today I begin... present tense	[R4,3]
be gan	Verb tense changes:	Yesterday I began... past tense	[R4]
be gun		I had begun before... past participle	[R4]
ex press	We often double S after a single vowel at ...		[R17]
false	Odd job E is added to keep the word from being mistaken for a plural word.		[R7]
earn	Add to **ER Page.**		
an oth er	[<ME an (an, one, the) + other]. Add to **ER Page.**		
a ble	A said /A/ at the end of a syllable. Every syllable must have a vowel.		[R4,7]
leaf	Plural: leaves. See SWR Step 27.		
feath er	Add to **ER Page** until the first column is filled. Especially seek more rare /ers/.		
right			
an y thing	1st syllable says /en/ in rhythm of speech. Y usually says /i/ at the end of a syllable.		[R5]
be cause	E said /E/ at the end of a syllable. This is an odd job E.		[R4,7]
her self	This /er/ is a dime a dozen. It's used 90% of the time. Especially seek more rare /ers/.		
glo ry	O said /O/ at the end of a... Y usually says /i/ at the end of... Y stands in for I.		[R4,5,6]
chee se	An odd job E.		[R7]
coal			
lead	lead (direct); lead (metal). Add *leadership* to **SH/TI Page.** Past tense: led		
worms	Add to **ER Page.** OR usually says /er/ when W comes before OR.		[R8]
fash i on	Think to spell /fash-i-on/. Say /fash-yon/. See SWR p. 85. Add to **SH/TI Page.**		[R10]

ANTONYMS. Teacher calls out the first word and student writes spelling word that is the opposite.

true/_____ *false*	incapable/_____ *able*	left/_____ *right*
ash/_____ *coal*	himself/_____ *herself*	shame/____ *glory*
stop/_____ *begin*	out of style/in ___ *fashion*	nothing/___ *anything*
regular/_____ *express*	in spite of/_____ *because*	inherit/____ *earn*

ANALOGIES. Teacher reads the analogy, and student writes the response using current spelling words.

Stove is to burner as tree is to _____ (leaf).   Beef is to hamburger as milk is to _ (cheese).
Dress is to fabric as pipe is to _____ (lead).   Flying is to bird as slithering is to _ (worm).
Dog is to fur as bird is to _____ (feathers).

COMPOUND WORDS. Join new, review (book, cut, down, fly, over, ring, up), or common words (pin, cake, birth, clover, cloth).

feather --	pinfeather	*worms* --	bookworms, cutworms, ringworms
fashion + able --	fashionable	*leaf* --	flyleaf, overleaf, cloverleaf
cheese -- cheesecake, cheesecloth		*right* --	birthright, downright, upright

Preliminaries. Phonograms: *ai, ay, ch, ck, ear, ee, er, ir, or, ou, ow, ng, th, ur, wor.*
Spelling Rules: In Section L we have taught or reviewed all rules except 15, 20, 21, 26!
Reference Pages: **Y's Exchanging** and **Plus Endings Pages**. See Steps 34 and 35 in SWR.

Words for Section L-6

621	third	Jesus announced before he died that on the *third* day he would raise himself from the dead.
622	or der	We see *order* in God's creation.
623	next	The lion has a mighty roar; I'm glad no lions live *next* door. --Ruth Echeles
624	ev er	The Bible is before all things true as no other book *ever* was or will be. --Thomas Carlyle
625	how ev er	I once was small, *however,* now I am tall.
626	be come	England has *become* great and happy by the knowledge of God through Jesus Christ. -Q. Victoria
627	be came	What *became* of kings who died in ages past?
628	such	*Such* dogs wag their tails when they are glad and seem to know when you are sad.
629	ear ly	The *early* bird catches the worm.
630	be fore	The ways of man are *before* the eyes of the Lord. --Proverbs 5:21
631	birth day	Many observe Christ's *Birthday* but few his precepts! --Benjamin Franklin
632	sil ver	No *silver* nor gold has obtained my redemption; no riches of earth can save my poor soul. -J. Gray
633	in deed	*Indeed,* I tremble for my country when I reflect that God is just. --Thomas Jefferson
634	small	You cannot help *small* men by tearing down big men. --Abe Lincoln
635	ti ny	When I was a little *tiny* boy, a foolish thing was but a toy. --Shakespeare
636	tall	Would you praise Him when you're *tall? --Children's Mother Goose*
637	fa ther	A wise son makes a glad *father,* but a foolish son is the grief of his mother. --Prov.10:1
638	world	The Bible is the best book in the *world.* --John Adams, 2nd president USA
639	morn ing	Weeping may endure for a night, but joy comes in the *morning.* --Psalm 30:5
640	peo ple	No *people* can prosper without His [God's] favor. --27th Congress of the USA

Spelling Enrichments

CREATIVE WRITING. Discuss favorite birthdays. Ask why they were special. Write down key words. After priming the pump in this way, have student write a paragraph starting with the topic sentence: "I will never forget one birthday." Use as many words from Section L as possible. Underline the spelling words.

SYNONYMS. Call out the first word and have students write the spelling word with the same meaning.
teeny / _____*tiny*   beforehand /___*early*   daddy /____*father*   lanky /__*tall*
daybreak /___*morning*   mankind /_____*people*   prior to /___*before*   earth/___*world*

DERIVATIVES. How many words can you make from *order?*   ordering   ordered
orderly   orderliness   orders   disorder   disordering   disordered
disorderly   disorderliness   reorders   reorder   reordering   reordered

COMPOUND WORDS. Dictate review words: *green, lasting, more, for, what, none, hand, land, grand, under, star, towns.* Students combine these with new spelling words to make compound words.
ever -- evergreen, everlasting, evermore, forever, whatever   *such* -- nonesuch
before -- beforehand   *father* -- fatherland, grandfather   *world* --underworld
morning --morningstar   *people* -- townspeople

Considering the sounds of the A.

What are the three sounds of the single letter A? (/a/-/A/- /ah/).   How can an A say /A/? (at the end of a syllable, with a silent final E). Give examples from Section L of A saying /ah/ *(water, talk, walk, watch, false)*. What does a single letter A say at the end of a word? (ah). How do we usually spell /A/ at the end of a word? (AY)

thi**r**d	Add to **ER Page** and **Number Page**.	
or d**er**		
next		
ev **er**		
h**ow** ev **er**		
b**e** come	E said /E/ at the end of a syllable. This is an odd job E.	[R4,7]
b**e** came	E said /E/ at the end of a syllable. A said /A/ because of the E.	[R4,7]
su**ch**		
ear ly	Y stands in for I; English words do not end with I. Add to **ER Page**.	[R5,6]
b**e** fore	E said /E/ at the end of a syllable. Use 1st type of E rather than OR + odd job E.	[R4,7]
bi**r**th day	Compound: birth + day. AY usually spells /A/ at the end. . . Add to **ER Page**.	[R18]
sil v**er**		
in d**ee**d		
sm**a**ll	We often double F,L,S after a single vowel at the end of a one-syllable word.	[R17]
t**i** ny	Y stands in for I; English words do not end with I.	[R5,6]
t**a**ll	We often double L after a single vowel at the end of a one-syllable word.	[R17]
fa **ther**		
w**or**ld	OR may say /er/ when W comes before OR. Add to **ER Page**.	[R8]
m**or**n ing	Root = morn. Abbreviation: a.m. (ante merideum -- midnight to noon).	[R12]
pe **o** ple	Think to spell pe-O-ple; say /pE-ple/. E said /E/ at the end... Every syllable must ...	[R4,7]

DEGREES OF COMPARISON.   Fold a notebook sheet of paper into three columns. Leave the first column blank. In the second column write **-er / more**. In the third column write **-est / most**. Skip a line and in the first column dictate *black*. In the next columns write: *blacker - blackest*. (We use -er to compare 2 things. We use *-est* to compare 3 or more things.)

Work together as a class to form degrees of comparison of words from Section K.

round - rounder - roundest	clean - cleaner - cleanest	clear - clearer - clearest
base - baser - basest [R16]	high - higher - highest	weak - weaker - weakest
grave - graver - gravest	light - lighter - lightest	easy - easier - easiest [R24]
evil - more evil - most evil	poor - poorer - poorest	watery - more - most watery
Add words from Section L-2, L-3:	mad - madder - maddest [R14]	warm - warmer - warmest

Assignment: Read through the current twenty words. Write any word that can be divided into degrees of comparison and give the forms. Watch out for E's dropping or Y's exchanging words.

early - earlier - earliest [R24]   small - smaller - smallest
tiny - tinier - tiniest [R24]   tall -taller - tallest

Complete these statements: Of all the people in the world I feel the *tallest* when ...
                                              Of all the people in the world I feel the *smallest* when ...

DICTATION FOR REVIEW. The following paragraph uses many of the spelling words in Section L. Dictate it for the students to write.

At the close of a war it is hard to buy food. Many fathers are dead from the battle. The butcher has few chicks or meat. The people are glad to buy flour, cheese, and honey.   In a Third-World country they may have to get their water from the stream. They wish for clothes like dresses, shoes, and suits. The power may be gone. People may have to walk down the road where once they drove their cars. The church people do see good as they each keep thinking of things above. Indeed, Christians know that nobody can keep them from one day meeting the God who has saved them.

DEAF SIGNING OF THE PHONOGRAMS.   This program involves all key avenues to the mind: the eye, ear, the mouth, and the hand. Vary writing as the physical response with either keyboard work (See page 34) or deaf signing of the phonograms. Use the chart below of the American Sign Language Alphabet as seen by the viewer.

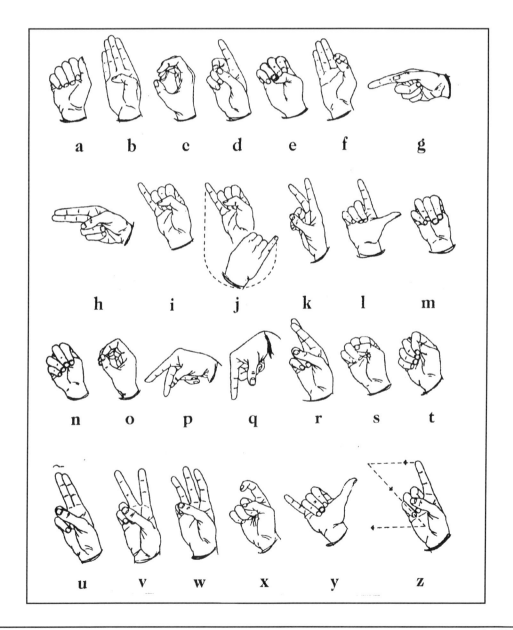

SPELLING
SECTION M

Do not expect the student scores on the spelling diagnostic test to accelerate as quickly now as they did in the beginning. While Sections J through S have more words per section, they are represented by the same number of words on the test as shorter sections. Progress at this midpoint in the program therefore may not be fully reflected by the student test scores. Don't let a slower jump or even a small drop in scores confuse you into thinking you are not gaining ground. Don't lose heart. This foundation is vital to prepare you for the next big jump.

In Sections M and N we include review words from Sections A-I. The words in A-I and their common derivatives compose 50% of all we write and read. This essential core of words should be totally mastered. Give the review words as a quiz. Any words that are misspelled on the quiz should be taught with standard spelling dictation. These review words do not occur in the same order as they are given in the Wise List. The fastest, easiest way to double check spelling markings for these words is with the BHI publication, The Alpha List which lists all the words in our program in alphabetical order.

The review words link as much as possible in some way to the new lesson in M and N. For example, the first set of words in Section M include: *color, wheel, yellow, orange,* and *purple*. The review words include: *red, white, green, black,* and *blue*. M-2 has new math-related words like *arithmetic, paid, stole, solution, account, thousand, less, ticket, money*. The new words include all the numbers taught prior to M. In M-3 we teach the 1-1-1 spelling rule. The review words can all be used to practice that rule. In M-4 the review words are used to help encourage the use of vivid words for effective composition. M-5 has a grammar lesson on adverbs and all the review words can be used as adverbs. M-6 has a lesson on personal pronouns. The review words include the personal pronouns. Several prepositions are new words in N-1. The review words are the other prepositions taught since the beginning of the program.

Preliminaries. <u>Reference</u>: Teach or review **Consonant/Vowel, Multi-letter Phonogram** and **Silent E Pages** (SWR Steps 9, 10, 17). Introduce **ER** and **E's Dropping Pages** (Steps 26, 29).

Words for Section M-1

641	col or	We will make a *color* wheel to help us learn to mix colors.
642	yel low	Color every other pie piece with a primary color: *yellow,* red, or blue.
643	or ange	The colors red and yellow mixed together make *orange.*
644	pur ple	Since red and blue together make *purple,* color the part between red and blue *purple.*
645	key	Prayer should be the *key* of the day and the lock of the night. --Thomas Fuller
646	heav en	*Heaven* cannot be bought with precious jewels or great riches.
647	for est	Yellow mixed with a double portion of blue makes *forest* green.
648	ho tel	The long *hotel,* acutely white, against the after-sunset light withers and takes the grass's tone. --Symons
649	who	He *who* wins souls is wise. --Proverbs 11:30.
650	sew	When you *sew,* match the color of thread to the color of the cloth.
651	wheel	Draw a circle to make the *wheel* and then divide it into six parts.
652	pen cil	With an orange *pencil,* color the section of the color wheel between yellow and red.
653	soil	Clay *soil* looks orange in color.
654	thread	America is not a blanket woven from one *thread,* one color, one cloth.--J. Jackson
655	change	Forgiveness does not *change* the past, but it does enlarge the future. --Paul Boese
656	chang ing	Trust in Him, ye saints, forever. He is faithful, *changing* never. --Thomas Kelly
657	change a ble	Man is *changeable,* only God changes not.
658	dough	Though through the tough sale I coughed, we bought many holiday boughs with my *dough.*
659	goes	What the mother sings to the cradle *goes* all the way down to the coffin. --Henry Beecher (1887)
660	snow	*Snow* covers the world with a sheet of white.

Spelling Enrichments

DICTATION. As a variation to regular spelling tests, call out whole sentences or even a paragraph composed of the words currently studied. Ideally, the students should learn to spell words by a kind of second nature like talking. This way their mental energies can focus on their expression of thought rather than just spelling mechanics.

Sentences: *The white snowman looked like a dough boy. Who says that this color needs to change?*

Paragraph: *Color is a gift from heaven. Who cannot find key colors everywhere from yellow corn, white milk, blue seas and lakes, green forests, red hotels, to orange clay soil? We can use pencils and paper of many colors or sew with many colors of thread. Seasons display changeable colors like a turning wheel. A summer plant may be green. In the fall it may change to yellows, purples, and oranges. In winter black branches may be covered with white snow.*

ALPHABETIZE. Put the twenty new words plus the fifteen review words in alphabetical order.

CONJUNCTIONS. Make phrases or sentences that link spelling words together by **and, or, but**:
> purple **or** orange thread, pencil **and** paper, red apple **or** yellow corn, forest green **or** snow white, snow **and** ice, not purple **but** blue, who **but** the key man. Change the hotel **and** the color.

Review Words from A-I. Quiz selected review words: *red, white, green, black, blue, sea, milk, corn, hair, robe, plant, lake, apple, house, paper, door, ice, stone, but, and, or.* Teach with full dictation any words missed. Use the *Alpha List* to check markings. Follow the same procedure throughout M and N.

col or   [GB colour] Americans may think /or/ for spelling but say /er/. See SWR p. 89.

yel low

or ange   G says /j/ because of the E.   [R3,7]

pur ple   [<Gk porphyra (purple dye)] Every syllable must have... Add to **ER Page**.   [R7]

key   EY as accented vowel may say /E/; as unaccented syllable we think /i/ (mon-key).

heav en

for est

ho tel   [<F hotel < OF hostel (inn)]. O said /O/ at the end of a syllable.   [R4]

who   Think to spell /wh-oo/; say /h-oo/. wh = /h/

sew   For EW to say /O/ is an eXception. *FEW sEW in a nEW pEW.*

wheel

pen cil   C says /s/ before I.   [R2]

soil

thread

change   A said /A/ because of the E. G says /j/ because of E. Mark first that applies.   [R3,7]

chang ing   Silent final E words are written without ... G may still say /j/ because of the I. [R16]

change a ble   Retain E so the G may still say /j/; Rule 3 overrides Rule 16.   [R7,4]

dough   This five-letter word has only two phonograms.

goes   Dictate /g/-/O/. Say, "add E-S." Say /g-O-z/.

snow

ART: Trace a circle in the middle of a sheet of paper. Write the title *Color Wheel*. Divide the circle into six equal parts. All of the colors in the world come from three basic colors. Can anyone name these colors? (yellow, red, blue). In the lower left corner write: *Pri-ma-ry Col-ors*. Below list: **yellow, red, blue**. Color every other pie wedge a primary color. In the lower right hand corner of the chart dictate *Sec-on-da-ry Col-ors*. What color do we get if we mix yellow and red? Color the wedge between yellow and red **orange**. What color do we get by mixing red and blue? Color the wedge between red and blue **purple**. What color is a mix between blue and yellow? Color that segment **green**. List under secondary colors: orange, purple, and green. In the bottom center write the spelling word **black** (darkness, no color hue) and **white** (lightness, no color hue).

Color Wheel

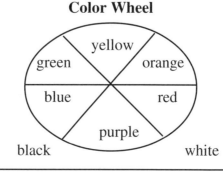

Pri-ma-ry Colors:
yellow
red
blue

Sec-on-da-ry Colors:
orange
purple
green

Preliminaries. Rules: Review 4, 7, 11, 12, 16, 17, 19, 25, 27, 28. Focus on rules, not rule numbers. Phonograms: Quiz on all 70. Reference Pages: Start or review **Number** and **AEIOU Pages**.

Words for Section M-2

661	a rith me tic	Reading, writing, and *arithmetic* are three subjects students need to study each day.
662	might	We *might* teach your little brother fractions after he learns to count past a thousand.
663	paid	She needs a thousand dollars for her large debt to be *paid*.
664	break	My covenant I will not *break*. --Psalm 89:34
665	hold	You can't *hold* a man down without staying down with him. --Booker T. Washington
666	stole	The bad boy who stood behind John *stole* his ticket and now John cannot go.
667	stood	John *stood* in line to buy an extra ticket to the next game.
668	heard	Judas *heard* all Christ's sermons. --T. Goodwin
669	o mit	If you *omit* a zero, the answer is wrong.
670	pass	Forget the troubles that *pass* your way, but never the blessing that come each day.
671	so lu tion	How might I find an easy *solution* to this math problem?
672	ac count	A charge *account* can be called the lie-awake plan.
673	thou sand	A *thousand* bales and a handful of hay is all the same at Doomsday.
674	less	People with tact have *less* to retract. --A. Glasow
675	tick et	He bought the baseball *ticket* on sale, and now both boys can go.
676	mon ey	No one can establish security on borrowed *money*. --A. Lincoln
677	spot	I never spoke with God, nor visited in heaven, yet certain am I of the *spot*... --E. Dickinson
678	an gle	The vase is leaning at an *angle* and may fall.
679	sight	The *sight* of God's glory humbles our pride like vanishing stars before a rising sun.
680	off	I owe, I owe, so it's *off* to work I go.

Spelling Enrichments

DERIVATIVES. Review from M-1 how "Silent final E words commonly lose the need for the E when adding a vowel suffix" [R16]. Look for potential E's dropping words in this spelling list: *stole/ stol-en; an-gle/ an-gled, an-gling, an-gler.*

COMPOSITION USING A MATH THEME. Dictate the title "Arithmetic Solutions" and some or all of the following sentences. Have students write several more word problems using as many new and review spelling words as possible. Ask students to solve these problems.

> *Add five and one. Is the sum less than seven?*
> *Is ten thousand less than nine thousand?*
> *If I omit a thousand from a six thousand dollar account, how much money is in the account?*
> *If five tickets sell for two cents, how much money do I need for ten tickets?*
> *I paid for nine tickets. Three were stolen. How many do I have?*
> *One solution took three days. How long might three solutions take?*
> *He sold four less than ten. How many does he hold?*
> *I paid ten thousand on the spot for five feet of gold. What would one foot cost?*

Dictate Review Words from A-L. If you have not already this year, add to **Number Page** the numbers taught so far: *one* [Think as in *lone* but say /wŏn/], *two, three, four, five, six, seven, nine, ten, eleven, twelve.* See sample on page 200. On separate paper dictate: *sold, add, how, many, much, than, short, trade, what, feet.*

Word	Note	Rule
a rith me tic	[<Gk arithmos (number, rhythm, order)].	[R4,2]
might		
paid	Irregular past tense for *pay*. See SWR p. 125. Abbreviation: pd.	[R12]
break		
hold	Two meanings: *keep (v.) part of ship (n.).* O may say /O/ before 2 consonants.	[R19]
stole	O said /O/ because of the E. Irregular past tense of steal. SWR p. 125.	[R7]
stood		
heard	Root = hear. Add to **ER Page**. Homophone: herd.	
o mit	O said /O/ at the end of a syllable.	[R4]
pass	We often double F, L, S after a single vowel at the end of a base word.	[R17]
so lu tion	O said /O/ and U said /U/.... TI can spell /sh/ at the beginning of...	[R4,11]
ac count	Think double consonants for spelling but not speech. Abbreviation: acct.	[R29,12]
thou sand	Add to **Number Page**.	
less	We often double F, L, S after a single vowel at the end of a base word.	[R17]
tick et	CK may be used only after a single vowel that says /a-e-i-o-u/.	[R25]
mon ey	Think to spell EY at the end of unaccented syllables as /i/.	
spot		
an gle	Every syllable must have a vowel.	[R7]
sight	The phonogram IGH follows the rule: I may say /I/ before 2 consonants.	[R19]
off	We often double F, L, S after a single vowel at the end of a base word.	[R17]

Spelling Enrichments

COMPOUND WORDS. Ask students to form as many compound words as possible based on the new spelling words.

paid --	overpaid, underpaid	*less* --	careless, headless, homeless, hopeless
break --	breakdown, breakwater, outbreak	*money* --	moneybag
hold --	behold, household, uphold, withhold	*spot* --	spotless, spotlight, sunspot
stood --	understood, withstood	*sight* --	eyesight, farsighted, insight, oversight, sightless
heard --	overheard		
pass --	overpass, passover, passport, -word	*off* --	cutoff, offhand, offset, -sides, -shore

THINKING OF A NUMBER. Play the game *I'm thinking of a number.* The person who thinks of the number has to spell any number from zero to twelve on a sheet of paper hidden from everyone else. Then others can ask questions to see who can guess the number. For example, they might say, "Is it five?" If you say no, they can ask, "Higher or lower?"

Preliminaries. Reference Page: If you haven't already this year, teach **1-1-1 Page**. See SWR Step 32.
  Phonograms: Practice reading the 70 phonograms. Time yourself. Can you do it in less than 75 seconds? Give quiz on: *ai, ay, ch, ci, ck, ea, ear, ed, er, ir, ng, ou, ow, ph, sh, si, tch, ti, ur, wor, wr.*
  Spelling Rule Cards: 4, 7, 10, 11, 14, 16, 17, 20, 25.

Words for Section M-3

681	swirl	My feet spin and spring, then I whirl and twirl as I swish and *swirl*.
682	fol low	The best leader is one who will faithfully *follow* the Lord.
683	pro vide	If God sends us on stony paths, He will *provide* us with strong shoes. --A. Maclaren
684	build	Anyone can kick a barn down, but it takes a carpenter to *build* it. --Sam Rayburn
685	re cov er	A slip of the foot you may soon *recover*, not a slip of the tongue.
686	re turn	To the Bible, men will *return*, and why? Because they cannot do without it. --Matthew Arnold
687	teach	Can anyone *teach* knowledge to God? --Job 21:22
688	speak	Liars are not believed even when they *speak* the truth. --Aesop
689	praise	Sweet is the work, my God, my King, to *praise* thy name, give thanks and sing. --McGuffey
690	solve	It is a satisfying feeling to *solve* a math word problem.
691	at tack	The word "*attack*" is related to "attach" which means to stick, to tack together.
692	dress	In winter I get up at night and *dress* by yellow candlelight. --Robert L. Stevenson
693	steam	Daniel Webster struck me much like a *steam* engine in trousers. --Sydney Smith
694	shop	If I read, much less answered, all attacks made on me, this *shop* might as well be closed. --Lincoln
695	file	Carefully *file* your school papers in the proper place in your notebook.
696	con tract	Poor Sally lost the money she collected for the sales *contract*.
697	drill	We want to *drill* the phonograms until we can say them all quickly and easily.
698	pitch	Miriam used *pitch* to help make the basket for baby Moses watertight.
699	swim	Mother, may I go out to *swim*? Yes, my darling daughter, just don't go near the water.
700	fix	If you *fix* your eyes on the past, you risk a collision with the future.

Spelling Enrichments

DERIVATIVES / -ER SUFFIX. Have students divide a loose-leaf sheet into three columns. In column one they should write the twenty spelling words. In column two, write a derivative of the word with the suffix -ER added. Remind the student to be alert for **E's Dropping** and **1-1-1 words**. In column three the student should define the new word. Example: hold / holder / a holder holds.

Note: *Contract* is a bonus challenge word. The suffix -er is for Anglo-based words. The Latin spelling for the same prefix meaning is -OR. *Contract* is a Latin-based word. One who contracts is a contractor.

SENTENCE DICTATION. Instead of a traditional test, dictate sentences which use the last forty words.

An <u>account paid</u> <u>teachers</u> <u>three</u> <u>thousand</u> <u>less</u> <u>tickets</u>.   *<u>Pass</u> a <u>short</u>, <u>swirling pitch</u> at an <u>angle</u>.*
A <u>builder heard</u> the <u>solution</u> for <u>fixing</u> the <u>contract</u>.   *A <u>swimmer</u> <u>followed</u> a <u>dog</u> and <u>stood</u> <u>off</u> shore.*
The <u>dressshop</u> <u>solved</u> a way to <u>recover</u> the <u>money</u> it <u>stole</u>.   *At the <u>sight</u> of pride <u>omit</u> <u>speaking</u> <u>praise</u>.*
A <u>steamship</u> will <u>attack</u> and <u>break</u> a <u>mighty</u> <u>foothold</u>.   *<u>Provide</u> <u>ten</u> <u>drills</u> in <u>arithmetic</u> and <u>find</u> a <u>file</u>.*

Dictate Review Words from A-I. Dictate: *run, top, cut, cat, let, pet, roll, dog, bog, row, flat, step, put, end, fun.* Add endings, doubling when needed: run (runner), top (topped), cut (cutting), cat (catty), let (letting), pet (petted), roll (roller) [not 1-1-1, ends with 2 consonants], dog (dogged), bog (boggy), row (rowing) [not 1-1-1, sounds like one vowel], flat (flattest), step (stepping), put (putting), end (ending) [not 1-1-1, ends with 2 consonants], fun (funny).

swirl	Add to **ER Page**.	
fol low	Think both L's for spelling but not for normal speech.	[R29]
pro vide	O said /O/ at the end of a syllable. I said /I/ because of the E.	[R4,7]
bu ild	One-syllable word. May exaggerate to 2 for spelling. See SWR p. 88.	
re cov er	E said /E/ at the end of a syllable.	[R4]
re turn	[<OF re- (again) + tourner (turn)]. E said /E/ at the end of a ... Add to **ER Pg**.	[R4]
teach		
speak		
praise	Odd job E.	[R7]
solve	An E is needed because English words do not end with V.	[R7]
at tack	CK may be used only after a single vowel that says /a-e-i-o-u/.	[R29,25]
dress	One reason we double the S is to indicate a nonplural base word.	[R17]
steam		
shop	SH may spell /sh/ at the beginning of a word. Add to **SH/TI Page**.	[R10]
file	Multiple meanings: folder/ steel tool/ material. I said /I/ because of the E.	[R7]
con tract	[<L com- (together) + trahere (to draw)].	
drill	We often double F, L, S after a single vowel at the end of a base word.	[R17]
pitch		
swim	Irregular past tense: swam.	
fix	Not a 1-1-1 word. X sounds like two consonants. See SWR p. 158.	[R20]

GRAMMAR/ SUBJECT & VERBS. Every sentence has a subject and a verb. The teacher will dictate potential subject-verb combinations made up of this set of spelling words. Sometimes the word is a derivative of the spelling word. Remind students to watch for **1-1-1** and **E's dropping** words. Teacher should carefully check each student's spelling.

shopper pitched	*builder contracted*	*pitch steams*	*shop returns*
dress swirled	*attack followed*	*teacher praises*	*drill provided*
follower solved	*speaker filed*	*swimmer recovered*	*attacker fixed*
attack swirled	*provider recovered*	*teacher drills*	*shopper returns*

Have students read the subject verb pairs and make an oral sentence using both words. Next have students write sentences. More than one combination can be used in a sentence. Examples: *The shopper pitched the attacker's gun out of the building. The long dress swirled around her ankles.*

VOCABULARY DEVELOPMENT. Consider multiple meanings in a simple word like "fix." As a verb 1. fix your eyes (focus) 2. fix dinner (prepare) 3. fix the car (repair) 4. fix the curtain (adjust) 5. fix your mistake (correct). As a noun: in a fix (a predicament). Can identify other meanings for "fix"?

Preliminaries. <u>Spelling Rule Cards</u>: Review 4, 5, 6, 7, 9, 12, 17, 19, 22, 24, 27. <u>Reference</u>: **Y's Ex Page**.
<u>Phonograms</u>: *ai, ay, ar, ch, dge, ea, ee, ei, eigh, er, ey, ie, kn, ng, oa, oi, oo, ou, ough, ow, oy, sh, th, wh.*

Words for Section M-4

701	ar my	An *army* marches on its stomach. --Napoleon
702	both	It can be said God is *both* near and far.
703	break fast	After a night without food, we break our fast at *breakfast.*
704	climb	Pride loves to *climb* up, not as Zaccheus to see Christ, but to be seen. --W. Gurnall
705	hap pen	There is a time to let things *happen* and a time to make things *happen.* --Hugh Prather
706	chil dren	Good *children* must parents obey. --New England Primer
707	grass	The *grass* looks greener on the other side of the hill.
708	broad	If we stand up to Hitler, the life of the world may move forward into *broad* sunlit uplands. --Churchill
709	noise	The Lord is mightier than the *noise* of many waters. --Psalm 93:4
710	read y	When our color wheel is *ready,* we should label each color.
711	brought	The angel *brought* Peter out of prison, but it was prayer that *brought* the angel.
712	be low	Being injured puts you *below,* revenging makes you even, forgiving sets you above your enemy.
713	while	You cannot get ahead *while* you are getting even. --Rep. Dick Armey
714	moun tains	*Mountains* are earth's undecaying monuments. -- Nathaniel Hawthorne
715	mon key	If you pay peanuts, you get *monkeys.* --James Goldsmith.
716	pull	If the best man's faults were written on his forehead, he would *pull* his hat over his eyes.---J. Trapp
717	be side	A spider sat down *beside* her to listen to Miss Muffet pray. --The Christian Mother Goose.
718	ea gle	Can you paint an *eagle* gliding across the azure sky?
719	thun der	Have you given the horse strength? Have you clothed his neck with *thunder?* --Job 39:19
720	pic ture	A *picture* is worth a thousand words.

Spelling Enrichments

ANALOGIES. Have students write the spelling word that completes the following analogies:

<u>Quiet</u> is to <u>loud</u> as <u>silence</u> is to __(noise).
<u>Evening</u> is to <u>morning</u> as <u>supper</u> is to _____ (breakfast).
<u>Washing machine</u> is to <u>clothes</u> as <u>lawn mower</u> is to ___(grass).
<u>Low</u> is to <u>high</u> as <u>valleys</u> are to ___(mountains).
<u>Bed</u> is to <u>ladder</u> as <u>sleep</u> is to ___ (climb).
<u>See</u> is to <u>hear</u> as <u>lightning</u> is to ___ (thunder).
<u>Ceiling</u> is to <u>floor</u> as <u>above</u> is to ___ (below).
<u>Forward</u> is to <u>backward</u> as <u>push</u> is to ___ (pull).
<u>Swim</u> is to <u>walk</u> as <u>navy</u> is to ___ (army).
<u>Father</u> is to <u>sons</u> as <u>parent</u> is to ____ (children).
<u>Spaghetti noodle</u> is to <u>lasagne noodle</u> as <u>narrow</u> is to ____ (broad).

METAPHORS. A metaphor is a comparison of two unlike things. Can you recognize the symbolic language
used in Alfred Lord Tennyson's poem *The Eagle?*

The wrinkled sea beneath him crawls;
He watches from his mountain walls, And like a thunderbolt he falls.

To what are wrinkles compared? (waves of the ocean)
To what does he compare the powerful, fast dive of an eagle? (lightning and thunder)

Dictate Review Words from A-I: *bacon, bread, bring, path, came, fish, food, home, jump, play, river, tree, summer, zoo, fall, ran, hill, wing, ball.* Follow the procedure described in M-1.

ar my	Y stands in for I; English words do not end with I.	[R5,6]
bo<u>th</u> ₂	O may say /O/ before 2 consonants.	[R19]
br<u>ea</u>k fast		
clim<u>b</u>	B is silent but helps make I say/ I/. I may say /I/ before 2 consonants.	[R19]
hap pen	Think /p/ twice for spelling but not for normal speech.	[R29]
<u>chi</u>l dren	Plural of child. We don't say "We have many childs."	[R22]
grass _x	We often double F, L, S after a single vowel at the end of a base word.	[R17]
br<u>oa</u>d ₂	Think to spell /b-r-O-d/; say /b-r-o-d/. See SWR p. 81.	
n<u>oise</u>_s	Odd job E	[R7]
r<u>ea</u>d y ₂ ₅	Y stands in for I; English words do not end with I.	[R5,6]
br<u>ou</u>ght		
be l<u>ow</u> ₂	Does E usually say /E/ at the end of a syllable? Yes. A-E-O-U usually say ...	[R4]
whil<u>e</u>	Not *wile*, but *while*. I said /I/ because of the E.	[R7]
m<u>ou</u>n tai<u>n</u>s ₂	Think "moun tAnz." Say whatever you say. <u>Abbreviation</u>: mts.	[R22,12]
mon k<u>ey</u> ₃	Think to spell EY at the end of an unaccented syllable as /i/.	
pull ₃	We often double F, L, S after a single vowel at the end of a base word.	[R17]
be sid<u>e</u>	E said /E/ at the end of a syllable. I said /I/ because of the E.	[R4,7]
<u>ea</u> gl<u>e</u>₄	Every syllable must have a vowel.	[R7]
thun d<u>er</u>		
pic tur<u>e</u>	Pronounce "pic-ture" and "pitch-er" differently. U said /U/ because of the E.	[R7]

DERIVATIVES. Teach (or review) the **Y's Exchanging Page**. See SWR Step 34. *The single vowel Y changes to I when adding any ending unless the ending starts with I* (happy/happiness) [R24].

Try to add -s, -es, -en, -er,- ed, -ing, -ness to these spelling words. Watch for words ending in Y.

climb	climbs, climbed, climber, climbing	picture	pictures, pictured, picturing
happen	happens, happened, happening	pull	pulls, pulled, pulling
monkey	monkeys, monkeyed, monkeying	broad	broader, broaden
ready	readies, readiness, readying, readied	eagle	eagles
thunder	thunders, thundering, thundered	army	armies

COMPOSITION. Good writers use vivid words, especially verbs and nouns. See SWR pp. 161-162. Dictate the following paragraph: *We are at the mountain. We have food. An eagle is there. Fish are in the river. Children are on the grass. A monkey is in the tree. I want to take a picture, but we go back home.*

Revise the paper trying to replace *is, are, was, were* with more active verbs. Use as many of the other spelling words as possible. Sample: *In the summer we went on a trip to the mountains. We brought bread and bacon for breakfast. We watched a broad eagle fall from heaven, fish jump in the river, and a boy pull a kite. Both our children climbed a tree after a monkey, then played with toy army men on the grass below. While taking a picture, we heard the noise of thunder and ran for home.* Draw a picture to illustrate.

Preliminaries. <u>Phonograms</u>: *ai, ay, ear, ed, er, gn, igh, ir, kn, oa, oe, oo, or, ou, ow, th, ui, ur, wh, wor.*
<u>Rules</u>: 8, 12, 13, 16, 18, 19, 21. <u>Reference Pages</u>: **Contraction, Dismiss L Pgs**. SWR Steps 28, 37.

Words for Section M-5

721	al most	You *almost* persuade me to become a Christian. --Acts 26:28
722	a gain	My sun sets to rise *again.* --Robert Browning
723	al so	Where your treasure is, there will your heart be *also.* --Matthew 6:21
724	dai ly	My mother had me learn *daily* long chapters of the Bible by heart. --J. Ruskin
725	rare ly	Children *rarely* play at being other children. --David Holloway
726	month	This is the *month,* and the happy morn, when the Son ... of virgin mother born. --Milton
727	sound	Some people talk because they think *sound* is more manageable than silence. --M. Halsey
728	true	A child should always say what's *true.* --Robert L. Stevenson
729	truth ful	Two half-truths do not make a *truthful* statement.
730	sol id	The car is painted a *solid* blue.
731	born	A man becomes a Christian; he is not *born* one. --Tertullian
732	en ter	Abandon hope all you who *enter* hell.
733	died	He lived by the sword and *died* by the sword.
734	re gret	We go to bed with reluctance, yet we quit it with *regret.*
735	col lect	The jolly usher waited to *collect* both tickets.
736	sow	Where there is hatred let me *sow* love; where injury, pardon. --Francis of Assisi
737	does	He who *does* not work *does* not eat! --2 Thess. 3:10
738	says	The fool *says* in his heart, "There is no God." --Psalm 14:1
739	driv en	Have you *driven* in the beautiful Blue Ridge Mountains of North Carolina?
740	learn	*Learn* to say no. It will be of more use to you than to be able to read Latin. --C. Spurgeon

Spelling Enrichments

HETERONYMS. Some words that are spelled alike have different meanings and sound differently.
      do   -- **Do** you know how to sing, "**Do**, ra, me, fa, so, la, ti, **do**?"
      lead   -- I am in the **lead** to sharpen my **lead** pencil.
      sewer   -- The **sewer** of the flag did not install the pipes for the **sewer**.
      lead   -- The man will **lead** the men in search of **lead.**

This lesson has two such words. See if the students can recognize them.
      sow   -- **Sow** the seed and feed slop to the **sow** with her piglets.
      does   -- **Does** the man like the picture I took of the buck and the **does**?

CROSSWORD PUZZLE. Make a crossword puzzle with the words. You may or may not require definition
down and across in the traditional format. All these words can fit together.

```
        s
    a l m o s t
        l     s o u n d
        i     a     i     a g a i n
        d a i l y     e     l
            s     d o e s
                      o
```

Dictate Review Words from A-I.

These review words can all be used as adverbs: *not, ever, very, when, soon, today, now, never, here, away, as, just, then, so, yet.*

al most (3)	*All* as a prefix uses one L. **Dismiss L Pg**. O may say /O/ before 2 consonants.	[R21,19]
a gain (3)	Exaggerate unaccented syllables to help with spelling. See SWR pgs. 79, 89.	[R4]
al so (3)	*All* as a prefix uses one L. **Dismiss L Pg**. O said /O/ at the end of a syllable.	[R21,4]
dai ly	root = day. Y stands in for I; English words do not end with I.	[R5,6]
rare ly	A said /A/ because of the E.	[R7,5,6]
month	[<OE mona (moon)]. <u>Abbreviation</u>: mo.	[R12]
sound		
true (=2)	English words do not end with U.	[R7]
truth ful (3)	E no longer needed, U not at end. *Full* as a suffix uses one L. **Dismiss L Pg**.	[R21]
sol id	[<L solidus (a Roman coin)].	
born		
en ter		
died (2)	English words do not end with I. For past tense of "die," drop the E and add -ED.	[R16,28]
re gret	E said /E/ at the end of a syllable.	[R4]
col lect	Think double consonants for spelling but not normal speech.	[R29]
sow (2)	<u>Homophones</u>: so, sew, sow. SOW a rOW of beans which will grOW slOWly.	
does (X 2)	Think to spell /d-o/ and add E-S. Say /duz/. <u>Contraction</u>: does not = doesn't.	[R13]
says (X 2)	Think to spell like Scottish /s-A-z/; say /sez/.	
driv en	Root = drive. Silent final E words commonly lose the need for the E when...	[R16]
learn	[American past tense: *learned.* British: *learnt*]. Add to **ER Page**.	

ADVERBS. Write on the board: *when? where? how? to what extent?* Adverbs can modify a verb, adjective or another adverb. They answer the questions when (run **soon**), where (run **there**), how (run **slowly**), to what extent (run **frequently, never** run). Adverbs can be either before or after a verb. They often end with -ly.

The quick boy came (Quick is an adjective. It modifies the noun boy and tells **what kind**).

The boy came quickly (Quickly is an adverb. It modifies the verb came and tells **how**).

Read the top line of words you just wrote in the spelling notebook: **almost** born; Almost tells what about born? (to what extent); **again** enter; tells what about enter? (when); **also** died; tells what about died? (to what extent); **daily** regrets; tells what about regrets? (when); **rarely** collect; tells what about collect? (how often).

Change these words into adverbs: *month, sound, true, truthful, solid, regretful, collectively.* How? (Add -ly). Why drop the E in **truly** if -LY is not a vowel suffix? (E not needed. U no longer at end.)

ADVERBIAL CLAUSES. Dictate the following clauses and have the student finish using spelling words.

I sow the seed when. . .   (the <u>month</u> is over.)
I sow the seed where. . .   (I was <u>born</u>.)

Preliminaries. Phonograms: Read all 70 by flipping through the cards and having students say only the sounds each phonogram can make (for AY say /A/). All 70 can be read in a minute and fifteen seconds. Save the letter E for last. Say, "Can you think of a third sound this one makes?" Write "false" on the board. "What does the E say in this word? (nothing). What do we call it? (A silent final E.) Review the five types of silent E's. This lesson contains spelling words using many of these reasons.

Words for Section M-6

741	nar row	Strait is the gate and *narrow* is the way that leads to life. --Matthew 7:14
742	ex tra	He did not have *extra* cash to buy another pass.
743	great	If America ceases to be good, America will cease to be *great.* ---Tocqueville
744	mid dle	People who stay in the *middle* of the road get run over.
745	past	Those who do not remember the *past* are condemned to repeat it. --George Santayana
746	wire	Match together the white *wire* and the red *wire.*
747	team	Our *team* colors were yellow and black.
748	those	It's tyranny to forcefully take money from *those* who work to give to the lazy.
749	few	*Few* are wise on their own. Anyone taught only by himself has a fool for a master.
750	liv ing	Our daily *living* depends on God.
751	fin ger	Clean your *finger* before you point at my spots. *--Poor Richard's Almanack*
752	chance	Never lose a *chance* to say a kind word. --W. Thackeray
753	heart	Works do not make the *heart* good, but a good heart makes works good. --S. Charnock
754	phrase	Explain the meaning of the *phrase,* "sink or swim together."
755	case	Keep your coloring pencils organized in a carrying *case.*
756	chick	The egg is no *chick* by falling from the hen, nor man a Christian till he's born again. --J. Bunyan
757	e vent	It is easy to be wise after the *event.*
758	col lar	She made her thousandth *collar* in the shirt factory.
759	rail road	Sally can't pay for the *railroad* trip.
760	mem ber	I wouldn't want to belong to any club that would accept a *member* like me. --Groucho Marx

Spelling Enrichments

SPELLING GRAPHIC. Title a page *Spelling Fingers*. With a pencil lightly in the center of the page trace around the fingers of each child's hand. On the perimeter of the sketch have the student write the spelling words around the outline like we did with the picture of a bow in Section I-4, page 32.

PERSONAL PRONOUNS. Dictate these review words from A-I to be written on a loose-leaf sheet of paper or as Reference Page 31 in the Black Learning Log. Divide the paper into three columns and dictate as follows. Teach the difference between subject and object pronouns. I can say, "I am your teacher." I should not say, "Me am your teacher." I can say, "Listen to me." I should not say, "Listen to I."

subject	object	possessive
I	me	my, mine
you	you	your, yours
he	him	his
she	her	her, hers
it	it	its
we	us	our, ours
they	them	their, theirs (will be taught in Q-6)

Dictate Review Words from A-I. It's one thing to learn words for a weekly test but another thing to learn each word for keeps. With every set of twenty new spelling words in Sections M and N, we will review 15 or so words taught earlier in this program. Write these review words on loose-leaf notebook paper, not in the Learning Log. For this lesson we will review the personal pronouns: *I, me, my, you, your, he, him, his, she, her, it, its, we, us, our, they, them.*

---

nar row	Think both R's for spelling but not for normal speech.	[R29]
ex tra	[<L extra- (outside of)] If a word ends with A it says /ah/.	[R18]
great		
mid dle	Sound double consonants for spelling... Every syllable must have a vowel.	[R29,7]
past	Homophone: passed (past tense of pass)	
wire	I said /I/ because of the E. See SWR p. 88.	[R7]
team		
those	O said /O/ because of the E.	[R7]
few		
liv ing	Root = live. Silent final E words commonly lose the need for the E when...	[R16]
fin ger		
chance	C says /s/ because of the E.	[R7]
he art	Spell HE-ar-t; say /h-ar-t/. Think one-syllable word as 2 for spelling.	
phrase	A said /A/ because of the E.	[R7]
case	A said /A/ because of the E.	[R7]
chick	CK may be used only after a single vowel that says /a-e-i-o-u/.	[R25]
e vent	[<L ex- (out) + venire (come)]. E said /E/ at the end of a syllable.	[R4]
col lar	Sound double consonants for spelling... Think to spell /ar/. See SWR p. 89.	[R29]
rail road	Compound word meaning "the road is laid with rails"	
mem ber	[<L membrum (limb, part)]	

Spelling Enrichments

ADJECTIVES. An adjective helps paint a picture by adding description. Read the top two words going across the page (narrow finger). How do these words go together? **Finger** is a naming word (a noun) and **narrow** tells what kind of finger. What other adjectives could modify finger? (skinny, pudgy, broken, bent, hurt, burnt, tan, fat, bronze, wrinkled). Continue to read the word pairs in like fashion.

extra chance	greater chance, lost chance, last chance
great heart	cold heart, hard heart, broken heart, strong heart
middle phrase	first phrase, last phrase, harsh phrase, forgotten phrase, etc.

Assignment. Either have students write sentences using the adjective noun combinations plus the personal pronouns in the review spelling words or dictate the following sentences:

*It has a **narrow finger**.*   *She needs an **extra chance**.*   *He has a **great heart**.*
*You say the **middle phrase**.*   *I will take the **past case**.*   *The **wire chick** belongs to him.*
*Go to my **team event**.*   *We lost **those collars**.*   *Few railroads are near to us.*
*His list is of **living members**.*

Preliminaries. Rules: Section M covers all rules except 15! Reference Page: **Plus Endings** (SWR Step 35) Phonograms: Review at least *ai, ar, au, aw, ay, ch, ea, ee, er, oo, or, ou, ough, oy, sh, th, ur.*

Words for Section M-7

761	in form	Let the reading of the Word not only *inform* you, but inflame you.
762	fur nish	A man saw what happened and decided to *furnish* a ticket for John.
763	charge	How much money do they *charge* for one child to go?
764	freeze	Cold prayers *freeze* before they reach heaven. --T. Brooks
765	took	He *took* the picture with color film.
766	trust	*Trust* in the LORD and do good; dwell in the land, and feed on His faithfulness. --Psalm 37:3
767	fas ten	Be FAST in learning to *FASTen* the tent.
768	bought	Sad Sally was unable to pay for all the pretty clothes she *bought.*
769	laid	Where were you when I *laid* the foundations of the earth? --Job 38:4
770	un a ble	Sally is *unable* to do many things she wants to do because of unpaid debts.
771	hur dle	Work hard to overcome that *hurdle.*
772	deal	*Deal* with another as you'd have another *deal* with you. --*New England Primer*
773	in come	You cannot keep out of trouble by spending more than your *income.* --A. Lincoln
774	please	Use magic words like these: thank you and would you *please*?
775	re cord	He will *record* the record-breaking time.
776	stare	It is not polite to *stare.*
777	gen tle	White added to the primary color red makes a more *gentle* pink color.
778	bur y	"We will *bury* you," said Nikita Khrushchev to the U.S.A. in 1956.
779	pret ty	There is only one *pretty* child in the world, and every mother has it.
780	un der stand	The passages in Scripture that trouble me most are those I *understand.* --Mark Twain

Spelling Enrichments

OXYMORONS. The Greek word *oxys* means "sharp" and *moros* means "stupid." An *oxymoron* is a figure of speech in which two words which are opposites are used together. *Shrimp* means something "small." *Jumbo* means "large." *Jumbo shrimp* is an oxymoron. Explain these examples: *small giant   good grief   wise fool   tight slacks   empty spot   almost exactly   soft rock*
Try to complete the following oxymorons. Give one word of the oxymoron and have the student finish it using one of the twenty spelling words above.

easy ____ (hurdle)   terribly __(pleased)   bad __ (deal)   __(bury) a find   spent __ (income)
blank ___ (record)   blind ___ (stare)   __(gentle) jolt   __ (pretty) ugly   __(understand) a puzzle

These can be tricky. Here is an example of how to guide the thinking:

easy hurdle	What are opposites of *easy*? (hard, difficult). *An obstacle* is what? *(a hurdle).*
terribly pleased	How do we feel when things are terrible? (sad).
	What are opposites of terrible and sad? (glad, happy, pleased).
bury a find	What are synonyms for find? (discover, unearth). What is the opposite? (hide, bury).
blind stare	A blind person cannot see. What words can mean see? (to look, gaze, stare).
gentle jolt	To jolt is to shake abruptly. What is the opposite of rough treatment? (gentle).
spent income	Where does money go after you spend it? (out)
	What is the opposite of money going out? (money coming in or income).

Dictate Review Words from A-I: *easy, day, find, form, heat, told, make, cold, see, like, live, lay, led, look, man, miss, Miss* [R26], *spent, zip* [R27].

---

in form		
fur nish	SH can spell /sh/ at the end of a word. Add to **ER Page** and **SH/TI Page**.	[R10]
charge₃	G says /j/ because of the E.	[R3,7]
freeze₅	Odd job E	[R7]
took		
trust	Root = true E no longer needed; U not at end.	
fas ten	Root = fast fasten = to hold fast	
bought	Irregular past tense of *buy*	
laid	Root = lay Word changes internally for past tense.	
un a ble₄	A said /A/ at the end of a syllable. Every syllable must have a vowel.	[R4,7]
hur dle₄	Add to **ER Page**. Every syllable must have a vowel.	[R7]
deal		
in come₅	Odd job E	[R7]
please₅	Odd job E	[R7]
re cord	E said /E/ at the end of a syllable. Homograph: rec-ord (n.)	[R4]
stare	A said /A/ because of the E. Homophone: stair	[R7]
gen tle₄	G may say /j/ before E. Every syllable must have a vowel.	[R3,7]
bur y	Y stands in for I; English words do not end with I. Think to spell /ber-i/.	[R5,6]
prĕt ty	Sound double consonants for spelling but not for normal speech.	[R29]
un der stand		

PREFIXES. Dictate the following prefixes to be written going down a page of loose-leaf paper. Make derivatives using as many new words as possible using a prefix with M-7 new and review words.

anti-	(against)	antifreeze
dis-	(the opposite)	discharge, dislike, dismiss, displease, distrust
mis-	(wrong or bad)	misinform, mislaid, mislay, misled, misrecord, misunderstand
out-	(away or more)	outlay, outlive, outlook, outspent, outlaid
over-	(higher / too much)	-bought, -charge, -heat, -lay, -laid, -look, -see, -spent, -took
re-	(again)	-charge, -deal, -fasten,-form, -heat, -line, -make, -miss, -told, -furish
super-	(over or above)	supercharge, superman
un-___	(not / opposite of)	unbought, unbury, unfasten, unfurnished, uninformed, unlike, unrecorded, unspent, untold, unzip

SUFFIXES. Add **-ing** and/or **-er** to spelling words. Watch for Y's Exchanging or E's Dropping rules.

furnish -- furnishing, furnisher   **inform** --informing, informer   **charge** -- charging, charger
break -- breaking, breaker   **freeze** --freezing, freezer   **trust** -- trusting
fasten -- fastening, fastener   **hurdle** --hurdling, hurdler   **deal** -- dealing, dealer
income -- incoming, incomer   **please** --pleasing, pleaser   **record** -- recording, recorder
stare --staring   **bury** --burying   **pretty** --prettying, prettier
understand --understanding   For a 1-1-1 word use review word -- **man** -- manning.

-able [-ible]	-age	-al
-ance	-ar	-ate
-ed	-ee	-en
-er	-ess	-est
-ful	-hood	-ic
-ing	-ion [-tion, -sion, -cion]	-ish
-ist	-ity	-ive
-ize	-less	-ly
-ment	-ness	-or
-ory [-tory]	-ous [-ious]	-y

Spelling
Section N

"Statistical evidence is overwhelming that millions of American children, including those graduating from high school, cannot read. When a disorder affects so many people, one calls it an epidemic.   An epidemic is always caused by external forces, not by defects in the individual. . . . When so many children are affected by the same disorder, the explanation cannot possibly be individual psychopathology."

-- Hilde Mosse, Ph.D.

Why does this program work when so many others fail?

"From research in the classroom and the clinic, we have discovered that when the sequence of reading and spelling instruction is compatible with the logic of the alphabet code **and** with the child's linguistic and logical development, learning to read and spell proceeds rapidly and smoothly **for all children** and is equally effective for poor readers of all ages."

--Diane McGuinness, Ph.D.

Preliminaries. Phonograms: *ea, ed, er, ng, oa, oe, ough, ph, th, wr.* Rules: 2, 4, 5, 6, 7, 12, 13, 17, 20, 22, 28. Reference Pages: Dictate **Consonant/Vowel, Multi-letter Phonogram** and **Silent Final E Pages** (SWR Steps 9, 10, 17) if you have not done so this year.

Words for Section N-1

781	stud y	In spiritual graces let us *study* to be great, and not to know it.
782	try	If at first you don't succeed, *try, try* again.
783	write	Into their mind I will put my laws and *write* them in their hearts. --Hebrews 8:10
784	hear	With my EAR I can *hEAR.*
785	be yond	*Beyond* the word of the LORD, I cannot go neither more nor less. --Num. 22:18
786	a mong	*Among* my most prized possessions are words that I have never spoken. --Sam Rayburn
787	bal ance	By truth is God pleased but a false *balance* is an abomination to the LORD. --Prov. 11:1
788	cry	To shut your ears to the *cry* of the poor is also to *cry* and not be heard. --Prov. 21:13
789	act	In prayer we *act* like men; in praise we *act* like angels. --Thomas Watson
790	use	With everything, *use* it as if it belongs to God; it does.
791	tax	With ease we can see the government *tax* is too high!
792	thought	At any man's wicked *thought* the Lord turns away His eyes.
793	size	On studying great men we learn they are but life-*size.*
794	rule	After men refuse God's *rule,* He lets them *rule* themselves. --Ruth Haycock
795	him self	For a man to have friends he must *himself* be friendly. --Proverbs 18:24
796	it self	In all things God's truth agrees with *itself.*
797	num ber	In the Bible we learn that God knows even the *number* of hairs on our head.
798	there	To a man *there* is a way that seems right, but its end is the way of death. --Prov. 16:25
799	cross	By crossing out "I" you form a *cross;* salvation requires death to self.
800	some thing	About two weeks passes between throwing *something* away and badly needing it.

Spelling Enrichments

COMPOUND WORDS. Identify the spelling words that are compound words *(itself, himself, something).* Many compound words are formed by merging a preposition with another word *(overhead, underage, afternoon).* Combine preposition review words with spelling words to make compound words:

study --	overstudy, understudy	*use* --	overuse	*cross* --	crossover
try --	tryout	*tax* --	overtax		
write --	overwrite, underwrite	*thought* --	afterthought		
hear --	overhear	*size* --	oversize		
balance --	overbalance	*rule* --	overrule		
cry --	outcry	*number* --	outnumber		
act --	overact	*there* ---	-abouts, -at, -by, -in, -with		

Other compound word possibilities: crybaby, taxpayer, crossbow, crossroad, thoughtless, numberless.

DERIVATIVES. Give students suffix cards (page 98) and prefix cards (page 116) and have them build from the base word *act.* There are at least 85 possibilities. See SWR pages 130-131 or *Alpha List* p. 72.

COMPOSITION. Use spelling words to write about your father at income tax time.

Dictate Review Words from A-I. See p. 83. These words can be prepositions: *about, after, at, by, down, for, in, into, of, on, out, over, to, up, under, with*. Prepositions are words that show the relationship to something. For example *beneath the boy* tells you where something is in relation to the boy. The expression *beside the boy* gives you a different picture. To illustrate prepositions in a fun way, team up as partners. Act out each preposition read by the teacher. Listen for two new prepositions in this list.

stud y	Y stands in for I; English words do not end with I.	[R5,6]
try	Y usually says /i/ at the end of a syllable but may say /I/.	[R5,6]
write	I said /I/ because of the E. Homophone: right. See Step 30 SWR.	[R7]
hear	Homophone: here	
be yond	E said /E/ at the end of a syllable.	[R4]
a mong	For spelling think A saying /A/ at... Bracket these two prepositions.	[R4]
bal ance	C say /s/ because of the E.	[R7]
cry	Y stands in for I; English words do not end with I.	[R5,6]
act		
use	U said /U/ because of the E. Spell the noun *use* the same but say it differently.	[R7]
tax	Plural: taxes	[R20,22]
thought	This word has seven letters but only three phonograms.	
size	Few words use Z within the word (dozen, organize, citizen). I said /I/ because of the E.	[R7]
rule	U said /U/ because of the E.	[R7]
him self		
it self	Bracket these two reflexive pronouns (personal pronoun + self or selves)	
num ber	Abbreviation: no. Homograph: numb + er (more numb)	[R12]
there	An odd job E. Contraction: there is = there's. See SWR Step 28.	[R7,13]
cross	We often double S after a single vowel at the end of a base word.	[R17]
some thing	Odd job E	[R7]

PREPOSITIONS. Build a list of prepositions through *beyond* and *among*. See SWR page 104.
Write sentences using new spelling words plus at least one review preposition in each sentence. Diagram the prepositional phrase portion of the sentence.

Example: Write the number *by* something.

The boy will balance himself *on* the bar.

Study something *with* careful thought.

SENTENCE STARTERS. Usually we make sentences that begin with a subject. *She left the room.* An effective writer learns to start sentences in a variety of ways. One pattern is to begin the sentence with a prepositional phrase. For example: *In a huff, she left the room.* For a bonus challenge assignment, have students use prepositional phrases for sentence openers as they write original sentences with these words.

Preliminaries. Spelling Rule Cards: 1, 2, 3, 4, 5, 7, 9, 12, 16, 17, 18, 19, 22, 24, 26, 28.
Phonograms: Review *ay, aw, ch, ci, ea, er, ie, ng, or, oy, qu, si, th, ti* and advanced *gu.* (SWR Step 38).
Reference Pages: Cover **E's Dropping Page** (SWR Step 29) and **ED Rule Page** (SWR Step 22).

Words for Section N-2

801	per son	It is not the talking but the walking and working *person* that is the true Christian. --Pres. Madison
802	press	A free *press* can be good or bad, but without freedom it will never be anything but bad. --Camus
803	guide	History is a better *guide* than good intentions. --Jeane Kirkpatrick
804	doc tor	An eye *doctor* wants to correct everything in sight.
805	teach er	A *teacher* is one who teaches.
806	priest	An ounce of mother is worth a pound of *priest.* --Spanish proverb
807	wo man	Once a *woman* has forgiven her man, she must not reheat his sins for breakfast. --M. Dietrich
808	wo men	*Women* take their being from men, men take their well-being from *women.* --T. Adams
809	vil lage	We shall defend every *village,* every town, and every city. --W. Churchill
810	an gel	A humble sinner is in a better condition than a proud *angel.* --Thomas Watson
811	de mand	The *demand* of the time is a young man grounded in Christianity and its Book. --Pres. McKinley
812	ex cuse	God will *excuse* those who trust in Jesus but allow no excuse for rejecting His Son.
813	of fer	By accepting Satan's *offer,* Adam got a taste of fruit but lost a paradise.
814	ques tion	The *question* is not whether God is on our side, but whether we are on His. --Pres. Reagan
815	pray	He that cannot *pray,* let him go to sea, and there he will learn.
816	con fess	*Confess* yourself to heaven; repent what's past; avoid what is to come. --Wm. Shakespeare
817	mum ble	When in doubt, *mumble.*
818	re pent	To *repent* is to alter one's thinking, to take God's point of view instead of one's own.
819	crit i cize	Don't *criticize* what you can't understand. --Bob Dylan
820	rea son	The *reason* people are down on the Bible is they are not up on the Bible. --William Ayer

Spelling Enrichments

DERIVATIVES. Write in a column going down on a blank piece of paper the review words *cry, study, tax, act, cross, try.* Ask, "Do we need to do anything before adding **-ing** to these words?" (No, just add the ending.) Dictate *size, write.* Repeat the **E's Dropping rule**. "Silent final E words commonly lose the need for the E when adding a vowel suffix." In the second column add **-ing** *(siz-ing, writ-ing).*

Use the cards on p. 98 or dictate a in a column on loose-leaf paper: *-ance, -ate, -ess, -ic, -ory, -ly, -hood, -able, -ed.*   Have the students find one or more spelling words that can use each suffix.

-ance	guidance		-ate	doctorate
-ess	priestess		-ic	angelic
-ory	offertory		-ly	priestly, womanly
-hood	priesthood, womanhood			
-able	personable, excusable, questionable, reasonable			
-ed	pressed, guided, doctored, demanded, excused, offered,			
	questioned, prayed, confessed, mumbled, repented, criticized, reasoned			

Organize the past tense examples by phonogram sound. See the Step 22 in SWR especially p. 124.

Dictate Review Words from A-I: *child, mother, loner, boy, thank, lord, read, ask, page, beg, sang, tell, call.* A good writer uses vivid words. Which words are a more vivid or precise word for "person?" *(child, mother, loner, boy, page, lord).* A more vivid word for "say?" *(read, ask, page, beg, sang, tell, thank, call).*

---

per son	[<L persona (person)].	
press	We often double F, L, S after a single vowel at the end of a base word.	[R17]
guide	gu = /g/ G may say /j/ before I but not before U.	[R3]
doc tor	Latin based words use -OR instead of -ER. <u>Abbreviation</u>: DR or Dr.	[R12,26]
teach er		
priest	IE is used more often than EI.	[R9]
wo man	Think to spell /wO-man/. Derived from "wife of man."	
wo men	Think as written for spelling /wO men/. Say /wim en/. This is a mutated plural.	[R11,22]
vil lage 2	A said /A/ because of the E and G says /j/ because of the E.	[R29,7]
an gel	<u>[<Gk angelos (messenger)]. A rarely says /A/ w/out R 4 or 7. G may say /j/ ...</u>	[R3]
de mand 2	E said /E/ at the end of a syllable.	[R4]
ex cuse	With the same spelling we can write the noun *ex cuse.*	[R7]
of fer	[<L ob- (to) +ferre (to bring)]. Sound double consonants for spelling.	[R29]
ques ti on	Think 3 syllables for spelling. See SWR p. 88. Root word "quest."	[R1]
pray	A-Y usually spells /A/ at the end of a word. If a word ends with A is says /ah/.	[R18]
con fess	[<L con- (together) + fateri (acknowledge)]. We often double S after ...	[R17]
mum ble 4	Every syllable must have a vowel.	[R7]
re pent	E said /E/ at the end of a syllable.	[R4]
crit i cize 2	Few words use Z within the word. British spelling: criticise.	[R5,2,7]
rea son		

PUNCTUATION--DIRECT QUOTES. Write original sentences using the spelling words and have each sentence contain a direct quote. Review the proper way to punctuate a direct quote. In addition to the new spelling words and this section's review words, include as many of the previously taught words in Section N as possible. Example: The woman demanded, "Try to write smaller-sized numbers."

VOCABULARY ENRICHMENT--VIVID WORDS. Fold a sheet of paper in half and title one column PERSONS (which may include groups of people, like class or government) and the other SAY. Add spelling words to the appropriate columns. Write the saying words in the past tense: *demanded, excused...*

CHARADES. This activity will use spelling words to demonstrate a dynamic writing principle. Explain that the expression, "The person did say," does not give a strong word picture. What kind of person? What manner of talking? More graphic words might include: "The doctor demanded" or "the guide mumbled." A fun way to help demonstrate the importance of using more vivid words in writing is with the game of charades. Prepare ahead 3x5 cards with expressions like: *Teacher excused, boy questioned, village criticized, guide demanded, mother prayed, boy mumbled, woman repented, angel called, doctor offered.* Have a student read the expression and without talking either act it out or illustrate it artistically on the board. When someone guesses a word correctly, he should come write it on the board.

Preliminaries. <u>Reference</u>: Introduce or review **Plural** and **Y's Exchanging Pages** (SWR Steps 27, 34). <u>Phonograms</u>: *ar, ch, ck, ea, ear, ee, er, kn, oi, oy, sh, th, ti, ur.* <u>Rules</u>: 3, 4, 5, 6, 7, 10, 11, 19, 22, 24, 25.

Words for Section N-3

821	clap	The ocean waves pound the beach like a boy will *clap* his hands.
822	crys tal	The difference between a *crystal* of sugar and a *crystal* of snow can be seen in the form.
823	sky	The rainbow in the *sky* followed the Ark when the earth was dry. --Christian Mother Goose
824	def i ni tion	The *definition* tells what a word is understood to express.
825	need	Work keeps us from three evils: boredom, vice, and *need.* --Voltaire
826	mat ter	Income is a small *matter* to me--especially after taxes.
827	pearl	The merchant found one *pearl* of great price and sold all that he had to buy it.
828	spir it	A man may be poor in purse, yet proud in *spirit.* --McGuffey's Third Reader
829	knee	If I fall down and scrape my *knee,* I ask Daddy to pray for me. --Christian Mother Goose
830	dol lar	Do you trash a good *dollar* because of a fake one? Don't reject Jesus because of a fake Christian!
831	chick en	Don't count the *chicken* before it hatches.
832	mis take	It would be a grave *mistake* to think that freedom requires nothing of us. --Margaret Thatcher
833	cat e go ry	Linnaeus knew God made each animal after its own kind, so he grouped them by *category.*
834	bur i al	Devout men carried Stephen to his *burial,* and made great lamentation over him. --Acts 8:2
835	bul le tin	A misprint in the church *bulletin* read, "I heard the bills on Christmas Day."
836	en er gy	All *energy* comes from God and was created by Him.
837	cus tom	Paul discouraged the Corinthian *custom* of men covering their heads for worship.
838	leath er	One misty morning with cloudy weather, I met an old man clothed all in *leather.*
839	emp ty	"God stretched out the north over the *empty* space and hung the earth upon nothing." --Job 26:7
840	oys ter	He was a bold man who first ate an *oyster.* --Jonathan Swift

Spelling Enrichments

GRAMMAR--ADJECTIVES. Make a list of possible adjective/noun combinations using review words from A-I (see top of page 105) modifying new spelling words. Some possible examples are given below:

long clap	soft clap	ice crystal	west sky
winter sky	a definition	each definition	long definition
that definition	all needs	other need	just matter
long pearls	oyster pearl	thick pearls	brave spirit
low spirit	odd knee	other knee	the dollar
other dollar	spring chicken	wild chicken	low mistake
each mistake	that mistake	wild category	odd category
late burial	spring bulletin	late bulletin	thick bulletin
low energy	other custom	wild custom	thick leather
just empty	an oyster	that oyster	thick oyster

Write at least five sentences using at least one of the pairs above and including other spelling words as well if possible. Example: *I need <u>a definition</u> for <u>brave spirits</u>.*

Dictate Review Words from A-I. These words can all be used as adjectives: *a, an, the, all, brave, each, ice, just, late, long, low, odd, other, soft, spring, that, thick, west, wild, winter.*

clap		
crys tal		
sk<u>y</u>	Y stands in for I; English words do not end with I.	[R5,6]
def i ni <u>ti</u>on	I usually says /i/ at the end of a syllable. TI may spell /sh/ at the beginning ...	[R5,11]
n<u>ee</u>d		
mat t<u>er</u>		[R29]
p<u>ea</u>rl 1	Add to **ER Page**.	
spir it	A one over the I indicates that we think the first sound of the vowel rather than /er/.	
kn<u>ee</u>	In the original Anglo-Saxon the K was voiced.	
dol l<u>ar</u>	<u>Think both L's for spelling but not for normal speech. Think /ar/ for spelling.</u>	[R29]
<u>chick</u> en	CK is used only after a single vowel that says /a-e-i-o-u/.	[R25]
mis tak͡<u>e</u>	A said /A/ because of the E.	[R7]
cat <u>e</u> g<u>o</u> ry		[R4,5,6]
b<u>ur</u> i al 3	[<OE beorg (to burrow), byrgen (grave)]. Root = bury. Add to **Y's Exchange Pg**.	[R5]
bul l<u>e</u> tin	Sound both L's for spelling but not normal speech. E said /E/ at the end...	[R29,4]
en <u>er</u> gy	G may say /j/ before Y. Y usually says /i/ at the end... English words...	[R3,5,6]
cus tom 2 2 l<u>ea</u>th er	Think to spell the unaccented syllable as /o/.	
emp ty	English words do not end with I. Y usually says /i/ at the end of a syllable.	[R5,6]
<u>oy</u>s t<u>er</u>	OY can be used within a word **or** at the end. OI is never used at the end.	

SUFFIXES. Review (or teach if you haven't done so already this year) the **Y's ExchangePage**. In column one dictate the following spelling words taught so far in Section N: *cry, study, try*. Repeat the rule together. *The single vowel Y changes to I when adding any ending unless the ending starts with I* [R24]. In the second column dictate the words *cried, studied, tried*. As you are sounding out the words repeat the phrase, "change the Y to I and add E-D." In the third column add the ending *-ing*. "Why don't we change the Y to I when we add -ing? " (English words do not have two I's together.)

PLURALS. "Divide paper in two columns. In the first column neatly write the spelling words. In the second write the plural form of the spelling words. Watch for Y's Exchanging Words (cries, studies, tries)."

clap --	claps	*spirit* --	spirits	*bulletin* --	bulletins
crystal --	crystals	*knee* --	knees	*energy* --	energies
sky --	skies	*dollar* --	dollars	*custom* --	customs
definition --	definitions	*chicken* --	chickens	*leather* --	leathers
need --	needs	*mistake* --	mistakes	*empty* --	empties
matter --	matters	*category* --	categories	*oyster* --	oysters
pearl --	pearls	*burial* --	burials		

Preliminaries. <u>Rules</u>: 1, 2, 4, 5, 6, 7, 10, 12, 14, 16, 17, 19, 24. <u>Reference</u>: **ER, 1-1-1, Plus Endings Pages.** (SWR Steps 26, 32, 35). <u>Phonograms</u>: Quiz all 70. *One makes a different sound in French-based words. Can you guess which one?* [QU -- SWR Step 38].

Words for Section N-4

841	curb	*Curb* and curve both come from the Latin word meaning bent.
842	car ry	Great rivers *carry* water into the sea, but so do little brooks.
843	sub ject	A Christian is free, *subject* to none [but] servant of all, and *subject* to everyone. --M. Luther
844	mis spell	Can you correct each word you *misspell?*
845	drug	A miracle *drug* is any *drug* that will do what the label says it will do. --Eric Hodgins
846	e rase	*Erase* the first and last letters in "sin" to find the root of sin.
847	fan cy	The *fancy* peacock utters a disgusting cry and cannot sing a pleasant song like other birds.
848	hem	Use a matching color of thread when you *hem* the pants for him.
849	dirt	Throw enough *dirt* and some will stick.
850	hur ry	*Hurry!* I never *hurry.* I have no time to *hurry.* --I. Stravinsky
851	con quer	I believe in the end truth will *conquer.* --John Wycliffe
852	pare	We will *PARE* the fruit to pre*PARE* it for the pie.
853	plan	Doing the will of God leaves me no time for disputing His *plan.* --George MacDonald
854	cen ter	Locate the *center* verse in Isaiah 53 and read the central theme of the Bible.
855	prove	*Prove* all things; hold fast that which is good. --1 Timothy 1:8
856	cop y	All art in some way is a *copy* of God's creation.
857	suf fer	We have joy when we *suffer* for Christ, but not when we *suffer* for sin.
858	sign	God gave the stars "for *signs* and for seasons" --Genesis 1:14
859	mar ket	To *market,* to *market,* to buy a fat pig; home again, home again, jiggety-jig.
860	voice	Whales all day, God's *voice* obey. --New England Primer

Spelling Enrichments

DERIVATIVES. Practice using the **1-1-1** rule using the review words from A-I on the facing page. Add the vowel suffix **-ing** to each word. To identify 1-1-1 words ask, "Is it one syllable? Can you see and hear one vowel then one consonant at the end?"

> **bag** *(bagging);* **belong** *(belonging -- 2 syllables);* **box** *(boxing -- X sounds like 2 consonants);* **bow** *(bowing -- OW sounds like 1 vowel);* **bug** *(bugging);* **cover** *(covering -- 2 syllables);* **gas** *(gassing);* **get** *(getting);* **hand** *(handing-- 2 consonants);* **hit** *(hitting);* **send** *(sending--ends with 2 consonants);* **show** *(see bow);* **sin** *(sinning);* **star** *(starring);* **tan** *(tanning);* **wash** *(washing-- ends with 2 consonants).*

Adding Endings Assignment: Have students add **ing** and **ed** to all the new spelling words plus the review words. With each spelling word the student needs to determine first if the word is an E's Dropping, Y's Exchanging, or a 1-1-1 word. If not, simply add the ending. See SWR Step 35.

+	E's	1-1-1	Y's
curb ing			
curbed			
car-ry ing			car-**ried**

© 2003, Wanda Sanseri

Dictate Review Words from A-I: *bag, belong, box, bow, bug, cover, gas, get, hand, hit, send, show, sin, star, tan, wash.* Follow the procedure described in M-1. (Option: Add *show, wash* to **SH/TI Page**.)

curb	Add to **ER Page**. British spelling: kerb.	
car ry	Y is a stand-in for I. We think to spell /i/--the unaccented sound of I.	[R29,5,6]
sub ject	[<L sub- (under) + jacere (throw)]. <u>Homograph</u>: *sub' ject* (n.), *sub-ject'* (v.).	
mis spell	[< mis- (bad, wrong) + (spell)]. We often double F, L, S after a single vowel...	[R17]
drug		
e rase	E said /E/ at the end of a syllable. A said /A/ because of the E.	[R4,7]
fan cy	C says /s/ because of the Y. Y stands in for I at the end of English words.	[R2,5,6]
hem		
dirt	Add to **ER Page**.	
hur ry	Y stands in for I at the end of English words. Add to **ER Page**.	[R29,5,6]
con quer	QU = /k/ as an advanced phonogram. See SWR p. 89.	[R1]
pare	[<L parare (prepare)]. A said /A/ because of the E.	[R7]
plan		
cen ter	British: cen tre₄. C says /s/ because of the E.	[R2]
prove	[<L probus (worthy)]. English words do not end with V.	[R7]
cop y		[R5,6]
suf fer	Double consonants are both sounded for spelling but not for normal speech.	[R29]
sign	I may say /I/ before 2 consonants.	[R19]
mar ket	Exaggerate the unaccented vowel as /e/ for spelling. <u>Abbreviation</u>: mkt.	[R12]
voice	C says /s/ because of the E.	[R7]

Spelling Enrichments

ALLITERATION. Write original spelling sentences using Section N-3, Section N-4 and review words. In each sentence group two or three spelling words that begin with the same sound. *Chicken* and *crystal* **do not** start with the same sound. *Knee* and *need* **do** start with the same sound. Small words (prepositions, pronouns, conjunctions, or articles) can separate the alliterated words.

Examples: The bag belonging to Ben was in the box by the bulletin at the burial.

                         The crystals cover that category in my rock class.

INTERROGATIVE SENTENCES. Write original questions using new spelling words and the A-I review words above. Punctuate correctly with a question mark at the end. Underline the spelling words.

Examples: In the <u>market</u> could you hear the <u>voice</u> that <u>belongs</u> to me?
                         Did you <u>carry</u> the <u>dirt</u> in the <u>box</u> to the house?
                         Did you <u>hurry</u> to make the <u>cover</u> <u>sign</u>?

LATIN ROOTS. See SWR pages 131-132. Illustrate how knowing that *jacere* means "throw" can help de-termine the meaning of many other Latin-based words. Start watching for other Greek and Latin roots.

Preliminaries. Phonograms: Review at least *ai, ay, ar, au, ea, ee, ei, eigh, er, ey, qu, th*.
Spelling Rules: 1, 2, 4, 5, 6, 7, 12, 18, 20, 27. Reference Page: **Number Page**. See SWR Step 15.

Words for Section N-5

861	been	Of all sad words of tongue or pen, the saddest are, 'It might have *been*.' --John Greenleaf Whittier
862	cap ture	The people an enemy can *capture* are called captives who are held in captivity.
863	broke	Jesus blessed and *broke* the little boy's loaves and fishes.
864	deed	It's a good *deed* to forget a poor joke. --Brenden Bracken
865	ex haust	We can never *exhaust* the wisdom of God.
866	in spect	It is the duty of parents to *inspect* the conduct or manners of their children. --Noah Webster, 1828
867	prac tice	First we *practice* sin, then defend it, then boast of it. --Thomas Manton
868	ex pect	I don't *expect* anyone just to sit there and agree with me, that's not their job. --M. Thatcher.
869	vote	Sink or swim, live or die, survive or perish, I give my hand and heart to this *vote*. --G. Peele, 1584
870	e quip	The soldiers needed to *equip* the fort with guns, bullets, and food.
871	feel	Hear reason, or she'll make you *feel* her. *--Poor Richard's Almanack*
872	di a ry	*Diary* comes from the Latin word meaning day and means a daily personal journal.
873	his to ry	Since Jesus Christ is the master over all time, *history* is known as His story.
874	doz en	Twelve eggs make one *dozen*.
875	sor ry	I never saw a wild thing *sorry* for itself. --David Lawrence
876	pear	A *pear* tree grows from the seed of a *pear*. --N. Webster's Bluebacked Speller
877	crit i cism	Most people don't mind *criticism* as long as it's about someone else. --Wiener
878	else	The aim of all music should be nothing *else* but the glory of God. --Bach
879	fifth	The cart has no place where a *fifth* wheel could be used. --Von Fritzlar
880	yes ter day	Remember *yesterday* for the sake of tomorrow.

Spelling Enrichments

DIARY. Dictate the following diary entry in place of a regular spelling test or have student create his own original diary entry using all the new and as many review words as possible. Underline the spelling words. As a bonus underline all verbs twice.

Dear <u>Diary</u>,

I <u>am</u> <u>sorry</u> I <u>broke</u> my promise. I <u>should have</u> written sooner but I <u>have been exhausted</u>. I <u>must</u> <u>have been</u> sad after I <u>had</u> a <u>fifth</u> <u>criticism</u> <u>yesterday</u> on my <u>history</u> paper. It <u>feels</u> more like a <u>dozen</u> complaints. I wonder what you <u>would</u> say if you <u>could</u> <u>inspect</u> my report. I <u>expect</u> you <u>might</u> <u>do</u> a good <u>deed</u> and <u>vote</u> for me. I <u>am</u> eating a <u>pear</u> as I write. I <u>would</u> hate to <u>be</u> <u>captured</u> by an enemy that <u>is</u> not <u>equipped</u> to feed me well. I <u>shall</u> <u>practice</u> writing to you again tomorrow or <u>else.</u>

P.S. I read a good <u>history</u> quote today from Thomas Jefferson. He said, "If we <u>expect</u> as a nation to <u>be</u> ignorant and free, we <u>expect</u> what never <u>was</u> and never <u>can</u> <u>be</u>."

DERIVATIVES. See SWR Step 35, after N-5 instructions on SWR page 172.

Dictate Review Words from A-I. On a loose-leaf sheet of paper have the students write the title HELPING VERBS. Dictate the review words in a column going down the page. These can all be helping verbs: *am, is, are, was, were, be, have, has, had, do, did, may, might, must, should, shall, can, could, will, would.*

be͜en	Think to spell with British pronunciation as /b-E-n/. Say whatever you say.	
cap tu͡re	U said /U/ because of the E.	[R7]
bro͡ke	O said /O/ because of the E. Irregular past tense of "break."	[R7]
de͜ed		
ex haust	[<L ex- (out) + haurire (draw)].	
in spect	[<L in- (upon) + specere (to view)].	
prac tic͜e 3	C said /s/because of the E.	[R7]
ex pect		
vo͡te	O said /O/ because of the E.	[R7]
e quip	E said /E/ at the end of a syllable. Q is always followed by U.	[R4,1]
fe͜el		
di a ry	Y stands in for I; English words do not end with I.	[R5,4,6]
his to ry	O said /O/ at the end....Y stands in for I; English words do not end with I.	[R4,5,6]
doz en	Z rarely used within common words. Add to **Number Page**. Abbreviation: doz.	[R12]
sor ry	Y stands in for I at the end of English words. Think to spell /s-o-r r-y/.	[R29,5,6]
pear		
crit i cism	[<Gk krinein (to judge)]. Root = critic.	[R5,2]
els͜e 5	Odd job E.	[R7]
fifth	Root = five. Add to **Number Page**. Abbreviation: 5th.	[R12]
yes ter day	A-Y usually spells /A/ at the end of a base word. If a word ends with A it says /ah/.	[R18]

GRAMMAR--HELPING VERBS. Some verbs can be added to the main verb to "help" express the meaning more exactly. For example: the man may vote, might vote, can vote, could vote, did vote, will vote, should vote. One of the new spelling words can also be a helping verb. Can you find it? (been)

Assignment. Find a main verb that can go with each helping word. The main verbs can come from either the current spelling words or from any of the words taught so far in Section N.   Examples:

am cross	have studied	must have broken	are exhausted	did hear
has cried	can suffer	is expected	had acted	do feel
should write	was inspected	shall number	will capture	could use
were practiced	might equip	would tax	may expect	be ruled

CONJUGATION. Select any verb and show the singular and plural present and past tense passive voice.

I am captured	we are captured	I was captured	we were captured
you are captured	you are captured	you were captured	you were captured
he (she, it) is captured	they are captured	he was sorry	they were captured

NUMBERS. If you have not done so already this year, add to the Number Page all the numbers taught so far. See SWR Step 15. *Eight, hundred, million, second, fourth,* and *ninth* will come up later.

Preliminaries. Phonograms especially: *ai, ay, ch, ck, dge, ea, ee, ew, igh, ng, oi, oy, oo, ou, ough, sh, tch, th.* Spelling Rules: 4, 7, 10, 19, 21, 25. Reference: **Dismiss L, Homophone** and **SH/TI Pages.**

Words for Section N-6

881	cheap	Election year is that period when politicians get free speech mixed up with *cheap* talk. --J. Kidd
882	cheer ful	God loves the *cheerful* giver. --2 Corinthians 9:7
883	hon est	Be *honest* and true in all you do and in all you say at work or play.
884	fresh	Many *fresh* waters meet in one salt sea. --Shakespeare
885	rough	Becoming a father is easy enough, but being one can be *rough.* --Busch
886	wise	He who walks with *wise* men will be *wise.* --Prov. 13:20
887	wide	A *wide* screen just made a bad film twice as bad.
888	plain	From shade of night to *plain* of light, O praise His name, Christ lifted me! --Charles Gabriel
889	ac tu al	Once begun, the *actual* task is easy; half the work is done. --Horace
890	sure	The less man knows the more *sure* he is that he knows everything. --Joyce Cary
891	de pend ent	The history of nations is *dependent* on their responses to God and His people. --Ruth Haycock
892	de light	I thank Thee, my Creator and Lord, that Thou hast given me this *delight* in the works of Thy hands. --Kepler
893	fu ture	The Bible is the only book by which you may know certainly the *future.*
894	choice	There is no small *choice* in rotten apples. --Shakespeare
895	least	He is the richest who is content with the *least.*
896	young	*Young* Timothy learned sin to flee. --New England Primer
897	pair	A *pair* is two of a kind and is spelled with the two-letter A.
898	faith	The author expressed deep *faith* in liberty.
899	al ways	Mercies are *always* greater for a Christian than his miseries.
900	steal	A man who will *steal* for me will *steal* from me. --Theodore Roosevelt

Spelling Enrichments

GRAMMAR. -LY ADVERBS. Half of the new spelling words can be made into adverbs which answer how by adding -ly. Write the spelling words in the adverbial form. Example: *cheap* -- cheaply

cheerful -- cheerfully	*rough -- roughly*	*plain* -- plainly	*dependent* -- dependently
honest -- honestly	*wise* -- wisely	*actual* -- actually	*delightful* -- delightfully
fresh -- freshly	*wide* -- widely	*sure* -- surely	*faithful* -- faithfully

COMPOSITION. Write sentences using all the spelling words. Include an LY adverb in each.

ANTONYMS. The teacher will call out the opposite for each new spelling word and the student will WRITE the spelling word that is the opposite. Be sure to check the spelling for accuracy.

fancy _____ *(plain)*	expensive _____ *(cheap)*	grief _____ *(delight)*
stale _____ *(fresh)*	dishonest _____ *(honest)*	smooth _____ *(rough)*
foolish ____ *(wise)*	uncertain _____ *(sure)*	independent ____ *(dependent)*
greatest ___ *(least)*	old _____ *(young)*	never _____ *(always)*
narrow ____ *(wide)*	grumpy _____ *(cheerful)*	past _____ *(future)*

Have the students arrange the A-I review words into related sets of opposites.

cold, hot;   come, go;   good, bad;   big, little;   give, take;   yes, no;   gave, got;   sick, well

Dictate Review Words from A-I. These review words can be used to form opposites: *bad*, *big*, *cold*, *come*, *gave*, *give*, *go*, *good*, *got*, *hot*, *little*, *no*, *sick*, *take*, *well*, *yes*.

cheap		
cheer ful	Add to **Dismiss L Page**. *Full* has one L when added to another syllable.	[R21]
hon est	Silent H. Think to spell /hon-est/; say /on-est/. See SWR p. 86.	
fresh	SH spells /sh/ at the end of a syllable. Add to **SH/TI Page**.	[R10]
rough		
wise	I said /I/ because of the E.	[R7]
wide	I said /I/ because of the E.	[R7]
plain	Homophone: plane	
ac tu al	U said /U/ at the end of a syllable.	[R4]
sure	Blended together fast /s/ + /U/ = /sh/ + /U/. U said /U/ because of the E.	[R7]
de pend ent	root = depend. E said /E/ at the end of a syllable.	[R4]
de light	E said /E/ at the end of a syllable. **Dismiss L** word: delightful	[R4,21]
fu ture	U said /U/ at the end of a syllable. U said /U/ because of the E.	[R4,7]
choice	C says /s/ because of the E.	[R7]
least		
young		
pair	Homophone: pear, pare, pair. See SWR Step 30.	
faith	**Dismiss L** word: faithful	[R21]
al ways	Add to **Dismiss L Page**. *All* is written with one L when added to another syllable.	[R21]
steal		

Spelling Enrichments

DERIVATIVES. Make derivatives from the words. Watch for E's Dropping Words. Possibilities include:

cheap --	cheapen, cheaper, cheapest		*future* --	futurist
cheerful --	cheerfulness		*choice* --	choicer, choicest
honest --	dishonest, honesty		*least* --	leastwise
fresh --	freshness, -er, -est, refresh(ed), refreshment		*young* --	younger, youngest, youngster
rough --	roughage, roughen, roughness, rougher, roughest			
wise --	un-, -crack, edge-, -ly, other-, over-, wiser, wisest		*pair* --	pairing, paired, unpaired
wide --	wideness, widespread, widening, wider, widest		*faith* --	faithless, faithful
plain --	plainness, plains, plainer, plainest		*steal* --	stealing
actual --	actuality			
sure --	ensure, insure, surer, surest, surely			
dependent --	independent, independently, dependently			
delight --	delightful, delighting, delighted			

DICTATION. "The *young* man had a *rough choice* to make for his *future*." Use as many spelling or review words as possible and explain what that rough choice might be.

Preliminaries. Phonograms: Review at least *ai, ar, au, ch, ck, dge, ea, er, oo, or, ou, ow, th, wor*.
Rule Cards: 2, 5, 6, 7, 8, 10, 12, 17, 18, 19, 20, 21, 23, 25, 28. Reference: **ED Page** (SWR Step 22.)

Words for Section N-7

901	mark	If you would hit the *mark*, you must aim a little above it. --Henry W. Longfellow
902	ar row	Like the *arrow* that has left the bow, we can never take back a spoken word.
903	blood	The *blood* of the martyrs is the seed of the Church. --Tertullian
904	front	Cannon to right, cannon to left, cannon in *front* volleyed and thundered. --Tennyson
905	won der	The earth shall be filled with His *wonder* and glory, as waters that cover the sea.
906	dair y	A *dairy* farm has cattle for producing milk products.
907	note	You don't get harmony when everybody sings the same *note*. --Doug Floyd
908	death	Let them fear *death* who do not fear sin. --Thomas Watson
909	cause	God is the *cause* of causes. --Christopher Nesse
910	bridge	Don't cross the *bridge* before you get to it.
911	court	You may fool a human *court* but in the Final Judgment there will be no appeal.
912	fair	A faint heart never won a *fair* lady.
913	smoke	There is no *smoke* without fire.
914	full	The trees of the Lord are *full* of sap. --Psalm 104:16
915	tire	We *tire* the night in thought, the day in toil. --Quarles
916	mean	Just because a person professes Christ does not *mean* he possesses Christ.
917	check	The teacher will *check* your paper for errors.
918	ex cept	I can resist everything *except* temptation. --Oscar Wilde
919	till	Idle men delay *till* tomorrow things that should be done today. --N. Webster
920	thus	Shall the thing formed say to him that formed it, 'Why hast thou made me *thus?*' --Romans 9:20

Spelling Enrichments.

SYNONYMS. Dictate in a column the following bolded words taught earlier in Section N or review words from A-K. Next ask the students to match each current spelling word to one of these review words that has a similar meaning or a common association.

underline	mark	**question**	wonder	**letter**	note
reason	cause	**cross**	bridge	**exhaust**	tire
low down	mean	**curb**	check	**all but**	except
burial	death	**box**	till	**in this way**	thus
bow	arrow	**red**	blood	**ahead**	front
love	court	**show**	fair	**gas**	smoke
equip totally	full	**milk**	dairy		

UNSCRAMBLED SENTENCE. Write a 5-to 10-word sentence using spelling words. Examples: *Check the tire marks on the bridge. I wonder what caused the smoke? The cause of death was an arrow to the front*. Write the words in miscellaneous order on the board. Students try to unscramble each sentence.

VERBS. Make as many new words as possible past tense. See format to use in SWR Step 22. -ed -- *fronted, noted, courted, excepted*; -ed2 -- *wondered, caused, bridged, tired, tilled*; -ed3 -- *marked, smoked, checked*, X -- *meant*. Note: The verb form of *blood* is bleed and *death* is die. Past tense = irregular *bled, died*.

Dictate Review Words from A-I. Cut 3x5 cards in half and dictate a word to a card: *back, bed, book, foot, head, house, land, let, like, shot, some, time, trade, way, yard.*

---

m**a**rk		
1 **2** ar row		[R29]
bl**oo**d	In Scotland many still say /oo/. Same as "flood." See SWR p. 81.	
front		
won d**er**		
d**air** y	Y stands in for I; English words do not end with I.	[R5,6]
n**o**t**e**	O said /O/ because of the E.	[R7]
d**ea**th		
cau**s**e	Odd job E	[R7]
bri**dge**	DGE is used only after a single vowel that says /a-e-i-o-u/.	[R23]
c**o**urt	Add *courtship* to **SH/TI Page**. Abbreviation: ct.	[R10,12]
f**air**		
smok**e**	O said /O/ because of the E.	[R7]
f**u**ll	The affix "-ful" has one L (fulfill, helpful). *Fully* avoids 3 L's	[R17,21]
tir**e**	Think 1 syllable to spell. I said /I/ because of the E. British spelling: tyr**e**	[R7]
m**ea**n		
ch**e**ck	[British: che**que**]. CK is used after a single vowel that says /e/.	[R25]
ex cept	X is never directly before S. C say /s/ before E.	[R20,2]
till	Two meanings: till tomorrow, till ground. We often double L after a single...	[R17]
t**h**us		

Spelling Enrichments

COMPOUND WORDS. Combine the review words with as many of the current spelling words as possible to make compound words. Most new words can be made into one or more compound words.

mark -- bookmark, landmark, trademark	*bridge* -- bridgehead
arrow -- arrowhead	*court* -- courthouse, courtyard, backcourt
blood -- bloodshot	*fair* -- fairway
front -- frontlet	*smoke* -- smokehouse
dairy -- dairyland	*full* -- fullback
note -- footnote, notebook	*tire* -- tiresome
death -- deathbed, deathlike	*mean* -- meantime
cause -- causeway	*check* -- checkbook

CLARITY. Dictate newspaper headlines with misplaced modifiers. Correct each to clarify the meaning.

Stolen Painting Found *by Bridge*   (Did the bridge find the painting?)
Court to Try *Shooting Defendant*   (Will the court shoot the defendant?)
Miners Refused to Work *after Death*   (Were dead miners resisting work?)

Watch for words with muliple meanings. An unclear use can create confusion. (*Check* the *check* for me.) An artistic use can produce a chuckle. (A bicycle can't hold itself up since it is *two-tired.*)

Preliminaries. Phonograms: Quiz all 70. Rules: 1, 2, 3, 5, 7, 8, 10, 11, 12, 16, 25. Reference: **SH/TI Page** (SWR Step 18.) Use derivatives of recent words: *inspection, exception, expression, confession.*

Words for Section N-8

921	poi son	The scheme of the wicked is deadly like the *poison* of a serpent.
922	chain	Pride compasseth them about like a *chain*. --Psalm 73:6
923	i ron	As *iron* sharpens *iron,* so a man sharpens the countenance of his friend. --Proverb 27:17
924	eve ning	At *evening* when the lamp is lit, around the fire my parents sit. --Robert L. Stevenson
925	light ning	A zipper of *lightning* opened a rain-filled sky. --Evelyn Lesch
926	bot tle	The rowboats bobbed like *bottle* corks on the lake.
927	strange	Humility, a *strange* flower, grows best in winter under storms of affliction. --Rutherford
928	sug ar	With devotion's visage and pious action we do *sugar* over the devil himself. --Shakespeare
929	in tent	A greater power than we can contradict hath thwarted our *intent. --Romeo & Juliet*
930	spa cious	Stars seem like lamps set in the *spacious* Hall of the Creator to show forth its grandeur. --McGuffey
931	cap i tal	Washington, D.C. is the *capital* of the United States of America.
932	range	The Creator moved over the *range* of the cosmos energizing "empty space."
933	fare	*Fare* thee well and if forever, still forever, *fare* thee well. --Byron
934	quart	One *quart* of milk will fill two pint cups. --Noah Webster
935	kit ten	See the *kitten,* how she starts, crouches, stretches, paws and darts. --Wordsworth
936	built	Love *built* on beauty, soon as beauty, dies. --John Donne
937	mix ture	The good things of life are not to be had singly, but come to us with a *mixture.* --Charles Lamb
938	nor	Give me neither poverty *nor* riches. --Proverbs 30:8
939	lin en	Joseph wrapped the body of Jesus in a clean *linen* cloth.
940	rope	We make *rope* of hemp and flax. --Webster's *Bluebacked Speller*

Spelling Enrichments

CONJUNCTIONS. Conjunctions connect sentence parts together. Common conjunctions are: *and, but, or, yet, so, nor.* Use a conjunction in sentences along with current spelling and review words.

> The kitten drank a strange mixture of poison **and** sugar.
> Men built a nice house with the intent for it to be the best **but** lightning hit it.
> The sick baby wanted a free ring, my lace doll **or** my best toy.
> She lived in this spacious capital *yet* missed the evening range back at the ranch.
> The rich man filled a quart bottle with water *so* he would not pay the fare at dinner.
> I have neither an iron chain ***nor*** a linen rope.

METAPHORS. Word imagery adds a dimension to writing. Consider the following:

> *A zipper of lightning opened a rain-filled sky.* Is the author, Evelyn Lesch, saying that a big zipper

was in the sky? No. She is comparing the lightning that zagged across the sky to a zipper. Other metaphors using spelling words include:

> *The rowboats bobbed like bottle corks on the lake.*
> *Stars seem like lamps set in the spacious Hall of the Creator.*

Students watch for examples of word imagery or try to write their own examples using spelling words.

Dictate Review Words from A-L.

Dictate review words paired in adjective/noun combinations:
this ring, free toy, sick baby, last dance, best doll, old lace, nice dinner, rich men.

poi son²	[< L potio < potionis (potion)].	
chain	[<F chaine (chain)].	
i ron	Think to spell /I-ron/. Say /i-ern/. I may say /I/ at the end of a syllable.	[R5]
eve ning	Short form: eve. E said /E/ because of the final E.	[R7]
light ning		
bot tle₄	Sound /t/ twice for spelling. Every syllable must have a vowel.	[R29,7]
strange	Silent final E type one can work over 2 consonants. See SWR top of p. 106.	[R7]
su gar	Blended together /s/ + /U/ = /sh/ + /U/. Think to spell /sU-gar/. Say /shoog-er/.	[R4]
in tent		
spa cious	A said /A/ at the end of a syllable. Root word: space. Add to **SH/TI Page**.	[R4,11,16]
cap i tal	[<L caput (head)]. I usually says /i/ at the end of a syllable.	[R5]
range	A said /A/ because of the E. G says /j/ because of the E.	[R7]
fare	A said /A/ because of the E. Homophone: fair. See SWR Step 30.	[R7]
quart	[<L quartus (fourth)]. Q always needs a U. Abbreviation: qt.	[R1,12]
kit ten	If we used a C as in "cat," the word would sound like /siten/.	[R2,29]
bu ilt	One syllable word. May exaggerate to 2 for spelling. See SWR p. 88.	
mix ture	Root = mix. U said /U/ because of the E.	[R7]
nor	[<OE ne- (not) + A (either)].	
lin en	[<OE lin (flax); linen is made from flax].	
rope	O said /O/ because of the E.	[R7]

Spelling Enrichments

KINDS OF SENTENCES. There are four kinds of sentences. Dictate the following list with examples.

1. State a fact.   *We make rope of hemp and flax.*
2. Ask a question.   *How many pints make a quart?*
3. Give a command.   *Sarah, iron the linen.*
4. Show strong feeling.   *It's poison!*

ORIGINAL SENTENCES. Have students write original sentences including one or more current spelling words. Illustrate each of the four types of sentences.

PUNCTUATION. Here's a novel way to practice proper end punctuation. Choose different sounds to represent a period, a question mark, and an exclamation point. Have a student read a sentence and wait for the class to end with the proper form of punctuation by making the appropriate noise. After a sentence that states a fact or gives a command we need what punctuation? (a period). After a sentence that asks a question we need what? (a question mark). After a sentence that shows strong feeling we need? (an exclamation point).

anti-	auto-	bi-
counter-	dec-	dis-
extra-	il-	in-
im-	ir-	inter-
mid-	mis-	non-
out-	over-	post-
pre-	pro-	re-
sub-	super-	trans-
tri-	ultra-	un-

Spelling
Section O

Even though the spelling list in this book progresses to freshman level in college and the work is beneficial as a remedial tool for all ages, there is great benefit for the student who can complete the work in the elementary grades. We want to introduce children to these words as early as possible. We do not expect the comprehension of all the words to keep pace with the student's ability to pronounce or spell them. If we introduce students to these words at a young age, we will quicken and sharpen their ability to understand them later.

The first 940 words in this program (A through N) and their derivatives include more than 75% of all the words we read or write.

Preliminaries. Spelling Rules: Review especially 1, 2, 4, 5, 6, 7, 9, 12, 17.
Phonograms: Quiz at least *ai, ay, au, aw, ch, ea, ie, or, ou, ow, qu, th, wr.*
Reference Pages: Dictate **Consonant, Multi-letter Phonogram, and Silent Final E Pages** if beginning a new year. See SWR Steps 9,10,17. Other reference pages will come up in the following lessons.

Words for Section O-1 (See SWR Step 12 for clarification of the dictation process.)

941	au thor	A bad novel tells us the truth about its *author*. --G.K. Chesterton
942	aunt	My *aunt* works hard at home like a wise ant laying up food for the winter.
943	un cle	My *Uncle* Robert was my mother's brother and his wife was my father's sister.
944	cap tain	The *captain* is the head of a group.
945	chief	The *chief* trouble with the church is that you and I are in it. --C. Heimsath
946	sail or	God made the stars constant enough to guide the *sailor* at sea.
947	no bod y	He who praises everybody praises *nobody*. --Samuel Johnson
948	po lice	*Police* are those who keep order in a city.
949	thief	A *thief* doth fear each bush an officer. --Shakespeare, *Henry VI*
950	friend	A *friend* loves at all times. --Proverbs 17:17
951	in di cate	A heavy swell of the sea in calm weather may *indicate* a storm at a distance.
952	re peat	He that knows little will often *repeat* it.
953	ex plain	"I can't *explain* myself," said Alice, "because I'm not myself." --Lewis Carroll
954	sen tence	A *sentence* should contain no unnecessary words or a drawing unnecessary lines.
955	re prove	*Reprove* not a scorner, lest he hate thee. --Prov. 9:8
956	re quest	A friend is someone who doesn't mind if you need to *request* help.
957	ob ject	No *object* created by God or man is to become an *object* of worship.
958	ad dress	Can you teach me how to properly *address* a letter to grandmother?
959	re fuse	Never *refuse* the sweet rebuke of him that is thy friend. *--New England Primer*
960	mourn	Rachel does *mourn* for her firstborn. *--New England Primer*

Spelling Enrichments

ORIGINAL SENTENCES.

a. Match words from the first column with words from the second column to make simple subject/verb combinations. We can retain the verb's actual spelling if we add a helping verb such as *can, did, may, will*. Examples: *Police can reprove. Captain did repeat. Chief may sentence.*

b. Match up words from the first column with words from the second column changing the verbs to the present tense. With singular subjects add an -s (or -es) to the verbs. For example: *Aunt explains. Chief sentences. Author addresses.* (If the verb ending hisses we add -es.) The word police is plural and we do not add an -s. *Police request.*

c. Make ten sentences using a vivid word for **person** as the subject and a vivid word for **says** for the verb. Example: *My aunt explains how to cook chicken. My friend objects to my plan.*

READING. Read aloud a book about sailors (like *Carry on, Mr. Bowditch* by Jean Latham or *The Vikings* by Elizabeth Janeway) or encourage the student to read independently an easy-to-read biography of Christopher Columbus.

Regional Pronunciations. The way we spell a word is more consistent and enduring against time and location than the way we say it. Some words are pronounced very differently depending on the region and period of history. For example the word *aunt* has been pronounced: aunt, ant, or aint. In any case we will all exaggerate to "think to spell" /au-n-t/. Spelling helps unite our ability to communicate.

au thor	Think to spell /or/. See SWR p. 89.	
aunt	Think to spell with British pronunciation as /au-n-t/. American homophone: ant	
un cle₄	C says /k/ before a consonant. Every syllable must have a vowel.	[R2,7]
cap tain	[<L *caput* (head)]. See *capital*, p. 115. Abbreviation: capt.	[R12]
chief	IE or EI? Remember IE is CHIEF, the phonogram used most often.	[R9]
sail or	Root = sail	
no bod y	O said /O/ at the end.... Y stands in for I. English words do not end with I.	[R4,5,6]
po lice₃	[<G polis (city)] O said /O/because... French I = /E/. C says /s/ because of E.	[R4,2,7]
thief	Introduce **IE/EI Page** before Q-1 only if the student has trouble with IE/EI.	[R9]
friend	IE says /e/ rather than a sound we learned. Mark an eXception with an X.	[R9]
in di cate	I usually says /i/ at the end of a syllable. A says /A/ because of the E.	[R5,7]
re peat	[<L re- (again) + petere (aim at)]. E said /E/ at the end of a syllable.	[R4]
ex plain		
sen tence₃	C says /s/ because of E.	[R2,7]
re prove₂	E said /E/ at the end of a syllable. English words do not end with V.	[R4,7]
re quest	[<L re- (again) + quaerere (ask)]. E said /E/ at the end of... Q always needs U.	[R4,1]
ob ject	[<L ob- (against) + jacere (throw)]. See SWR "jactum" p. 132.	
ad dress	Sound /d/ twice for spelling but not in normal speech. We often double S after...	[R29,17]
re fuse₂	Verb form *re-fuse* is spelled the same way as the noun *ref-use*.	[R4,7]
mourn	Homophone: morn (as in morning)	

Spelling Enrichments

LITERATURE AND COMPOSITION. Dictate the question, "What is a friend?" Discuss. Have student read *Thy Friend Obadiah* by Briton Turkle. Ask the student to find and write down Obadiah's definition of friendship. This Caldecott Honor book should be in your public library.

VIVID WORDS. Good writers use more vivid words, especially nouns and verbs. Have the student head a page in the notebook, "Vivid Words." Fold the paper in half to make two columns. At the top of the first column write the word: person. At the top of the second write: speaks. Have student write appropriate spelling words under each column.

POETRY. Read the poem, "Mr. Nobody," author unknown. What does Mr. Nobody do in your home?
> It's he who always tears our books, who leaves the door ajar;
> He pulls the buttons from our shirts, and scatters pins afar;
> That squeaking door will always squeak, of course now, don't you see,
> We leave the oiling to be done by Mr. Nobody.

Challenge students to add a verse to the poem using spelling words. Keep the same rhythm and use rhyme.

Preliminaries.

Review especially the following <u>Spelling Rule Cards</u>: 4, 5, 6, 7, 9, 10, 11, 12, 25.
<u>Phonograms</u>: *ai, ay, ck, ea, ee, eigh, ei, er, ew, ey, ie, oa, oe, or, ough, ow, sh, th, ti, ui, wh.*
<u>Reference Page</u>: If you haven't this year, start **Number, SH/TI Pages**. SWR Steps 15,18.

Words for Section O-2

961	waste	To be upset over what you don't have is to *waste* what you do have. --K. Keyes
962	ate	Nate *ate* dates late one night.
963	hole	When you've got yourself in a *hole*, stop digging.
964	throw	Don't *throw* the baby out with the bath water.
965	threw	As if someone *threw* a switch, the world turned crimson and gold.
966	slide	Fall leaves *slide* down banisters of air.
967	struck	The clock collected in the tower its strength and *struck*. --A.Housman, 1936
968	weath er	Friends in fine *weather* only are not worth much. --Aesop
969	sec ond	Resurrection means a *second* rising. --Thomas Aquinas
970	wea ry	Though my heart grows *weary*, I never will despair. --Ackley
971	waist	*Waist* comes from the Welsh word meaning "to squeeze."
972	eight	Fall seven times, stand up *eight*. --Japanese proverb
973	whole	God made the *whole* world in six days.
974	nee dle	Gravity causes the *needle* of a compass to point north.
975	through	Two men look *through* the same bars. One sees mud; the other sees stars.
976	board	We go aboard the ship on a *board*.
977	port	A *port* is a harbor where ships can enter.
978	sta tion	When vice prevails the post of honor is a private *station*. --Joseph Addison, 1719
979	rate	We often *rate* each other by appearance and not by character.
980	shine	A good deed will *shine* in a naughty world! --William Shakespeare

Spelling Enrichments

COMPOUND WORDS. Dictate review words: *air, band, hand, land, man, moon, out, over, paper, work* plus common words: *sale, teen*. Combine with the current spelling words to make compound words.

waste	wastepaper	*weather*	weatherman	*needle*	needlework
ate	overate	*second*	secondhand	*board*	overboard
hole	manhole	*weary*	overweary	*port*	airport
threw	overthrew	*waist*	waistband	*station*	outstation
throw	overthrow	*eight*	eighteen	*rate*	overrate
slide	landslide	*whole*	wholesale	*shine*	outshine
struck	moonstruck	*through*	throughout		moonshine

Bonus: Dictate additional review words: *above, back, base, basket, birth, bill, coat, key, line, way*. Compound word possibilities: aboveboard, backslide, baseboard, wastebasket, birthrate, billboard, waistcoat, keyhole, waistline, throughway.

NUMBER PAGE. If you have not done so already this year, fill in all the numbers taught to date on a page such as introduced in Section A. See SWR, Step 15. At this point all the number words have been taught except: *fourth, ninth, hundred, million.* Teach the days and months any time now.

Homophones Many words in English sound the same but are spelled differently and have different meanings. This lesson has some of these homophones but instead of teaching them one after the other (which sometimes creates confusion), we separate the initial presentation. The similar word is taught in the second column for later comparison. A Reference Page can be built using a form in the SWR Chart pack or in the reference section of a Black Log. See SWR Step 30.

waste	First kind of silent final E can work with 2 consonants *(paste, clothe)*.	[R7]
ate	A said /A/ because of the E. Food we EAT gets jumbled around (ATE).	[R7]
hole	O said /O/ because of the E.	[R7]
throw	Present tense.	
threw	Irregular past tense of throw (not throwed).	
slide	I said /I/ because of the E.	[R7]
struck	CK said /k/ after a single vowel that says /u/.	[R25]
weath er	Add to ER Page if er column is not full.	
sec ond	Add to **Number Page**. <u>A</u>bbreviation: sec.	[R12]
wea ry	Y usually says /i/ at the end of a syllable. Y stands in for I.	[R5,6]
waist	Welsh word origin meaning "to squeeze." A girdle was tied in the waist.	
eight	Add to **Number Page**.	
whole	wh = /h/. O said /O/ because of the E.	[R7]
nee dle	Every syllable must have a vowel.	[R7]
through	Add to preposition list *through, throughout*. See SWR p. 104.	
board	[<OE bord (plank)]. Add *aboard* to the preposition list.	
port		
sta tion	A said /A/ at the end of a syllable. TI can spell /sh/... **SH/TI Page**.	[R4,11]
rate	[<L rata (fixed)]. A said /A/ because of the E.	[R7]
shine	SH can spell /sh/ at the beginning... I said /I/ because of the E. **SH/TI Page**.	[R10,7]

Spelling Enrichments

DICTATION or ADVANCED ORIGINAL SENTENCES. Use homophone sets to make sentences. Try to include as many of the other current spelling words as possible.

Example:
waste / waist   Don't *waste* time worrying about your *waist*.
ate / eight   *Eight* people *ate* dinner at my house.
whole / hole   The *whole* needle had one *hole*.
threw / through He *threw* eight balls *through* my uncle's window.
bored / board   He *bored* a hole in the *board*.

ART. Illustrate and label the homonyms.

o o o o
o o o o
eight

ate

waste

waist

SCIENCE. Link as many spelling words as possible to the weather. *It is <u>weary</u> <u>weather</u>. Will the sun <u>shine</u> the <u>second</u> day in <u>port</u>? I am <u>weary</u> after snow <u>boarding</u>. Did the car <u>slide</u> on ice before it <u>struck</u> the <u>station</u>?*

Preliminaries

Review especially the following <u>Spelling Rule Cards</u>: 1, 4, 5, 6, 7, 8, 12, 26.

<u>Phonograms</u>: *ai, ar, ear, ee, er, ew, gn, ie, igh, ir, kn, or, ou, ough, ph, qu, tch, th, ur, wor.*

<u>Reference Page</u>: If you haven't this year already, introduce **ER Page**. See SWR Step 26.

Words for Section O-3

981	north	*North* is the direction to the right of one facing the setting sun.
982	south	*South* is the direction to the left of one facing the setting sun.
983	fourth	Character consists of what you do on the third and *fourth* tries. --James Michener
984	four teen	God gave Heman *fourteen* sons and three daughters. --1 Chron. 25:5
985	for ty	Five words cost Zachariah *forty* weeks' silence. --See Luke 1
986	di rects	If Washington *directs* us when to sow and reap, we will soon want bread. --T. Jefferson
987	sur face	An egg has a smooth *surface*.
988	quite	There are none *quite* so blind as those who will not see.
989	con firm	We should *confirm* all truth by the Word of God.
990	none	Prayer is the burden of a sigh...when *none* but God is near. --J. Montgomery
991	far ther	If I could find a higher tree *farther* and *farther* I should see. --Robert L. Stevenson
992	cel lar	A root *cellar* is a cold place in the ground for keeping vegetables.
993	quar ter	One fourth of something is the same as one *quarter*.
994	un til	No one knows how bad he is *until* he has tried to be good. --C.S. Lewis
995	knew	Bill *knew* the correct answer.
996	pub lic	The rule of law helps protect *public* liberty.
997	na vy	My favorite skirt is *navy* blue.
998	e nough	A government big *enough* to give you all you want can take everything you have.
999	wor ry	Why *worry* when you can pray?
1000	de part	Fear the Lord and *depart* from evil.

Spelling Enrichments

COMPASS ACTIVITY. Have students write the heading, *Compass*, on the top of a sheet of notebook paper. Dictate: *A compass with a magnetic needle pointing north can direct us where to go.* Have student trace a circle and divide it evenly in quarters. Label each of the four points: North, East, South, and West. (East and west are review spelling words.)

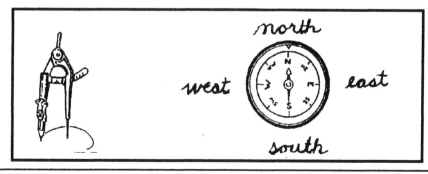

Watch for a Change in the Base Word when Making a Derivative. Normally we retain the spelling of the base word when we add an ending.   Watch for an unusual case in this spelling list *(four -- forty)*. Why do we drop the U? *Forty* was spelled with the U until the middle of the eighteenth century when the U suddenly disappeared. Some suggest that the vanishing U reflected a slight change in pronunciation. Maintaining the U in *four* helps distinguish it clearly from the preposition *for.*

north	Abbreviation: N	[R12]
south	Abbreviation: S	[R12]
fourth	Abbreviation: 4th Add to **Number Page**.	[R12]
four teen	four + ten = fourteen.	
for ty	Y stands in for I. Y usually says /i/ at the end of a syllable.	[R5,6]
di rects	I usually says /i/ at the end of a syllable. Some say /I/. Either is correct.	[R5]
sur face	Two reasons for E: A says /A/ and C says /s/. Add to **ER Page**.	[R2,7]
quite	Q always needs a U. I said /I/ because of the E.	[R1,7]
con firm	Add to **ER Page**.	
none	[<OE ne- (no) + an (one)]. No one = none. Think to spell /n-O-n/; say /nun/.	[R7]
far ther	Root = far. Add to **ER Page** (if still room in the first column).	
cel lar	[< L cella (small room, hold)]. Think /l/ twice for spelling, not speech.	[R2,29]
quar ter	[<L quartus (fourth)]. See SWR p. 132 for other words based on quartus.	[R1]
un til	One L; *till* and *until* have the same meaning. *Un-* doesn't mean "not" here.	
knew	EW can be marked as the second sound. Homophone: new.	
pub lic		
na vy	A said /A/ at the end ... Y usually says /i/ at ... English words do not end...	[R4,5,6]
e nough	E said /E/ at the end of a syllable.	[R4]
wor ry	Add to **ER Page**.	[R8,5,6]
de part	E said /E/ at the end of a syllable.	[R4]

Spelling Enrichments

COMPOSITION. Research the meaning of compass and write several sentences summarizing what you learn. Be sure to use spelling words like *directs, north, south, east,* and *west.*

LITERATURE. Read a fictional account or a biography of a great naval hero such as Nathaniel Bowditch *(Carry on Mr. Bowditch)* or a story about someone getting lost in the wilderness.

ANTONYMS. Say the first word in each pair and have the students write the spelling word that forms the opposite. Example: admit/ deny.

private / *public*	underside/ *surface*	north / *south*	attic / *cellar*
nearer / *farther*	feel at ease/ *worry*	after/ *until*	all / *none*
indirect/ *direct*	insufficient / *enough*	arrive / *depart*	army / *navy*

Preliminaries

Spelling Rule Cards: Review especially 1, 2, 3, 4, 5, 6, 7, 8, 10, 11, 16, 18, 23, 24, 28.
Phonograms: Quiz at least *ai, ay, ar, dge, ea, er, ie, or, qu, th, sh, ti, ci, si, wor.*
Reference Page: If you haven't this year, dictate sample words for **SH/TI Page** (SWR Step 18).

Words for Section O-4

1001	worth	The Bible is a book *worth* all other books ever printed. --Patrick Henry
1002	shed	Jesus *shed* His blood to redeem His people.
1003	judge	Never *judge* from appearances because appearances are deceptive.
1004	pleas ure	He who loves *pleasure* will be a poor man. --Proverbs 21:17
1005	ap pear	To establish himself a man does everything he can to *appear* established.
1006	lo cate	We can *locate* the church with the help of a map.
1007	con tained	The Bible already *contained* many facts "discovered" by scientists only recently.
1008	qui et	A *quiet* conscience sleeps in thunder. *--Poor Richard's Almanack*
1009	o ce an	Blue the sky spread like an *ocean* hung on high. --Byron
1010	per fect	Every good gift and every *perfect* gift is from above. --James 1:17
1011	fig ure	Do not make for yourselves an idol in the form of any *figure.*
1012	per son al	God gave Cain the *personal* warning, "If thou doest well."
1013	prop er	Be careful to use *proper* manners.
1014	reg u lar	A *regular* habit is a steady, uniform practice governed by a rule or rules.
1015	a fraid	I'm not *afraid* to die, I just don't want to be there when it happens. --Woody Allen
1016	shrink	Truth will *shrink* if it is stretched.
1017	ho ly	Better a *holy* discord than a profane concord. --Thomas Adams
1018	hol i day	The word *holiday* comes from the two words "holy" and "day."
1019	com fort	The God of all *comfort* comforts us in all our tribulation. --2 Corinthians 1:4
1020	pop u la tion	*Population* means a number of people in an area.

Spelling Enrichments

PREFIXES. See SWR, Step 24. Teach the following prefixes:

dis-	opposite of	*pre-*	before	*mis-*	wrong
ir-, in-, im-	not	*mid-*	middle	*un-*	not

DERIVATIVES. Change *worth* into *worthy* then add prefixes to spelling words to build derivatives.

worthy --	unworthy	*figure* --	disfigure, prefigure, misfigure
shed --	unshed	*personal* --	impersonal
judge --	misjudge, prejudge	*proper* --	improper
pleasure --	displeasure	*regular* --	irregular
appear --	disappear	*afraid* --	unafraid
locate --	dislocate	*shrink* --	preshrink
contained --	precontained	*holy* --	unholy
quiet --	disquiet	*holiday* --	preholiday
ocean --	midocean	*comfort* --	discomfort
perfect --	imperfect	*population* --	mispopulation

Ti-Ci-Si   Dictate on loose-leaf review words such as: *subject, face, express.*   Now dictate for the TI Page derivatives of these words with correct suffix: *-tion, -cial, -sion.*

     sub-jec-tion   *fa-cial*   *ex-pres-sion*

After teaching *perfect* and *locate,* add *per-fec-tion* and *lo-ca-tion.* Notice how the root word will **often** indicate which /sh/ to use. A word ending with T (or T + silent E) usually takes TI: C -- CI, and S -- SI.

worth	Add to **ER Page.**	
shed	Use the /sh/ we can use at the beginning... Add to **SH/TI Page.**	[R10]
judge	DGE is used only after a single vowel that says /a-e-i-o-u/.	[R23,3]
pleas ure	/z/ before /U/ often sounds like /zh/. Root word = please.	[R16,7]
ap pear	Think /p/ twice for spelling but not for normal speech.	[R29]
lo cate	O said /O/ at the end...A said /A/ ... Add *location* to **SH/TI Page.**	[R4,7]
con tained		[R28]
qui et	[<L quietus (rest)]. Q always needs U. I usually says /i/ at the end...	[R1,5]
o ce an	Think to spell /O- sE-an/; say /O shun/.	[R4,2]
per fect	per' fect (adj.) per-fect' (verb) Perhaps add *perfection* to **SH/TI Page.**	[R11]
fig ure	U said /U/ because of the E.	[R7]
per son al	Root = person. Add to **ER Page** (if room).	
prop er	Add to **ER Page** (if room).	
reg u lar	[<L regula (a rule)]. U said /U/ at the end of a syllable.	[R4]
a fraid	A said /A/ at the end of a syllable.	[R4]
shrink	SH can spell /sh/ at the beginning of a word. Add to **SH/TI Page.**	[R10]
ho ly	*Holy* is the base word for *holiday.*	[R4,5,6]
hol i day	Y changes to I when adding ... AY usually spells /A/ at ...	[R24,18]
com fort		
pop u la tion	TI can spell /sh/ beginning any syllable after the first. **SH/TI Page.**	[R4,11]

Spelling Enrichments

COMPOSITION. Write about a holiday adventure at the beach using all the spelling words. You may use derivatives of the words. *(I tried to figure how much our week at the beach was* worth*. Our* personal *cabin was small as a* shed*. . .)*

ANALOGY. Have the student write the spelling word that completes the analogy.

Inhale is to exhale as enlarge is to _____(shrink).   Bad is to good as sinful is to _____ (holy).
Irritate is to encourage as annoy is to ___(comfort).   Peaceful is to scared as calm is to __(afraid).
Routine is to special as regular day is to __ (holiday).   Loud is to silent as noise is to __(quiet).
Can you make your own analogies?

DERIVATIVES. Can do SWR Step 35 after O-4. See Plus Endings Page, SWR page 173.

Preliminaries

Spelling Rule Cards: Review especially the following 2, 4, 5, 6, 7, 14, 16, 28.
Phonograms: *ai, ea, ed, ee, er, ir, ng, oi, ou, ow, oy, ti, th, ur.*
Reference Page: Introduce or review **E's Dropping** and **1-1-1 Pages** (SWR Steps 29, 32).

Words for Section O-5

1021	con fuse	Anyone I did not *confuse* does not really understand what's happening.
1022	en dure	What we can't cure, we must *endure.*
1023	pro ject	*Project* comes from Latin *pro-* (before) and *ject* (to throw).
1024	re ject	Men *reject* the Bible because it contradicts them.
1025	skirt	A *skirt* is so feminine on a young lady.
1026	ca noe	Every man should paddle his own *canoe.*
1027	e lect	The people did not *elect* a ruler with integrity.
1028	pic nic	Oh, tough as a steak was Yukon Jake--hard-boiled as a *picnic* egg. --Paramore
1029	re tire	*Retire* comes from the Latin *re-* (back) and *tirer* (back).
1030	raise	God will *raise* up all who believe in Christ some day.
1031	at tend	My son listen, pay attention, *attend* to my words.
1032	dur ing	God sees you *during* the dark, as well as in the daylight. --McGuffey
1033	re mains	One never notices what has been done, only what *remains* to be done. --Marie Curie
1034	jail	*Jail* is a place for lawbreakers.
1035	get ting	*Getting* into debt is getting into a tanglesome net. --Benjamin Franklin
1036	dis tant	Our sympathy is cold to *distant* misery. --Edward Gibbon, historian
1037	sweep ing	At the Boston Tea Party the Americans could be seen *sweeping* the ship.
1038	sud den	The *sudden* call surprised me.
1039	roy al	Queen Esther comes in *royal* state, to save the Jews from dismal fate. *--New England Primer*
1040	tru ly	She *truly* desires to do what is right.

Spelling Enrichments

ORIGINAL SENTENCES. Have the student write original sentences using either all the spelling words or derivatives of the words. He may combine as many spelling words in one sentence as he can and still make a logical sentence. As a start dictate to him a student sample: "The Christians *during* the Reformation *endured* many things because they would not *reject* their faith to avoid *jail.*"

DERIVATIVES. Practice applying the **E's Dropping Rule**. On a blank sheet of paper give a quiz on the first ten spelling words. Fold the paper in half vertically. In the second column have the student write each word adding the suffix -ing. Alert them to watch for two challenge words in the list.

confuse -- confusing	*reject* -- rejecting	*elect* -- electing	*raise* -- raising
endure -- enduring	*skirt* -- skirting	*picnic* -- picnicking**	
project -- projecting	*canoe* -- canoeing*	*retire* -- retiring	

* canoeing -- Retain the E. The need for clarity overrides Rule 16.
** picnicking -- Change the C to CK to separate C and I. See Rule 2.

E's Dropping Page. If you have not done so already this year present the **E's Dropping** Rule.   Select sample silent final E words. Either use examples from SWR Step 17, or pick words taught in Section O that your student needs reinforced: *indicate, sentence, reprove, refuse, waste, slide, needle, measure, rate, locate, figure.*   Dictate the selected silent E words for placement in column one of the Reference Page. Dictate derivatives using a vowel suffix for the next column: *in-di-ca-tor, sen-tenc-er, re-proved,* etc.

con fuse	U said /U/ because of the E.	[R7]
en dure		[R7]
pro ject	[<L pro- (forward) + jacere (throw)]. pro-ject (v.); proj-ect (n.)	[R4]
re ject	[<L re- (back) + jacere (throw)]. See SWR "jactum" p. 132.	[R4]
skirt	Add to **ER Page**.	
ca noe	A said /A/ at the end of a syllable. Odd job E.	[R4,7]
e lect	E said /E/ at the end of a syllable.	[R4]
pic nic		[R2]
re tire	E said /E/ at the end of a syllable. I says /I/ because of the E.	[R4,7]
raise	Odd job E.	[R7]
at tend	Double consonants in multisyllable words ... sounded for spelling but...	[R29]
dur ing	Root = dure. Silent final E word commonly lose the need for the E...	[R16]
re mains	[<L re- (back) + manere (to stay)]. E said /E/ at the end of a syllable.	[R4]
jail	British spelling: *gaol.* We cannot use G in American spelling. Why?	[R3]
get ting	Root = get. With a *1* syllable word, ending in *1*vowel then *1* consonant...	[R14]
dis tant		
sweep ing		
sud den	Double consonants in multisyllable words ... sounded for spelling but...	[R29]
roy al		
tru ly	Root = true. E is no longer needed. U is not the end of the word, but the end of a syllable.	[R4,16,5,6]

Spelling Enrichments

ADVERBS.   An adverb modifies (or restricts the meaning) of a verb, adverb, or another adjective. Adverbs are often formed by adding -ly. Title a paper " -LY Adverbs" and dictate spelling words 1036-1039: *distant, sweeping, sudden, royal.* (You may wish to also add these words from earlier in Section O: *public, chief, quiet, personal, perfect, regular.*) Double-check the student's spelling. Now in the next column have students make these words -LY adverbs.

Add *true* and *whole* to the first column. In the second column dictate the words with the proper spelling: *truly, wholly.*   These words seem to violate the E's Dropping Rule. Ask the students why these words can drop the E before a CONSONANT suffix. The secret is the use of other spelling rules.

In **truly** the U is no longer at the end of a word AND it can say /U/ at the end of a syllable [R. 4].

In **whole** O says /O/ because of the E. In **wholly** the O may say /O/ before 2 consonants [R. 19].

Preliminaries

Phonograms: Review especially *ai, ci, ea, ee, er, ie, igh, ir, ng, si, th, ti, ur.*
Spelling Rule Cards: 2, 4, 5, 6, 7, 9, 10, 11, 12, 13, 19, 22, 24.
Reference: Introduce or review **Plural** and **Y's Exchanging Pages.** See SWR Steps 27, 34.

Words for Section O-6

1041	fact	To imagine a *fact* is a lie.
1042	lie	A half-truth is a whole *lie.* --Yiddish proverb
1043	dis trict	A *district* is a portion of a country, a region.
1044	du ty	Fear God and keep His commandments, for this is the whole *duty* of man. --Ecc. 12:13
1045	lib er ty	The love of *liberty* is the love of others; the love of power is the love of self. --W. Hazlitt
1046	crea ture	Little *creature* buzzes merrily, "God made me!"
1047	pal ace	What can you build with your blocks? Castle or *palace,* temple or dock. --R. Stevenson
1048	com pan y	In this electronic age, a man is known by the *company* he beeps. --Dratwa
1049	cur tain	Branches meet above our heads and shut out the sun like a green *curtain.* --McGuffey
1050	pen ny	A *penny* saved is a *penny* earned. --Benjamin Franklin
1051	res ur rec tion	Christianity begins where religion ends, with the *resurrection.*
1052	ly ing	All sin is a kind of *lying.* --Augustine
1053	rath er	To get understanding is to be chosen *rather* than silver. --Proverbs 16:16
1054	re strain	He who can *restrain* his lips is wise.
1055	in stead	Everything points to the resurrection as fact *instead* of fiction. --H. Peters
1056	don't	*Don't* let ghosts of unforgiven crimes murder your rest. --McGuffey
1057	mu sic	Bells are like the laughter of *music.*
1058	stir	Tall oaks, charmed by earnest stars, dream all night without a *stir.* --Keats
1059	ev er y thing	You can't have *everything.* Where would you put it? --S. Wright
1060	re deem	Our Redeemer died to *redeem* us from eternal punishment.

Spelling Enrichments

ALLITERATION. Alliteration is when two or more words start with the same first sound. For example: *royal remains, picnic project, company curtains.* A sentence may gain a lyrical quality when alliteration is sparingly used. Beware of overuse. Too many S's in a row are difficult to read without hissing.

ORIGINAL SENTENCES. When student writes the original sentences using these spelling words, have him try to use some alliteration in each sentence.

You may read or dictate the following sentences to help demonstrate how to do this. Note the alliterating spelling words from 1021-1060:

The <u>penny</u> <u>project</u> promoted the <u>palace</u> <u>picnic.</u>
<u>During</u> <u>duty</u> in Dan's <u>distant</u> <u>district</u> the doctor dozed.
The <u>rejected</u> <u>royal</u> ruler <u>remained</u> <u>retired</u> <u>rather</u> than recruit a <u>redeemer.</u>

The Y's Exchanging Rule

Dictate for Y's Exchanging Page: wor-ry   wor-ries   wor-ry-ing.

Write rule: *The single vowel Y changes to I when adding any ending unless the ending begins with an I.* Clarify the meaning by asking questions. Example: Is the word *toy* a Y's exchanging word? (No, it doesn't end with a single vowel Y. It ends with OY.) This lesson will have some **Y's Exchanging** words.

---

fact

lie   Think /L-I/ and add E. English words do not end with I.   lie (v.) liar (n.)   [R6,9]

dis trict

du ty   U said /U/ at the end of a syllable. English words do not end with I.   [R4,5,6]

lib er ty   [<OF liber (free)]. Y usually says /i/ at the end of a syllable.   [R5,6]

crea ture   Root = create. U said /U/ because of the E.   [R7]

pal ace   A said /A/ because of the E. C says /s/ because of the E.   [R7]

com pan y   Y usually says /i/ at the ...English words do not end... Abbreviation: co.   [R5,6,12]

cur tain   Think to Spell /ker-tAn/. Add to **ER Page**.

pen ny   Sound double consonants for spelling but not normal speech. Y stands in for I.   [R29,5,6]

res ur rec tion   [<L re- (again) + surgere (to rise)]. Add to **ER, SH/TI Pages**.   [R29,11]

ly ing   Root = lie. Drop E and change I to Y to add -ing.   [R24]

rath er   Add to **ER Page**.

re strain   E said /E/ at the end of a syllable.   [R4]

in stead

don't   Contraction for *do not*. O may say /O/ before 2 consonants.   [R19,13]

mu sic   U said /U/ at the end of a syllable.   [R4]

stir   Add to **ER Page**.

ev er y thing   Compound word: every + thing.   [R5]

re deem   [R4]

Spelling Enrichments

PLURALS. Ask the student to write the first ten words on a loose-leaf sheet of paper and in the second column make each of these words plural. Be careful to watch for **Y's Exchanging Words**: *facts, lies, districts, duties, liberties, creatures, palaces, companies, curtains, pennies.*

COMPOSITION. Dictate the sentence: *A half truth is a whole lie.* Have student explain orally the meaning. Assign a paragraph using the dictated sentence as the topic sentence. Example:

A half-truth is a whole lie. Partial truth that misleads is not real truth. We must explain everything using all the important facts. That is the whole truth.

ART CLUES. Give student a card with one of the following spelling words from Section O: *picnic, squirm, canoe, jail, sweeping, resurrection, penny, curtain, music, palace, creature, company,* etc. Student is to draw pictures on the board without talking to see if someone can guess the word he is illustrating.

Memory Devices to Help with Homophones

When we have two or more different spellings for words that sound the same, how can we remember which spelling to use for which meaning? Sometimes students can have fun making up visual reminders.

Consider the following:

ant / aunt	*a n t* (drawing of ants)	(drawing of a figure) *aunt*
board / bored	*board* (drawing of a board)	(drawing of a bored face) *bored*
cheap / cheep	*Cheap* (with cent sign)	(drawing of a bird) *cheep*
mourn / morn	*mourn*	(drawing of a sunrise) *morn*
new / knew	(drawing of a coin) *new*	(drawing of a face) *knew*
pare / pear / pair	*pare* (drawing of a peeler)	*pear* (drawing of a pear)	*pair* (drawing of glasses)
rain / rein / reign	(drawing of an umbrella) *rain*	*rein*	(drawing of a crown) *reign*

Spelling
Section P

A small number of words account for a high percentage of all written material. The student who has mastered the Wise Guide Spelling Words through Section O and can spell their variants (derivatives built from these words) has learned the words for 65% of all written material. (See *3000 Instant Words* for documentation.)

Don't feel like you have to be a slave to always repeat a rule every time it applies to a new word. The student who has done this program from the beginning may not need that. All spelling rules are listed each time they occur for those who may need them. Some teachers and tutors resume teaching a group someone else taught earlier. Some students begin this program in later grades and do not necessarily start at Section A. After a student has mastered a common concept like rule 4, you may check periodically for understanding but don't necessarily recite the rule every time. The student will demonstrate recognition of rule 4 at work when he tells the teacher the correct spelling marking for a word.

"Education is not the filling of a pail, but the lighting of a fire," said William Butler Yeats. Kindle rather than extinguish the love of learning. Drill for mastery but don't overdo it.

Preliminaries.

Phonograms: Do fast-paced review reading all 70. Quiz especially: *ai, ar, ay, gn, igh, kn, or, ou, ow, tch.* Introduce advance phonogram-- *augh.* (SWR Step 38).

Reference: If beginning a new year, dictate **Consonant/ Vowel, Multi-letter Phonogram,** and **Silent Final E Pages**. See SWR Steps 9, 10, 17.   Other reference pages will come up in subsequent lessons.

Words for Section P-1

1061	im por tant	Forgetting can be just as *important* as remembering and more difficult. --H. Mier
1062	but ton	Why is the sea urchin called a *button?* [Show a picture of a sea urchin.]
1063	hu man	God established *human* government as a means of controlling sinful man.
1064	match	No settled senses of the world can *match* the pleasure of that madness. -Shakespeare
1065	set tle	Kind words are the music of the world to *settle* hard and angry hearts.
1066	re gard	God does not *regard* workless faith or reward faithless work.
1067	val ue	Teach children the *value* of a dollar; give them a dime.
1068	u su al	The one most full of himself is the *usual* one to be most empty.
1069	for tune	He that waits upon *fortune* is never sure of a dinner. *--Poor Richard's Almanack*
1070	count	Don't *count* your chickens before they hatch. -- Aesop -- *The Milkmaid and Her Pail*
1071	re pair	It is better to build children than to *repair* men. --Bob Peterson
1072	caught	Some things are better *caught* than taught.
1073	taught	I am always ready to learn although I do not always like being *taught.* -- Churchill
1074	flight	A hundred of you shall put ten thousand to *flight.* --Leviticus 26:8
1075	tri al	One can learn more from a *trial* in life than in a triumph.
1076	scale	Who has weighed the mountains in a *scale* and the hills in a balance? --Isaiah
1077	sup port	He who robs Peter to pay Paul will always have the *support* of Paul.
1078	fa vor	A good man obtains *favor* from the Lord. --Proverbs 12:2
1079	known	Even a child is *known* by his doings." --Proverbs 20:11
1080	dou ble	If man could have half his wishes he would *double* his trouble. --Ben Franklin

Spelling Enrichments

HOMOGRAPHS.   Words with the same spelling can have distinctly different meanings depending on the etymology: *scale, match, count.* Write original sentences using both meanings in the same sentence. For example: I struck a *match* at the tennis *match.*   The *count* learned to *count.* See SWR Step 30.

GRAMMAR. Make the verbs past tense. See **ED Page**, SWR Step 22, p. 124. Omit *settle, value, scale, double* unless you have already taught the E's Dropping Rule earlier this year.

COMPOSITION. Write original sentences with a values theme that describes important things that count.

SUFFIXES. Teach suffixes *-less, -ly, -ment,* and *-ness.* You may use the cards on page 98. Have students make as many derivatives as possible by combining these with the current spelling.

-less	*without*	buttonless, matchless, regardless, valueless, fortuneless, countless
-ly	*in a manner, like*	importantly, humanly, usually
-ment	*act, or state, or condition of being*	settlement
-ness	*quality, state, or condition of being*	humanness, usualness

Watch for Possible Themes with Spelling Words

The word *flight* jumps out of this list. An interesting read-aloud assignment could be one of the many excellent biographies of the famous brothers, Orville and Wilbur Wright. Have students try to use some aspect of flight in each of the original sentences with these spelling words.

---

im por tant		
but ton	[<F bouton < OF boton (nob)]. Sound /t/ twice for spelling but not normal speech.	[R29]
hu man	U said /U/ at the end of a syllable.	[R4]
match	[<Gk myxa (a candle)] or [<OE gemaecca (companion)]. Meanings trace to root word.	
set tle₄	Sound /t/ twice for spelling but not normal speech. Every syllable must have a vowel.	[R29,7]
re gard	E said /E/ ... Add *regarding* to **Preposition Page**. See SWR p. 104.	[R4]
val ue₂	[<L valere (to be worth)]. English words do not end with U.	[R7]
u su al	U said /U/ at the end of a syllable. /Z/ before U may say /zh/ in the rhythm of speech.	[R4]
for tune	U said /U/ because of the E.	[R7]
count	To compute [< L com- (with) + putare (reckon)]. A noble [<F counte (companion)].	
re pair	[< L re- (again) + parare (prepare)]. E said /E/ at the end of a syllable.	[R4]
caught	augh = /aw/. Advanced phonogram. GH is silent as in *ough* of *bought*.	
taught	augh = /aw/. Bracket because both have same uncommon phonogram.	
flight	Root = fly. [< OE flyht (flight)].	
tri al	Root = try. I may say /I/ at the end of a syllable.	[R5]
scale	(n.) on fish [< G scala (husk)], measuring tool [<ME skal (balance)], (v.) to step [< L scalae (ladder)].	[R4]
sup port	Sound both P's for spelling but not normal speech.	[R29]
fa vor	A said /A/ at the end of a syllable. British spelling: fa-vour.	[R4]
known	Root = know.	
dou ble₄	Every syllable must have a vowel.	[R7]

PREFIXES. Teach prefixes *mid-, pre-, re-, super-*. You may use the cards on page 116. Have students independently make as many derivatives as possible by combining these with the current words.

mid-	*middle*	midflight
pre-	*before*	preflight, pretrial
re-	*again, once more*	rebutton, rematch, resettle, revalue, recount, recaught, retaught, retrial, rescale, redouble
super-	*above, over*	superhuman

ANTONYMS. Express the opposite of words by adding a negative prefix *(de-, dis-, in-, mis-, non-, un-)*.

de-	*to do the opposite*	devalue
dis-	*opposite of*	disregard, discount, disrepair, disfavor
in-	*not*	inhuman
mis-	*wrong*	mismatch, misfortune, mistaught, mistrial
non-	*not, opposite of, lack of*	nonhuman, nonsupport
un-	*not*	unimportant, unbutton, -matched, -settled, -usual, -counted, unrepaired, -caught, -taught, -scaled, -known, -doubled

Preliminaries.

Rules addressed in P-1, P-2 words and phonograms: 1, 2, 3, 4, 5, 6, 7, 8, 9, 10,11, 16, 18, 23, 28.
Phonograms: Quiz *ai, ay, ea, er, ie, ng, oa, or, ough, sh, ed, ph.* Advanced: *aügh* (SWR Step 38).
Reference Pages: If beginning a new year, teach **SH/TI, E's Dropping Pages**. SWR Steps 18, 29.

Words for Section P-2

1081	no tice	Did you *notice* the sunbeams dancing, or hear leaves sing a rustling song?
1082	no tic ing	Have you been *noticing* the change in the weather?
1083	no tice a ble	You have made *noticeable* improvement in your studies.
1084	ob tain	Whoever finds wisdom will find life and *obtain* favor from the LORD.
1085	es cape	He who speaks lies will not *escape.* --Proverbs 19:5
1086	vis it	What is the son of man that you *visit* him? --Psalms 8:4
1087	coast	At the *coast* I saw the ocean waters stopped at God's appointed place.
1088	com pli cate	Honesty pays; telling a lie will only *complicate* the problem.
1089	de sire	*Desire* of having is the sin of covetousness. --Shakespeare
1090	pro duce	It takes a great deal of history to *produce* a little literature. --Henry James
1091	trace	I could *trace* the crumbs you dropped from the kitchen to the living room.
1092	cough	Your *cough* and sneezes spread diseases.
1093	style	*Style* is the dress of thought, a modest dress, neat but not gaudy. --Samuel Wesley
1094	re treat	Dear night is my soul's calm *retreat* which none disturb! --Henry Vaughan, 1695
1095	pat tern	The detailed *pattern* of the Master Builder is seen in nature.
1096	shield	Prayer is a *shield* to the soul, a sacrifice to God, and a scourge for Satan. --Bunyan
1097	o blige	God makes it an obligation for children to *oblige* the rules of their household.
1098	trou ble	Let unjust praise *trouble* you as much as unjust slander.
1099	laugh	A *laugh* is a smile that burst --Patricia Nelson
1100	laugh ter	*Laughter* is the brush that sweeps away the cobwebs of the heart. --M. Walker

Spelling Enrichments

SENTENCE DICTATION. In spelling tests of individual words, also dictate sentences that contain the new spelling words as well as review words from recent lessons.

Example: I *desire* to *trace* a *complicated pattern* using a *noticeable* old *style.*

BIBLICAL INSIGHTS.

Read and discuss together Job 38:1-11. Try to express what you've learned using spelling words. For example: It did not *escape* my *notice* on my *visit* to the *coast* that the ocean comes only so far and then *retreats.* God tells the waves, "You can come this far and no farther."

Read and discuss Proverbs 17:22. She encouraged me in my time of *trouble* by helping me *laugh.*

READING. Read the story of a man who made a great escape from trouble like Martin Luther. Many excellent biographies of the great reformer are available on a variety of reading levels.

E's Dropping Rule: If you haven't already this year, teach the **E's Dropping Page**. With red, underline the silent final E markings. You may chose to use review words from P-1:

hope	hop ing	hope ful
scale	scaled	scale less
set tle	set tler	set tle ment
val ue	val u a ble	val ue less

no tice₃	O said /O/ at the end of a syllable. C says /s/ because of the E.	[R4,2,7]
no tic ing	Silent final E words may lose the need for the E when adding...	[R2,16]
no tice₃ a ble₄	Do not drop the E. C would say /k/ before an A. Rule 2 overrides 16.	[R2]
ob tain	[<L ob- (to) + tenere (hold)]	
es cape	[< L ex- (out of) + cappa (cloak)] A said /A/ because of the E.	[R7]
vis it		
coast	2 meanings: (v.) *coast* down hill, (n.) beach on the *coast*.	
com pli cate	I usually says /i/ at the end of a syllable. A said /A/ because of the E	[R5,7]
de sire	E said /E/ at the end of a syllable. I said /I/ because of the E.	[R4,7]
pro duce	O said /O/ at the end.... U said /U/ because...	[R4,7]
trace	A said /A/ and C says /s/ because of the E.	[R2,7]
cough	This word has 5 letters but only 2 phonograms.	
style	Y stands in for I in Greek-based word. Y says /I/ because of the E.	[R7]
re treat	[<L re- (back) + trahere (draw)] E said /E/ at the end of a syllable.	[R4]
pat tern	Sound both T's for spelling but not for normal speech.	[R29]
shield	SH can spell /sh/ at the beginning.... Add to **SH/TI Page.**	[R10,9]
o blige	O said /O/ at the end... I says /I/ and G says /j/ because of the E.	[R4,3,7]
trou ble₄	Every syllable must have a vowel.	[R7]
laugh	Second sound of advanced phonogram. *augh* = /aw-af/.	
laugh ter	*augh* = /aw-af/	

DERIVATIVES. All of these spelling words (except *laughter*) can take at least one of the following suffixes: *-ed, -ing, -able, -ible, -ation*. Have the students write the spelling words and as many derivatives as possible. Remind them to ask E's dropping questions: *Does it end with E? Are we adding a vowel suffix? Does it harmonize with other rules* [See rules 2, 3]? If the answer to all three questions is "yes," drop the E before adding an ending.

notice	noticing, noticeable, noticed	-->	*obtain*	obtained, obtaining, obtainable
escape	escaped, escaping, escapable		*visit*	visited, visiting, visitation
coast	coasted, coasting		*complicate*	complicated, complicating
desire	desired, desiring, desirable		*produce*	produced, producing, producible
trace	traced, tracing, traceable		*cough*	coughed, coughing
style	styled, styling		*retreat*	retreated, retreating
pattern	patterned, patterning		*shield*	shielded, shielding
oblige	obliged, obliging, obligation*		*laugh*	laughing, laughable
trouble	troubled, troubling			

*We can drop the E before A because we want to change the sound to /g/.

Preliminaries. Spelling Rules: Review P-2 rules plus new rules in this lesson 12, 14, 15, 25, 26.
Phonograms: Quiz *ai, ar, ay, ck, ear, er, ie, ir, ou, ow, qu, sh, th, ti, ur, wor.*
Teach advanced phonogram *gu.* SWR Step 38.
Reference: Teach (or review) TI side of **SH**, **ER**, **1-1-1**, and **2-1-1** **Pages** (SWR, Steps 18, 26, 32, 39).

Words for Section P-3

1101	wait	They that *wait* on the Lord shall renew their strength. --Isaiah 40:31
1102	quit	You're never a loser until you *quit* trying. --Mike Ditka
1103	thumb	The thimble protects the *thumb* of the seamstress.
1104	blur	The ink spill caused a *blur* on my paper.
1105	lack	Fools die for *lack* of wisdom. --Proverbs 10:21
1106	sig nal	Petting her kitty the child said, "I can hear a busy *signal.*"
1107	lev el	Levelers wish to *level* you down as far as themselves. --Samuel Johnson
1108	ad mit	Christianity includes: *admit*, submit, commit, and transmit. --S. Wilberforce
1109	shad ow	I have a little *shadow* that goes in and out with me. --Robert L. Stevenson
1110	trav el	Pass on kindness; let it *travel* down the years; let it wipe another's tears.
1111	Mrs.	*Mrs.* is a title of courtesy for a married woman.
1112	cow ard	A *coward* dies many times before his death. --William Shakespeare
1113	pris on	The Bible is the window to eternity in this *prison* world. --Dwight
1114	lan guage	A different *language* is a different vision of life. --F. Fellini
1115	verb	A *verb* tells what is or what is done, expressing action or being.
1116	noun	A *noun* names a person, place, thing, or idea.
1117	rap id	You have made *rapid* improvement in spelling.
1118	grief	A foolish son is the *grief* of his mother. --Proverbs 10:1
1119	red dish	At sunrise the sky is often covered with bright *reddish* clouds.
1120	e lec tion	Corruption in an *election* is the great enemy of freedom. --Pres. John Adams

Spelling Enrichments

LITERATURE. Dictate parts of R. L. Stevenson's poem, "My Shadow."

I have a little shadow that goes in and out with me,/ What can be the use of him is more than I can see.
He is very, very like me from the heels up to the head; / I see him jump before me, when I jump into my bed.

He hasn't got a notion of how children ought to play, / And can only make a fool of me in every sort of way.
He stays so close beside me, he's a coward you can see: / I'd think shame to stick to nursie as that shadow sticks to me!

One morning, very early, before the sun was up,/ I rose and found the shining dew on every buttercup;
But my lazy little shadow, like an errant sleepy-head, / Had stayed at home behind me and was fast asleep in bed.

Ask: *Why does a shadow stay close? How is he like a coward? Why was he still in bed before sunrise?*

COMPOSITION. Write original sentences about **an election** using as many spelling words as possible.
Example: I can't *wait* for the next *election.* The last leader caused much *grief.* He lied to the people and misused the *language.* Respect for his job has *rapidly* fallen to a low *level.* He *lacks* integrity and may go to *prison.* This new *election* will hopefully *signal* that change is on the way.

1-1-1 Rule: Dictate words such as *clap, drug, hem, plan, spot, stop, swim*. Add some sample endings that require the **1-1-1** rule. Teacher can select derivatives from below.

clap	clapped	clapper	clapping	*spot*	spotty	spotting	spotted
drug	druggist	drugger	drugged	*stop*	stopped	stoppable	stopper
plan	planner	planning	planned	*swim*	swimmer	swimming	swimmable

w<u>ai</u>t		
q<u>ui</u>t	[<L quietus (rest)]. Q always needs U. U is not a vowel here.	[R1]
thum<u>b</u>	Dictate /thum/; say, "Add /b/." See SWR p. 86. A thimble sits on a thum**b**.	
bl<u>ur</u>	Add to **ER Page**.	
la<u>ck</u>	CK is used after a single vowel saying /a-e-i-o-u/ at the end of a base word.	[R25]
sig nal	Root = sign. In *signal* the G and N split into two phonograms.	
lev el		
ad mit		
shad o̲w̲²	[< OE sceadu (shade)]. Add to **SH/TI Page**.	[R10]
trav el	Exaggerate the unaccented vowel within a syllable. See SWR p. 87.	
Mrs.	<u>A</u>bbreviation of *Mistress*, the female variant of *master*. SWR Step 25.	[R26,12]
c<u>ow</u> ard²		
pris on²	[<L prehendere (seize)].	
lan gu̲a̲g̲e̲²	g̲u̲² = /gw/. U in this advanced phonogram says /w/ as it did in QU.	[R3,7]
ve<u>r</u>b	This word is a noun! Isn't that funny?	
n<u>ou</u>n	[<L nomen (name)].	
rap id		
gr<u>ie</u>f	<u>Oxymoron</u>: good grief. We usually use IE. We can but don't have to double F...	[R9,17]
red d<u>ish</u>	Dictate *red*. Use 1-1-1 questions for adding -ish. Add to **1-1-1, SH/TI Pages**.	[R14,10]
e̲ lec ti̲o̲n	[<L ex- (out) + legere (to choose)]. E said /E/ at ... Add to **SH/TI Pg.** (if room)	[R4,11]

SHADOW ART. Shine a flashlight in a dark room. Between the source of light and the wall, shape your hand to look like different animals. Two fingers can represent bunny ears, a thumb can form the head of a turtle, etc. Students can write sentences describing the activity.

DERIVATIVES. Students write the first ten words on a loose-leaf sheet of paper and beside each word write a derivative formed by adding **-ING.** Identify 1-1-1 or 2-1-1 words. Be prepared to defend conclusions.

waiting	(not a single vowel)	*signaling**	(accent on first syllable)	
quitting	(U is not a vowel here.)	*leveling**	(accent on first syllable)	
thumbing	(not a single consonant)	*admitting*	(2-1-1-Accent word)	
blurring	(UR = 1 vowel + 1 consonant)	*shadowing*	(ow = /O/, no consonant sound)	
lacking	(not a single consonant)	*traveling**	(accent on first syllable)	
Bonus: *acquitting*	(2-1-1-Accent word)	* British double consonant regardless of accent.		

ALPHABETIZING. Put the spelling words in alphabetical order. Words that begin with the same first letter must be lined up by subsequent letters: *admit, blur, coward, election, grief, lack, language, level, Mrs., noun, prison, quit, rapid, reddish, shadow, signal, thumb, travel, verb, wait.* (SWR Step 36.)

Preliminaries

Phonograms: Especially review: *ar, ai, ay, ch, ck, ea, ear, er, ew, ng, ou, ow, ough, qu, th, wh.*
Rules: 1, 2, 4, 5, 7, 12, 13, 16, 19, 25, 27. Students repeat the actual rule, not the number.
Reference: Teach or review **Number**, **A-E-I-O-U**, **Contraction Pages** (SWR Steps 15, 19, 28).

Words for Section P-4

1121	sale	A *sale* item is not a bargain if you don't need it.
1122	sub tract	God does not *subtract* our bad deeds from our good deeds.
1123	near ly	It is *nearly* bedtime.
1124	sev er al	To *several* subjects heaven hath my empty words. --Shakespeare
1125	e qual	Much prayer is *equal* to much victory; little prayer is *equal* to big defeats.
1126	since	*Since* by man came death, by Man also came the resurrection. --1 Corinthians 15:21
1127	an i mal	God made each *animal,* bird, fish, and creeping thing. --McGuffey Reader
1128	cu ri ous	*Curious* things, habits. People themselves never know they had them. --Agatha Christie
1129	ninth	Would you like to bat in the *ninth* inning when your team is down by one point?
1130	which	Things *which* hurt, instruct. --Benjamin Franklin
1131	sail	Columbus gained a world. He gave that world its grandest lesson: "On! *sail* on!" -Miller
1132	hun dred	One joy scatters a *hundred* griefs. --Chinese proverb
1133	o' clock	Napoleon described two *o'clock* in the morning courage as "unprepared courage."
1134	dec i mal	A *decimal* part is a tenth.
1135	a mount	The *amount* of seven and nine is sixteen.
1136	com plaint	You raise dust and then make the *complaint* we cannot see.
1137	strength	The *strength* of a country is the *strength* of its religious convictions. --C. Coolidge
1138	cat er pil lar	"Who's tickling my back?" said the wall. "Me," said a *caterpillar* learning to crawl.
1139	news pa per	My Bible tells what people ought to do, and my *newspaper* what they do.
1140	hearse	A *hearse* is a vehicle for transporting a casket.

Spelling Enrichments

LITERATURE. Read Aesop's Fable, "The Bundle of Sticks." Story summary: After one particularly violent argument, a father asked his sons who frequently quarreled to bring him a bundle of sticks. He handed the tied bundle to each son in turn and asked him to break it. They each tried to outdo the other but to no avail. The father then untied the bundle and gave the boys the sticks one by one and they easily broke them. Have students sketch the story and underneath write the moral: *In unity is strength.*

Dictate Christina Rossetti's poem "Caterpillar."

Brown and furry   *No toad may spy you,*
Caterpillar in a hurry,   *Hovering bird of prey pass by you;*
Take your walk   *Spin and die,*
To the shady leaf, or stalk.   *To live again a butterfly.*

SCIENCE. Read material on caterpillars and butterflies. An excellent resource on the subject is *From Darkness to Light to Flight: Monarch--the Miracle Butterfly* by Jules H. Poirier. The photographs are spectacular. The teacher can read aloud from this material and have the students take notes and write several sentences on what they learned. They may enjoy illustrating their work.

Homophones and Not Quite

Homophones are words that sound alike but are spelled differently and mean different things. See SWR Step 30. Watch for a homophone pair in this list (sale/ sail), but also be alert for accurate pronunciation of a word that is often mistakenly pronounced like a similar, but distinctly different, word (which/ witch).

---

sal̄e	A said /A/ because of the E. *A SALE is addicting like ALE.*	[R7]
sub tract	Could we pronounce the S as /z/? No.	[R27]
ne͟ar ly		[R5,6]
sev e͟r al	Add to **ER Page** (if any room is left. This ER is a dime a dozen).	
e͟ qual	E said /E/ at the end of a syllable. Q always needs U.	[R4,1]
sinc̲e₃	C says /s/ because of the E. Add to preposition list. SWR p.104.	[R2,7]
an i mal	[<L anima (air, breath)]. I usually says /i/ at the end of a syllable.	[R5]
cu͟ ri o͟u͟s⁴	U said /U/ at the end of a syllable. I usually says /i/ at the end...	[R4,5]
nin͟t͟h	Root = nine. E no longer needed for I to say /I/ before 2 consonants.	[R16,19]
whi͟c͟h	Say *which*, not *witch*. Put you hand out. Feel the breath of /wh/.	
sa͟il	Homophone: sale.	
hun dred	Add *ninth* and *hundred* to **Number Page**.	
o͟' cloc͟k	Contraction:*of the clock.* O said /O/ at ... CK after a single ... /o/	[R13,4,25]
dec i mal	[<L decimus (tenth)].	[R2,5]
a̲ mo͟unt	A said /A/ at the end of a syllable. Abbreviation: amt.	[R4,12]
com pla͟int	Root = complain. [<L com- (with) + plangere (to strike)].	
stren͟g͟t͟h	This is the longest syllable in English!	
cat e͟r pil la͟r²	Say AR distinctly for spelling. See SWR p. 89.	[R29]
ne͟w͟s pa̲ pe͟r	A said /A/ at the end of a syllable.	[R4]
he͟ars̲e₅	Add to **ER Page**. [*Rehearse* and *hearse* are from Latin root meaning "harrow," a farming implement that looks like a hearse. *Re-* means "again." A *harrow* breaks up the sod making it finer and finer. *Rehearse* means "to harrow" or refine a presentation.]	

ORIGINAL SENTENCES. Write original sentences with the spelling words using a math theme. Review words can also be used such as: *match, count, double, scale, value, fortune, four, fourteen, forty.*

You may select some of the following sentences for examples or for dictation.

> I have *subtracted four* from *fourteen since* the *complaint* at *four o'clock.*
> *Which hearse* held the *ninth newspaper?*   *Match* the *value* to make an *equal amount.*
> I bought *several sails* for my boat on *sale.*   I saved *nearly* a *hundred* dollars.
> The *animal's strength doubles* his *value.*   The *curious caterpillar* climbed *nearly forty* feet.

NUMBERS. Add *ninth* and *hundred* to the **Number Page**. See sample on page 200. Every number has been taught by now except *million.* Some add word #1434 *decade* (ten years) here as well. The Latin word *decimus* meaning "ten" is the source of many words such as: *December* (the tenth month of the Roman calendar), *Decalog* (the 10 commandments), *decimate* (to kill one in ten), *decathlon* (an athletic contest with ten parts), and *decameter* (10 meters).

Preliminaries. Phonograms: *dge, ea, ee, ew, ie, ng, oi, oo, ou, ow, oy, th, ui, wr.*
    Advanced phonograms: *augh, gu.* See SWR Step 38.
    Review Spelling Rules: 2, 3, 4, 5, 6, 7, 9, 16, 23, 24.
    Reference Pages: Teach (or review) **Y's Exchanging Page**. See SWR Step 34.

Words for Section P-5

1141	length y	Only God can control how *lengthy* your life will be.
1142	loud	The pride of dying rich raises a *loud* laugh in hell. --John Foster
1143	naugh ty	A *naughty*, worthless, wicked person devises evil continually.
1144	hun gry	An idle person may go *hungry*.
1145	heav y	He's not *heavy*; he's my brother.
1146	brief	Happiness like a butterfly delights us for one *brief* moment, but soon flits away. --Anne Pavalova
1147	sim ple	There is no vice so *simple* but assumes some mark of virtue on his outward parts. --Shakespeare
1148	guilt y	Whoever shall keep the whole law and yet stumble in one point, he is *guilty* of all. --James 2:10
1149	slow	*Slow* and steady wins the race. -- Aesop, *The Hare and the Tortoise*
1150	strong	A chain is only as *strong* as its weakest link.
1151	en trance	The *entrance* of Your words gives light; it gives understanding to the simple.--Ps. 119:130
1152	cloth	Every *cloth* will cover our sores, but the finest silk will not cover our sins. --Henry Smith
1153	spend	You can *spend* your money more wisely than the government can spend it for you.
1154	cat tle	He causes the grass to grow for the *cattle,* and herb for the service of man. --Ps. 104:14
1155	steel	Three things are extremely hard: *steel,* a diamond, and to know one's self. --B. Franklin
1156	view	Noah did *view* the old world and new. *--New England Primer*
1157	pie	Sing a song of sixpence, a pocket full of rye, four and twenty blackbirds, baked in a *pie.*
1158	de stroy	One leak will sink a ship; and one sin will *destroy* a sinner. --John Bunyan
1159	spread	God made mountains rise, *spread* the flowing seas abroad, and built the lofty skies.--Watts
1160	bot tom	Success is how high you bounce when you hit *bottom.* --Gen. George Patton

Spelling Enrichments

COMPOUND WORDS. Dictate the following: *bed, broad, dish, land, head, hold, oil, over, pot, man, way, yard.* Combine with the last eleven spelling words to make new compound words:

strong	headstrong, stronghold	*view*	overview
entrance	entranceway	*pie*	potpie
cloth	broadcloth, dishcloth, oilcloth	*destroy*	--
spend	overspend	*spread*	bedspread, overspread
cattle	cattleman	*bottom*	bottomland
steel	steelhead		

SENTENCES. Write original sentences linking the word in first column with the word across from it. Usually these are adjective/ noun combinations. Examples:

lengthy entrance:	The mansion had a *lengthy entrance.*
loud cloth:	The *loud* red *cloth* stood out.
naughty spend:	It was *naughty* of him to *spend* his money on gambling.

Teach Y's Exchanging Rule. If you haven't this year, introduce **Y's Exchanging Page**. *The single vowel Y changes to I when adding any ending unless the ending starts with I.* Dictate the following:

cry	cried	cry ing
wea ry	wea ri er wea ri est	wea ry ing

leng̲th y	[<OE lang (long)]. Y usually says /i/ ... English words do not end in I.	[R5,6]
lou̲d		
na̲ugh ty	augh = /aw/	[R5,6]
hun gry		[R5,6]
hĕav y	[<OE hebban (heave)]	[R5,6]
bri̲ef	[<L brevis (short)] We usually use IE. Add to IE Page later.	[R9]
sim ple̲ ₄	Every syllable must have a vowel.	[R7]
gu̲ilt y	gu = /g/	[R3,5,6]
slŏw		
stro̲ng		
en trance̲ ₃	C says /s/ because of the E. Otherwise C would say /k/.	[R2,7]
clo̲th		
spend		
cat tle̲ ₄	Double consonants in multi-syllable words.... Every syllable must...	[R29,7]
ste̲el	Homophone: steal	
vi ĕw	[<Russian viju] 1 syllable; may exaggerate to 2 for spelling.	[R5]
pĭe	We usually use IE. Wait to build IE/EI Page with our first EI word.	[R9]
de stroy̲	E said /E/ at the end ... Change Y to I if we added -ed? No. OY not single Y.	[R4,24]
sprĕad		
bot tom	Double consonants in multi-syllable words should both...	[R29]

Spelling Enrichments

DEGREES OF COMPARISON. "Weary, wearier, weariest" are called degrees of comparison. The endings **-er** and **-est** show degrees of something. *I am weary. Samuel is wearier than me. Jane is the weariest of all.* The first ten words above can all be written in this form, but some words are Y's Exchanging Words and some are E's Dropping words, so be careful to follow the spelling rule that applies.

lengthy	lengthier	lengthiest	*brief*	briefer	briefest
loud	louder	loudest	*simple*	simpler	simplest
naughty	naughtier	naughtiest	*guilty*	guiltier	guiltiest
hungry	hungrier	hungriest	*slow*	slower	slowest
heavy	heavier	heaviest	*strong*	stronger	strongest

SUFFIX. Add -ness (meaning *the quality of, or the act of*) to as many of the same words as possible: *lengthiness, loudness, naughtiness, hungriness, heaviness, simpleness, guiltiness, slowness.* Notice that the "quality of being brief" is *brevity* and of "being strong" is *strength*.

Preliminaries

Spelling Rules: 3, 4, 5, 6, 7, 10, 14, 15, 16, 24, 25.
Phonograms: Quiz at least *ai, ay, ci, eigh, er, ew, oa, oe, or, ou, ph, sh, si, ti, ur, wh.*
   Advanced: *gu, augh.* See SWR Step 38.
Reference Page: Review or teach **Plus Endings Page**. See SWR Step 35.

Words for Section P-6

1161	cous in	A *cousin* is the child of an aunt and uncle.
1162	pas sen ger	I was the last *passenger* on the airplane.
1163	nurse	Florence Nightingale was a famous *nurse.*
1164	may or	You may become the *mayor* of our city when you grow up.
1165	tail or	A *tailor* is one who cuts and sews fabric.
1166	daugh ter	An undutiful *daughter* will prove to be an unmanageable wife. --B. Franklin
1167	guest	A constant *guest* is never welcome.
1168	neph ew	Usually a *nephew* is younger than his aunt or uncle, but not always.
1169	hus band	An excellent wife is the crown of her *husband.* --Proverbs 12:4
1170	clerk	The *clerk* of court processed the adoption.
1171	ex hort	I *exhort* my children to guide themselves by the teachings of the New Testament. -Dickens
1172	coun sel	Blessed is the man who walks not in the *counsel* of the ungodly. --Psalm 1:1
1173	an swer	If I speak what is false, I must *answer* for it; if truth, it will answer for me. --T. Fuller
1174	im i tate	The end of learning is to know God, and out of the knowledge to love and *imitate* Him.--Milton
1175	cor rect	How much easier it is to be critical than to be *correct.* --B. Disraeli
1176	com mit	*Commit* your works to the Lord. --Proverbs 16:3
1177	ap prove	The bank slogan said, "We *approve.*"
1178	share	The miracle is this--the more we *share,* the more we have. --L. Nimoy
1179	re ply	Theirs not to make *reply*/ Theirs but to do and die. --*Charge of the Light Brigade*
1180	whis per	Stay, let me weep while you *whisper,* 'Love paid the ransom for me!' --Fanny Crosby

Spelling Enrichments

COMPOSITION. Good writers use vivid words. See SWR pp. 161-2. In Section O-1 we listed some "Vivid Words." Either add to that list or begin a new one. Make two columns. At the top of the first column write, *person.* At the top of the second column write *speaks.* Add new spelling words to the appropriate column.

person	speaks	person	speaks
cousin	exhorts	daughter	commits
passenger	counsels	guest	approves
nurse	answers	nephew	shares
mayor	imitates	husband	replies
tailor	corrects	clerk	whispers

ANALOGIES. Teacher reads analogy and student writes on the board the spelling word that completes it.

Country is to president as city is to _____(mayor).   Woman is to man as wife is to _____ (husband).
God is to man as create is to_____ (imitate).   Dentist is to hygienist as doctor is to ___(nurse).
Loudest is to softest as shout is to is to__(whisper).   Ball is to athlete as needle and thread are to__ (tailor).

Adding Endings to Words.   See Rules for Adding Endings Reference Page in SWR.
When we add a suffix to a word what do we usually do? We usually just add the suffix.
Who can name one of four cases where we must do something more? (Rules 14, 15, 16, 24).
Add -er to the following review words: *red, travel, produce, guilty.*

| red | **redder** (1-1-1) | travel | **traveler** (accent on first syllable) |
| produce | **producer** (E's dropping) | guilty | **guiltier** (Y's exchanging) |

cous in	See SWR p. 87 for a Think to Spell note.	
pas sen ger	Sound /s/ twice for spelling... Could we spell /er/ with UR here? No.	[R29,3]
nurse	Add to **ER Page**. Odd job E.	[R7]
may or	AY may be used anywhere. AI cannot. Add *mayorship* to **SH/TI Page**.	
tail or	The root *tailor* comes from a Latin word for cut. Think to spell note SWR p. 89.	
daugh ter	augh = /au/.	
guest	gu = /g/. Silent U separates G and E so the G will clearly say /g/.	[R3]
neph ew		
hus band		
clerk	Add to **ER Page**. Could we use CK? No, it's not after a single vowel.	[R25]
ex hort	H is the ghost of a forgotten sound. See SWR pp. 85-86.	
coun sel		
an swer	[<OE **and**- (against) + **swer**ian (swear)] W is in the origin of the word.	
im i tate	I usually says /i/ at the end of a syllable. A said /A/ because of the E.	[R5,7]
cor rect	Sound /r/ twice for spelling but not for normal speech.	[R29]
com mit	Sound /m/ twice for spelling but not for normal speech.	[R29]
ap prove	Sound /p/ twice for spelling but... English words do not end with V.	[R29,7]
share	SH at the beginning. Add to **SH/TI Page**. A said /A/ because..	[R10,7]
re ply	E said /E/ at the end of a syllable. Y stands-in for I at the end of...	[R4,5,6]
whis per	Add to **ER Page**.	

Spelling Enrichments

WORD ANALYSIS. Have students turn the verbs that are synonyms for *speaks* into past tense ending. Organize the words by spelling rule category. Use the format of the **Plus Endings Page**.

Word + ending: *exhorted, counseled, answered, corrected, whispered*
E's Dropping: *imitated, approved, shared*   Y's Exchanging: *replied*   2-1-1: *committed*

ORIGINAL SENTENCES. Write original sentences combining the synonyms for *person* with the synonyms for *speaks*. You may change the verb tense. Example: The *clerk* will *correct* his *nephew*. The *passenger shared* her story. For an extra challenge have the student start each sentence with a prepositional phrase. Example: After the election, the *mayor approved* the bill.

ANTONYMS: Listen to the word and write the spelling word that forms the opposite.

son / *daughter*	hostess / *guest*	wife / *husband*	wrong / *correct*
driver / *passenger*	citizen / *mayor*	niece / *nephew*	shout / *whisper*
ask / *answer*	conductor/ *passenger*	reject / *approve*	originate / *imitate*

Preliminaries

Phonograms: Review especially phonograms: *au, aw, ea, ee, ei, ey, ie, ng, ough, oy, th, ti, wr.*
Rules: 2, 3, 4, 5, 6, 7, 11, 17, 20, 21, 22, 24.
Reference Pages: Teach or review **Plural** and **Dismiss L Pages**. See SWR Steps 27, 37.

Words for Section P-7

1181	fam i ly	Proverbs, the book on wisdom, views the *family* as the place of instruction.
1182	care ful	Those who have believed in God should be *careful* to maintain good works. --Titus 3:8
1183	bea u ty	Charm is deceptive and *beauty* is fleeting --Proverbs 31:30
1184	loss	She dropped her toy down a deep hole and now mourns her *loss*.
1185	wrong	Instead of complaining about what's *wrong*, be grateful for what's right. --Z. Fisher
1186	en gine	The *engine* itself almost seemed to hear her. --E. Nesbit, *The Railway Children*.
1187	be neath	The LORD Himself is God in heaven above and on the earth *beneath*. --Deut. 4:39
1188	though	*Though* I am young, yet I may die. --New England Primer
1189	cab bage	I thought I planted *cabbage* in my garden, but it grew into brussel sprouts.
1190	awe	Let all the earth fear the LORD; let all the world stand in *awe* of Him. --Psalms 33:8
1191	va ca tion	We vacate our house when we go away on a *vacation*.
1192	de gree	A *degree* indicates a step, a portion of progression, a measure, the extent.
1193	beau ti ful	The Bible grows more *beautiful* as we grow in our understanding of it. --Goethe
1194	en joy	Learn to *enjoy* doing those things that help others.
1195	voy age	It is not the going out of port, but the coming in, that determines the success of a *voyage*.--Beecher
1196	car ries	The wise man *carries* his possessions within him. --Bias of Priene
1197	cit ies	Jesus went about all the *cities* and villages teaching and preaching the gospel. --Matt. 9:35
1198	em pire	The Holy Roman Empire is neither holy, nor Roman, nor an *empire*.
1199	in dus try	*Industry* pays debts while idleness or despair will increase them. --Noah Webster, 1828
1200	aw ful	*Awful* referred to God and meant "full of awe, fear, and reverence."
		Over time this word has degenerated to mean "something very unpleasant."

Spelling Enrichments

PLURALS. Locate the spelling words that can be used as nouns: words that name a person, place, thing, or idea. Write the spelling word in the singular and then the plural form. Watch for Y's Exchanging Rule.

family	families	*engine*	engines	*voyage*	voyages
beauty	beauties	*cabbage*	cabbages	*city*	cities
loss	losses	*vacation*	vacations	*empire*	empires
wrong	wrongs	*degree*	degrees	*industry*	industries

COMPOSITION. Title a paper *Family Vacation*. Write a creative story C.S. Lewis- style about adventures on a pretend *vacation*, a *voyage* that takes you to see both *beautiful* and *awful* things in *cities beneath* the *empire*. You must learn to be *careful* about making *wrong* turns with the *cabbage* -shaped *engine* that *carries* you below the sea. This is an exercise to *enjoy*.

Teach the Dismiss L Rule.

Teach the suffix -ful, meaning *full of.*   Add -ful to *mourn* and *duty* (*mournful, dutiful*).
Watch for additional words that could be added to the **Dismiss L Page** from the P-7 list:

careful	*wrongful*	*although*	*beautiful*	*awful*

fam i ly	I and Y usually say /i/ at the end of a syllable. English words do not end with I	[R5,6]
care ful		[R7,21]
bea u ty	Two-syllable word; exaggerate to three for spelling. See SWR p. 88.	[R4,5,6]
loss		[R17]
wrong		
en gine	G may say /j/ before I. Odd job E	[R3,7]
be neath	Add *beneath* and *underneath* to **Preposition Page**. See SWR p.104.	[R4]
though	*Though* and *although* have the same meaning.	
cab bage	[<L caput (a head)]. Think to spell note SWR p. 87.	[R29,7]
awe	Odd job E. E adds significance to word. See SWR p.108.	[R7]
va ca tion	Root = vacate. A said /A/ at the end of a syllable. Add to **SH/TI Page**.	[R4,11]
de gree	E said /E/ at the end of a syllable.	[R4]
bea u ti ful	Root = beauty. See SWR p. 88. Add to **Dismiss L** and **Y's Exchanging Pgs**.	[R4,5,24,21]
en joy	Root = joy.	
voy age	A said /A/ because of the E. Think to spell note SWR p. 87.	[R7]
car ries	Root = carry. Change Y to I and add ES. Add to **Y's Exchanging Pg**.	[R29,24,22]
cit ies	Root = city. Change Y to I and add ES. Add to **Y** or **Plural Page**.	[R2,24,22]
em pire	I said /I/ because of the E.	[R7]
in dus try	Y stands in for I at the end of English words.	[R5,6]
aw ful	Root = awe. See SWR p. 148 for explanation of why we drop the E here.	[R21]

Spelling Enrichments

ALPHABETIZE.	awe	awful	beautiful	beauty	beneath	cabbage
careful	carries	cities	degree	empire	engine	enjoy
family	industry	loss	though	vacation	voyage	wrong

WORD FAMILIES. *Hill* and *kill* look and sound alike, but have no relationship in meaning. Words in the *hill* family include *hillside, hilly, hilltop.* Find root words and non-plural derivatives for P-7 words.

family	familial		*voyage*	voyager
care	careful(ness), (over)careful, carefully, careless		*carry*	carrier, carried
beauty	beautiful, beautify, beautifully		*city*	citizen(ship),
wrong	wrongly, wrongfully, wronged			citify, citified
engine	engineer, engineering		*empire*	emperor
awe	awesome, awful, overawed, awfully		*industry*	industrial,
joy	joyful(ness), overjoy, joyfully, enjoy(ed), enjoyment			industrious(ness)

MEMORY CONCENTRATION GAME

Have student make two sets of small cards of different colors. On one set of cards he should write spelling words and on the other set simple definitions of those words. Scramble and spread out the cards face down in two sets. Play the memory game. The student will select a card from the word set, turn it over and then try to select its match in the definition set. If he matches a pair correctly he can continue taking turns until he misses. The winner is the one making the most matches.

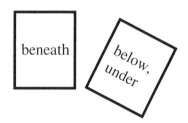

SENTENCE BUILDING

Teacher selects spelling words previously taught, especially those needing extra review. She reads aloud one word to each player who writes it down. (The teacher should be carefully scanning student work for possible misspellings that need correction.) She continues assigning various words to each player until everyone has at least six words. The teacher then writes an unassigned word on the board for all to see.

The object is to see who can create a complete (even if ludicrous) sentence using all his words. The first player can either read his statement or trade one of his words in exchange for either the word on the board or the next unknown word in the teacher's list. When trading the student must cross out the surrendered word from his list and add the replacement word. The teacher erases her word on the board and writes the surrendered word in its place. If a player trades a word he must wait until his next turn to suggest a sentence. Play continues until someone has an understandable (even if silly or weird) complete sentence.

PHONOGRAM GUESSING GAME

The teacher says, "I'm thinking of a phonogram. Who can name it first?" Students are allowed one at a time to ask yes or no questions. Examples below include advanced phonograms through Section P.

Is it a single-letter phonogram? Can it represent two different sounds? *c, e, g, i, s.*
Is it a vowel? *a, e, i, o, u, y.*

Is it a two-letter phonogram that we do not use at the end of English words?
Possible answers: *ai, au, ci, kn, oa, oi, ou, si, ti* (advanced -- *gu, eu).*

Is it a two-letter phonogram that we may use at the end of English words?
Possible answers: *aw, ay, ck, ee, ed, er, gn, ir, ng, oe, or, ow, oy, ph, sh, ur.*

Is it a two-letter phonogram that represents one sound? *ai, ar, au, aw, ay, ci, ck, ee, er, gn, ir, kn, ng, oa, oe, oi, or, oy, ph, qu (as a basic phonogram), sh, ti, ui, ur, wh, wr.*

Is it a two-letter phonogram that represents two sounds? *ew, ow, si, th* (advanced -- *qu, gu).*

Is it a two-letter phonogram that can make three sounds? *ch, ea, ed, ei, ey, ie, oo.*

Is it a three-letter phonogram? *dge, ear, tch, wor.*

Is it a four-letter phonogram? Possible answers: *eigh, ough* (advanced -- *augh).*

Spelling
Section Q

Charles Weisman, the editor of a facsimile edition of Noah Webster's *Blue-backed Speller,* expresses a philosophy we share when he says, "It is useful to teach children the signification of words, as soon as they can comprehend them; but the understanding can hardly keep pace with the memory, and the minds of children may well be employed in learning to spell and pronounce words whose signification is not within the reach of their capacities; for what they do not clearly comprehend at first, they will understand as their capacities are enlarged."

Preliminaries. Spelling Rules: Review especially 2, 4, 5, 7, 9, 11, 28.
   Phonograms: *ai, ar, ay, ch, ci, ea, ed, ei, eigh, er, ie, ng, oi, or, ou, ow, oy, si, ti.*
   Reference Pages: Introduce **IE/ EI Page** SWR Step 40. If beginning a new year, teach **Consonant/Vowel, Multi-letter Phonogram** and **Silent Final E Pages**. Delay SH/ TI Page until Q-6.

Words for Section Q-1

1201	claim	Nothing good have I, whereby Thy grace to *claim.* --Elvine Hall
1202	meas ure	Like doth quit like and *measure* still for *measure.* --Shakespeare, *Measure for Measure*
1203	rep re sent	The fifty stars in the flag *represent* the fifty states in the United States.
1204	po si tion	What *position* do you play in basketball?
1205	sup pose	Happiness depends less on exterior things than most *suppose.* --William Cowper
1206	ar range	She took care to *arrange* the flowers artistically.
1207	sim i lar	In what ways are a frog and a toad *similar?*
1208	con tin ue	As the Father has loved me, so have I loved you: *continue* in my love. --John 15:9
1209	ap point	God did long ago *appoint* the day on which he will judge the world. --Acts 17:13
1210	touch	He who strives to *touch* the stars oft stumbles at a straw. --Edmund Spenser
1211	ac tion	Suit the *action* to the word, the word to the *action.* --Shakespeare, *Hamlet*
1212	im por tance	All other books in comparison to the Bible are of minor *importance.* --Rob. E. Lee
1213	jus tice	Sin is the dare of God's *justice.* --J. Bunyan
1214	sec tion	Your sister will divide the candy into two but you can get first pick of a *section.*
1215	con nect	Blocks are fun because we can *connect* them to make many different things.
1216	con nec tion	There is a *connection* between virtue and happiness.
1217	field	There's as much dignity tilling a *field* as writing a poem. --Booker T. Washington
1218	di rec tion	The actions of believers can change the *direction* of government. --Ruth Haycock
1219	term	The president of the United States can twice serve a *term* of four years.
1220	veil	The bride wears a *veil* as a symbol of her submission to her husband.

Spelling Enrichments

PREFIXES. Combine prefixes with the current spelling words to make as many new words as possible. *dis-* (opposite), *inter-* (between, among), *im-* (not), *in-* (not, in), *mid-* (middle), *mis-* (wrong), *pre-* (before), *pro-* (forward, forth), *trans-* (across), *re-* (back, again), *sub-* (under), *un-* (not)

claim	reclaim, proclaim, disclaimer	*action*	inaction, interaction, reaction, trans-
measure	remeasure	*importance*	unimportance
represent	misrepresent	*justice*	injustice
position	reposition, imposition	*section*	midsection, subsection
suppose	presuppose	*connect*	reconnect, disconnect, interconnect
arrange	rearrange, disarrange, prearrange	*connection*	reconnection, disconnection
similar	dissimilar	*field*	midfield, infield
continue	discontinue	*direction*	misdirection
appoint	reappoint, disappoint, preappointed	*term*	midterm
touch	retouch	*veil*	unveil

Introduce IE / EI Page.

Hold up the two phonograms IE and EI. How do we know when to use which? Most of the time we use IE, BUT we use EI **after** C, **if** we say /A/ or **in** some exceptions we learned. Dictate for the IE column the following review words from Sections O and P: *chief, thief, friend, lie, shield, grief, brief, pie.* These all use IE, "the ch**ie**f of the two choices." Now we will watch for our first examples of EI which we can add to our IE / EI Reference Page.

---

cl**ai**m		
me**as** ure	/Z/ before /U/ often blends into /zh/. U said /U/ because of the E.	[R7]
rep re sent	E said /E/ at the end of a syllable.	[R4]
po si tion	If beginning new year, add /sh/ samples to **SH/TI Page** after Q-6 words.	[R4,5,11]
sup pose	Think /p/ twice for spelling but not in normal speech.	[R29,7]
ar range	[<OF a- (to) + rang (rank)]. 2 consonants between vowels are ok in first type E.	[R7]
sim i lar	[<L similis (like)]. See SWR p. 89 for think to spell note.	[R5]
con tin ue	English words do not end with U.	[R7]
ap point	Think /p/ twice for spelling but not in normal speech.	[R29]
t**ou**ch		
ac tion	TI can spell /sh/ at the beginning of any syllable after the first one.	[R11]
im por tance	Root = important. C says /s/ because of the E.	[R2,7]
jus tice	Root = just. C says /s/ because of the E.	[R2,7]
sec tion	TI can spell /sh/ at the beginning of any syllable after the first one.	[R11]
con nect	Think /n/ twice for spelling but not in normal speech.	[R29]
con nec tion	[<L con- (together) + nectere (tie)].	[R29,11]
f**ie**ld	Use IE, not EI. It's not after C, doesn't say A, and not an exception. Add to **IE/EI Pg.**	[R9]
di rec tion	The dictionary allows I in the first syllable to sound as either /I/ or /i/.	[R5,11]
te**r**m		
v**ei**l	Use EI here because it says /A/. Add to **IE/EI Page.**	[R9]

Spelling Enrichments

DERIVATIVE CHALLENGE. Can you make the base word "act" into eighty-five different words *(acting, reacting, transacting, counteracting, interacting, enacting, acted, action, active, inactive,* etc.)? See SWR pages 130-131 and the Alpha List p. 72.

GRAMMAR. See SWR pp. 103, 219. All these words can be what part of speech: *represent, arrange, continue, appoint, connect, direct?* (verbs) Direct can also be an adjective. Add a suffix ending to each word to change it to a noun. *(representation, arrangement, continuation, appointment, connection, direction).*
> Make a sentence using the following words as both a noun and a verb: *claim, field, veil, direct.*
> He *claimed* he made the *claim* for the land.   He *fielded* the ball in the *field* behind me.
> The *veil veiled* her hair for worship. A *director directed* with *direct directions* (n.,v., adj., n.).
Note: A verb is a word that shows action or state of being and can change tense. A noun is a naming word that can be accompanied by one of the articles (a, an, the) and can be either singular or plural.

COMPOSITION. Write original sentences relating all spelling words to a sport such as baseball or soccer.

Preliminaries. <u>Spelling Rules</u>: 1, 4, 5, 6, 7, 14, 20, 21, 22, 25.
> <u>Phonograms</u>: Quiz *ar, au, aw, ch, ck, ea, ee, er, gn, kn, oo, ou, ough, ph, qu, th, tch, ur, wh.*
> <u>Reference Page</u>: If you haven't already this year, dictate **Plural Page**. See SWR Step 27.

Words for Section Q-2

1221	whose	Blessed is he *whose* transgression is forgiven, *whose* sin is covered. --Psalm 32:1
1222	quick	He that is extravagant will be *quick* to become poor.
1223	en tire	Let patience have her perfect work, that you may be perfect and *entire,* wanting nothing.
1224	ter ri ble	The *terrible* grumble, rumble, and roar, told the battle was on once more. --T. Read
1225	prompt	The whispering angels *prompt* her golden dreams. --Alexander Pope
1226	won der ful	All things wise and *wonderful,* the Lord God made them all. --Cecil F. Alexander
1227	se lect	Be careful how you *select* friends.
1228	calm	A man of understanding is of a *calm* spirit. --Proverbs 18:27
1229	smooth	*Smooth* seas do not make skillful sailors.--African proverb
1230	pri vate	*Private* property rights are essential to freedom.
1231	branch	The tree *branch* formed a cozy nook for dreaming dreams and reading books.
1232	pri ma ry	The *primary* comes before the general election.
1233	fac to ry	A *factory* is a place for making things.
1234	mur der	Malice is mental *murder.* --Thomas Watson
1235	gen tle man	Anyone can be a hero sometime, but a *gentleman* is something to be all the time.
1236	self	To thine own *self* be true, and thou canst not then be false to any man.--Shakespeare
1237	calf	Better is a dinner of herbs where love is, than a fatted *calf* with hatred. --Prov. 15:17
1238	com mand	He that cannot obey, cannot *command. --Poor Richard's Almanack*
1239	beg gar	Do not be made a *beggar* by banqueting upon borrowing.
1240	prop er ty	The Ten Commandments reinforce *property* rights by forbidding stealing.

Spelling Enrichments

PLURALS. After building Plural Page with at least the samples on the top of page 151, quiz the students on words #1231-1240.   Assign them to write the plural forms watching for words ending with Y and F. *(branches, primaries, factories, murders, gentlemen, selves, calves, commands, beggars, properties)*

ADJECTIVES. An adjective describes a noun or pronoun. The first ten words can be used as adjectives modifying (restricting the meaning of) words in the second column.   Write original sentences using adjective/noun spelling words in each row. Example: *whose branch*. -- <u>*Whose branch* is this?</u>

-LY ADVERBS. An adverb describes a verb, adjective, or another adverb. Some words can be changed into an adverb by adding -ly (gentle/ gently).   Which spelling words can become -ly adverbs?

quick -- quickly	*entire* -- entirely	*terrible* -- terribly*	*prompt* -- promptly
wonderful --wonderfully	*select* -- selectly	*calm* -- calmly	*smooth* -- smoothly
private -- privately	*primary* --primarily		

*Notice: *ter-ri-ble* becomes *ter-ri-bly.* We merely drop the E to add -Y probably to avoid the more cumbersome ter-ri-ble-ly. The tendency is to find the easiest way to say things.

Plurals

Review the rule for making words plural [R22]. *To make a word plural just add an -S, UNLESS the word ending hisses (ch, s, sh, x, z), changes (life / lives; fly / flies), or just stops with O (hero / heroes). In these cases add -ES. Occasional words have no change (dust / dust), an internal change (man /men), or a foreign spelling (solo / solos).* Most music terms use Italian spelling.

whose	wh = /h/ Don't confuse with contraction for who is = who's. Odd job E.	[R7]
quick	Q always needs U. Two-letter /k/ can be used after a single vowel that says /i/.	[R1,25]
en tire	I said /I/ because of the E.	[R7]
ter ri ble	I usually say /i/ at the end of a syllable. Every syllable must have a vowel.	[R29,5,7]
prompt	For spelling carefully sound the final /p/ and /t/.	
won der ful	*Full* is written with one L when added to another syllable. Add to **Dismiss L Page**.	[R21]
se lect	[<L se- (apart) + legere (choose)]. E said /E/ at the end of a syllable.	[R4]
calm	L is the ghost of a forgotten sound.	
smooth		
pri vate	Think to spell /prI-vAt/.	[R5,7]
branch		
pri ma ry	I said /I/ & A said /A/ at the end of a syllable. English words do not end with Y.	[R4,5,6]
fac to ry	O said /O/ at the end of a syllable. Y stands-in for I at the end of a word.	[R4,5,6]
mur der	Add to **ER Page**.	
gen tle man	Silent E helps give every syllable a vowel.	[R7]
self		
calf	For spelling sound the silent letter L.	
com mand	[<L com- (with) + mandare (give to the hand)]. Sound /m/ twice for spelling.	[R29]
beg gar	[< Middle Dutch beggaert (monk)]. Root = beg See the **1-1-1 Page**.	[R29,14]
prop er ty	Think to spell the unaccented Y as /i/. See *SWR* pp. 82-85.	[R5,6]

Spelling Enrichments

RHYMING SYNONYMS. An ill bird is **a sick chick.** Orally finish the following: a joyful papa -- **a glad __(dad)**; a sulky boy-- **a mad __(lad)**; a midday beverage--**lunch __(punch)**; a quick explosion -- **a fast __ (blast)**; a large hog -- **a big __ (pig)**; a rodent home -- **a mouse __(house)**; furnace border-- **foundry ___ (boundary)**; count joy-- _____ (measure) **pleasure.** Have students number a sheet of paper from 1 to 10 and write the spelling word that completes the following. The rhyme portion is in bold.

1. **damp tramp** is a wet _____ *(beggar)*
2. **sweet treat** is a _____*(wonderful)* dessert
3. **hill kill** is a mountain _____ *(murder)*
4. **main stain** is a _____ *(primary)* blotch
5. **scream dream** is a ____ *(terrible)* nightmare
6. divided cow is a **half** ___ *(calf)*
7. steady hand-- ____ *(calm)* **palm**
8. slippery glide-- _____*(smooth)* **move**
9. rapid kiss--____ *(quick)* **lick**
10. unidentified footwear--____ *(whose)* **shoes**

Can you think of any more rhyming synonyms using current spelling words?

ORIGINAL SENTENCES. Write original sentences using each pair of the words across from each other.
Example: *whose branch.* *Whose tree branch broke last night?*

Preliminaries.

Review especially the following Spelling Rules: 2, 3, 5, 6, 7, 14, 15, 16, 17, 23.
Phonograms: *ar, dge, ea, er, ew, ir, ng, ow, th, ui, wh, wr.*
Reference Pages: If you have not done so this year, dictate **1-1-1 Page** and at least a sample word of **2-1-1**. Also dictate **ER Page** (at least the top sentence). See SWR Steps 32, 39, 26.

Words for Section Q-3

1241	ledge	The wind went sighing over the rocky *ledge*, causing the flowers to wave at me.
1242	toss	I saw you *toss* the kites on high and blow the birds about the sky. --R. L. Stevenson
1243	ten der	God's *tender* mercies are over all His works.
1244	run ning	The kite is *running* away to visit the lost balloons that made little children cry.
1245	al low	God will not *allow* you to be tempted beyond what you are able. --1 Cor. 10:13
1246	crowd	All at once I saw a *crowd*, a host, of golden daffodils. --Wordsworth
1247	firm	True believers can rejoice in hope, *firm* to the end.
1248	dew	Has the rain a father? Or who has begotten the drops of *dew?* --Job 38:28
1249	writ ten	As it is *written,* "The just shall live by faith." --Romans 1:17
1250	pride	*Pride* is tasteless, colorless, and sizeless but hard to swallow.
1251	some times	It rained all night long, *sometimes* soft, sometimes loud, like a choir's song.
1252	whom	He who loves not his brother *whom* he has seen, how can he love God?
1253	state ment	A *statement* once let loose cannot be caught by four horses. --Asian Proverb
1254	ex er cise	Laughing is good *exercise* like jogging on the inside.
1255	breath	The Spirit of God made me, and the *breath* of the Almighty gave me life. --Job 33:4
1256	gram mar	*Grammar* can govern even kings. --Moliere
1257	an kle	A strong, firm *ankle* is needed for ice skating.
1258	con fi dence	Be certain to glorify the Lord with *confidence* in His faithful care for you.
1259	glo ri fy	Man's chief end is to *glorify* God and enjoy Him forever. --Westminster Catechism
1260	weap on	Prayer is a fortress of the church and a goodly Christian *weapon.* --Martin Luther

Spelling Enrichments

COMPOUND WORDS. Dictate the following review words: *bone, drop, ever, hand, hearted, less, over, taking, under.* Combine these words with the new spelling words to make as many compound words as possible. Not all of the spelling words can be used for this activity.

running	overrunning	*exercise*	overexercise
crowd	overcrowd	*breath*	breathless, breathtaking
dew	dewdrop	*tender*	tenderhearted
written	handwritten, underwritten	*ankle*	anklebone
whom	whomever	*confidence*	overconfidence
statement	overstatement, understatement	*weapon*	weaponless

COMPOSITION. See point 4 in SWR p.163. Use spelling words to construct an attention-getting first sentence to a novel you plan to write. Examples: 1. *Pride* is like a *weapon* which destroys the soul.
2. *Running* for safety I lost my *breath.* 3. The *weapon* peered over the *ledge.*

Apply Rules for Adding Endings to New Spelling Words

After teaching the first ten base words (#1241-1250), on the blackboard beside the word, form a derivative by adding an ending of your choice. Ask, *Is this a 1-1-1 or 2-1-1 word if we add the ending ___?* *Why or why not?* Possible words: *ledger, tossed, tenderly, run --running, allowance, crowded, firmest, dewy, writ --written, prided.* Erase your words and assign for the students to independently make derivatives of these words. They can add a different ending for run like -er *(runner),* or -y *(runny).*

ledge	Does this word follow a rule? Yes, DGE follows a single vowel saying /e/.	[R23,3]
toss	We often double S after a single vowel at the end of a base word.	[R17]
ten der		
run ning	First dictate *run.* Ask the **1-1-1** questions for adding -ing.	[R14]
al low	Not Rule 15. W is not a consonant here in the same way U is not a vowel in QU.	[R29]
crowd		
firm	Add to the **ER Page**.	
dew		
writ ten	First dictate *writ* (as in Holy *Writ*). Ask the **1-1-1** questions for adding -en.	[R14]
pride	I said /I/ because of the E.	[R7]
some times	Treat O as a French overtone. See SWR p. 82. Compound word with 2 types E.	[R7]
whom	*Who* is a subject pronoun, *whom* is an object pronoun. Ex.: *Who* sat with *whom*?	
state ment	A said /A/ because of the E.	[R7]
ex er cise	C says /s/ because of the I. I said /I/ because of the E.	[R2,7]
breath		
gram mar	Sound /m/ twice for spelling. Hint: Don't MAR it by bad gramMAR.	[R29]
an kle	Every syllable must have a vowel.	[R7]
con fi dence	I usually says /i/ at the end of a syllable. C says /s/ because of the E.	[R5,2,7]
glo ri fy	root = glory. Four spelling rules apply to this word. What are they?	[R4,5,24,6]
weap on		

Spelling Enrichments

DICTATION. Instead of a regular spelling test, dictate the following paragraph.

A Painful Way to Overcome Pride

I had written a firm but foolish statement about how brave I am. Pride sometimes allows me to glorify myself, but after pride comes a fall. I lost confidence when I saw someone toss a weapon in a crowd. I started running but was soon out of breath because I haven't had much exercise lately. The morning dew made me slip and I tripped on a ledge and twisted my tender ankle.

GRAMMAR. Discuss subject and object pronouns to explain when to use the words *who* and *whom*.

	Subject		Object
I	I am your teacher.	me	Listen to me.
he	He is your friend.	him	Be nice to him.
she	She is your sister.	her	Look out for her.
who	Who is your teacher?	whom	We listen to whom?

Preliminaries. Spelling Rules: Review especially 2, 4, 5, 6, 7, 8, 9, 12.
Phonograms: Review *ai, ar, ay, ea, ear, ee, ei, eigh, er, ew, ey, ie, igh, ir, ou, th, ur, wh, wor, wr.*
Reference Pages: Review **IE/ EI Page** SWR Step 40.

Words for Section Q-4

1261	pres i dent	Our first *president* was "first in war, first in peace, and first in the hearts of his countrymen."
1262	rel a tive	The arguments may be good, but they are not *relative* to the subject.
1263	bound a ry	The special quilt indicates a *boundary* for the toddler during family devotions.
1264	thir teen	A bright cold day in April the clocks were striking *thirteen*. --George Orwell, *1984*
1265	mice	Beneath her skirt, her feet, like little *mice,* peeped in and out, as if they feared the light.
1266	cir cus	A *circus* of acrobats, animals, and clowns usually performs in a circular tent.
1267	ei ther	God has no grandchildren; you *either* know Him firsthand or not at all.
1268	crit ic	A *critic* evaluates the work of others and may either praise or criticize.
1269	cul ture	To destroy a *culture* just get people to stop reading. --Bradbury
1270	prob lem	Not the greatness of our *problem* but the smallness of our faith makes us complain.
1271	pre side	The president will *preside* over the meeting.
1272	re late	If you are a relative then you *relate* to me in some way.
1273	con vict	When He has come, He will *convict* the world of sin. --John 16:8
1274	re mem ber	*Remember* that time is money. --Benjamin Franklin
1275	at tempt	He had decided to live forever or die in the *attempt*. --Joseph Heller
1276	de clare	The morning light, the lily white *declare* their Maker's praise. --M. Barcock
1277	ar rest	*Arrest* comes from the Latin word *rest,* meaning "to stop, stay, wait."
1278	en close	Her smile like double rows of rosebuds *encloses* orient pearls.
1279	a wait	We eagerly *await* the birth of the baby.
1280	con sent	Purity of the soul cannot be lost without *consent*. --Augustine

Spelling Enrichments

GRAMMAR. A noun can be preceeded by one of the three articles (a, an, the). A verb can change tense. Write original sentences using a noun from the first column preceeded by one of the articles and a verb from the second column used in the present tense. Put a check mark over the article. Underline the spelling word noun once and the spelling word verb twice .

> ✓
> Examples: A <u>president</u> <u>presides</u> over the meeting.
>
> ✓
> The <u>thirteen</u> <u>remember</u> to be polite.
>
> ✓
> The <u>relatives</u> <u>related</u> the story to me.

Warning. At least one of the words in the first column is not a noun. Can you identify it? (Either)

IE / EI? Many current spelling words can be added to the **IE/EI Page**. Remember IE is the chief phonogram, the one used more than EI.

When do we use EI? 1) After C. 2) If we say /A/. 3) In some exceptions we learned. *Either weird foreign sovereign forfeited leisure. Neither heifer seized counterfeit protein.* [R9]. Later, on a more advanced level we can introduce another sentence that covers foreign spellings.

pres i dent	Root = *preside*. [<prae (before) + federe (to sit)]. Abbreviation: pres.	[R5,12,16]
rel a tive	Root = *relate*. In unaccented syllable think to spell /A/.	[R4,16,7]
bound a ry	Root = *bound* (limit).	[R4,5,6]
thir teen	Add to **ER Page**.	
mice	With 2 reasons for a silent E we mark the first one that works.	[R2,7]
cir cus	[<L circus (ring)]. C says /s/ because of the I. Add to **ER Page**.	[R2]
ei ther	Uses EI instead of IE because it's an exception we learned. Add to **IE/EI Page**.	[R9]
crit ic		
cul ture	U said /U/ because of the E.	[R7]
prob lem		
pre side	E said /E/ at the end of a syllable. I said /I/ because of the E.	[R4,7]
re late	E said /E/ at the end of a syllable. A said /A/ because of the E.	[R4,7]
con vict		
re mem ber	E said /E/ at the end of a syllable. Add to **ER Page**.	[R4]
at tempt	Think to spell /at-tempt/; say /a-tempt/.	[R29]
de clare	E said /E/ at the end of a syllable. A said /A/ because of the E.	[R4,7]
ar rest		
en close	O said /O/ because of the E.	[R7]
a wait	A said /A/ at the end of a syllable.	[R4]
con sent	[<L com- (with) + sentire (to feel)].	

Spelling Enrichments

ALLITERATION. When two words together start with the same initial sound we say they have alliteration. Sometimes alliteration can add poetic flavor to our writing. Combine spelling words or their derivatives into pairs that use alliteration.

president's problem	cultures consent	president's progress
relative remembers	critic convicts	relative relates
circus critic	attempted arrest	await arrest

ORIGINAL SENTENCES. Write original sentences with the spelling words, trying as much as possible to use alliteration. Underline the spelling words.

Example: My <u>relative relates</u> concern over the <u>president's problem</u>.

Preliminaries. <u>Rules</u>: 4, 5, 6, 7, 10, 11, 16, 24, 28. Students learn concepts, not rule numbers.
<u>Phonograms</u>: *ci, ea, er, oa, oe, oi, or, ou, ow, oy, sh, si, th, ti.* Advanced: *gi, our, yr.* SWR Step 38.
<u>Reference Pages</u>: Teach or review **E's Dropping**, **Y's Exchanging Pages**. See SWR Steps 29, 34.

Words for Section Q - 5

1281	pub lish	Maybe some day someone will *publish* some of your writing.
1282	man u fac ture	A factory is a place where the *manufacture* of things takes place.
1283	im pris on	Try to *imprison* the restless winds. --Dryden
1284	pre sent	*Present* the present to her on her birthday.
1285	breathe	*Breathe* Thy loving Spirit into every troubled breast. --C.Wesley
1286	em ploy	*Employ* a portion of time each day in reading the Scriptures.
1287	serve	True happiness comes when we *serve* others.
1288	brace	A *brace* holds anything tight from crooked teeth to a falling building.
1289	mag ni fy	*Magnify* means to make large.
1290	en gage	If we *engage* in giving we can gain joy in living.
1291	jour nal	A *journal* gives a daily record of what one thinks, feels, or notices.
1292	in for ma tion	Other books give *information*, but the Bible brings transformation.
1293	re gion	The word of the Lord was being spread throughout all the *region*. --Acts 13:49
1294	pe ri od	Where God places a *period,* don't put a question mark.
1295	cour age	You cannot build *courage* by taking away initiative and independence. --Lincoln
1296	de bate	I love argument, I love *debate*. --Margaret Thatcher
1297	ad di tion	It is a destructive *addition* to add anything to Christ. --Richard Sibbes
1298	nerve	Stretch every *nerve* with vigor for a heavenly race demands your zeal.
1299	fame	Physicians of *fame* replied as they collected fees, "There is no cure for this disease."
1300	fa mous	*Famous* remarks are very seldom quoted correctly. --Simeon Strunsky

Spelling Enrichments

ANTONYMS. Give the spelling word that is the opposite of:

absent /_____ (present)	diminish/____(magnify)	disengage/____ (engage)
subtraction/___ (addition)	release/_____ (imprison)	choke/_____ (breathe)

DERIVATIVES. Words in the first column (#1281-1290) can all take the endings **-ed** and **-ing**. Students should write the spelling words and then derivatives using these endings. Warn them to watch for Y's Exchanging and E's Dropping words.

publish	published, publishing	*employ*	employed, employing
manufacture	manufactured, manufacturing	*serve*	served, serving
imprison	imprisoned, imprisoning	*brace*	braced, bracing
present	presented, presenting	*magnify*	magnified, magnifying
breathe	breathed, breathing	*engage*	engaged, engaging

COMPOSITION: Write original sentences on the theme of courage.

Two More Spellings for /ER/

We initially learned a guide sentence for five spellings of /er/. Do you know any other spellings for /er/? Hint: Greek words use Y where we often use I. What would be the Greek form of IR? (YR--*martyr*, *myrtle*, *zephyr*, *myrrh*). The French phonogram, OUR, can also spell /er/ as in *journey* or *adjourns*. Add these to the **Multi-letter Phonogram** and **ER Pages** (SWR Steps 10, 26).

pub lish	SH spells /sh/ at the end of a syllable. Wait until Q-6 for SH/TI Pg.	[R10]
man u fac ture	[<L manu (hand) + facere (make)] Name 2 reasons U says /U/ in this word?	[R4,7]
im pris on		
pre sent	The noun form is spelled the same but pronounced /preZ-ent/.	[R4]
breathe 5	Compare with spelling word taught earlier, *breath* (1255).	[R7]
em ploy		
serve 2	English words do not end with V.	[R6,7]
brace	With two reasons for a silent final E, mark the first type.	[R2,7]
mag ni fy	[<L magna (large) + facere (make)]	[R5,6]
en gage	A said /A/ because of the E._____	[R7]
jour nal	[<F jour (day)] our = /er/ Add to **ER Page**.	
in for ma tion	Root = *inform*	[R4,11]
re gion	gi = /j/ Without I, the G would say /g/.	[R4,3]
pe ri od	[<Gk peri- (around) + hodos (going)]	[R4,5]
cour age	our = /er/ Add to **ER Page**.	[R7]
de bate	A said /A/ because of the E.	[R4,7]
ad di tion	Sound /d/ twice for spelling. I usuallys says /i/... TI can spell ...	[R29,5,11]
nerve 2	English words do not end with V.	[R6,7]
fame	A said /A/ because of the E.	[R7]
fa mous 4	A said /A/at the end of a syllable. Add to **E's Dropping Page**.	[R4,16]

Spelling Enrichments

SUFFIXES. Add endings to the new spelling words. Watch for **E's dropping** or **Y's exchanging** words.

-able	-- able to be__, deserving to be	*-er*	-- a person or thing that___.
-al	-- of, like, having the nature of	*-ment*	-- act, state, or fact of ___ing.
-ical	-- specialized	*-ness*	-- quality, state, condition of being___.
-ism	-- the study of	*-ous*	-- having much, full of
-ist	-- one who does, knows, makes		

publish	publisher	*journal*	journalist, journalism
imprison	imprisonment	*region*	regional
present	presentable, presenter	*period*	periodical
breathe	breather, breathable	*courage*	courageous (R3 overrides R16.)
employ	employment, employer	*debate*	debater, debatable
serve	server, servable	*addition*	additional
brace	braceable (R2 overrides R16.)	*nerve*	nervous
magnify	magnifier	*fame*	famous
engage	engagement	*famous*	famousness

Preliminaries. Review Spelling Rules: 3, 4, 5, 7, 10, 11, 12, 17, 18, 21, 24, 25, 28.
Phonograms: *ai, ar, ci, ck, ed, ei, er, or, ough, ow, th, ur,* and advanced phonogram *gi*. SWR Step 38.
Reference Pages: If you haven't yet this year, dictate **SH/TI** and **Dismiss L Pages**, SWR Steps 18, 37.

Words for Section Q-6

1301	al though	*Although* the bird flew through the rough trough, he thought of the bough.
1302	sur prise	God is never taken by *surprise*. Things happen to fit His plans.
1303	re li gion	No sciences are better attested than the *religion* of the Bible. --Isaac Newton
1304	es tate	I found some wonderful books to read at the *estate* sale.
1305	back ward	To hiccup is to cough *backward*.
1306	pro gress	As we *progress* through time we can make progress.
1307	tow el	Jesus began to wash the disciples' feet, and to wipe them with the *towel*.
1308	ef fort	What is written without *effort* is in general read without pleasure. --Samuel Johnson
1309	spe cial	God made you *special*; no one else is just like you!
1310	in clude	Duty will *include* what we owe to God, to our fellow men, and to ourselves. --N. Webster
1311	their	People who do what seems right in *their* own eyes will do what's wrong in God's eyes.
1312	ex am ple	*Example* is the school of mankind and they will learn at no other. --E. Burke
1313	debt	A promise made is a *debt* unpaid --Robert W. Service
1314	deb it	A *debit* is an item of debt recorded in an account.
1315	for ward	We look *forward* to the time we exclaim, 'Christ first, country next!' --Pres. A. Johnson
1316	um brel la	The *umbrella* moved down the street like a dancing ball.
1317	dry	Better is a *dry* morsel with quietness than a house full of feasting with strife.
1318	dried	The Lord rebuked the Red Sea and it *dried* up for Israel to cross.
1319	re sult	All growth, including political growth, is the *result* of risk-taking. --J. Wanniski
1320	per haps	This is not the end. It is not even the beginning of the end. But it is, *perhaps*, the end of the beginning. --Churchill

Spelling Enrichments

FLAIR IN WRITING STYLE. Effective writers vary sentence patterns. Start each of your original sentences this week using one of these adverbial clause starters: *when, while, since, as, if, although*.
Be sure to place a comma between the clause *(When I go to the store,)* and the main sentence *(I will be sure to buy milk)*. Underline all the spelling words used. Circle the adverb clause.

When the *example* of *religion* came up, I was thankful for your *effort* to help me.

Although it rained hard, I have tried to *dry* the *umbrellas* with a *towel*.

While the long-term *result* is not clear, their *debt* is growing each day.

Since *their estate* went into *debt*, the bank awaits payment.

POETRY. Dictate and have students illustrate the classic poem "Rain" by Robert Louis Stevenson.

The rain is raining all around
It falls on field and tree,
It rains on umbrellas here
And on the ships at sea.

TI, CI, SI. Write on the board: sh, ti, ci, si. Which /sh/ can we use to begin a word? (sh -- share). At the end of a word? (sh -- publish). With ending -ship? (sh -- courtship). At the beginning of any syllable after the first one? (ti, ci, si). How do we know which of the three to use? Ninety percent of the time we use TI. We memorize the others, putting them on the TI page to help reinforce the spelling. Add *share, publish, courtship* along with the following words taught earlier in Section Q to the **SH/TI Page**: *position, action, section, connection, direction, information, addition.* With red, underline SH or TI.

al though	*All* is written with one L when added to another syllable. Add to **Dismiss L Page**.	[R21]
sur prise	I said /I/ because of the E. Add to **ER Page**.	[R7]
re li gion	gi = /j/. The I lets the G say /j/. E said /E/ at the end... I usually says /i/ at the end...	[R4,5,3]
es tate	A said /A/ because of the E.	[R7]
back ward	[<ME bak- (back) + ward (toward)]. CK is used after /a/.	[R25]
pro gress	We often double S after a single vowel... Add *pro-gres-sion* to **TI/SH Page**.	[R4,17,11]
tow el		
ef fort	[<L ex- (out) + fortis (strong)]. Sound /f/ twice for spelling, not normal speech.	[R29]
spe cial	Not rule 4. The 1 reminds us to say /e/ not /E/. Add to **TI/SH Page**.	[R11]
in clude	U said /U/ because of the E. Add *in clu sion* to **TI/SH Page**.	[R7,11]
their	Root = *they*. Use EI here because it says /A/. Add to **EI Page**.	[R9]
ex am ple	Every syllable must have a vowel. Abbreviation = ex.	[R7,12]
debt	[<L debitum (owed)]. *Debt* is taken from a Latin word that contained a B.	
deb it	B in *debt* is easier to remember when linked to *debit* from the same Latin root.	
for ward		
um brel la	Sound /l/ twice for spelling ... At the end of a word A usually says /ah/.	[R29,18]
dry	Y usually says /i/ at the end of a syllable. English words do not end with I.	[R5,6]
dried	Change the Y to I. Add to **Y's Exchanging Page**.	[R24,28]
re sult	E said /E/ at the end of a syllable.	[R4]
per haps	Always ends in S.	

Spelling Enrichments

ANALOGIES. Complete comparisons using spelling words. Ex.: <u>Box</u> is to <u>square</u> as <u>bowl</u> is to ___ (circle).

<u>Sun</u> is to <u>sunglasses</u> as <u>rain</u> is to _____ (umbrella).   <u>Ocean</u> is to <u>wet</u> as <u>desert</u> is to _____ (dry).
<u>Regress</u> is to <u>backward</u> as <u>progress</u> is to ___ (forward).   <u>Wet</u> is to <u>washcloth</u> as <u>dry</u> is to ___ (towel).
<u>Ordinary</u> is to <u>important</u> as <u>okay</u> is to _____ (special).   <u>Start</u> is to <u>cause</u> as <u>end</u> is to _____ (result).
<u>Anticipate</u> is to <u>shock</u> as <u>expect</u> is to _____ (surprise).   <u>Yes</u> is to <u>maybe</u> as <u>surely</u> is to _____ (perhaps).

Can you think of additional analogies using the spelling words?

ALPHABETIZE. Put the words in alphabetical order (*although, backward, debit, debt, dried, dry, effort, estate, example, forward, include, perhaps, progress, religion, result, special, surprise, their, towel, umbrella*).

GRAMMAR. Find words in this lesson that can be used as more than one part of speech depending on the sentence. Can you use each word as each part of speech? See SWR Step 16. Students can use dictionary.

> *surprise* -- n, v, adj, interj   *estate* -- n, adj   *backward* -- adj, adv
> *prog-ress* -- n; *pro-gress* -- v)   *towel* -- n, adv   *special* -- n, adj
> *debit* -- n, v   *forward* -- adj, adv   *dry* -- v, adj   *result* -- n, v

An Old-Fashioned Spelling Bee

Since initially we teach students to spell by sound, not by letter name, how can we think of encouraging a spelling bee? Once a child has learned to naturally think words by sound, this student can, without harming that process, enjoy participation in a spelling bee. James A. Bowen in his book published in 1900, *English Words as Spoken and Written,* explains the benefits of this activity and the rules for doing so effectively.

The Benefit
To know a word we must learn it by the sense of hearing, the sense of sight, and the sense of muscular perception. Oral spelling acquaints the pupil with a word through the ear and the vocal organs, as written spelling does through the eye and finger.

The Procedure
In oral spelling, the letters of the syllable should be named in their order, but those of each phonogram should be grouped in the naming, so as to show that they are recognized as members of a phonetic element and, together, equal to a letter.

Format for one-syllable words: *The pupil should not say b-a-i-t, but should say b-ai-t, thus indicating the three phonetic elements of the word. The "ai" together should have about the same stress and time utterance, as each of the other letters. Briefly, oral spelling is calling, in their order, the phonograms of a word, rather than the letters.*

DIRECTIONS FOR ONE-SYLLABLE WORDS
        optional -- ask for a sentence
        repeat the word
        spell the word phonogram by phonogram

Format for multi-syllable words: *The syllable is the unit element of words, as the phonogram is of syllables. From a thousand given syllables, many thousands of words may be made; hence, knowledge of syllables is a knowledge of the structure of words. In oral spelling the pupil should* **spell by syllables,** *pronouncing each one as he spells it, in the old-fashioned way.*

DIRECTIONS FOR MULTI-SYLLABLE WORDS
        optional -- ask for a sentence
        repeat the word
        say the word in syllables
        say the syllable, spell the word phonogram by phonogram

Slowing children down to spell syllable by syllable is very important. The application of the spelling rules are more apparent if they are considered syllable by syllable versus considering the word as a whole unit.

Spelling
Section R

Even though the spelling list in this book progresses to freshman level in college and the work is profitable as a remedial tool for all ages, there is great benefit for the student who can complete the work in the elementary grades. We want to introduce children to these words as early as possible. We do not expect the comprehension of all the words to keep pace with the student's ability to pronounce or spell them. If we introduce students to these words at a young age, we will quicken and sharpen their ability to understand them later.

Preliminaries. Review especially the following Spelling Rules: 2, 4, 5, 7, 10, 11, 17, 19, 25.

Phonograms: *ch, ci, ck, ee, er, gn, kn, oo, or, ou, ow, sh, si, th, ti, wr.*

Reference Pages: Introduce **SH/TI Page**, SWR Step 18. Select review words for SH portion. If beginning a new year, dictate **Consonant/ Vowel, Multi-letter Phonogram,** and **Silent Final E Pages**.

Words for Section R-1

1321	loose	I watched his eyebrows prying *loose* an idea. --Richard T. Johnson
1322	sweet	Our present joys are more *sweet* because of past sorrow.
1323	com mon	If you can walk with kings nor lose the *common* touch, you'll be a man my son! --R. Kipling
1324	stage	All the world's a *stage* and all the men and women merely players. --W. Shakespeare
1325	re sign	I *resign* my soul to the Almighty...relying on the merits of Jesus Christ for the pardon of my sins.-S. Adams
1326	pre cious	Holy Bible, book divine, *precious* treasure, thou art mine. --John Burton
1327	pro vi sion	A *provision* is something set aside by planning ahead.
1328	hon or	*Honor* your mother and your father that your days may be long upon the earth.
1329	con grat u late	When we *congratulate* someone, we show our joy for him.
1330	ten sion	Much stress and *tension* come from a prideful heart.
1331	tooth	Judge to dentist: "Please pull the *tooth*, the whole *tooth*, and nothing but the *tooth*."
1332	pa tient	We'd never learn to be brave and *patient*, if there were only joy in the world. --H. Keller
1333	sword	The pen is mightier than the *sword*.
1334	wreck	*Wreck* comes from a Swedish word meaning "to throw away" and a Dutch word meaning "broken."
1335	pro fes sion	Homemaking, though underrated, is an essential and challenging *profession*.
1336	con ven tion	When will we convene the homeschool *convention?*
1337	tempt	Idleness tempts the devil to *tempt*. --Thomas Watson
1338	fa cial	I could tell he was pleased by his *facial* expression.
1339	at ten tion	My son, give *attention* to my words. --Proverbs 4:20
1340	ex per i ment	After a fiftieth failed *experiment*, Edison said, "I know one more way it will not work."

Spelling Enrichments

COMPOUND WORDS. Dictate the following review words: *ache, back, eye, fish, foot, hand, heart, leaf, less, pick, place, play, ship.* For a bonus you can also dictate: **bitter, brush, coach, wealth.** Make as many compound words as possible by combining these words with the current spelling words.

common	commonplace, **commonwealth**	*loose*	footloose, loose-leaf
sword	swordfish, swordplay	*sweet*	sweetheart, **bittersweet**
stage	backstage, stagehand, **stagecoach**	*wreck*	shipwreck
tooth	eyetooth, toothache, toothpick, **toothbrush**	*honor*	honorless

ANALOGIES. Write the spelling word that completes the following:

A teacher has a student; a doctor has a _____ (patient).

Loss is to comfort as victory is to _____ (congratulate).

Garbage is to worthless as ruby is to _____ (precious).

Inspiring good is to encourage as enticing bad is to ___(tempt).

An audience is to seats as an actor is to _____ (a stage).

Diamond is to gravel as precious is to _____(common).

A lemon is sour; a pie is _____ (sweet).

Bullet is to gun as blade is to _____ (sword).

Paper is to wad as car is to _____ (wreck).

Cement is to jelly as firm is to _____ (loose).

Chef is to bake as scientist is to___(experiment).

Hand is to finger as gum is to _____(tooth).

As a bonus try to make your own analogies using these or other spelling words.

SH/TI Page. Hold up phonogram cards: SH, TI, CI, SI, CH. These can all say /sh/. SH is used at the beginning of a word (share), at the end of a syllable (wash), with the ending -ship (friendship). In Latin-based words TI, CI, and SI can spell /sh/ at the beginning of any syllable after the first one (action, special, tension). CH is the French way of spelling /sh/ (chef). After dictating the below words add examples of /sh/ words to the SH page.

loose	Show how it cannot be one of the first four types of silent final E's.		[R7]
sweet	Oxymoron: sweet sorrow. Can we begin this word with C? Why not?		[R2]
com mon	Sound /m/ twice for spelling. With one M this might say /cO-mon/.		[R29]
stage	A said /A/ and G says /j/ because of the E.		[R3,7]
re sign	Why does the E say /E/? Why does the I say /I/?		[R4,19]
pre cious	The 1 shows to think the first phonogram; not R4.	ci = /sh/	[R11]
pro vi sion	[<L pro- (before) + visio (see)].		[R4,5,11]
hon or	British spelling: hon our.		
con grat u late	U said /U/ at the end of.... A said /A/ because of the E.		[R4,7]
ten sion	[<L tendere (stretch)]. Root = tense.	si= /sh/	[R16,11]
tooth	Plural: teeth.		[R22]
pa tient	A said /A/ at the end of a syllable.	ti = /sh/	[R4,11]
sword	W is the ghost of a forgotten sound.		
wreck	Does the rule work here? Yes, /e/ comes before CK.		[R25]
pro fes sion	Root = *profess*. O said /O/ at the end of a syllable.	si = /sh/	[R4,17,11]
con ven tion	[<L con- (together) + venire (come)]. Root = *convene*.	ti = /sh/	[R11]
tempt	Carefully pronounce the consonants!		
fa cial	Root = face. A said /A/ at the end of a syllable.	ci = /sh/	[R4,11]
at ten tion	Sound /t/ twice for spelling but not for normal speech.	ti = /sh/	[R29,11]
ex pe ri ment	[<L experiri (to test)].		[R4,5]

Spelling Enrichments

SAME SOUND, DIFFERENT SPELLING. Although 90% of the time we use TI to spell /sh/ at the beginning of any syllable after the first one, we must remember when to use the other forms. Have students add to TI Page as many new words as possible. This can be assigned as homework or filled in as taught.

ti	ci	si	si
pa tient	*pre cious*	*ten sion*	*pro vi sion*
con ven tion	*fa cial*	*pro fes sion*	
at ten tion			

Add -*ation* and -*tion* to current spelling words: *resignation, congratulation, temptation, experimentation*.

COMPOSITION. Dictate the following in lieu of a regular spelling quiz.

Congratulate a child who overcame the *common temptation* of a *sweet tooth*. She saw a *tooth*less man *resign* at the *honor convention*. She had a *loose tooth* from a *wreck*. *Tension* grew when she learned that not all enjoy the *provision* of teeth that cut like a *sword*. She saw how *precious* her teeth could be when she noticed the *facial* change in the man on *stage* without teeth. Now she gives *patient attention* to the *experiment* to use her *toothbrush* like a *professional*.

Preliminaries. Spelling Rule Cards: 2, 4, 5, 6, 7, 10, 17, 18, 20, 22.
      Phonograms: *au, aw, ch, ee, er, ey, sh, oi, oo, ou, ough, ow, oy.*
      Reference Pages: If you haven't yet this year, build **Plural** and **Y's Exchanging Pages**. See
SWR Steps 27, 34.

Words for Section R-2

1341	ra di o	Why do you think the word *radio* is not listed in Webster's 1828 Dictionary?
1342	vid e o	We must be careful what we watch on *video.*
1343	shelf	An actual newspaper headline goof said, "Eye Drops off *Shelf.*"
1344	val ley	The sun cut itself on a steep hill and bled into the *valley.* --John Steinbeck
1345	mouse	We say mice to refer to more than one *mouse.*
1346	ech o	Our love for God is like an *echo*; we return what we receive.
1347	di a mond	Common is to gravel as rare is to *diamond.*
1348	sal a ry	*Salary* has two A's as in "Appreciate A good *salAry*!"
1349	law yer	A *lawyer* is one who deals with the law.
1350	pris on er	The *prisoner* with wistful eye looked upon that tent of blue called the sky.
1351	pre fix	A *prefix* like "un-" is added to a word like "happy" to change the meaning.
1352	suc cess	The only thing that ever sat its way to *success* was a bird.
1353	va ri e ty	*Variety* is the very spice of life that gives it all its flavor. --William Cowper
1354	sheep	When it rains why don't *sheep* shrink?
1355	moose	The *moose* has a loose tooth.
1356	pi an o	Owning a *piano* doesn't make one a famous musician.
1357	e ter ni ty	To the godly *eternity* is day with no sunset; to the wicked night with no sunrise. -Watson
1358	to ma to	Never ask a three-year old to hold a *tomato.*
1359	i de a	Write down a good *idea* before it gets lost.
1360	en e my	There is no little *enemy.* *--Poor Richard's Almanack*

Spelling Enrichments

COMPOSITION. Dictate the sentences used above with *diamond, eternity, valley, video.* Discuss together
the meanings of these sentences. Have the student select one as a topic sentence for which they write several
more related sentences. If possible use other spelling words. Underline the spelling words.

ART. Illustrate and label as many spelling words as possible.

GRAMMAR. All of the above spelling words can be used as nouns. What is a noun? (A word that names
a person, place, thing, or idea).   Ask students to organize the spelling words into these categories. Some
words could be used as more than one part of speech.

person--	*lawyer, prisoner, enemy*
place--	*valley, shelf*
thing--	*radio, video, echo, mouse, moose, salary, tomato, prefix, sheep, piano, diamond*
idea--	*success, variety, eternity, idea*

Review Spelling Rules.

Teach the set dialog for spelling rules but occasionally ask questions to check for understanding such as: "Would the word *ma* be an exception to rule 4?" (No, the rule says, "A **usually** says /A/ at the end of a syllable. Usually means that it will most of the time, but it can make a different sound as well.) "Do we use SH to spell /sh/ at the beginning of the second syllable in a base word?" (No, we use ti-, ci-, or si- there.)

ra di o	[<L radius (ray)]. A and O usually say /A/ and /O/ at ... I usually says /i/ at ...	[R4,5]
vid e o	[<L videre (see)]. E and O usually say /E/ and /O/ at the end of a syllable.	[R4]
shelf	SH can spell /sh/ at the beginning of a word. Add to **SH/TI Page**.	[R10]
val ley	Think to spell /i/ with EY at the end of an unaccented syllable.	[R29]
mouse	Odd job E helps us see this is not a plural word.	[R7]
ech o	O usually says /O/ at the end of a syllable.	[R4]
di a mond	I usually says /i/ at the end of a syllable. A usually says /A/ at ...	[R5,4]
sal a ry	A usually says /A/ at the end of... Y stands-in for I at the end of a word.	[R4,5,6]
law yer	Root = law.	
pris on er	[<L prehendere (seize)]. Root = prison.	
pre fix	E usually says /E/ at... X is never directly before S. Add -es for plural.	[R4,20,22]
suc cess	C says /s/ before E. Double S for nonplural base words.	[R2,17]
va ri e ty		[R4,5,6]
sheep	SH can spell /sh/ at the beginning.... Add to **SH/TI Page**.	[R10]
moose	What would this word be without the odd job E? (moos) Plural: moose.	[R7,22]
pi an o	I usually says /i/ at the end of a syllable. O usually says /O/ at ...	[R5,4]
e ter ni ty	E usually says /E/ at the end of a syllable. I usually says /i/ at ...	[R4,5,6]
to ma to	O usually says /O/ and A usually says /A/ at the end of a syllable.	[R4]
i de a	Why doesn't A say /A/? At the end of a word A says /ah/.	[R5.4.18]
en e my	[<L in- (not) + amicus (friendly)].	[R4,5,6]

Spelling Enrichments

PLURALS. Work through the spelling rule for plurals writing the words on the board. Establish the 5 categories. To make a word plural just add an -s UNLESS the word ending hisses (ch, s, sh, x, z), changes (wife/wives; fly/ flies), or just stops with O (tomato/tomatoes). In these cases add -es. Occasional words have no change (sheep/sheep), an internal change (man/men) or a foreign spelling (solo/ solos). Musical terms ending with O are often foreign words (*altos, cellos, banjos, trios, concertos*). Some of us can only play the *radios* and *videos*.

-s	radios, videos, pianos, valleys, lawyers, prisoners, ideas, diamonds, valleys
hisses	successes, prefixes
changes	shelves, salaries, varieties, eternities, enemies
O	(not musical terms) echoes, tomatoes
other	mouse/ mice; sheep/ sheep; moose/ moose

Erase board. Have students write the spelling words in first the singular form and then the plural form.

Preliminaries. Review <u>Spelling Rules</u>: 1, 3, 4, 5, 6, 7, 9, 11, 12, 14, 16, 21, 23, 24.
<u>Phonograms</u>: Quiz especially *ai, ar, ay, ci, dge, ea, er, ie, igh, ng, oa, oe, or, ou, ow, qu*.
<u>Reference Pages</u>: If you have not done so this year, present **E's Dropping** and **1-1-1 Pages**. See SWR Steps 29, 32.

Words for Section R-3

1361	bar gain	She haggled for a *bargain* at the garage sale.
1362	fierce	No beast is so *fierce* but knows some touch of piety. --Shakespeare
1363	gra cious	What plea so tainted and corrupt, but being seasoned with a *gracious* voice, obscures the evil? Shakespeare
1364	hum ble	The Lord, to whom I drew near in *humble* and child-like faith, suffered and died for me. --Mozart
1365	bright	*Bright* star, would I were steadfast as thou art. --John Keats
1366	bus y	Martha was *busy* and troubled about many things. --Luke 10:40
1367	gen er al	No *general* in the midst of battle has a great discussion about what to do if defeated. --Owen
1368	square	Three *square* meals a day can make a person round.
1369	ac cord ing	Our zeal should be *according* to knowledge.
1370	an gry	He that will be *angry,* and not sin, must not be *angry* but for sin. --John Trapp
1371	to mor row	The fool does say, "*Tomorrow* I'll reform." --Poor Richard's Almanack
1372	se cure	No nation is *secure* if it exalts itself above God.
1373	man ner	The *manner* of giving is worth more than the gift. --Pierre Corneille
1374	in creas es	He gives power to the faint; and to them that have no might he *increases* strength. --Isa. 40:29
1375	com bine	When bad men *combine,* the good must associate. --Edmund Burke
1376	due	You have a library book *due* today.
1377	re lease	Pilate, wishing to *release* Jesus, again called out to them, but they shouted, "Crucify Him!"
1378	wear	In 1797 the first man to *wear* a top hat was arrested for disturbing the peace.
1379	lose	Much wants more and will *lose* all. --Aesop, *The Goose that Laid the Golden Egg*
1380	al read y	When something is ready all the way, it is *already* done.

Spelling Enrichments

-LY ADVERBS. Change as many spelling words as possible into -LY Adverbs. Watch for rules.

Do we change a single Y to I when adding -LY?   (Yes, Y's Ex Rule works w/ ANY not I suffix--R24.)
Do we drop a silent E when adding -LY?   (No, E's Drop Rule applies to vowel suffixes--R16.)
Do we double a consonant before adding -LY?   (No, 1-1-1 Rule applies to vowel suffixes--R14.)

Which adverbs answer **How?** *fiercely, graciously, humbly* (shortened from humble + ly for ease in speech), *brightly, busily, generally, squarely, accordingly, angrily, securely, mannerly, duly* (E not needed; U not at end of word <u>and</u> U can say U at the end of a syllable). **How often?** *increasingly.* What spelling words are adverbs without needing -LY and answer **When?** *tomorrow, already.*

COMPOSITION. Write original sentences with the new words (or an -LY Adverb derivative). Include an adverb in each sentence. Underline the adverb and write ADV over it. Example: He <u>*fiercely*</u> controls the game. Esther <u>*graciously*</u> appealed to the king. She <u>*humbly*</u> increases her tasks. <u>*Tomorrow*</u> they will *lose.* Note: an adverb can appear on either side of the verb *(angrily appealed/ appealed angrily).*

POETRY. Dictate the poem *Lazy People* by Shel Silverstein. *Let's write a poem about lazy people/ Who lazily laze their lives away;/ Let's finish it **tomorrow**. / I'm much too tired today.*

Adverbs. The base word for adverb is "verb." Adverbs answer questions about verbs (or adjectives and other adverbs) like: **when? where? how? how much? how often?** Examples: *arrived* yesterday (**when** it arrived); pushed *backward* (**where** *it was pushed); rapidly* ate (**how** he ate); rained *slightly* (**how much** it rained); studied *continually* (**how often** he studied). Many adjectives (*polite* boy) can be turned into adverbs by adding -LY (spoke *politely).*

bar gain	Think to spell /bar-gAn/. See SWR p. 89.	
fierce	Use IE, not EI; it's not after C, doesn't say A, and not an exception.	[R9,2,7]
gra cious	Root = grace A said /A/ at the end of a syllable. Add to **SH/TI Page.**	[R4,11]
hum ble	Every syllable must have a vowel.	[R7]
bright		
bus y	Think to spell /buz-i/. Say /biz-i/. See SWR p. 81.	[R5,6]
gen er al	G may say /j/ before E.	[R3]
square	Q always needs U. A said /A/because of the E. <u>Abbreviation</u>: sq.	[R1,7,12]
ac cord ing	Sound /k/ twice for spelling but not for normal speech.	[R29]
an gry	Y usually says /i/ at the end of a syllable. See SWR pp. 82-85.	[R5,6]
to mor row	Sound /r/ twice for spelling but not for normal speech.	[R29]
se cure	E said /E/ at the end of a syllable. U said /U/ because of the E.	[R4,7]
man ner	Sound /n/ twice for spelling but not for normal speech.	[R29]
in creas es		
com bine	I said /I/ because of the E.	[R7]
due	English words do not end with U. <u>Homophone</u>: dew See SWR p.150	[R7]
re lease	E said /E/ at the end of a syllable. Odd job E	[R4,7]
wear	A one-syllable word that some treat as two! <u>Homophone</u>: ware	
lose	Show how odd job E cannot be any of the other four kinds.	[R7]
al read y	*All* is written with one L when... Add to **Dismiss L Page.**	[R21,5,6]

SIMILES. A simile compares two unlike things using the words *like* or *as: wise as an owl, sick as a dog, hairy as an ape, proud as a peacock, as tough as nails, as stiff as a board.* Complete the following similes. A good writer looks for fresh, original comparisons. Try to add a new twist.

The cake was as *square* as ____   The chrome shined as *bright* as___
The princess was as *humble* as ___   The knight was as *fierce* as ___
The maid was as *busy* as a ___   The *general* was as *angry* as _____
Mother was as *gracious* as ____   The mayor was as *controlling* as ___

PERSONIFICATION. Give an inanimate object qualities usually given to people. "The maples *wear* a gayer scarf, the field a scarlet gown"-- E. Dickinson.   Use personification with new spelling words. (The *bright* sun appealed to the *busy* girl to come out and play.)

DEGREES OF COMPARISON. Illustrate with R-1 words (**loose**, looser, loosest/ **sweet**, sweeter, sweetest). Create degrees of comparison with seven adjectives in R-3. Watch for R16,24. See SWR p. 130.

fierce, fiercer, fiercest   **bright**, brighter, brightest   **angry**, angrier, angriest
gracious, more gracious, most gracious   **busy**, busier, busiest
humble, less humble, least humble   **square**, squarer, squarest

Preliminaries. <u>Spelling Rules</u>: Review especially 4, 5, 6, 7, 8, 11, 16, 19, 28.

<u>Phonograms</u>: Quiz especially *ar, ch, ci, ea, ear, ed, er, ir, ph, si, th, ti, ur, wor.*

<u>Reference Pages</u>: If you have not done so already this year, teach **A-E-I-O-U Page** and the top part of **ER Page**. See SWR Steps 19, 26.

Words for Section R-4

1381	mod ern	No idea is so antiquated that it was not once *modern*. --Ellen Glasgow
1382	pop u lar	It may be *popular*, but it is not wise.
1383	com plete	He who has begun a good work in you will *complete* it. --Phippians 1:6
1384	a dopt	To *adopt* means to take or receive as one's own that which is not naturally so.
1385	re vealed	All that I am I owe to Jesus Christ, *revealed* to me in His divine Book. -D. Livingston
1386	dis trib ute	Of great riches there is no real use, except to *distribute*. --Francis Bacon
1387	pur pose	A Church exists for the double *purpose* of gathering in and sending out.
1388	dif fer ent	It is one thing to say that something should be done, but a *different* matter to do it. --Aesop
1389	sat is fy	*Satisfy* us early with Your mercy that we may rejoice and be glad all our days! -Psalm 90:14
1390	con trol	God is in *control* of the rise and fall of rulers.
1391	pub li ca tion	A magazine is a *publication* to keep the **public** informed.
1392	vir tue	*Virtue* is its own reward.
1393	search	Truth hurts, not the *search* for it, but the run from it!
1394	to geth er	A good conscience and a good confidence go *together*. --Thomas Brooks
1395	pa tience	The *patience* of God towards evil is not necessarily everlasting.
1396	con sid er	You may *consider* the bearing of many children an investment. --India's Gandhi
1397	in jure	A man may *injure* himself by wounds, his estate by negligence, or his happiness by vice. -Webster
1398	in jur y	An *injury* is much sooner forgotten than an insult. --Philip Chesterfield
1399	in ter est	And can it be that I should gain an *interest* in the Savior's blood? --Charles Wesley
1400	ed u ca tion	Honesty is the beginning of *education*. --John Ruskin

Spelling Enrichments

PREFIXES. Dictate the following prefixes: *al-, dis-, post-, pre-, re-, im-, in-, ultra-, un-.* Add these prefixes to current spelling words to make new words. (Two words will not take a prefix: *purpose* and *virtue*.) Be prepared to explain the meaning of the newly formed words.

modern --	ultramodern, postmodern	*publication* --	prepublication, republication
popular --	unpopular	*search* --	research
complete --	incomplete	*together* --	altogether
adopt --	readopt	*patience* --	impatience
revealed --	unrevealed	*consider* --	reconsider, inconsiderate
distribute --	redistribute	*injure* --	reinjure, uninjured
different --	indifferent	*injury* --	reinjury, post-injury
satisfy --	dissatisfy, unsatisfied	*interest* --	reinterest, disinterest, uninterested
control --	ultracontrol, uncontrolled	*education* --	re-education (some dictionaries omit hyphen)

CLARITY OF THOUGHT. This actual newspaper headline can be misinterpreted. "Enraged cow *injures* farmer with ax." How can it be made more clear? Farmer with ax *injured* by enraged cow.

How many types of silent E's?

This lesson illustrates most of the types of silent final E's. Which one do you think will be used the most? Which one will not be represented? The teacher can write numbers one through 5 in a line on the corner of the board and place a tally mark under the appropriate number each time a word uses that type of E. Students get excited to see which E wins.

---

mod ern	[<L modo (just now)].	
pop u lar	[<L populus (people)]. U said /U/ at the end of a syllable.	[R4]
com plete	Use French overtone. See SWR p. 82. E said /E/ because of the E.	[R7]
a dopt	[<L ad- (to) + optare (choose)]. A said /A/ at the end ... Root word = opt	[R4]
re vealed	[<L re (back) + velare (to cover)]. Base word didn't end with /d/ or /t/; ED says /d/.	[R4,28]
dis trib ute	U said /U/ because of the E.	[R7]
pur pose	Odd job E. Add to **ER Page**.	[R7]
dif fer ent	Root word = differ. Think /f/ twice for spelling, but not normal speech.	[R29]
sat is fy	English words do not end with I.	[R5,6]
con trol	O makes 2nd sound but not for any of the reasons we learned.	[R4,7,19]
pub li ca tion	I said /i/ at the end ... A said /A/ at the... Add to **SH/TI Page**.	[R5,4,11]
vir tue	English words do not end with U. Add to **ER Page**.	[R6,7]
search	[<L circus (circle)]. Add to **ER Page**.	
to geth er		
pa tience	Homophone: patients.	[R4,11,7]
con sid er		
in jure	U said /U/ because of the E.	[R7]
in ju ry	What rules apply to this word?	[R4,16,11]
in ter est		
ed u ca tion	Root = educate. U and A said /U/ and /A/ ... Add to **SH/TI Page**	[R4,11]

Spelling Enrichments

LITERATURE. Read the Aesop's Fable "Belling the Cat" prior to teaching this set of spelling words. In the story, one mouse suggested that a protection against the cat would be to hang a bell around his neck so they would hear when he was coming. The young mice all thought this was an excellent idea. An old mouse asked one important question, "Who will put the bell on the cat?" Dictate the moral: "It's one thing to say that something should be done, but a different matter to do it."

ANTONYMS. [<Gk anti- (opposite) + onyma (word)] Ex. shame/ honor; rejected/ chose.

collect -- *distribute*	ancient -- *modern*	ignore -- *consider*
disappoint -- *satisfy*	conceal -- *reveal*	separated -- *together*
same -- *different*	reject -- *adopt*	heal -- *injure*

SYNONYMS. [<Gk syn- (together) + onyma (name)] Ex. esteem/ *honor*

forbearance -- *patience*	select -- *adopt*	contemporary -- *modern*	total -- *complete*
well liked -- *popular*	hurt -- *injury*	disperse -- *distribute*	hunt -- *search*
uncover-- *reveal*	unlike -- *different*	motivation -- *purpose*	please -- *satisfy*

Preliminaries. Review especially <u>Phonograms</u>: *ai, ay, ch, ea, eigh, er, ew, ir, oo, ough, qu, tch, ti, ur.*
<u>Spelling Rules</u>: 1, 4, 7, 11, 14, 15, 16, 18. What restriction do we learn on rule 4 from rule 18?
When does A not say /Ā/ at the end? <u>Reference Page</u>: **Plus Ending Page**. See SWR Step 35.

Words for Section R-5

1401	choose	*Choose* this day whom you will serve. --Joshua 24:15
1402	en ter tain	Dwelling in a house by the side of the road, he used to *entertain* all comers. -Homer
1403	weigh	Every way of a man is right in his own eyes, but the LORD will *weigh* the hearts.
1404	im prove	Man's 32,600,000 laws do not *improve* on the Ten Commandments.
1405	prom ise	Our Lord has written the *promise* of the resurrection. . . in every leaf in spring. -M. Luther
1406	pre fer	To *prefer* something is to want it before other things.
1407	chose	God *chose* the foolish things of the world to confound the wise.
1408	il lus trate	To *illustrate* means to make clear by stories or examples.
1409	pre pare	The Bible can fit a man for life and *prepare* him for death. --Daniel Webster
1410	sol dier	I watched my leaden *soldier* go with different uniforms and drills. --R.L. Stevenson
1411	ma chine	No *machine* can do the work of one extraordinary man. --Hubbard
1412	trea son	To betray one's country is to commit *treason.*
1413	ob jec tion	God has an *objection* when any created thing is used as an object of worship.
1414	a re a	The *area* of a rectangle is the height times the base.
1415	serv ice	Till men have faith in Christ, their best *service* is but glorious sin. --Thomas Brooks
1416	treas ure	Forsaking Christ for the world is to leave a *treasure* for a trifle. --W. Jenkyn
1417	cre ate	Only God can *create* something out of nothing.
1418	cre a tion	The whole of *creation* groans and travails in pain because of sin.
1419	quiz	The word *quiz* comes from a root word meaning "to question."
1420	ef fect	Nature is but a name for an *effect* whose cause is God. --William Cowper

Spelling Enrichments

SUFFIXES. Use *-able, -ed, -en, -ful, -ing, -ist, -ive, -ly, -ment, -ous, -y* to make derivatives.
Watch for rules 14, 15, 16.

E's Dropping Words [R16]

choose --	choosing, choosy
improve --	improving, improved, improvable, -ment
promise --	promising, promised
chose --	chosen
illustrate --	illustrating, illustrative, illustrated
prepare --	preparing, prepared
machine --	machinist
service --	servicing, served, serviceable*
treasure --	treasury, treasured
create --	creating, creative, created

*R2 overrides R16. See SWR p. 147.

1-1-1 [R14] / 2-1-1 Words [R15]

quiz --	quizzing, quizzed
prefer --	preferred, preferable,* preferring*

* note accent shift: pre'fer able, pre fer'ring

Word + ending:

entertain --	-ed, -ing -ment
weigh --	weighable, weighed
soldier --	soldierly
treason --	treasonous, -able
objection --	objectionable
creation --	creationist
effect - -	effective

20

Homophones [<Gk homos (same) + phone (sound)]
Homophones sound the same but have different spellings and different meanings. Examples: *ant/ aunt; ate/ eight; be/ bee.*   Read through the words taught so far in Section R looking for examples of words that have a homophone (patients/ patience; wear, ware). Listen for words that can be homophones in this lesson. See SWR Step 30.

choose	Tally silent E's again as on p.169. Irregular verb form. See SWR p. 125.	[R7]
en ter tain		
weigh	Homophone: way.	
im prove	English words do not end with V.	[R6,7]
prom ise	Odd job E.	[R7]
pre fer	[<L prae (before)]. E said /E/ at the end of a syllable.	[R4]
chose	O said /O/ because of the E. Odd job E shows word not plural.	[R7]
il lus trate	[<L lustrum (to light up)]. A said /A/ because of the E.	[R29,7]
pre pare	E said /E/ at the end of a syllable. A said /A/ because of the E.	[R4,7]
sol di er	[OF soldier (pay) <L solidus (Roman coin)]. See SWR p. 88.	[R5]
ma chine	Retains French influence: ch = /sh/; i = /E/ Alter. marking: 3rd sound of A.	[R4,7]
trea son		
ob jec tion	Use Latin spelling for /sh/. Add to **SH/TI Page**. See SWR "jactum" p. 132.	[R11]
a re a	A said /A/ at the end of a syllable, but not at the end of a word.	[R4,18]
serv ice	Root = serve. Drop the E to add a vowel suffix. Add to **E's Dropping Page**.	[R16,7]
treas ure	U said /U/ because of the E. /Z/ followed by /U/ may sound like /zh/.	[R7]
cre ate	E said /E/ at the end of a syllable. A said /A/ because of the E.	[R4,7]
cre a tion	E and A said /E/ and /A/ at the end of a syllable. Add to **SH/TI Page**.	[R4,11]
quiz	Q always needs U.	[R1]
ef fect	Think /f/ twice for spelling but not for normal speech.	[R29]

Spelling Enrichments

SYNONYMS. What spelling word most closely matches the following words in meaning? test -- *quiz*
        prize -- *treasure*   draw -- *illustrate*   amuse -- *entertain*   design -- *create*
        select -- *choose*   assistance -- *service*   better -- *improve*   pledge -- *promise*

MULTIPLE MEANINGS FOR SAME WORD. Some words have many, seemingly unrelated meanings. *Service* can describe: a move in tennis, silverware, a type of industry, repair for purchased article, the delivery of a legal document, a branch of armed forces, a formal meeting, devotion to God, quality of assistance, a special entrance. How many current spelling words can combine with *service* to illustrate these meanings?

choose reliable **service**	*illustrate* difference between goods and **services**
*entertain*ment is a **service** profession	*prepare* to **service** legal papers
weigh the meaning of the **service** contract	*soldiers* are in the armed **services**
improve my tennis **service**	**service** the *machine*
promise a church wedding **service**	*treasure* silver table **service**
prefer the **service** entrance	*objection* to jury **service**

Can you think of a way to link service to the words: *treason, create, creation,* and *quiz?*

Preliminaries. <u>Spelling Rules</u>: Review especially 1, 4, 5, 6, 7, 9,12, 25, 26, 27.
<u>Phonograms</u>: *ai, ar, ck, ea, ee, ei, eigh, er, ie, th, or, ow, ui, wh.*
<u>Reference Pages</u>: Introduce or review **Number** and **IE/EI Pages**. See SWR Steps 15, 40.

Words for Section R-6

1421	fea ture	We *FEATure* the FEATs of others.
1422	neigh bor	If your *neighbor* has a nicer house than you do, it may help when you sell.
1423	beige	I spilled spaghetti sauce on my *beige* slacks.
1424	sleeve	I will wear my heart upon my *sleeve.* --William Shakespeare, *Othello*
1425	pov er ty	*Poverty* and affliction take away the fuel that feeds pride. --Sibbes
1426	vis i tor	A *visitor* should not make his visit too long. --Noah Webster's *Bluebacked Speller*
1427	to ward	Does the hawk fly by your wisdom, and spread its wings *toward* the south? --Job 39:26
1428	pick le	We *pickle* cucumbers. We should be "DILL-igent" not to get ourselves in a *pickle.*
1429	ad vice	You don't need to take a person's *advice* to make him feel good, just ask for it. --L. Peter
1430	to bac co	Teens smoke *tobacco* thinking they look mature but they really look insecure.
1431	ar ti cle	I adopted no *article* from creeds but such as confirmed by the Bible. -John Jay, S. C. Justice
1432	drown	Many waters cannot quench love, neither can the floods *drown* it. --Song of Solomon 8:7
1433	li quid	Let the rain beat upon your head with silver *liquid* drops. --Langston Hughes
1434	dec ade	A *decade* is ten years.
1435	dis as ter	The truly noble spirit becomes more conspicuous in times of *disaster.* --Plutarch
1436	ves sel	A fool, like an empty *vessel*, makes the loudest sound.
1437	av e nue	*Avenue* is a French word for street.
1438	jan i tor	The word *janitor* comes from a Latin word meaning "doorkeeper."
1439	a gainst	No sin *against* a great God can be strictly a little sin. --Ralph Venning
1440	meth od	Though this be madness, yet there is *method* in it. --Shakespeare's *Hamlet*

Spelling Enrichments

FLAIR IN WRITING STYLE. Write original sentences using the new spelling words. In the middle of each sentence use an adverbial clause starting with one of these clause signal words: *where, when, while, since, if, although.* Underline all the spelling words used. Circle the adverbial clause.

For extra fun try to make every sentence include the word "pickle."

The <u>visitor</u> dropped a <u>pickle</u> (<u>where</u> I just mopped the floor.)

Note: A dependent clause is a set of words that have a subject and verb but does not make sense by itself. An adverbial clause is like a stretched-out adverb starting with one of the adverb signal words above plus a subject and a verb. The first sentence could have read: *She dropped a pickle there.* The adverb *there* would modify the verb *dropped.* Likewise the clause *where I just mopped the floor* modifies the verb dropped.

The <u>janitor</u> cried (when he dropped his <u>pickle</u>.) I can pass the <u>quiz</u> (if I eat a <u>pickle</u>.)

© 2003, Wanda Sanseri

Silent Final E Review

These twenty words have an example of every kind of Silent Final E. Watch for them as you go and chart them on the board in the same format at the original Silent Final E reference page. Write only the first example that illustrates each separate category (*feature, sleeve, avenue, advice, beige, pickle, where*).

fea ture	U said /U/ because of the E.	[R7]
neigh bor		
beige₃	Use EI; it says /A/. Add to **IE/EI Page**. G says /j/ because of the E.	[R9,3,7]
sleeve₂	English words do not end in V.	[R6,7]
pov er ty	Y usually says /i/ at the end of ..... English words do not end with I.	[R5,6]
vis i tor	I usually says /i/ at the end of a syllable.	[R5]
to ward		
pick le₄	CK is after a single vowel saying /i/. Every syllable must have a ...	[R25,7]
ad vice	I says /I/ and C says /s/ because of the E.	[R2,7]
to bac co	O said /O/ at ... Think /k/ twice for spelling but not normal speech.	[R4,29]
ar ti cle₄	I usually says /i/ at ... Every syllable must have a vowel.	[R5,7]
drown		
li quid	I usually says /i/ at ... Q always needs U. Dictionary splits *qu*.	[R5,1]
dec ade	[< Gk deka (ten)] A says /A/ because of the E. Add to **Number Page**.	[R7]
dis as ter	[<L dis (without) + aster (star)]	
ves sel	Think /s/ twice for spelling but not for normal speech.	[R29]
av e nue₂	E says /E/ at the end... English words do not end in U. Abbreviation: Ave.	[R4,7,12]
jan i tor	I usually says /i/ at the end of a syllable.	[R5]
a gainst	Think to say as A saying /A/ at the end of a syllable.	[R4]
meth od		

Spelling Enrichments

GRAMMAR. Nouns: Which spelling words can be used as nouns? Categorize them as a person (*janitor, visitor, neighbor*), place (*avenue, vessel*), thing (*sleeve, pickle, article, liquid, tobacco*) or idea (*disaster, poverty, method, advice*). Prepositions: Dictate the preposition list in SWR p.104 through *against*.

JOURNALISM. Dictate the following: *Newspapers use different types of writing. A news story may report a disaster such as the drowning of a neighbor. A feature article might give advice for making a better type of pickle or tell how a janitor provided poverty relief.*

Have students write an original human interest story about how a janitor arrived in time to save a child from drowning in beige liquid. Use as many spelling words as possible.

TIMED READING. Time the student reading Section R spelling words going across each two columns. For example: *prepare machine, entertain treason.* If the student stumbled over any words, have him read it again and try to beat his time. For a variation, take turns reading the two adjoining words and then make up an original oral sentence using the two words. Ex.: *prepare machine. I will prepare the sewing machine.*

Development of the English Language

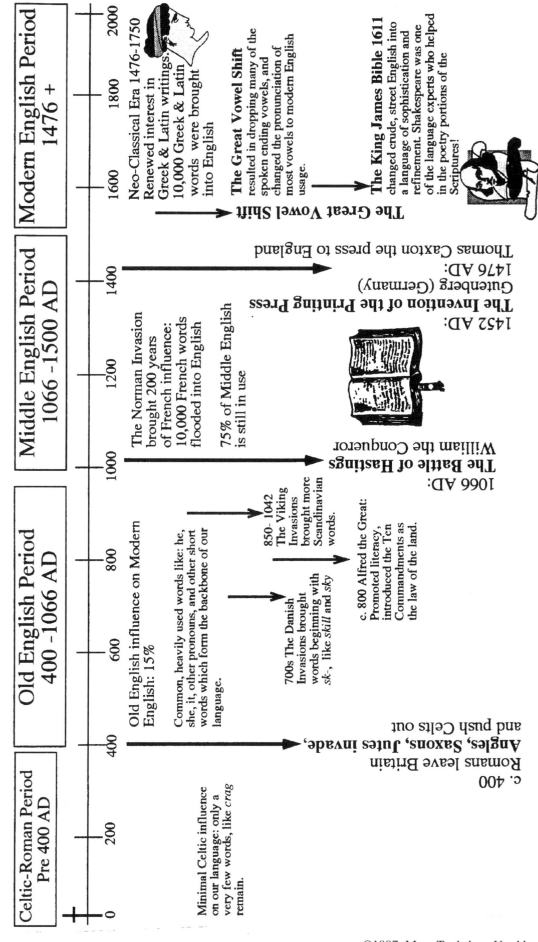

Celtic-Roman Period Pre 400 AD	Old English Period 400 -1066 AD	Middle English Period 1066 -1500 AD	Modern English Period 1476 +

0   200   400   600   800   1000   1200   1400   1600   1800   2000

Minimal Celtic influence on our language: only a very few words, like *crag* remain.

c. 400
Romans leave Britain
Angles, Saxons, Jutes invade,
and push Celts out

Old English influence on Modern English: 15%

Common, heavily used words like: he, she, it, other pronouns, and other short words which form the backbone of our language.

700s The Danish Invasions brought words beginning with *sk-*, like *skill* and *sky*

850- 1042 The Viking Invasions brought more Scandinavian words.

c. 800 Alfred the Great: Promoted literacy, introduced the Ten Commandments as the law of the land.

The Norman Invasion brought 200 years of French influence: 10,000 French words flooded into English

75% of Middle English is still in use

1066 AD:
The Battle of Hastings
William the Conqueror

1452 AD:
The Invention of the Printing Press
Gutenberg (Germany)

1476 AD:
Thomas Caxton the press to England

Neo-Classical Era 1476-1750 Renewed interest in Greek & Latin writings. 10,000 Greek & Latin words were brought into English

The Great Vowel Shift
resulted in dropping many of the spoken ending vowels, and changed the pronunciation of most vowels to modern English usage.

The Great Vowel Shift

The King James Bible 1611
changed crude, street English into a language of sophistication and refinement. Shakespeare was one of the language experts who helped in the poetry portions of the Scriptures!

Sources:
Children's: *Sumer is icumen in*, by Howard Greenfeld
The Story of English, by McCrum
Talk About English, by Janet Klausner

174

©1997, Mary Tanksley   Used by permission.

Spelling
Section S

"English spelling is like a map of the history of English words; it continues to carry letter groups that are leftovers from their Greek, Roman, Celtic, German, and, of course, English origins. They represent sounds long since forgotten. The spelling remained static while the sound of the words has changed. Each variation of the spelling of the same sound therefore indicates the historic derivation of the word that requires this particular spelling. Where the "f" sound, for instance, is spelled "ph," or the "s" sound "ps," the word has a Greek origin. In modern Greek and in some other derivative languages the "p" and the "s" are still both pronounced separately in words such as psychiatry."

--Dr. Hilde L. Mosse

"Words introduced from a foreign language into English generally retain the orthography of the original... The northern nations of Europe originally spoke much in gutturals. Thus *k* before *n* was once pronounced as in *knave, know,* the *gh* in *might,* and the *g* in *reign.* Pronunciation of words is softened in proportion to a national refinement of manners. In this progress, the English have lost the sound of most of the guttural letters, softening the sound of letters or suppressing those which are harsh or disagreeable."

--Noah Webster, 1789

The first 1560 words in this program (A through S) and their derivatives include more than 80% of all words we read and write.

Preliminaries. Phonograms: *ai, ar, ay, ea, er, ti, ou, ow.* Rules: 2, 3, 4, 5, 6, 7, 11, 16, 18, 20, 21, 24. Reference: Introduce **E's Dropping** and **Y's Exchanging Pages** SWR Steps 29, 34. If starting a new year, reteach **Consonant/Vowel, Multi-letter Phonogram** and **Silent Final E Pages**.

Words for Section S-1

1441	im par tial	He was not partial for one or the other; he was *impartial.*
1442	pos si ble	With God all things are *possible.*
1443	to tal	We cannot hide from God even in *total* darkness.
1444	par tic u lar	It is smart to be *particular* about the friends you choose.
1445	nat u ral	The great *natural* world is but another Bible. --Beecher
1446	tem po ra ry	The use of force alone is but *temporary.* --Edmund Burke
1447	pleas ant	How *pleasant* it is for brothers to dwell together in peace!
1448	grate ful	When we ATE we were *grATEful.*
1449	cer tain	We brought nothing into this world and it is *certain* we carry nothing out.
1450	se ri ous	Lord, help me be *serious* about more things, especially laughter.
1451	lo cal	Under what seemed to be a *local* dust cloud, the day grew darker and darker.
1452	op po site	The *opposite* of thoroughly is incompletely, carelessly, or partially.
1453	pe cu liar	There is a *peculiar* grace which boldest painters cannot trace. --Somerville
1454	bril liant	*Brilliant* scientists like George Washington Carver had lowly beginnings.
1455	di vine	The Hand that made us is *divine.* --Joseph Addison
1456	fer tile	A young mind is a *fertile* field to sow.
1457	o rig i nal	Adam is responsible for the *original* sin.
1458	hand y	I always keep a book *handy* so I can read when I have a spare moment.
1459	con stant	There is nothing more *constant* than change.
1460	anx ious	She is *anxious* to do the wrong thing correctly. --Saki

Spelling Enrichments

-LY ADVERBS. All these spelling words can be used as adjectives. By adding an -LY we can often change an adjective into an adverb. On a separate sheet of paper have the student first write the spelling words in the adjective form and then make the word into an adverb. Watch for Y's Exchanging words.

impartial -- impartially	*possible* -- possibly	*total* -- totally
particular -- particularly	*natural* -- naturally	*temporary* -- temporarily
pleasant -- pleasantly	*grateful* -- gratefully	*certain* -- certainly
serious -- seriously	*local* -- locally	*opposite* -- oppositely
peculiar -- peculiarly	*brilliant* -- brilliantly	*divine* -- divinely
fertile -- *fertilely*	*original* -- originally	*handy* -- handily
constant -- constantly	*anxious* -- anxiously	

ORIGINAL SENTENCES. Make sentences with all the spelling words. Use at least two of the spelling words in each sentence. Make one of them into an -LY Adverb. For example: *locally impartial, possibly opposite, totally peculiar, particularly brilliant, naturally divine, temporarily fertile, pleasantly original, gratefully handy, certainly constant, seriously anxious.*

Examples: The issue did not affect us so we could be *locally impartial.* That play was *particularly brilliant.* The *fertile* land *opposite* the river *originally* belonged to a *peculiar* family.

Y's Exchanging: If you haven't done so already, add these review words to the Y's Exchanging Page.

cry	cried	cry ing	Advanced Note: "injuring"
in ju ry	in ju ri es		follows R16 with the base word
bus y	bus i ly		"injure" rather than R24.
sat is fy	sat is fied	sat is fy ing	

im par tial	TI = /sh/. Delay introducing SH/TI Page until S-3.	[R11]
pos si ble	Think /s/ twice for spelling but .... Every syllable must have a vowel.	[R29,5,7]
to tal	O said /O/ at the end of a syllable.	[R4]
par tic u lar	U said /U/ at the end of a syllable.	[R4]
nat u ral	Root = nature. See **E's Dropping Page.**	[R4,16]
tem po ra ry	O said /O/ at the end.... English words do not end with I.	[R4,5,6]
pleas ant	please + -ant. Silent final E words commonly lose need for E when ...	[R16]
grate ful	A said /A/ because of the E. Dismiss L word.	[R7,21]
cer tain	C says /s/ before E. Think to spell /ser-tAn/. See SWR p. 89.	[R2]
se ri ous	E said /E/ at the end of a syllable. I usually says /i/ at the end...	[R4,5]
lo cal	[<L locus (place)]. O said /O/ at the end of a syllable.	[R4]
op po site	Think /p/ twice for spelling but ... O said /O/ at the end.... Odd job E.	[R29,4,7]
pe cu li ar	Think to spell /pE-cU-li-ar/; say /pE-cUl-yar/. See SWR p. 85.	[R4,5]
bril li ant	Think to spell /bril-li-ant/; say /bril-yant/. See SWR p. 85.	[R29,5]
di vine	I usually says /i/ at the end of a syllable. I said /I/ because of the E.	[R5,7]
fer tile		[R7]
o rig i nal	O said /O/ at the end... G says /j/ because of the I. I usually says /i/ at ...	[R4,3,5]
hand y	Unaccented Y stands in for I at the end of the word.	[R5,6]
con stant	[< L com- (together) + stare (to stand)].	
anx ious	x = /ks/; si = /sh/. The /s/ slides over to I to make /si/. /ank-sious/	[R20]

Spelling Enrichments

ANTONYMS. Prefixes meaning "not" include *im-, in-, non-, un-*. Reverse the meaning of as many spelling words as possible by simply adding or removing one of these prefixes.

partial --	impartial	pleasant --	unpleasant	possible --	impossible
grateful --	ungrateful	original --	unoriginal	fertile --	infertile
constant --	inconstant	local --	nonlocal	natural --	unnatural
particular --	nonparticular	certain --	uncertain		

Identify the spelling word that is the opposite of the following:

fake --	(original)	joking --	(serious)
permanent --	(temporary)	ordinary ---	(brilliant or peculiar)
calm --	(anxious)	inconvenient --	(handy)
partial --	(total)		

WRITE FOR CLARITY. These newspaper headlines can be easily misinterpreted because of misplaced modifiers. Can you make them more clear? *Local* high school dropouts cut in half. (The number of high school dropouts cut in half). Kids make *pleasant* snacks. (Pleasant snacks are made by kids.)

Preliminaries. Spelling Rules: Give timed review of 2, 4, 5, 6, 7, 9, 11, 12, 14, 16, 23, 24, 27, 28.
Phonograms: Quiz *ai, ar, ay, dge, ea, ed, ee, er, ew, gn, ie, kn, oa, oe, oi, or, ou, ow, oy, ph, th, ti*.
Reference Pages: Introduce or review **Number** and **1-1-1 Pages**. See SWR Steps 15, 32.

Words for Section S-2

1461	cen tu ry	Cent means a hundred, and *century* means a hundred years.
1462	cen ten ni al	*Centennial* means every hundred years.
1463	cen ti me ter	*Centimeter* means 1/100th of a meter.
1464	ex am ine	*Examine* me, O LORD, and prove me; try my mind and my heart. --Psalm 26:2
1465	ex am i na tion	*Examination* of the acts of government should be encouraged. --W. Henry Harrison
1466	mar ry	It is good to *marry* but be wary.
1467	mar riage	God by *marriage* makes two become one.
1468	con di tion	The *condition* upon which God hath given liberty to man is eternal vigilance. --J. Curran
1469	gov ern ment	A *government* should protect its people from foreign invasion.
1470	stopped	The mouth of those who speak lies shall be *stopped*. --Psalm 63:11
1471	knowl edge	He who has *knowledge* spares his words. --Proverbs 17:27
1472	the a ter	It seems nobody goes to the *theater* unless he has bronchitis.
1473	meg a phone	A *megaphone* is a large cone-shaped object that increases speech sound.
1474	be lief	The more I know of astronomy, the stronger my *belief* in God. --Heber Curtis
1475	be lieve	Give me liberty to know, to think, to *believe*, and to speak freely.
1476	a bil i ty	They gave after their *ability* to the work. --Ezra 2:69
1477	un ion	The motto of the USA is: *Union* means "out of many, one."
1478	be have	People respect a child who knows how to *behave*.
1479	be hav ior	Character is *behavior* a person exhibits when only God sees.--Dr. J.Kennedy
1480	course	Words are, of *course*, the most powerful drug used by mankind. --Rudyard Kipling

Spelling Enrichments

GRAMMAR. List the spelling words that can be used as nouns to identify a person, place, thing, or idea.
Nouns: *century, centennial, centimeter, examination, marriage, condition, government, knowledge, theatre, megaphone, belief, ability, union, behavior, course.*

Verbs: *examine, marry, stopped, believe, behave.*

MODIFIERS. The first set of words in section S are all adjectives that can be changed into adverbs by adding -LY. Use those words to modify these spelling words. Be sure to use the correct form. Remember adjectives modify nouns and adverbs modify verbs, adjectives, or other adverbs. Adjectives usually preceed nouns while adverbs can be either before or after the words modified. There are numerous possibilities. Examples:

impartial examination	*possibly believe*	*total behavior*	*peculiar marriage*
particular theater	*brilliant course*	*temporarily examine*	*pleasant union*
behave gratefully	*certain century*	*serious centennial*	*marry seriously*
local government	*naturally stopped*	*opposite belief*	*divine ability*
fertile condition	*originally stopped*	*handy megaphone*	*behave anxiously*
constant knowledge	*total centimeters*		

Root Words and Derivatives: We often make derivatives from English root words *(temporary: tempo-rariness, temporarily, contemporary)* . We can also use Greek and Latin word parts to make derivatives. For example *mega* means "large" in Greek. We do not consider *mega* a word in English but we have words like: megatons (a million tons), megameter (a million meters), megabucks (a great deal of money).

cen tu ry	[<L centum (hundred)]. Add to **Number Page**.	[R2,4,5,6]
cen ten ni al	C says /s/ because of the E.	[R2,29,5]
cen ti me ter	British = cen ti me tre ₄ Abbreviation: cm	[R2,5,4,12]
ex am ine₅	Odd job E. None of the first four types apply.	[R7]
ex am i na tion	Latin spelling for /sh/.	[R5,4,11]
mar ry	The 1 over the A shows we think /a-r/ and not /ar/.	[R29,5,6]
mar ri age	2-syllable, exaggerate to 3, See SWR p.88. **Y's Ex Page**.	[R29,24,5,7]
con di tion	I usually says /i/ at.... Use Latin spelling for /sh/.	[R5,11]
gov ern ment	Abbreviation: gov't.	[R12]
stopped	Add to **1-1-1 Page**.	[R14,28]
knowl edge	3-letter /j/ is after a single vowel that says /e/.	[R23]
the a ter	British: the a tre ₄ E said /E/ and /A/ at the end of...	[R4]
meg a phone	[<Gk. mega (large) + phone (sound)].	[R4,7]
be lief	E said /E/ at the end ... We use I before E except after C, if ...	[R4,9]
be lieve₂	English words do not end with V.	[R4,9,6,7]
a bil i ty	A said /A/ at the end... I usually says /i/ at ... English words...	[R4,5,6]
un i on	[<L unus (one)]. Think /Un-i-on/; say /Un-yon/. See SWR p. 85.	[R5]
be have	A said /A/ because of the E. English words do not end with V.	[R4,6,7]
be hav i or	Add a syllable for spelling. See SWR p. 85. **E's Dropping Page**.	[R4,5,16]
course₅	[<F cours (a running)]. Odd job E shows word is not plural.	[R7]

Spelling Enrichments

PREFIXES. Most of these spelling words can take one or more of these prefixes:
   amphi- (around, on both sides), *bi-* (two), *dis-* (not), *fore-* (before), *in-* (in), *inter-* (between), *mis-* (incorrectly, wrongly), *non-* (not), *pre-* (before), *re-* (back, again), *super-* (over, above), *tri-* (three), *un-* (not).

bicentennial, tricentennial, re-examine, re-examination, intermarry, remarry, remarriage, precondition, recondition, misgovernment, unstopped, foreknowledge, amphitheater, unbelief, disbelief, disbelieve, inability, disability, reunion, disunion, nonunion, misbehave, misbehavior, discourse.

Bonus: Can you think of other words using bi- and tri-? See SWR page 132 for more examples.

bicycle (2 wheels)	tricycle (3 wheels)
bisect (divide into 2)	triangle (3 sides and 3 angles)
bicuspid (double-pointed tooth)	tricuspid (three-pointed tooth)
biceps (2-headed muscle)	triceps (3-headed muscle)
bifocal (2 focuses)	trigraph (3 letters used to spell a single sound--igh, dge)
bilateral (2 sides)	trimonthly (every 3 months)

Preliminaries. Review especially Spelling Rules: 2, 4, 5, 6, 7, 9, 11, 16, 19, 25, 27.
      Phonograms: *au, aw, ch, ci, ck, ei, eigh, er, ey, gn, ie, igh, oo, ou, ough, sh, si, tch, th, ti.*
      Reference: Review or introduce **SH/TI, AEIOU,** and **IE/EI Pages**. See SWR Steps 18, 19, 40.
Space permitting add S-1, S-2 review that apply (impar**ti**al, examina**ti**on, condi**ti**on, bel**ie**ve, bel**ie**f).

Words for Section S-3

1481	doubt	Through the night of *doubt* and sorrow, onward goes the pilgrim band. --Gould
1482	mo tion	Let a good man obey every good *motion* rising in his heart.
1483	snooze	He who would *snooze* in church will lose a blessing.
1484	crawl	Below the cliff I could see the wrinkled sea *crawl.*
1485	wound	God's *wound* cures, sin's kiss kills. --W. Gurnall
1486	de sign	Great *design* demands a Designer.
1487	tie	I myself on a swiftly tilting planet stand before a glass and *tie* my *tie.* --C. Aiken
1488	men tion	Praise the Lord, make *mention* that His name is exalted. --Isaiah 12:4
1489	as sist	I need for you to *assist* me with this math problem.
1490	nick el	What this country needs is a good five-cent *nickel.* --Franklin Adams, 1932
1491	con fes sion	*Confession* is good for the soul.
1492	e mo tion	*Emotion* (fear, sorrow, envy, and hatred) causes most sickness. --Dr. McMillan
1493	mo ment	He who plans for now but not eternity, is wise for a *moment*, but a fool forever.
1494	con cert	I heard a beautiful violin concerto at the *concert.*
1495	sym pa thy	*Sympathy* means to feel with someone else.
1496	fi nal	Do you know five reasons for a silent *final* E?
1497	sys tem	Can you name in order the nine planets in the solar *system*?
1498	maj es ty	O Lord, the *majesty* and glory of Your name fills the earth and overflows heaven.
1499	bank rupt	*Bankrupt* literally means "bank broke." A bankrupt person cannot pay his debts.
1500	mil lion	A *million* dollars and a pound of hay are worth the same on Judgment Day.

Spelling Enrichments

SUFFIXES. Make as many derivatives of the current spelling words as possible with these suffixes.

     vowel suffixes: -aire, -al, -ant, -ary, -atic, -ed, -er, -ic, -ing, -ism, -ist, -ity, -ize, -o
     consonant suffixes: -cy, -ful, -less, -ly

doubt -- doubter, doubting, doubtless, doubtful, doubted
snooze -- snoozing, snoozed
wound -- wounded, wounding
tie -- tied, tying (to avoid 2 I's we change I to Y)
assist -- assisting, assisted, assistant
confession -- confessional
moment -- momentary
sympathy -- sympathize
final -- finalize, finalist, finally, finality
bankrupt -- bankruptcy, bankrupted, bankrupting

motion -- motionless, motioned, motioning
crawl -- crawled, crawling, crawler
design -- designer, designing, designed
mention -- mentioning, mentioned
nickel -- nickeled, nickeling [GB nickelled]
emotion -- emotional, emotionalism
concert -- concerto, concerted, concerting
majesty -- majestic, majestically
system -- systematic, systematize
million -- millionaire

Dictionary Skills

Teach the students how to look up a word in the dictionary and determine its part of speech. The part of speech is an italicized abbreviation. *v.* (verb), *n.* (noun), *pron.* (pronoun), *prep.* (preposition), *adj.* (adjective), *adv.* (adverb), *conj.* (conjunction), *interj.* (interjection).

doubt	[<L duo (2) + bito (go)]. Think silent B for spelling.		
mo tion	O said /O/ at the end ... Use Latin spelling for /sh/.	**SH/TI Page**	[R4,11]
snooze₅	Show how odd job E is not one of the first four kinds.		[R7]
crawl			
wound³	Same spelling, different sound: wound (a clock); wound³ (hurt).		
de² sign	E said /E/ at end of a syllable. I said /I/ before 2 consonants.		[R4,19]
tie²	Use I before E except...	**IE/EI Page**	[R9]
men tion	Use Latin spelling for /sh/.	**SH/TI Page**	[R11]
as sist	Think /s/ twice for spelling but not ... Add *assistantship* to **SH/TI Page**.		[R29]
nick el	2-letter /k/ is used after a single vowel that says /i/.		[R25]
con fes sion	[<L com- (together) + fateri (acknowledge)]. Root = confess.	**SH/TI Page**	[R11]
e mo tion	[<L e- (out) + movere (move)].	**SH/TI Page**	[R4,11]
mo ment	O said /O/ at the end of a syllable.		[R4]
con cert	[<L con- (together) + certo (strive)]. C says /s/ because of the E.		[R2]
sym pa thy	[<Gk syn- (together) + pathos (suffering)].		[R4,5,6]
fi nal	I usually says /i/ at the end of a syllable, but may say /I/.		[R5]
sys tem	Y = Greek I.		
maj es ty	Y usually says /i/ at the end of a syllable. English words do not end with I.		[R5,6]
bank rupt			
mil li on	[<G mille (thousand)]. See SWR p. 85.	**Number Page**	[R29,5]

Spelling Enrichments

GRAMMAR. Many words can be used as more than one part of speech. For example, the words *scale* and *count* can be used either as a noun or a verb.

> I'd rather look at the *scale* after I *scale* the mountain.
> I would rather meet the *count* than *count* my gold.

Make as many sentences as possible containing new spelling words used as both nouns and verbs. Check the dictionary to see which words can be both.

Do you *doubt* the man's *doubt*?
I *motion* that we accept the *motion*.
I'll *snooze* while you're taking a *snooze*.
Can the baby *crawl* the crab *crawl*?
You can *wound* my heart as easily as you *wound* a clock.

I can *design* a colorful floral *design*.
He can *tie* the *tie*.
Did you *mention* my honorable *mention*?
Will you *assist* the coach in demonstrating a basketball *assist*?

Preliminaries. Review <u>Spelling Rules</u>: 2, 4, 5, 6, 7, 9, 10, 11, 12, 17, 19, 24, 25.

   <u>Phonograms</u>: *ai, au, aw, ck, eigh, er, ie, gn, kn, oo, or, ou, ough, ow, ph, sh, si, tch, ti, th, wh, wr.*
   <u>Reference Pages</u>: Review or introduce **Plural Page** from SWR Step 27.

Words for Section S-4

1501	sleigh	The horse knows the way to carry the *sleigh* through the white and drifted snow --Child
1502	af fair	Stay out of trouble. A bad *affair* is easier to enter than to exit. --Aesop
1503	par a graph	A *paragraph* should have more than one sentence on the same topic.
1504	is land	The silent "s" in *island* was added by a scribe mistaking "insula" for the root word.
1505	am bi tion	*Ambition* is the grand enemy of all peace. --John Cowper Powys
1506	tem per a ture	By God's design a *temperature* triggers our immune system.
1507	o pin ion	Refusing to have an *opinion* is a way of having one, isn't it? --Luigi Pirandello
1508	dif fer ence	Old boys have playthings as well as young ones; the only *difference* is the price.
1509	on ion	To rain a shower of commanded tears, an *onion* will do. --Shakespeare
1510	pis tol	At the beginning of a new year, some ring a bell or fire a *pistol.*
1511	re cess	Milton considered a quiet spot for meditation a "happy place, our sweet *recess."*
1512	can vas	*Canvas,* a coarse cloth made of hemp, is used to make tents or sails for ships.
1513	dic tion a ry	I begin with the Bible to learn a new language, which I can read without a *dictionary.* -Macaulay
1514	com mu ni ty	A *community* is made up of people with common interest or common laws.
1515	van i ty	*Vanity* plays tricks on our memory. --Joseph Conrad
1516	gro cer y	A *grocery* is a grocer's store where originally spices and vegetables were sold.
1517	your self	You need to see *yourself* as God sees you in order to experience His forgiveness.
1518	mush room	A bedroom is a room with a bed but a *mushroom* is not a room with a mush.
1519	cel er y	I like to crunch on carrot sticks and *celery.*
1520	gal lows	So they hanged Haman on the *gallows* that he had prepared for Mordecai. --Esther

Spelling Enrichments

PLURALS.   Student should write the spelling rule for plurals skipping four lines between each phrase to save room for examples:
   To make a word plural just add an -S. . .
   UNLESS the word ending hisses. . .
   Changes. . .
   Or Just ends with O. In these cases add -es.
   Occasional words have no change, an internal change, or a foreign spelling.

Write the plural form of each spelling word, placing the word under the related phrase.
   To make a word plural just add an -S: sleighs, affairs, paragraphs, islands, ambitions, temperatures, opinions, differences, onions, pistols, mushrooms.
   UNLESS the word ending hisses: recesses, canvases
   Changes: dictionaries, communities, vanities, groceries, yourselves
   Occasional words have no change: celery, gallows

Dictionary Skills. Teach the students to find the etymology of words. This information will be in square brackets. Ex. **church** . . . [OE *circe* <Gk. *kyriakon (doma)* (house) of the Lord < *kyrios* lord < *kyros* power]. The word *circe* from which church developed was used in Old English and came from the Greek word *kyriakon* (appearing in *kyriakon doma* meaning "house of the Lord"), which was derived from the word *kyrios* meaning "Lord," which came from another Greek word *kyros* meaning "power."

sleigh		
af fair	Think both F's for spelling but not for normal speech.	[R29]
par a graph	[< Gk para- (beside) + graph (write)] A said /A/ at the end of a syllable.	[R4]
is land	I may say /I/ before two consonants. Abbreviation: Is.	[R19,12]
am bi tion	[<L ambi- (around) + ire (go)] I usually says /i/ at ... TI spells /sh/ at ...	[R5,11]
tem per a ture	[<L temperatura <tempus (time, season)] A said /A/ ... . U said /U/...	[R4,7]
o pin i on	Think to spell /O-pin-i-on/. Say /O-pin-yon/. See SWR p. 85.	[R4,5]
dif fer ence	[< L dif (apart) + ferre (carry)] Oxymoron: same difference	[R29,2,7]
on i on	Think to spell /on-i-on/. Say /on-yon/. See SWR p. 85.	[R5]
pis tol		
re cess	E said /E/ at the end... C says /s/ before E. We often double S...	[R4,2,17]
can vas	[<OF canevas (hemp)]	
dic tion a ry	[<L dictio (diction)]	[R11,4,5,6]
com mu ni ty	[<L com- (together) + men (people)]	[R29,4,5,6]
van i ty	Y usually says /i/ at the end of a word. English words do not end with I.	[R5,6]
gro cer y		[R4,2,5,6]
your self	Compound: your + self	
mush room	[< F mousseron] *Mushroom* is NOT the compound for mush + room.	[R10]
cel er y	C says /s/ because of the E. English words do not end with I.	[R2,5,6]
gal lows	Think /l/ twice for spelling, but not for normal speech.	[R29]

Spelling Enrichments

ALPHABETIZE. Organize the spelling words in alphabetical order. Write them neatly in a column going down the page:

affair, ambition, canvas, celery, community, dictionary, difference, gallows, grocery, island, mushroom, onion, opinion, paragraph, pistol, recess, sleigh, temperature, vanity, yourself

ETYMOLOGY. Beside the alphabetized list of words, write the etymology (word origins) given in the dictionary. The meanings of the abbreviations are given in the front of the dictionary.

ORIGINAL PARAGRAPH. Write from dictation the following paragraph titled "A Hot Island."

In the *island community* the *temperature* sizzled. Crops like *celery, mushrooms,* and *onions* grew well, but so did tempers. Two *grocery* workers with great *vanity* and strong *ambition* foolishly tried to settle a *difference* with *pistols*. This sad *affair* ended with one man killed and the other sentenced to the *gallows*. The moral of the story is to stay cool even when it's hot.

Preliminaries Rules: 2, 3, 4, 5, 6, 7, 8, 9, 11, 12, 23, 24. Reference: **ER** and **Plus Endings Pages.**
Phonograms: *ar, au, ch, ci, dge, ear, ei, er, ie, igh, ir, kn, or, ph, th, ti, ur, wor.* Advanced: *ge.* Step 38

Words for Section S-5

1521	el e phant	God made the great whale, the *elephant,* and the little worm. --McGuffey
1522	ser geant	Conscience is God's *sergeant* He employs to arrest the sinner. --William Gurnall
1523	com pan ion	Sin has the devil for its father, shame for its *companion,* and death for its wages.
1524	af flic tion	*Affliction* may be lasting, but it is not everlasting. --Thomas Watson
1525	au di ence	An auditorium enhances the auditory part of a program for an *audience.*
1526	mu si cian	A *musician* is commended not that he played long, but that he played well. -Shute
1527	niece	My *nIEce* wants a pIEce of pIE.
1528	bach e lor	HE was a *bacHElor* until he was blessed with a wife.
1529	col lege	Not everyone needs to go to *college* to be successful.
1530	so ci e ty	As are families, so is *society* --W.M. Thayer
1531	fright en	He who sings will *frighten* away his ills. --Cervantes
1532	ac knowl edge	In all your ways *acknowledge* Him. --Proverbs 3:15
1533	pur chase	You cannot *purchase* wisdom with gold. --Job 28:15
1534	ac cuse	Do not *accuse* others falsely.
1535	pres sure	*Pressure* can make a man or a diamond. --M. Alcala
1536	ar rive	Our guests are expected to *arrive* before dinner.
1537	af fect	Cold will *affect* the body.
1538	lis ten	God does not *LISTen* to the prayer LIST of the proud. --Hebrew proverb
1539	in ves ti gate	Sherlock Holmes loves to *investigate* strange crimes.
1540	sup ply	My God shall *supply* all your needs.

Spelling Enrichments

DICTATION. Dictate either some of the sentences above or some sentences you compose using as many spelling words as possible. Examples: The *audience listened* to the *musician.* The *sergeant purchased* a *supply* of *elephants.* Neither *companion arrived* at *college.* Her *frightened niece accused* the *bachelor. Investigate* the way *affliction affects society. Acknowledge* the *pressure* caused by the *sergeant's arrival.*

SUBJECT AND VERB AGREEMENT. The first ten words can be used as subjects in a sentence and the words in the facing column can be used as verbs. Combine these words to make original sentences, taking care to make the subjects and verbs agree. If the subject is singular, the verb must also be singular. If the subject is plural the verb must also be plural.

We CANNOT say:	elephant frighten	(singular subject/ plural verb)
We CAN say:	elephant frighten**s**	(singular subject/ singular verb)
	elephant**s** frighten	(plural subject/ plural verb)

Does adding an -S make elephant plural? (yes) Does adding an -S make frighten plural? (no)

Adding an -S to a noun makes it plural *(girl/girls).* Adding an -S to a third person verb usually makes it singular *(Girl sings/girls sing).*

Homographs. Homographs are spelled the same but have different meanings and different origins. Examples: ball (round object), ball (formal dance); bowl (round dish), bowl (play game with a ball); list (series of words), list (tilt to one side); unaffected (not influenced), unaffected (sincere).

el e phant	E said /E/ at the end of a syllable.	[R4]
ser geant	er = /ar/; ge = /j/. See SWR p. 81. Abbreviation: sgt.	[R3,12]
com pan i on	Root = company Change Y to I. Add syllable for spelling (SWR p. 85).	[R24]
af flic tion	Root = afflict. **SH/TI Page.**	[R29,11]
au di ence₃	[<OF audire (hear)] I usually says /i/ at... C says /s/ because of the E.	[R5,2,7]
mu si cian	U said /U/ at the end... I usually says /i/ at... CI says /sh/ at...**SH/TI Pg.**	[R4,5,11]
niece₃	Use I before E except... Add to **IE/EI Pg**. C says /s/ because of the E...	[R9,2,7]
bach e lor	Think to spell /bach-E-lor/.	[R4]
col lege₃	Think /l/ twice for spelling... G says /j/ because of the E.	[R29,3,7]
so ci e ty	O said /O/ at the end...C says /s/... Y stands in for I at the end.	[R4,2,5,6]
fright en	Root = fright	
ac knowl edge	Root = know G says /j/ because... 3 letter /j/ is used after /e/.	[R3,23]
pur chase	Think A saying /A/ because of the E. Add to **ER Page**.	[R7]
ac cuse	Think /k/ twice for spelling... U said /U/ because of the E.	[R29,7]
pres sure	S before U can say /sh/. U said /U/ because of the E.	[R7]
ar rive	2 reasons for E: I said /I/... English words do not end with V.	[R6,7]
af fect	[<L ad- (to) + facere (do)]	[R29]
lis ten	Think silent T for spelling. *A good LISTener may LIST to one side.*	
in ves ti gate	I usually says /i/ at the end... A says /A/ because of the E.	[R5,7]
sup ply		[R29,5,6]

Spelling Enrichments

SUBJECT/ VERB AGREEMENT. Write the simple subject/ verb combinations making them first present tense singular and then present tense plural. Watch for the **Y's Exchanging Rule**.

singular	plural	
elephant frightens	elephants frighten	
sergeant acknowledges	sergeants acknowledge	
companion purchases	companions purchase	
niece affects	nieces affect	
audience pressures	audiences pressure	
musician arrives	musicians arrive	
niece accuses	nieces accuse	
bachelor listens	bachelors listen	
college investigates	colleges investigate	
society supplies	societies supply	(Remember to change the Y to I!)

Note: The problem of subject-verb agreement does not arise when we use simple past verbs except the verb "be" (elephant frightened/ elephants frightened; elephant **is** frightened/ elephants **are** frightened).

Preliminaries. Review <u>Spelling Rule Cards</u>: 1, 2, 3, 4, 5, 7, 9, 17, 22, 24. <u>Phonograms</u>: Read all 70 in 75 seconds. Quiz *ar, au, ch, ea, ee, ei, er, ie, ng, oo, or, qu, th, ti, ur.* <u>Reference</u>: **Homophone Page.** SWR Step 30.

Words for Section S-6

1541	there fore	God made him; *therefore*, let him pass for a man. --Shakespeare
1542	wis dom	Value *wisdom* over gold. --New England Primer
1543	peace	Some people sell their *peace* in eternity to get a toy. --Shakespeare
1544	a bun dance	Out of the *abundance* of the heart the mouth speaks.
1545	too	The Bible is all pure, all sincere; nothing *too* much; nothing wanting. --J. Locke
1546	quar rel	He who forgives ends the *quarrel.* --African proverb
1547	hand ker chief	Her *HANDkerchief* is in my HAND.
1548	ceil ing	How did God design the fly so it could walk on the *ceiling?*
1549	rein	We need to *rein* our tongues so they will heal and help and not hurt others.
1550	nei ther	Changing countries or beds cures *neither* a bad manager nor a fever. --B. Franklin
1551	fur ther	You are to follow no man *further* than he follows Christ.
1552	teeth	Baby *teeth* are drop-outs. --Marjorie Frank
1553	piece	The woman rejoiced greatly when she found the gold *piece* she had lost.
1554	steak	Tough as a *steak* was Yukon Jake, hard-boiled as a picnic egg. --Paramore
1555	of ten	The most rewarding things in life are *often* ones that look impossible.
1556	mor sel	He rolls it under his tongue as a sweet *morsel.* --Matthew Henry
1557	ox y gen	We must have *oxygen* to breathe.
1558	car riage	We look for happiness in boats and *carriage* rides. --Horace
1559	sauce	The best *sauce* in the world is hunger. --Miguel de Cervantes
1560	wit ness	The *WITness* had dry WIT.

Spelling Enrichments

COMPOUND WORDS. Dictate to loose leaf paper the following review words:
 apple, beef, buck, cross, eye, head, master, more, pan, some, time, times, under, work.

On a new sheet of paper, quiz the new words in a single column. Correct spelling. Have students combine review words with new words to make as many compound words as possible.

peace --	peacetime		*steak* --	beefsteak
quarrel --	quarrelsome		*often* --	oftentimes
further --	furthermore		*carriage* --	undercarriage
teeth --	eyeteeth, buckteeth		*sauce* --	applesauce, saucepan
piece --	cross-, eye-, head-, master-, -meal, -work		*witness* --	eyewitness

POETRY. Dictate the following poem by Christina Rossetti titled "Who Has Seen the Wind?"
Who has seen the wind?
Neither I nor you;
But when the leaves hang trembling,
The wind is passing through.

Homophones [homo (same) + phone (sound)]

Often words sound the same but are spelled differently and have different meanings.   At least four of these words have homophones: *piece, peace*; *too,* two, to; *rein,* rain (after T-2 reign); *steak,* stake.

there, fore	O said /O/ because of the E.		[R7]
wis dom	[<OE wis (wise)]		
peace,	C says /s/ because of the E; otherwise it would say /k/		[R2,7]
a bun dance,	A said /A/ at the end of a syllable. C says /s/ because of the E.		[R4,7]
too	An added O means *also*.		
quar rel	Q always needs U. Think /r/ twice for spelling but not for normal speech.		[R1,29]
hand ker chief	I before E ...	**IE/EI Page**	[R9]
ceil ing	Except after C... C says /s/ before E.	**IE/EI Page**	[R2,9]
rein	If we say /A/... [< L retinere (hold back)]	**IE/EI Page**	[R9]
nei ther	Exceptions we learned... [<ME ne- (not) + either (either)]	**IE/EI Page**	[R9]
fur ther		**ER Page**	
teeth	Mutated plural of *tooth*.		[R22]
piece,	I before E... C says /s/ ...	**IE/EI Page**	[R9,2,7]
steak			
of ten	[<OE oft (often)] If you can hear /t/ you don't have to mark it silent.		
mor sel	[<OF mors (a bite)]		
ox y gen	Y usually says /i/ at... G may say /j/ before E.		[R5,3]
car ri age	Root = carry 2-syllable word; exaggerate to 3 for spelling. SWR p. 88.		[R29,24,7]
sauce,	C says /s/ because of the E.		[R2,7]
wit ness	Often double S after a single... -SS used to end non-plural base words.		[R17]

Spelling Enrichments

GRAMMAR.   Look up the parts of speech for the spelling words in the dictionary.

Adverbs. List any words that can be used as an adverb *(further, often, too)*.

Nouns / verbs. Find words that can be both nouns and verbs. Hint: A noun can take an article (a, an, the); a verb can be made into past tense: witness (a witness, witnessed); piece (a piece, pieced); quarrel (a quarrel, quarreled); sauce (a sauce, sauced); rein (a rein, reined).

ANTONYMS. Teacher should call out the following words and have student write the spelling word that means the opposite.) Can you do others?

ignorance / _____ (wisdom)	rarely /_____ (often)	scarcity /_____ (abundance)
carbon dixoide /_____ (oxygen)	war / _____ (peace)	big portion/__ (morsel)
floor / _____ (ceiling)	agree / _____ (quarrel)	whole / _____ (piece)

COMPOSITION. Make a proposal using as many spelling words from Section S as possible. Example: *Acknowledge* the *wisdom* of avoiding needless *quarrels*.   List three reasons to hold the *rein* on anger. Use the word *therefore* to summarize the value of *peace*.

Advanced Phonograms with Word Examples

ae	Greek and Latin = /A/ Greek and Latin = /E/	aerospace (1867) algae	aerosol (1868) archaeology	aerobics Caesar
ah	Hebrew = /ah/ Swedish/ Native American	hallelujah (2000) dahlia	Jehovah Utah	Jonah
ai[2]	Old French/ Polynesian /I/	aisle (1719)	Hawaii	aioli
aigh	Old English = /A/	straight (1572)		
au[2]	French = /O/	chauffeur (1975)	chauvinism	
augh	Old English = /aw/ Old English = /af/	caught (1072) laugh (1099)	taught (1073) laughter (1100)	naughty (1143)
ay[2]	Native American = /I/	bayou	cayenne	kayak
cu **cu**[2]	/k/ U added so C = /k/ /kw/ U = /w/ as in QU.	biscuit (1602) cuisine	circuit	
eau	French = /O/	bureau (1824)	plateau	chateau
et	French = /A/	bouquet (1673)	ballet	gourmet
eu **eu**[2]	/OO/ /U/	neutral (1691) Europe	amateur (1908) eulogy	sleuth feud
ge	French G = /j/	sergeant (1522)	pigeon (1701)	surgeon (1770)
gh	Italian G = /g/ Old English = /g/	spaghetti (1779) ghost	ghetto ghastly	aghast
gi	French G = /j/	region (1293)	religion (1303)	allegiance (1998)
gu	French = /g/	guide (803) guess (1647) guarantee (1964)	guilty (1148) vague (1886) rogue	guest (1167) fatigue (1959) tongue
gu[2]	/gw / U = /w/ as in QU	language (1114) anguish	distinguish (1731) languish	jaguar penguin
pn **ps** **pt**	Greek = /n/ Greek = /s/ Greek = /t/	pneumonia (1996) pneumatics psalm, psychic, psychiatrist (No examples in *Wise Guide*.) ptomaine, Ptolemy (No examples in *Wise Guide*.)		
qu[2]	Spanish / French = /k/	conquer (851) mosquito (1773)	liquor (1639) critique	bouquet (1673) antique (1851)
rh	Greek = /r/	rhyme (1860)	rhinoceros (1982)	myrrh
sc	Latin = /s/	scissors (1620) descent (1680)	science (1671) consciousness (1803)	descend (1679) scepter
x[2]	Greek = /z/	Xerox®	xylophone	Xerxes

Spelling
Section T

Some teachers add dictionary work at these upper levels. Students can check words for word derivation, meaning, and part of speech. We especially desire to impart an appreciation for the rich heritage of the language.

"The great quality of English is its teeming vocabulary, 80 percent of which is foreign-born. Precisely because its roots are so varied -- Celtic, Germanic (German, Scandinavian, and Dutch), and Romance (Latin, French, and Spanish) -- it has words in common with virtually every language in Europe: German, Yiddish, Dutch, Flemish, Danish, Swedish, French, Italian, Portuguese, and Spanish. In addition, almost any page of the *Oxford English Dictionary* or *Webster's Third* will turn up borrowings from Hebrew and Arabic, Hindi-Urdu, Bengali, Malay, Chinese, the languages of Java, Australia, Tahiti, Polynesia, West Africa, and even from one of the aboriginal languages of Brazil. It is the enormous range and varied source of this vocabulary, as much as the sheer numbers and geographical spread of its speakers, that makes English a language of such unique vitality."

--The Story of English
by Robert McCrum, William Cran, and Robert MacNeil

Preliminaries

Phonograms: Quiz *ar, ch, ci, ear, ee, er, ir, or, sh, si, ti, ur, wor.* Introduce *aigh* (SWR Step 38).
Review Spelling Rule Cards: 2, 3, 4, 5, 6, 7, 8, 10, 11, 16, 24.
Reference Pages: If beginning a new school year at this point, first rebuild **Consonant/Vowel, Multi-letter Phonogram, Silent Final E, SH/TI** and **ER Pages** (SWR Steps 9, 10, 17, 18, 26).

Words for Section T-1

1561	com mence	Eighth grade *commence*ment celebrates when a student can *commence* high school.
1562	cru cial	Reading is *crucial* to education.
1563	re cent	The *recent* eruption of Mt. Saint Helens validates creation science.
1564	se vere	When the darkness is the most *severe,* the promises of God shine more brightly.
1565	en ti tle	The sacrifices Jesus made for me *entitle* Him to my praise.
1566	fa mil iar	Many with whom we are *familiar* become like family.
1567	im pos si ble	With God nothing is *impossible.*
1568	a muse	Some people *amuse* themselves with sports, music, games, or fishing.
1569	ac com pa ny	Will you *accompany* us on the piano?
1570	gen u ine	Virtue and piety are the *genuine* fruits of holiness. --Noah Webster, 1828
1571	e lec tri cal	The *electrical* effects added excitement.
1572	straight	The crooked shall be made *straight* and the rough places plain. --Isa. 40:4
1573	po lit i cal	When *political* leaders show integrity, the people live in peace.
1574	ra cial	The early church unleashed a flood of kindness in a world of *racial* strife.
1575	u ni ver sal	It's a *universal* law: the other line moves faster.
1576	speech	Let your *speech* always be with grace, seasoned with salt. --Colossians 4:6
1577	cir cu lar	Something *circular* is shaped round like a circle.
1578	ar gue	To *argue* from mercy to sin is the devil's logic. --James Janeway
1579	re al	The *real* problem is in the hearts and minds of men. --Albert Einstein
1580	wor ship	It's only when men begin to *worship* that they begin to grow. --Pres. Coolidge

Spelling Enrichments

CONSONANT SUFFIXES. These words can take one or more of these consonant suffixes: -ful, -less, -ly, -ment, -ness. Write the spelling words and then the derivative(s).

commence	commencement	*electrical*	electrically
crucial	crucially	*straight*	straightly, straightness
recent	recently, recentness	*political*	politically
severe	severely	*racial*	racially
entitle	entitlement	*universal*	universally
familiar	familiarly	*speech*	speechless, speechlessly
impossible	impossibly*	*circular*	circularly
amuse	amusement	*argue*	argument **
accompany	accompaniment [R24]	*real*	really
genuine	genuinely	*worship*	worshipful

* After word endings like -BLE, we utilize the L in the word for part of the -LY. Not *im-pos-si-ble-ly,* but *im-pos-si-bly.*
** We normally don't drop E before a consonant suffix. U is no longer at the end. U says /U/ at the end of a syllable [R4].

Ti...Ci...Si. If you haven't already this year, format the **SH/TI Page**. Discuss the ways to spell /sh/. Hold up the SH card. "Used at the beginning of a word *(shoes)*, the end of a syllable *(finish)*, but not at the beginning of any syllable after the first one except for the ending -ship *(hardship)*." Hold up TI, CI, SI. (Used at the beginning of any syllable after the first one). Under TI dictate several review words from Section S: *affliction, ambition, motion, mention*. Under CI add: *musician*. Under SI add: *confession*. Watch for more words to add to this page from Section T. Focus on CI and SI. TI words are a dime a dozen.

com menc̣e̱ ⁻₌3	Sound /m/ twice for spelling but ... C says /s/ because....	[R29,2,7]
cru̱ c̣ial	[<L crux (cross; like the fork in a road)]. **SH/TI Page**	[R4,11]
re̱ cent	E said /E/ at the end of a syllable. C says /s/ before E.	[R4,2]
se̱ vére̱	E said /E/ at the end of a syllable. E said /E/ because	[R4,7]
en ti tle̱ ₌4	I said /I/ at the end of a syllable. Every syllable must have a vowel.	[R5,7]
fa̱ mil i ar	Think to spell /fA-mil-i-ar/; say /fA-mil-yar/. See SWR p. 85.	[R4,5]
im pos si ble̱ ₌4	Each letter in SI is sounded separately.	[R29,5,7]
a mus̃e̱	A said /A/ at the end of a syllable. U said /U/ because of the E.	[R4,7]
ac com pa̱ ny	Root = *company*. See SWR p.82.	[R29,4,5,6]
gen u̱ ine̱ ₌5	[<L genuinus (natural)]. G said /j/... U said /U/... Odd job E.	[R3,4,7]
e̱ lec tri cal	Root = *electric*. E said /E/ at the end of ... I said /i/ at ...	[R4,5]
straight	aigh = Old English /A/.	
po̱ lit i cal	[<Gk. polis (city)]. O said /O/ and I said /i/ at the end....	[R4,5]
ra̱ c̣ial	Root = *race*. A said /A/ at ... CI can spell /sh/ at ... **SH/TI Page**	[R4,11]
u̱ ni ver sal	[<L unus (one) + vertere (to turn)]. U said /U/ at the end ...	[R4,5]
speech	Can S say /z/ here? Why not?	[R27]
cir cu̱ lar	[<L circus (ring)]. C said /s/ because .... U said /U/ at ... **ER Page**	[R2,4]
ar gue̱ ₂	English words do not end with U.	[R6,7]
re̱ al	Oxymoron: real phony. E said /E/ at the end of a syllable.	[R4]
wor ship	OR may say /er/ when W comes before OR. **ER, SH/TI Pgs**.	[R8,10]

Spelling Enrichments

ALPHABETIZE. Ask the students to organize the words into alphabetical order: *accompany, amuse, argue, circular, commence, crucial, electrical, entitle, familiar, genuine, impossible, political, racial, real, recent, severe, speech, straight, universal, worship*. (See SWR Step 36.)

ALLITERATION. In alliteration two or more words start with the SAME FIRST SOUND. For example: *Sally sold sea shells*. Combine spelling words that alliterate *(severe speech, real recent racial, accompany amusement)*. Look for words in Section S to form more examples: *genuine general, universal union, finally frighten the familiar, serious century, circular system*.

Dictate sentences with spelling words using alliteration. Students can also compose their own examples.

It is <u>impossible</u> to sew <u>straight</u> <u>circular</u> seams.   <u>Commence</u> the <u>crucial</u> craft class.

The <u>severe</u> snow storm swirled <u>straight</u> to Salem.   <u>Recently</u> Ryan had <u>real</u> <u>racial</u> rage.

ORIGINAL SENTENCES. Make original sentences using the words across from each other. Underline the words. Example: *<u>Commence</u> the <u>electrical</u> project. It is <u>crucial</u> to draw the line <u>straight</u>.*

Preliminaries. Review especially <u>Spelling Rules</u>: 2, 4, 5, 7, 9, 11, 12, 16, 18, 23, 28.

<u>Phonograms</u>: *ai, au, aw, ay, dge, ea, ed, eigh, ei, er, ey, gn, ie, igh, ir, kn, ou, ph, si, ti.*

<u>Reference</u>: Introduce or review **IE/ EI Page** and possibly the **Abbrev. Page** (SWR Steps 40, 25).

<u>Motivational Tip</u>: "This list has words we can abbreviate, a homophone, and a homograph. Can you spot them?" SWR p.133 (minute -- min; television -- t.v. or TV). SWR p. 150 (*reign* -- rain, rein).

Words for Section T-2

1581	pierced	The scripture said, 'They shall look on him whom they *pierced.*" --John 19:37
1582	de ceived	The world is still *deceived* with ornament...a gracious voice obscures the show of evil. --Shakespeare
1583	reign	The kingdom of God *reigns* wherever God rules over human heart as King.
1584	weird	Either *weird* foreign sovereign forfeited leisure.
1585	di vi sion	*Division* is better than agreement in evil. --George Hutcheson
1586	ac cel er ate	Unpunished sin will *accelerate* the ruin of a people.
1587	ap pear ance	The *appearance* of religion only on Sunday proves that it is only an *appearance*. --J. Adams
1588	ab sence	We missed you in your *absence*.
1589	cir cle	Sin is like a *circle* in water when a stone is thrown into it; one produces another.--P. Henry
1590	source	The Creator God is the *source* of all things and upholds all things by His power.
1591	na tion	No man or *nation* can overrule God.
1592	na tion al	The more the Bible enters our *national* life, the grander, purer, and better will that life become.
1593	min ute	Lots of people know a good thing the *minute* the other fellow sees it first. --J. Hedges
1594	mi nute	Computer chips are *minute*.
1595	au to graph	A person's handwritten signature is an *autograph*.
1596	au to mo bile	An *automobile* was known as the horseless carriage because it moved by itself.
1597	tel e vi sion	A *television* helps us see things from far away.
1598	tel e phone	A *telephone* brings sound from far away.
1599	mi cro phone	A *microphone* magnifies small sounds.
1600	di lem ma	A strong *dilemma* in a desperate case, to act with infamy or quit the place! --Swift

Spelling Enrichments

PREFIXES. Identify the spelling words that can take one of these prefixes: *de-* (opposite of), *dis-* (opposite of), *inter-* (together), *re-* (again, back), *semi-* (half), *sub-* (further division), *un-* (not).

deceive	undeceived	*pierced*	unpierced, repierced
division	subdivision	*circle*	semicircle
accelerate	decelerate	*appearance*	disappearance, reappearance
source	resource	*national*	international

DICTATION. The *national dilemma,* since the official's *appearance* on *television*, is should we impeach him? He *deceived* the people. He has been the tragic *source* of *division* in the land. The *absence* of truth *accelerates* the *reign* of evil in a *nation*.

ANTONYMS. multiplication / __ (division)   ordinary/ _____ (weird)   huge/ __ (minute)
              disappearance/ __ (appearance)   international/ __ (national)   slow/ ___(accelerate)

IE or EI? If you have not done so already this year, format the IE Page. On the first base line write the titles:

      ie   *cei*   *ei says /A/*   *exceptions*

Write the rule three lines from the bottom of the page lining each phrase up under the related column.

    Use I before E   *except after C*   *if we say A*   *and in some exceptions.*

Under the IE column write *chief*. Between IE and EI, IE is used the most; it is the *chief* one. The first four spelling words below will use either IE or EI. Ask the elimination questions to determine which phonogram to use. If it is not after C, does not say /A/, and is not one of the memorized exceptions, use IE.

pierced	**I before E...** Root = pierce. Drop E... ED says /t/ ...	**IE/EI Page**	[R9,2,16,28]
de ceived	**EI after C.** Root = deceive. Drop E... ED says /d/...	**IE/EI Page**	[R4,2,9,16,28]
reign	**EI if we say /A/.** Homophones: rein, rain	**IE/EI Page**	[R9]
weird	**EI with exception words.**	**IE/EI Page**	[R9]
di vi sion	I said /i/ at ... SI spells /zh/ at the beginning of...	**SH/TI Page**	[R5,11]
ac cel er ate	C says /s/ before E. A said /A/ because of E..		[R2,7]
ap pear ance	Root = appear.		[R29,2,7]
ab sence	[<L ab-(away) + esse (to be)]. C says /s/ because of E.		[R2,7]
cir cle	C says /s/ before I [R. 2]. Every syllable must ...	**ER Page**	[R2,7]
source	C says /s/ because of the E.		[R2,7]
na tion	[<L natio (race), ult. <nasci (be born)]. A said /A/ at...	**SH/TI Page**	[R4,11]
na tion al	Accent shifts w/ suffix added to Latin-based word.	**SH/TI Page**	[R11]
min ute	[<L minuta (small part)]. Abbrev.: min.		[R7,12]
mi nute	[<L minutus (made small) <minus (less)]. Homograph: min-ute.		[R5,7]
au to graph	[<Gk auto (self) + graph (write)].		[R4]
au to mo bile	[<Gk auto (self) + mobile (move)].		[R4,7]
tel e vi sion	[<Gk tele- (far away) + video (see)]. Abbrev. = t.v.	**SH/TI Page**	[R4,5,11,12]
tel e phone	[<Gk tele- (far away) + phone (sound)].		[R4,7]
mi cro phone	[<Gk micro- (small) + phone (sound)].		[R5,4,7]
di lem ma	[<Gk di- (two) + lemma (premise)].		[R5,29,18]

Spelling Enrichments

GREEK ROOTS. Identify the spelling words using these Greek roots:

auto- (self)	--autograph, automobile	mobile (move)	--automobile
di- (two)	--dilemma, division	micro- (small)	--microphone
phone (sound)	--telephone, microphone	graph- (write)	--autograph
tele- (far away)	--television, telephone	video (see)	--television
			--division

Can you identify other words combining these roots? autobiography, telegraph, interphone, phonograph, telephony, videotelephone.

GRAMMAR. Conjugate the present tense of the verbs *pierce, deceive, reign,* and *accelerate.*

    Example: I pierce   we pierce

                  you pierce   you pierce

                  he, she, it pierces   they pierce

Preliminaries. Review especially <u>Spelling Rules</u>: 2, 4, 5, 6, 7, 11, 12, 16, 17, 22, 24, 25.
<u>Phonograms</u>: *ar, ch, ci, er, ey, or, ough, ti, ui, ur.* Advance Phonograms. See SWR Step 38. How can C say
/k/ before /i/? A silent letter can separates the two *(cu)*. What sound would advance phonogram *sc* make?
(/s/). <u>Reference</u>: Introduce or review **Plural** and **Y's Exchanging Pages**. SWR Steps 27, 34.

Words for Section T-3

1601	bus i ness	Your *business* is to put me out of *business*. --Dwight Eisenhower
1602	bis cuit	A *biscuit* in the States is a piece of quick bread, in England it is a cookie.
1603	stom ach	A hungry *stomach* has no ears. --Jean de La Fontaine
1604	proc ess	Happiness is a by-product in the *process* of making something else.--Huxley
1605	chim ney	Fire in the *chimney* is the best of servants but out of the *chimney* is the worst of masters.
1606	choir	In heaven everyone in the *choir* will sing on-key.
1607	cho rus	One girl can be pretty, but a dozen are only a *chorus*. --F. Scott Fitzgerald
1608	drought	Though we survived through rough coughing, we sought relief from the *drought*.
1609	med al	A design or words stamped on metal in memory of an event is called a *medal*.
1610	fa vor ite	"My *favorite* spot," said the frog, "is a knotty log near a pool where the water is cool." Groh
1611	con ver sa tion	Reading good books is like a *conversation* with men of past centuries.
1612	bur glar	A *burglar* is unable to steal treasures stored in heaven.
1613	ache	Wash the root of a tooth in vinegar and dry it in the sun and it will never *ache* again. -Franklin
1614	e lec tri cian	Never hire an *electrician* with scorched eyebrows. --Cooper
1615	bruise	It pleased the LORD to *bruise* Him for your sins and mine.
1616	vol ume	Upon that sacred *Volume* I rest my hope of eternal salvation through Jesus Christ. -A. Jackson
1617	hymn	Christ, our God, to Thee we raise this our *hymn* of grateful praise. --F. Pierpoint
1618	lil y	The Lord compares His people to a *lily* among thorns. --Song of Solomon 2:2
1619	dis cov er y	A *discovery* is usually not made by one man alone. --Henry Segerist
1620	scis sors	We are two halves of a pair of *scissors*, together we are something. --Dickens

Spelling Enrichments

DERIVATIVES. Suffixes *-ant, -er, -ar, -or, -ist, -ee* can mean "a person or thing that." In a similar way *man*
can be used to make a compound word. A *showman* is "one who shows." Review **E's Dropping Rule**. Find
examples in Section T of words that can be made into derivatives with one of these endings.

deceive-- deceiv**er**	*accelerate*-- accelerat**or**	*worship* -- worship**er**	*real* -- real**ist**
straight-- straight**ener**	*commence*-- commenc**er**	*minute* -- minute**man**	

Show current words (or forms of them) that indicates "a person or thing that."

business --	business**man**, business**woman**	*process* --	process**or**, process**er**
conversation -- conversational**ist**		*bruise* --	bruis**er**
electric --	*electri**cian***	makes a *discovery* --	discover**er**

SYNONYMS. Write the spelling word that means the same as the following:

			loudness -- *volume*
robber -- *burglar*	religious song -- *hymn*	singing group -- *choir*	pain -- *ache*
company -- *business*	British cookie -- *biscuit*	tummy -- *stomach*	shears -- *scissors*
Easter flower --*lily*	front-runner -- *favorite*	talk -- *conversation*	a find -- *discovery*
procedure -- *process*	smokestack -- *chimney*	injure -- *bruise*	dryness -- *drought*

Greek and Latin Roots

Write on the board *graph, phone, tele, video, scopeo, auto, micro.* Ask students to use these foreign word parts to make English words *(telegraph, autograph, telephone, microphone, television, telescope).* Write *verti.* This Latin root means "to turn." We will have a new spelling word today that uses that Latin root. See if you can be the first to identify it.

bus i ness	Root = busy. Think to spell /u/ and /i/. See SWR p. 81.	[R24]
bis cuit	cu = /k/. Silent U allows C to say /k/. C says /s/ before E, I, or Y.	[R2]
stom ach		
proc ess	C says /s/ ... We often double S... British alternative: pro cess.	[R2,17]
chim ney	Think to spell 3rd sound EY with an unaccented syllable at end of word.	
cho ir	[<L chorus <Sax. chor (choir)]. Think to spell "K-O I-r." Say /quire/.	[R4]
cho rus	O said /O/ at the end of a syllable.	[R4]
drought		
med al	[<L metallum (metal)].	
fa vor ite	British spelling: fa vour ite _____	[R4,7]
con ver sa tion	[<L con- (with) + verti (turn)]. Root = converse.	[R16,4,11]
bur glar	[<G berg (dwelling) + L latro (robber)]. **ER Page.**	
ache	A said /A/ because of the E. Works w/ 2 consonants. SWR p. 106.	[R7]
e lec tri cian	Root = electric. **SH/TI Page.**	[R4,5,11]
bruise	Odd job E. Show how *not* one of first four types of silent Es.	[R7]
vol ume	U said /U/ because of the E. Abbreviation: vol.	[R7,12]
hymn	[<G hymnos (hymn)]. Silent N is voiced in "hymnal." Homophone: him.	
lil y	English words do not end with I. For spelling connect sounds of Y and I.	[R5,6]
dis cov er y	[< L dis- (not) + cooperire (to cover)].	[R5,6]
scis sors	Latin: SC says /s/ before E, I, Y. SC = /s/ in same way CK = /k/.	[R2,29]

Spelling Enrichments

PLURALS. Make the spelling words plural using Rule 22.

To make a word plural just add an -S:

biscuit/ biscuits	*chimney/ chimneys*	*choir/ choirs*
drought/ droughts	*medal/ medals*	*favorite/ favorites*
burglar/ burglars	*ache/ aches*	*conversation/ conversations*
electrician/ electricians	*bruise/ bruises*	*volume/ volumes*
hymn/ hymns	*stomach/ stomachs*	

UNLESS

the word ending hisses:	*business/ businesses*	*process/ processes*	*chorus/ choruses*
changes:	*lily/ lilies*	*discovery/ discoveries*	
has no change:	*scissors/ scissors*		

COMPOSITION. Compose oral sentences using the words across from each other (examples: business conversation; biscuit burglar; stomach ache). Write down your four best sentences. Examples: *The biscuit burglar got a stomach ache in the business meeting. A dreadful drought killed the lovely lily.*

Preliminaries. <u>Phonograms</u>: *ci, ck, ea, ed, ee, ei, er, ey, gn, kn, oa, oe, oi, or, ou, ough, ow, oy, qu, th, ti, wh, wr.* Advanced: a second sound for one of the basic 70 phonograms-- $\overset{2}{qu}$ (SWR Step 38).
<u>Spelling Rules</u>: 1, 2, 4, 5, 6, 7, 9, 11, 14, 16, 18, 19, 20, 21,24. <u>Reference Pages</u>: Teach or review
AEIOU, E's Dropping, and **Dismiss L Pages** SWR Steps 19, 29, 37.

Words for Section T-4

1621	wheth er	It is not *whether* God is on our side, but *whether* we are on His. -- Ronald Reagan
1622	com pete	He broke his leg and did not know whether he could *compete* in the final race.
1623	wres tle	We do not *wrestle* against flesh and blood, but against ... the rulers of the darkness.
1624	re al ize	The wise *realize* that the great use of life is to spend it for something that lasts.
1625	folks	A Christian is the keyhole through which other *folks* see God. --R. Gibson
1626	con cern	A compassionate person shows *concern* for others.
1627	whis tle	I tried to *whistle* but nothing came. Can people swallow a *whistle?*
1628	suc ceed	It takes as much courage to have tried and fail as it does to have tried and *succeed.* --A. Lindbergh
1629	for feit	If you *forfeit* the confidence of your fellow citizens, you can never regain their respect. --A. Lincoln
1630	of fice	To show unfelt sorrow is an *office* which the false man does easily. --Shakespeare
1631	ought	We *ought* to obey God rather than man.
1632	al to geth er	When something is together completely, it is *altogether.*
1633	wreath	Decorate a Christmas *wreath* with symbols of Jesus: a star, a shepherd, a lamb.
1634	ex cep tion	Everyone has to die, but I always believed an *exception* would be made in my case. --Sanoyan
1635	va ry	Fear and anger, with alternate grace, pant in her breast and *vary* in her face. --Addison
1636	'va ri ous	I gave a *various* gift to each, to charm, to strengthen and to teach. --Longfellow
1637	nine ty	Since the time of Noah's Flood, few people have lived past *ninety* years of age.
1638	er ror	It is one thing to show a man his *error,* and another the truth. --John Locke
1639	li quor	Drunkenness from too much *liquor* is sinful.
1640	of fi cial	Undercover policemen do not wear their *official* uniforms.

Spelling Enrichments

CONJUNCTIONS. Conjunctions are connecting words such as: *and, but, or, so, yet.* Some conjunctions work in pairs *(either. . . or; neither. . . nor; whether. . . or; both . . . and).* Write original sentences using these spelling words. Include a conjunction or a conjunction pair in each sentence. Circle the conjunctions and underline the spelling words. For a bonus include other words from Section T. See the examples below.

> I can't tell *whether* the <u>concern</u> of the <u>folks</u> will <u>succeed</u> *or* not.
> Do you know *whether* the man should <u>forfeit</u> his <u>office</u> *or* not?
> The <u>official</u> <u>error</u> is *either* <u>ninety</u> *or* <u>ninety</u>-one.
> We will go <u>altogether</u> to *either* the <u>office</u> *or* to my house.
> Do you think one <u>ought</u> to *either* drink <u>liquor</u> in moderation *or* not at all?
> Can you see *whether* the <u>various</u> <u>concerns</u> make sense *or* if we need to explain the <u>exceptions</u>?
> We <u>realize</u> that *neither* the boys who <u>wrestle</u> *nor* the girls who play volleyball <u>succeeded.</u>
> Can you *both* <u>whistle</u> a hymn *and* pat your stomach at the same time?
> *Both* the boys' team and the girls' team <u>competed,</u> *and* each one of them won a <u>wreath.</u>

E's Dropping Rule

If you have not done so already this year, review Rule 16. Format E's Dropping Page. You could use two or more of the following recent review words for examples:

argue	argued	severe	severest
ache	aching	deceive	deceiver
bruise	bruised	minute	minutest

wheth er	Not "weather"	
com pete	[<L com- (together) + petere (drive toward)] E said /E/ because of the E.	[R7]
wres tle	Root = wrest (to twist or pull). Every syllable must have a vowel.	[R7]
re al ize	E said /E/ at the end of a syllable. I said /I/ because of the E.	[R4,7]
folks	[<OE folc] Once pronounced L still needed so O can say /O/.	[R19]
con cern	C says /s/ before E. SWR p. 104. Add *concerning* to **Preposition Page**	[R2]
whis tle	Every syllable must have a vowel. *Play Whist without whisTling.*	[R7]
suc ceed	[<L sub- (up) + cedere (go)] C says /s/ before E.	[R2]
for feit	I before E, **except** ...in some exceptions we learned **IE/EI Page**	[R9]
of fice	Think /f/ twice for spelling but not for normal speech. C says /s/...	[R29,7]
ought		
al to geth er	*All* as a prefix uses one L. **Dismiss L Page**	[R21]
wreath		
ex cep tion	X is never directly before S. **SH/TI Page**	[R20,2,11]
va ry	English words do not end with I. Treat Y as stand-in for I. SWR pp. 82-85.	[R4,5,6]
va ri ous	Root = vary. Single Y changes to I when adding any ending unless...	[R24]
nine ty	I said /I/... Y stands in for I; English words do not end with I.	[R7,5,6]
er ror	Root = err. Think /r/ twice for spelling but not for normal speech.	[R29]
li quor	qu = /k/. Dictionary splits QU (liq-uor). I usually says /i/... Q always...	[R5,1]
of fi cial	**SH/TI Page**	[R29,5,11]

Spelling Enrichments

SUFFIXES. Add suffixes -al, -ed, -es, -ial, -ing, -ly to as many of the spelling words as possible. Watch for E's dropping or Y's Exchanging words. See SWR p. 173 for a way to review rules for adding endings.

compete -- competed, competing
wrestle -- wrestled, wrestling
realize -- realized, realizing
concern -- concerned, concerning

whistle -- whistled, whistling
succeed -- succeeded, succeeding
forfeit -- forfeited, forfeiting
office -- official, officially

exception -- exceptional(ly)
vary-- varied, varying
various -- variously
ninety -- nineties

WORD SEARCH. Words beginning with WR- have a meaning related to twisting. How is this true with *wrestle* and *wreath*? What about: *wrap, wrench, wreck, wrest, wring, wrinkle, wrist, wrong, write?*

POEM. Whether the weather be fine or whether the weather be not,
    Whether the weather be cold or whether the weather be hot,
    We'll weather the weather, whatever the weather, whether we like it or not.

Preliminaries.

Phonograms: Quiz *ar, ed, er, ew, ng, oo, ou, ti, th, ui, wh, wr*. Advanced *gu*. See SWR Step 38.
Review Spelling Rule Cards: 2, 3, 4, 5, 6, 7, 11, 14, 15, 16, 17, 18.
Reference Pages: Introduce or review **1-1-1** and **2-1-1 Pages**. See SWR Step 32, 39.

Words for Section T-5

1641	ac ci dent	An *accident* is something sad that was not planned.
1642	slipped	The hills and valleys have *slipped* into gentle sleep.
1643	de cide	Before you borrow money from a friend, *decide* which you need more.
1644	con fer	God did not *confer* the responsibility for education to the government.
1645	ac cept	When you *accept* my view we will be in full agreement.
1646	re fer	If you are not sure how to spell a word you can *refer* to the dictionary.
1647	guess	There, I *guess* King George can see that. --Hancock signing Declaration of Independence.
1648	sum mon	When I *summon* remembrance of things past, I sigh the lack of many a thing I sought. --Shakespeare
1649	in vite	All occasions *invite* God's mercy and all times are His seasons. --John Donne
1650	es ti mate	When do you *estimate* that the estimate will be ready?
1651	vic tim	A nation... will more easily fall *victim* to a big lie than to a small one. --A. Hitler
1652	ba nan a	We have one foot in heaven and the other on the *banana* peel of self-interest. --Bash
1653	med i cine	A faithful friend is the *medicine* of life.
1654	con fer ence	A *conference* is a place where people gather to confer.
1655	ar gu ment	An *argument* would not last so long if the fault were only on one side.
1656	prod uct	No *product* enters this country untaxed except the answer to prayer. --Mark Twain
1657	frac tion	The *fraction* 3/4 is what percent of one hundred?
1658	cel e bra tion	When was the 500-year *celebration* of Columbus' discovery of America? (1992)
1659	in vi ta tion	Do you have your *invitation* to the party?
1660	sta tion ar y	The statue is *stationARy;* it cannot move fAR like a cAR.

Spelling Enrichments

SUFFIXES. Write all the spelling words in a column on a loose-leaf sheet of paper. Identify words that can take one or more of the following suffixes: *-able, -al, -ally, -ance, -ation, -ative, -ed, -ee, -ence, -er, -ing, -ion, -ive, -ize, -y*. Write word and derivatives. Watch for **1-1-1, 2-1-1** and **E's Dropping** words.

accident -- accidental, accidentally
slip --   *slipped,* slipping, slipper, slippery
decide --   decided, deciding
confer --   conferring, conferred
accept --   accepted, accepting, acceptable, acceptance
refer --   referred, referring, referral, reference,* referee*
guess --   guessing, guessed, guesser
summon -- summoner, summoning, summoned
invite -- invited, inviting, invitation
estimate -- estimated, estimating, estimation

victim -- victimize, victimization
banana --
medicine -- medicinal, medicinally
*conference** -- conferencing
argument -- argumentation
           argumentative
product -- production, productive
fraction -- fractional, fractionally
celebration --
invitation --
stationary--

*Not rule 15; accent on 1st syllable.

Invitation to a Celebration

In this lesson we will receive an invitation to what I hope will be a celebration, but you must pay close attention and learn these words. Are you ready? (Invitation and celebration are spelling words on this list. The invitation is to learn the words. The celebration is when the student does so.)

ac ci dent	[<L ad- (to) + cadere (fall)] C says /s/ before I.		[R2]
slipped	Root = slip. With a 1-syllable word... ED says /t/ ... **1-1-1 Page**		[R14,28]
de cide	E said /E/ at the end... C says /s/ before I. I said /I/ because of the E.		[R4,2,7]
con fer	[<L con- (together) + ferre (bring)]		
ac cept	[<L ad- (to) + capere (take)]. *Accept (A-o.k.); eXcept (Xed out).* C says /s/...		[R2]
re fer	E said /E/ at the end of a syllable.		[R4]
guess	gu = /g/. Without the U, G could say /j/. We often double S.		[R3,17]
sum mon	[<L sub (secret) + monere (warn)] Think /m/ twice for spelling but not ...		[R29]
in vite	I said /I/ because of the E.		[R7]
es ti mate	Es-ti-mAte (to guess); es-ti-mate (price proposed). I usually ... A said /A/...		[R5,7]
vic tim			
ba nan a	How do we know the final A doesn't say /A/?		[R18]
med i cine	[<L medicus (doctor)] I usually says /i/ ... C says /s/... Odd job E		[R5,2,7]
con fer ence	Root = confer. Not rule 15; accent shifts to 1st syllable. C says /s/ ...		[R2,7]
ar gu ment	Root = argue. E not needed; U not at the end of word. SWR p.148.		[R4]
prod uct			
frac tion	TI usually spells /sh/ beginning any syllable after the first.	**SH/TI Page**	[R11]
cel e bra tion	Root = celebrate	**SH/TI Page**	[R2,4,16,11]
in vi ta tion	Root = invite	**SH/TI Page**	[R5,4,11]
sta tion a ry	*A stationAry thing stAnds still.*	**SH/TI Page**	[R4,11,5,6]

PREFIXES. Make as many of the words or their derivatives **negative** by adding a prefix.
        undecided   unacceptable   uninvited   unproductive

VIVID WORDS. Add as many spelling words (or derivatives) as possible to the vivid words chart from p.142. See SWR pp. 161-2. Dictate review words (see * below) as examples. Use these pairs *(electrician argues)* and other new spelling words to write original sentences. (Example: *The electrician argues about the celebration.*)

person/group	*speaks*	
electrician*	argues*	about medicine
choir*	worships*	at the conference
business*	deceives*	its victims
folks*	accept	the invitation
office*	refers	its products
official*	guesses	at the estimate
officer*	summons	accident victims
wrestler*	invites	friends for a banana split
victim	estimates	the fraction of banana remaining
referee	confers	with the stationary coach

Numbers			Months of Year	Days of Week
0	ze ro			
1	one	1st	first	Jan u a ry	Sun day
2	two	2nd	sec ond	Feb ru a ry	Mon day
3	three	3rd	third	March	Tu es day
4	four	4th	fourth	A pril	Wed nes day
5	five	5th	fifth	May	Thurs day
6	six	6th	sixth	June	Fri day
7	sev en	7th	sev enth	Ju ly	Sat ur day
8	eight	8th	eighth	Au gust	
9	nine	9th	ninth	Sep tem ber	Period of Years
10	ten	10th	tenth	Oc to ber	dec ade
11	e lev en	11th	e lev enth	No vem ber	
12	twelve	12th	twelfth	De cem ber	doz en

100	hun dred	(ten X ten)		cen tu ry
1,000	thou sand	(ten X hundred)		mil len ni um
1,000,000	mil li on	(thousand X thousand)		

Spelling
Section U

One outstanding aspect of this program is the scope of possible applications. The same basic phonograms and spelling rules that work with beginning first-grade words still work with higher level vocabulary whether it be the names of the states in the United States, the names of the continents, the days of the week, the months of the year, the elements on the chemistry periodic table, or the names of the books in the Bible.

Even though the above words are not actual spelling words, suggested markings for them are provided in various places in the program. See SWR pages 57-58 for alternative versions of teaching the Consonant/Vowel Reference Page using some of these words. For the markings of the remaining states, the days of the week, the months of the year, and the continents, see The Alpha List. Months and days are also marked on the Number Page in SWR Step 15. The names of the books of the Bible are covered in the SWR Chart Masters packet.

Even intelligent, bright students with high literacy skills will benefit by having this program fill gaps in their education. If, however, you are beginning for the first time SWR/WISE with an older student who demonstrated mastery on the diagnostic test to this point in the list, we suggest that you drop back to Section T in order to cover in application all of the phonograms and spelling rules addressed in the program.

Preliminaries. Spelling Rules: 1, 3, 2, 4, 5, 6, 7, 8, 11, 14, 15, 16, 22, 24, 28.
Phonograms: *ear, ed, er, ie, ir, ng, or, ou, ur, wor.* Advanced: *our, et, sc, qū* (SWR Step 38).
Reference Pages: If beginning a new year, build **Consonant/ Vowel, Multi-letter Phonograms, Silent Final E Pages**. Introduce **ER** (top line), **1-1-1, Y's Exchanging Pages**.(SWR Steps 9, 10, 17, 26, 32, 34)

Words for Section U-1

1661	con serve	Learn to *conserve* before you consume.
1662	sur vive	As the seventh of nine children, I had to struggle to *survive.* -Robert Kennedy
1663	cir cum fer ence	God's center is everywhere, His *circumference* nowhere. --Thomas Watson
1664	cir cum stance	The real you is revealed when you face a difficult *circumstance.* --Neander
1665	ear li est	The *earliest* one is the one to do something in advance of others.
1666	re hearse	Look in the dictionary for the relationship between hearse and *rehearse.*
1667	ad journ	Her church first worships early, then they *adjourn* for fellowship time.
1668	dropped	The heavens *dropped* rain at the presence of God. --Psalm 68:8
1669	for get ting	*Forgetting* the past, I press toward the mark for the prize. --Philippians 3:14
1670	be gin ning	The fear of the LORD is the *beginning* of wisdom. --Proverbs 9:10
1671	sci ence	The Bible and the finds of true *science* do not conflict.
1672	cer e mo ny	Their wedding *ceremony* reflected their love for Christ and each other.
1673	bou quet	I gave Mother a *bouquet* of flowers for her birthday.
1674	col o ny	The foreign *colony* began with difficulty.
1675	col o nies	The early Puritan *colonies* settled in New England.
1676	co lo ni al	*Colonial* people live in a colony, land governed by a faraway nation.
1677	col o nel	In the colony are there enough kernels of corn for the *colonel?*
1678	ker nels	The pilgrims lived for months on a ration of only five *kernels* of corn a day.
1679	de scend	The Lord Himself will *descend* from heaven with a shout. --1 Thess. 4:16
1680	de scent	*Descent* means passing from a higher to a lower place or from an ancestor to an heir.

Spelling Enrichments

ALLITERATION. List the spelling words that have alliteration (start with the same first sounds).

/b/ -- beginning, bouquet
/d/ -- dropped, descend, descent
/k/ -- conserve, colony, colonies, colonial, colonel, kernels
/s/ -- survive, circumference, circumstance, science, ceremony

Write spelling sentences using the new words. Let each sentence have at least two words that have alliteration.

Example: Father bought me a bouquet for the beginning of my birthday.
Dan descended carefully because the deep descent dropped abruptly.
The concerned colonies needed to conserve kernels of corn.
Sally's science studies helped her sister survive a sad circumstance.
Always adjourn by afternoon.
The flowers faded, but we are not forgetting their fragrance.

1-1-1 / 2-1-1-Accent Pages.

If you have not done so already, dictate the top guide words (get/ getting; forget/ forgetting) and write on the bottom of the pages the rules. Otherwise, review these pages and be ready to teach additional words that follow these rules.

con serve₂	English words do not end with V.	**ER Page**	[R6,7]
sur vive	[<L super- (over) + vivo (live)].	**ER Page**	[R6,7]
cir cum fer ence₃	[<L circum- (around) + ferre (bear in a direction)].	**ER Page**	[R2,7]
cir cum stance₃	[<L circum- (around) + stantia (stand)].	**ER Page**	[R2,7]
ear li est	Root = early	**ER,Y's Ex Page**	[R5,24]
re hearse₅	See *hearse* (1140).	**ER Page**	[R4,7]
ad journ	[<L ad- (for) + jour (day)]. our = /er/.	**ER Page**	
dropp³ed	Root = drop.	**1-1-1 Page**	[R14,28]
for get ting	Root = forget.	**2-1-1 Page**	[R15]
be gin ning	Root = begin.	**2-1-1 Page**	[R4,15]
sci ence₃	sc = /s/.		[R2,4,7]
cer e mo ny	Y stands in for I.		[R2,4,5,6]
bou quet	et = /A/. qu = /k/.		[R1]
col o ny	[<L colonia (farm)]. Y stands in for I.		[R4,5,6]
col o nies	[<L colonia (farm)]. Root = colony.		[R4,24,22]
co lo ni al	[<L colonia (farm)]. Root = colony.		[R4,5,24]
col o nel	Spell "col-O-nel." Say /ker-nel/. See SWR p. 81.		
ker nels		**ER Page**	
de scend	[L <de- (down) + scandere (climb)]. sc = /s/.		[R4,2]
de scent	[L <de- (down) + scandere (climb)]. sc = /s/.		[R4,2]

Spelling Enrichments

DICTATION. Dictate the following paragraph instead of a regular spelling test. All new words are included.

The earliest colonies had to conserve each kernel of food to survive. In one colony a maiden hunted flowers to make a bouquet for her colonial wedding to the colonel. When she tried to descend a cliff she dropped her basket. The descent was so rough that she barely made it for the beginning time to rehearse for the ceremony. Under the circumstance she was happy that the practice had not adjourned without her, but she kept forgetting her lines. Later she walked the circumference of the colony rehearsing until she had her part down to a science.

ER WORD SENTENCES. Make up sentences with words that contain examples of the first five ER's. See SWR Page 137. Examples: Kernels survived circumstance worded earlier. Mother nurtures virtues worth rehearsing. Nervous disturbing squirming worsens learning.

DERIVATIVES. See Plus Endings Page, Step 35, especially notes on U-1 on page 173 of SWR.

Preliminaries. Review especially <u>Spelling Rules</u>: 2, 3, 4, 5, 6, 7, 9, 12, 15, 16, 24.
<u>Phonograms</u>: *ch, ei, eigh, ey, gn, kn, ie, oi, oo, or, ou, ow, oy, th, ui, wh.* Advanced: *eu* (SWR Step 38).
<u>Reference Pages</u>: If you haven't yet this year, dictate **IE/EI Page**. See SWR Step 40.

Words for Section U-2

1681	yield	*Yield* to all and you will soon have nothing to yield. --Aesop
1682	siege	The *siege* of Troy lasted ten years.
1683	a chieve	No matter what you *achieve,* somebody helped you.
1684	re ceive	The wise in heart will *receive* commands, but a prating fool will fall. --Prov. 10:8
1685	con ceit	The smaller the mind, the greater the *conceit.* -- Aesop, *The Gnat and the Bull*
1686	vein	I'm not in the giving *vein* today. --Shakespeare, *Richard III*
1687	for eign	Humor is the first of gifts to perish in a *foreign* tongue. --Virginia Woolf
1688	de scribe	A scribe is one who can *describe* what he observes.
1689	re sponse	Happiness is a joyful *response* to something good that happens.
1690	re bel lious	The *rebellious* rebel soldiers plan to rebel tonight.
1691	neu tral	It is not the *neutral* or the lukewarm who make history. --Adolf Hitler
1692	sug gest	A wise child will listen to what older people *suggest.*
1693	pe na lize	We will have more of what we subsidize and less of what we *penalize.*
1694	un for tu nate	The *unfortunate* one who lacks tact has more to retract.
1695	height	The Bible is the only book to embrace all the *height* and depth of human nature. -Darlow
1696	re vere	A woman is to *revere* her husband.
1697	mere	Repentance must be something more than *mere* remorse for sins. --Ben Hur
1698	nec es sar y	All that is *necessary* for the triumph of evil is that good men do nothing. --Burke
1699	en vel op	The fog will *envelop* the ship, but a letter will be mailed in an envelope.
1700	com pute	The meaning of *"compute"* has changed since the creation of the computer.

Spelling Enrichments

COMPOSITION. Dictate the following paragraph which includes seventeen of the spelling words.

<u>Describe</u> our <u>response</u> to people with <u>conceit</u>. The <u>height</u> of our feelings is not <u>neutral</u> even though the <u>vein</u> of the problem is not <u>foreign</u> to us. How does God <u>penalize</u> the <u>unfortunate</u> one who practices this sin likened to <u>rebelliousness</u>? <u>Suggest</u> ways one can <u>receive</u> victory over vanity. What is <u>necessary</u> to lay <u>siege</u> to this problem? We need to <u>revere</u> God and <u>yield</u> to Him. Without Him we could not <u>achieve</u> anything.

SILENT FINAL E WORDS. List silent final E spelling words so far in Section U. Organize them by types.

1		2	3	4	5
survive *unfortunate*		*conserve*	*circumference*		*rehearse*
describe *revere*		*achieve*	*circumstance*		*response*
penalize *mere*		*receive*	*science*		
compute			*siege*		

ANTONYMS. Write the spelling word that is the opposite.

unneeded/ *necessary*	demand/ *suggest*	reward/ *penalize*	despise/ *revere*
native/ *foreign*	blessed/ *unfortunate*	fail/ *achieve*	humility/ *conceit*
		resist/ *yield*	depth/ *height*

IE/ EI?   If you have not already done so this year, dictate the top guide words for IE Page and write the rule.   Under IE write *chief.* When choosing between IE and EI, IE is the chief one used.   Practice every day saying the exception senences orally.   Under the exception column add the review words *either* and *weird.* Practice the elimination questions with the first seven words below.

yield	After C?	Says /A/?	Exception?	No, use IE.	**IE/EI Page**	[R9]
siege ₃	After C?	Say /A/?	Exception?	No, use IE.	**IE/EI Page**	[R9,3,7]
a chieve ₂	After C?	Say /A/?	Exception?	No, use IE.	**IE/EI Page**	[R4,9,6,7]
re ceive ₂	After C?	Yes, use EI.			**IE/EI Page**	[R4,2,9,6,7]
con ceit	After C?	Yes, use EI.			**IE/EI Page**	[R2,9]
vein	Says /A/?	Yes, use EI.			**IE/EI Page**	[R9]
for eign	Exception?	Yes, use EI.			**IE/EI Page**	[R9]
de scribe	[<L de- (down) + scribere (write)]					[R4,7]
re sponse ₅						[R4,7]
re bel li ous	Root = rebel See SWR p. 85.					[R4,15]
neu tral	eu = /U/		[<L < ne- (not) +uter (either)]			
sug gest						[R3]
pe nal ize	Root = penal	British = penalise				[R4,7]
un for tu nate	Root = fortune					[R4,16,7]
height	eigh = /I/. root = high. See SWR p. 81. Abbreviation: ht.					[R12]
re vere	[<L re- (again) + vereri (in awe of, fear)]					[R4,7]
mere	[<L merus (pure, unmixed)]					[R7]
nec es sa ry						[R2,29,4,5,6]
en vel op	Do not confuse this verb with the noun *envelope.*					
com pute	U said /U/ because of the E.					[R7]

Spelling Enrichments

SUFFIXES. Each of these spelling words can take one to four suffixes. Review Rules16, 24. Use these suffixes: *-able, -ed, -en, -ence, -er, -est, -ing, -ible, -ity, -ive, -ize, -less, -ly, -ment, -ness.*

yield	yielding, yielded, yielder		*suggest*	suggested, suggesting, suggestive, suggestible
siege	sieged, sieging			
achieve	achieving, achiever, achievable, achievement		*penalize*	penalized, penalizing
receive	receiving, received, receiver, receivable		*unfortunate*	unfortunately
conceit	conceited, conceitedness		*revere*	revered, revering, reverence
vein	veined, veining, veinless		*mere*	merely, merest
foreign	foreigner		*height*	heighten
describe	described, describing, describable		*necessary*	necessarily
response	responsive		*envelop*	enveloping, enveloped
rebellious	rebelliousness		*compute*	computer, computing, computed
neutral	neutrality, neutralize, neutralizer			

Preliminaries. Spelling Rule Cards: 2, 3, 4, 5, 6, 7, 9, 10, 11, 12, 18, 20, 22, 23, 24.
Phonograms: *ai, ay, ch, ci, dge, ei, er, ey, ie, oa, or, sh, si, ti.* Advanced: *ãi, ge, our, sc* (Step 38).
Reference Page: If you haven't yet this year, teach **Plural Page** (SWR Step 27).

Words for Section U-3

1701	pi geon	Horse and chariot flashed its splendor, then disappeared like a wild *pigeon.*
1702	heir	The *heir* inherits the estate.
1703	em per or	The child saw that the *emperor* had no clothes.
1704	cit i zen	What makes a man a good Christian makes him a good *citizen.* --Daniel Webster
1705	at tor ney	I do not care to speak ill behind his back, but I believe he is an *attorney* .-S. Johnson
1706	cus tom er	The *customer* is always right. --Gorden Selfridge
1707	ma jor i ty	The pervading evil of democracy is the tyranny of the *majority.* --Lord Acton
1708	is sue	She shouldn't make a big *issue* about the torn tissue.
1709	tis sue	We often use *tissue* paper in place of handkerchiefs to wipe our tears.
1710	scene	Keep thou my feet: I do not ask to see the distant *scene;* one step enough for me. --John Newman
1711	jour ney	All along my pilgrim *journey,* Savior, let me walk with Thee. --Fanny Crosby
1712	com pli ment	*Compliment* someone over something they can control, like a cheerful spirit.
1713	ap pe tite	Riches enlarge rather than satisfy the *appetite.* --Thomas Fuller
1714	ap pa ra tus	No man-made *apparatus* can create life; only God can.
1715	en ve lope	Can you fold paper to make an *envelope?*
1716	veg e ta ble	Only fruit and *vegetable* plants can make food from nonliving matter.
1717	ap proach	Do good to all men, and much the more as you see the day *approach.*
1718	dif fi cul ty	To encourage is to help a friend see *difficulty* from God's point of view.
1719	aisle	The bride glowed as she marched down the *aisle.*
1720	i ci cle	You will hang like an *icicle* on a Dutchman's beard. --Shakespeare

Spelling Enrichments

PLURALS. Each of these spelling words can be used as a noun. After teaching these words, have the student close his spelling book and take out a blank piece of paper. Dictate the same words for him to test and reinforce his short-term memory. Have him proofread the test against the words in his notebook. The teacher should also double-check the work. Ask him to write each word again in the plural form.

customer	customers	*vegetable*	vegetables
heir	heirs	*compliment*	compliments
emperor	emperors	*appetite*	appetites
citizen	citizens	*apparatus*	apparatus or apparatuses
attorney	attorneys (not a single vowel Y)	*envelope*	envelopes
pigeon	pigeons	*journey*	journeys (not a single vowel Y)
majority	majorities (single vowel Y changes to I)	*approach*	approaches (the *ch* hisses)
issue	issues	*difficulty*	difficulties (single vowel Y changes to I)
tissue	tissues	*aisle*	aisles
scene	scenes	*icicle*	icicles

Review Advanced Phonograms Taught So Far

Ask student, "How many advanced phonograms (additional to the 70 basic ones) can you name? Five advanced phonograms have a G or C plus a silent letter. Explain the reason for the silent letters in these cases: **gu** (guest), **cu** (biscuit), **gh** (spaghetti), **gi** (region), **ge** (first example will be taught in this lesson)." See Rules 2 and 3 and SWR page 181.

pi geon	ge = /j/. Without the E, G would say /g/.		[R5,3]
heir	Think /h-A-r/ ; say /A-r/. Homophone: air.	**IE/EI Page**	[R9]
em per or	[<OF empereor (the ruler of an empire)].	**ER Page**	
cit i zen	Root = city. Few words use Z within the word.		[R2,5,24]
at tor ney	Abbreviation: atty.		[R29,12]
cus tom er	Root = custom.	**ER Page**	
ma jor i ty	[<OF majeste <L majus (great)]. Root = major.		[R4,5,6]
is sue	S before U can say /sh/.		[R29,7]
tis sue	S before U can say /sh/.		[R29,7]
scene	sc = /s/. C says /s/ before E. Homophone: seen.		[R2,7]
jour ney	our = /er/ as in *adjourn*.	**ER Page**	
com pli ment	I usually says /i/ at the end of a syllable.		[R5]
ap pe tite	[<L appetitus (longing or desire)].		[R4,7]
ap pa ra tus	[<L ad- (to) + parare (to prepare)].		[R29,4]
en ve lope	Noun. See verb *envelop* (1699).		[R4,7]
veg e ta ble	[<L vegetus (vigourous)].		[R4,7]
ap proach			[R29]
dif fi cul ty			[R29,5,6]
aisle	[<F aile <GB isle; influenced "alley"]. ai = /I/. Homophone: isle.		[R7]
i ci cle	[<OE is (ice) + gicel (icicle)]. Root = ice.		[R5,2,7]

Spelling Enrichments

ARTICLES/ POSSESSION. The articles (a, an, the) are called noun indicators because they indicate the presence of a noun. If the initial sound of the word after the article is a vowel sound, we use **an.** If it is a consonant sound, we use **a.** If the first letter is a silent consonant and the next letter is a vowel, then the word will take the article an (an herb garden.) When we add an apostrophe and an -S to a noun, we indicate ownership of the following noun. Example: *Sue's bouquet; a colonel's kernel; an odd colony's ceremony.* Add the article (a, an) and an apostrophe to the first eight spelling words to have them show ownership of the adjoining words in the next column.

a pigeon's journey   *an heir's compliment*   *an emperor's appetite*
a citizen's apparatus   *an attorney's envelope*   *a customer's vegetable*
a majority's approach   *an issue's difficulty*

ART. Use your imagination and draw an elaborate apparatus. Describe the purpose and function of this thing using as many Section U spelling words as possible. Don't stretch the words to the point of being ridiculous. Have fun but be logical. Write the title "An Elaborate Apparatus" at the top of the page. See if others can guess how your invention can benefit mankind. Be prepared to give a viable answer.

Preliminaries. Rules: Do a spelling rule warm-up review of 1, 2, 4, 5, 6, 7, 10, 11, 12, 15, 16, 20, 25.
Phonograms: Read all 70 in 75 seconds. Discuss advanced phonogram *gu*. See page 188.
Reference Page: Introduce or review **SH/TI** and **E's Dropping Pages**. See SWR Steps 18, 29.

Words for Section U-4

1721	sen ate	At the U.S. capitol we ATE *SenATE* bean soup, a dish served daily since 1901.
1722	sen a tor	In Rome a *senator* was required to own property of a certain value.
1723	ex pense	The final *expense* is due today.
1724	ac quire	Poor men and rich may possess what they rightly *acquire*. --Edgar, King of England, 975 AD
1725	e lab o rate	The architect will *elaborate* on the elaborate architecture.
1726	el e gant	This body one day will appear in a more *elegant* edition, revised and corrected by the Author.
1727	an cient	With the *ancient* is wisdom; and in length of days is understanding. --Job 12:12
1728	de li cious	It is quiet here and restful and the air is *delicious*. --Gorky
1729	con fi den tial	He was confident that his friend could keep the secret *confidential*.
1730	con ver sion	Noah Webster experienced Christian *conversion* at fifty.
1731	dis tin guish	I can *distinguish* proper and improper fractions by actions. --Ogden Nash
1732	ig nore	Men of ill judgement oft *ignore* the good. --Ajax
1733	ig nor ance	The greater our knowledge increases, the more our *ignorance* unfolds. -- J.F. Kennedy
1734	ne ces si ty	Lighting a candle is not a *necessity* for seeing the sun. --English proverb
1735	ex cel lence	The same man cannot well be skilled in everything; each has his special *excellence*. --Euripides
1736	meant	I *meant* what I said and I said what I *meant* . -- Dr. Seuss
1737	prov i dence	*Providence* has been my only dependence. All other resources seem to have failed. -G. Washington
1738	fi nal ly	*Finally,* brethren, pray for us that the word of the Lord may have free course. --2 Thess. 3:1
1739	in ter fere	A person known to *interfere* is called a busybody.
1740	in ter fer ence	I could not hear the radio clearly because of the *interference*.

Spelling Enrichments

COMPOSITION.   Write a paper on how a senator overcame wasteful spending on antiques and gourmet cooking when he realized the need to allot funds more wisely.

SYNONYMS. Have the student read each word from his notebook and, when possible, say another word that means the same thing. The next day give a quiz where you, the teacher, call out a synonym and have the student identify a spelling word that means the same, and then write the word. Check spelling.

tasty -- *delicious*	intended -- *meant*	disregard --*ignore* change -- *conversion*
intricate -- *elaborate*	divine intervention -- *providence*	cost -- *expense*
congressman -- *senator*	lastly -- *finally*	essential need -- *necessity*
greatness -- *excellence*	lacking information -- *ignorance*	very old -- *ancient*
set apart -- *distinguish*	posh -- *elegant*	obstruct -- *interfere*
obtain, get -- *acquire*	secret -- *confidential*	obstruction -- *interference*

Root Words and Derivatives

A root word is the smallest form of a word from which other words are made. This lesson has many derivatives. Challenge student to identify as many root words as possible. Sometimes words can be spelled the same but be pronounced differently. Watch for a word that does this.

sen ate			[R7]
sen a tor	Root = senate. Abbreviation: Sen.	**E's Drop Pg.**	[R4,16,12]
ex pense	[<L ex- (out) + pendere (pay)].		[R7]
ac quire	[<L ad- (to) + quarere (seek)].		[R1,7]
e lab o rate	(v.) Homograph: (adj.) e lab o rate₅ Root = labor.		[R4,7]
el e gant	Think /el E gant/. In the rhythm of speech say /el e gant/..		[R4]
an cient	Rare place where A says /A/ without using rules 4 or 7.	**SH/TI Page**	[R11]
de li cious	Related to "delight."	**SH/TI Page**	[R4,5,11]
con fi den tial	Root = confident. [<L con- (completely) + fidere (trust)].	**SH/TI Page**	[R5,11]
con ver sion	Root = converse. [<L con- (around) + versio (turn)].	**SH/TI Page**	[R11]
dis tin guish	gu = /gw/. U says /W/ as in QU.	**SH/TI Page**	[R10]
ig nore	[<L ig- (not) + gnarus (aware)].		[R7]
ig nor ance	Root = ignore.	**E's Drop Pg**.	[R4,16,2,7]
ne ces si ty	[<L necesse (unavoidable)].		[R4,2,29,5,6]
ex cel lence	Root = excel. X is never directly before S.	**2-1-1 Page**	[R20,2,15,7]
meant	Root = mean. [<OE maenan (to tell or say)].	**ED Page**	
prov i dence	Root = provide.	**E's Drop Pg.**	[R5,16,2,7]
fi nal ly	Root = final.		[R5,6]
in ter fere	[< L inter- (between) + ferir (strike)].		[R7]
in ter fer ence	Root = interfere.	**E's Drop Pg.**	[R16,2,7]

Spelling Enrichments

ANTONYMS. Identify opposites using spelling words. Examples:

rotten --	*delicious*	simple --	*elaborate*
house of representatives --	*senate*	lose, sell --	*acquire*
luck --	*providence*	initially --	*finally*
inferiority --	*excellence*	common --	*elegant*
public --	*confidential*	knowledge --	*ignorance*
luxury --	*necessity*	modern --	*ancient*

Can you name others?

ORIGINAL SENTENCES. Write original sentences using as many spelling words as possible. Underline the spelling words. As a member of the <u>distinguished</u> <u>senate</u>, the <u>ancient</u> <u>senator</u> made an <u>elaborate</u> plan with great <u>expense</u> to <u>acquire</u> an <u>elegant</u> but pointless <u>apparatus</u> for his <u>senate</u> office.

Preliminaries. Review especially <u>Spelling Rules</u>: 2, 4, 5, 6, 7, 9, 11, 12, 15, 16, 21, 22, 24, 28.
<u>Phonograms</u>: *ti, ci, si, ea, ee, ed, er, ie, ei, kn, gn, ough, ph, wr.* Advanced: *our* (SWR Step 38).
<u>Reference Page</u>: If you haven't yet this year, teach the **Dismiss L Page.** See SWR Step 37.

Words for Section U-5

1741	so cial	What book in the Bible teaches the most about good *social* skills and education? (Prov.)
1742	com mu ni cate	Learn to *communicate* graciously with others.
1743	rev er ence	We should *reverence* God, that is display fear mingled with respect and affection.
1744	prob a bly	He will *probably* go to college after he finishes homeschooling.
1745	cal cu late	*Calculate* the cost before you begin.
1746	ap pli ca tion	Had his *application* been equal to his talents, his progress might have been greater. -J. Jay
1747	ad mit tance	He gained *admittance* into church. --Noah Webster
1748	oc cu py	We should be careful what we let *occupy* our time.
1749	ma te ri al	*Material* things are not as important as spiritual things.
1750	re lief	How oft in grief hath not He brought thee *relief.* --Joachim Neander
1751	cour te sy	Someone who is courteous will show *courtesy* to others.
1752	re spect ful	He who is *respectful* of others is respected by them.
1753	de vel oped	Gossip, like a snapshot, begins with a negative, is *developed* and is often enlarged. -Knight
1754	re spon si ble	Be *responsible* for your own actions.
1755	a gree ment	False doctrines, like false witnesses, do not have *agreement* among themselves.
1756	con sid er a tion	She took my needs into *consideration* when she planned the trip.
1757	as sured	*Assured* through only the merits of Christ, I partake life everlasting. -- Shakepeare's will
1758	vi sion	*Vision* refers to the ability to see (from Latin root video, meaning "to see.").
1759	di vid ed	Though Christ's coat was once *divided*, He will never suffer His crown to be divided. --Brooks
1760	con ceal	You cannot *conceal* your sins from an all-seeing God.

Spelling Enrichments

QUIZ SPELLING USING SENTENCES. *<u>Social</u> <u>courtesy</u> probably assures <u>respectful</u> <u>consideration.</u>
<u>Communicate</u> <u>reverence</u> to those <u>responsible</u> for <u>admittance.</u> <u>Calculate</u> <u>materials</u> needed for <u>relief.</u>*

GRAMMAR. Use present tense form of verbs to create ED Page similar to examples in SWR Step 22.

PREFIXES. Combine the following prefixes with current words to make thirty new words: *anti-, dis-, ex-, im-, ir-, mis-, pre-, re-, sub-, tele-, un-.*

social	antisocial	*courtesy*	discourtesy
communicate	_excommunicate	*respectful*	disrespectful
reverence	irreverence	*developed*	undeveloped, pre-, re-
probably	improbably	*responsible*	irresponsible
calculate	miscalculate, precalculate	*agreement*	disagreement
application	misapplication, reapplication	*consideration*	reconsideration
admittance	preadmittance, readmittance	*assured*	reassured
occupy	preoccupy, reoccupy	*vision*	television, revision
material	immaterial	*divided*	undivided
relief	unrelief	*concealed*	preconcealed, un-

Building Blocks to Making Words

With the use of a dozen common prefixes and nine basic suffixes, you can turn these twenty words into a hundred different words. Just as we can make many words from 70 phonograms, we can make many words from using basic word parts. Watch for rules on adding suffixes (Rules 14, 15, 16, 24).

so cial	[<L socialis (companion)]	**SH/TI Page**	[R4,11]
com mu ni cate			[R29,4,5,7]
rev er ence	[<L re- (back) + vereri (stand in awe)] Root = revere		[R16,2,7]
prob a bly	Root = probable		[R4,16,5,6]
cal cu late			[R4,7]
ap pli ca tion	Root = apply	**SH/TI Page**	[R29,5,4,24,11]
ad mit tance		**2-1-1 Page**	[R15,7]
oc cu py		**ED Page**	[R29,4,5,6]
ma te ri al			[R4,5]
re lief		**IE/EI Page**	[R4,9]
cour te sy	our = /er/	**ER Page**	[R4,5,6]
re spect ful	Root = respect	**Dismiss L Pg.**	[R4,21]
de vel oped	[<F de- (un) + enveloper (wrap)]	**ED Page**	[R4,28]
re spon si ble			[R4,5,7]
a gree ment	[<L gratum (pleasing)]		[R4]
con sid er a tion	Root = consider	**SH/TI Page**	[R4,11]
as sured	Blended /s/ + /U/ = /sh/ + /U/.	**ED Page**	[R29,16,28]
vi sion	[<L video (to see)]	**SH/TI Page**	[R5,11]
di vid ed	Root = divide	**ED Page**	[R5,16,28]
con ceal			[R2]

Spelling Enrichments

SUFFIXES. By just adding some of the following suffixes to the current spelling words you can make over twenty new spelling words: *-ary, -ed, -ing, -ism, -ist, -ize, -ly, -ment, -ness, -tion, -y.*

social	socialism, socialist, socialize, socially	*respectful*	respectfully, respectfulness
communicate	communicated, communicating, communication	*responsible*	responsibleness, responsibly
		assured	assuredly
reverence	reverencing	*vision*	visionary
calculate	calculated, calculating, calculation	*conceal*	concealed, concealing, concealment
occupy	occupied, occupying		
material	materialism, materialist, materialize, materially		

BOTH PREFIX & SUFFIX ADDED. *excommunicated, excommunication, miscalculated, miscalculating, miscalculation, precalculated, precalculating, precalculation, uncalculated, preoccupied, preoccupying, reoccupied, reoccupying, unoccupied, disrespectfulness, disrespectfully, irresponsibly, reassuredly, revisionist, preconcealed, preconcealing, preconcealment, unconcealed, unconcealing.*

PHONOGRAM OR SPELLING REVIEW USING MORSE CODE

Use early consistent drill with multi-sensory reinforcement for the highest level of spontaneous response to written language. Enhance the involvement of kinestetic learners by adding a physical variation to normal writing. Anyone interested in ham radios will be motivated to learn Morse Code. Phonogram drills or spelling drills could be practiced by sending or receiving flashlight responses. The code must be internalized for instant recall to be used properly. The student should learn to think of the code by phonograms, not just letters. Build a chart with all the phonograms written into the code. Below are the individual letters.

a . _	**h**	**o** _ _ _	**v** . . . _
b _ . .	**i** . .	**p** . _ _ .	**w** . _ _
c _ . _ .	**j** . _ _ _	**q** _ _ . _	**x** _ . . _
d _ . .	**k** _ . _	**r** . _ .	**y** _ . _ _
e .	**l** . _ . .	**s** . . .	**z** _ _ . .
f . . _ .	**m** _ _	**t** _	
g _ _ .	**n** _ .	**u** . . _	

Spelling
Sections V through Z

If you are beginning SWR/WISE for the first time with an older student who demonstrated mastery to this point in the list on the diagnostic test, we suggest that you drop back to Section T in order to cover in application all of the phonograms and spelling rules addressed in the program.

Even intelligent, bright students with high literacy skills will benefit by having this program fill gaps in their education. Consider the report called Illiteracy in America by the National Advisory Council on Adult Education. "Since 1911, a total of 124 studies have compared the look-say eclectic approaches with phonics-first programs. Not one found look-say superior." Yet, "since 1955 approximately 85 percent of our 16,000 school districts have been using this eclectic approach..... Regardless of labels, only about 15 percent of the nation's primary age children have received instruction in direct, systematic, and intensive phonics."

Preliminaries.

Review <u>Spelling Rule Cards</u>: 1, 2, 3, 4, 5, 6, 7, 8, 9, 10, 11, 12, 16, 22, 23, 25.

<u>Phonograms</u>: Quiz all 70 plus advanced phonograms: *ge, gi, gu, gh, qu*². See SWR Step 38.

<u>Reference</u>: Teach or review **SH/TI, ER, Plural, IE/EI Pages** (SWR Steps 18, 26, 27, 40).

Words for Section V-1

1761	ce re al	Some boxed *cereal* contains less food value than the cardboard package.
1762	prin ci pal	The *principal* is my PAL.
1763	prai rie	They needed to PRAY to cross the *PRAIrie* in covered wagons.
1764	ca reer	The word "car" is the root word for *"career."* Where is the job taking you?
1765	vol un teer	One *volunteer* is worth two forced men.
1766	as so ci a tion	A wise man avoids deep *association* with fools.
1767	yacht	They discovered the principal's valise on the *yacht* of a questionable individual.
1768	mis sion ar y	God had only one son and he was a *missionary* and a physician. --David Livingston
1769	man sion	I have a *mansion* in Heaven.
1770	sur geon	A *surgeon* must be careful when he takes the knife! --E. Dickinson
1771	li cense	Liberty is not *license* to sin.
1772	pi an ist	I don't play the notes as well as most *pianists,* but I excel at the pauses.
1773	mos qui to	A nervous *mosquito* is a jitterbug. --Marjorie Frank
1774	sec re tar y	A *SECRETary* can keep a SECRET well.
1775	ar til ler y	His report compared the *artillery* used in World War I and World War II.
1776	griev ance	Men often bear a little *grievance* with less courage than they do large misfortunes.
1777	berth	The seventy-year-old man died on his *berth.*
1778	prin ci ple	The Boston Tea Party was conducted as a matter of *principle.*
1779	spa ghet ti	*Spaghetti* is an Italian food that Americans enjoy.
1780	su per sti tion	The *superstition* of science scoffs at the *superstition* of faith.--James

Spelling Enrichments

COMPOSITION. Assign a paragraph using the current spelling words. Read or dictate sample paper.

Use spelling words to describe <u>grievances</u>. You could list an itchy <u>mosquito</u> bite, a goof as a <u>pianist</u> at a recital, a harmful <u>association</u> with someone, a leaky <u>yacht</u>, mushy <u>spaghetti</u>, or stale <u>cereal</u>. Before you get too negative in your thoughts, list blessing like your <u>missionary</u> friend, an outstanding <u>principal</u>, the comfortable <u>berth</u> on your train trip, the helpful work of the <u>surgeon</u>, or your victory over silly <u>superstition</u>.

SENTENCE DICTATION. Dictate the following quote from Aesop. "Men often bear a little *grievance* with less courage than they do large misfortunes." Discuss the meaning of this profound quote.

POSSESSION. Match up spelling words to make one word show possession of another. Examples:

| *principal's principle* | *missionary's cereal* | *volunteer's career* |
| *secretary's spaghetti* | *surgeon's yacht* | *association's pianist* |

Play on Words

Writers often get our attention by purposefully switching a word with another word that sounds the same but has a different meaning. Example: *Seven days without prayer makes one weak*. Thomas Hood uses one of this week's new words in a similar way. *The old man's death happened in his berth*.

---

ce re al	[<L Ceres (grain) Roman goddess of agriculture]		[R2,4]
prin ci pal	Chief (principal sum) or chief person (head administrator)		[R2,5]
prai rie		**IE/EI Page**	[R9]
ca reer	[<MF carriere (race course) sense of running]		[R4]
vol un teer	related to voluntary		
as so ci a tion	Root = associate	Abbrev.: assoc. [R29,4,2,5,16,11,12]	
yacht	[<O Dutch jaght (yacht)]		
mis sion a ry	[<L missio (send)] Root = mission	**SH/TI Page**	[R29,11,4,5,6]
man sion	[<L manere (stay)] Root = manse	**SH/TI Page**	[R11]
sur geon	ge = /j/. Without the E, G would say /g/.	**ER Page**	[R3]
li cense	[<L licere (to be allowed)]		[R5,2,7]
pi an ist	piano + ist = pianist		[R5]
mos qui to	[<mosca (fly)] Spanish: qu = /k/ i = /E/		[R1,4]
sec re ta ry	[<L secretarius (confidential officer, keeper of secrets)]		[R4,5,6]
ar til ler y	Y stands in for I at the end of a word.	**ER Page**	[R29,5,6]
griev ance	[<L gravis (weighty)] Root = grieve	**IE/EI Page**	[R9,16,7]
berth	Homophone: birth	**ER Page**	
prin ci ple	A noun meaning "the basis of truth."		[R2,5,7]
spa ghet ti	gh = /g/ Italian, but not English words, can end with I.		[R29,3,6]
su per sti tion	[< L super- (over) + stare (stand)]	**ER,SH/TI Pgs.**	[R4,5,11]

NOUNS. Organize the spelling words into the categories of:

person	place	thing	idea
principal	*prairie*	*cereal*	*grievance*
volunteer	*yacht*	*career*	*principle*
missionary	*mansion*	*association*	*superstition*
surgeon	*berth*	*mosquito*	*license* (or a thing)
pianist		*artillery*	
secretary		*spaghetti*	

PLURALS. Make words plural. Review the rule for plurals. Watch for Y's Exchanging words.

cereal -- cereals   *principal* -- principals   *prairie* -- prairies   *career* -- careers
volunteer -- volunteers   *association* -- associations   *yacht* -- yachts   *missionary* -- missionaries
mansion -- mansions   *surgeon* -- surgeons   *license* -- licenses   *pianist* -- pianists
mosquito -- mosquitoes   *secretary* -- secretaries   *artillery* -- artillery   *grievance* -- grievances
berth -- berths   *principle* -- principles   *spaghetti* -- spaghetti   *superstition* -- superstitions

---

Preliminaries. Review especially <u>Spelling Rules</u>: 2, 3, 4, 5, 6, 7, 9, 11, 12, 16, 24, 25.
<u>Phonograms</u>: Read all 70 phonograms and give written test on *ck, er, ei, ie, oa, oe, ou, ough, si*.
<u>Reference Pages</u>: Teach or review **E's Dropping**, **Y's Exchanging Pages** (SWR Steps 29, 34).

Words for Section V-2

1781	mys te ri ous	Much discussion centered around his *mysterious* trip to the prairie.
1782	re lieve	We should help *relieve* the burdens of others.
1783	ad vise	To *advise* is to help sell your view.
1784	sol emn	I bear *solemn* testimonial of reverence and gratitude to the Holy Bible.-- John Q. Adams
1785	ap par ent	Good writing treats something difficult with *apparent* ease.
1786	im age	Behavior is a mirror in which every one displays his own *image*. --Goethe
1787	im ag ine	I can only *imagine* what heaven will be like.
1788	col umn	May our daughter be like a support *column* carved to adorn a palace. --King David
1789	in de pen dent	Lord, let me be less *independent*, but let me do it my way.
1790	ev i dence	Faith is the substance of things hoped for, the *evidence* of things not seen.
1791	tes ti mo ny	The *testimony* of the Lord is sure, making wise the simple. --Psalm 19:7
1792	in di vid u al	The desire to get "something for nothing" can destroy an *individual*, a family, or a country.
1793	in no cence	*Innocence* is better than repentance. --McGuffey
1794	sac ri fice	I admired the principal's *sacrifice* in standing for the principle of honesty.
1795	prej u dice	Someone who has *prejudice* judges before they know someone.
1796	coarse	Soft and easy is your cradle, *coarse* and hard your Savior lay. --*New England Primer*
1797	lei sure	Marry in haste and repent in *leisure*.
1798	ref er ence	Learn the *reference* to the Bible verses you memorize.
1799	oc ca sion	Any *occasion* is an occasion for kindness.
1800	a cre	An *acre* used to be the area a man could plow in one day.

Spelling Enrichments

SUFFIXES. Students should build derivatives of the current spelling words by adding suffixes. They can use the suffix cards from page 98 or you can dictate the following suffixes: *-able, -age, -al, -ary, -ation, -ative, -ed, -er, -ery, -ing, -ion, -ism, -ist, -ity, -ive, ize, -ly, -ness, and -y*.   Review the E's Dropping Rule [R16] and the Y's Exchanging Rule [R24] before proceeding.

mysterious -- mysteriously, mysteriousness
advise -- advising, advised, advisable
apparent -- apparently
imagine -- imaginative, imagination
independent -- independently
testimony -- testimonial
innocence -- innocency
prejudice -- prejudiced
leisure -- leisurely
occasion -- occasional, occasionally

relieve -- relieved, relieving, reliever
solemn -- solemnly, solemnness, solemnity
image -- imaging, imaged
column -- columnist, columned
evidence -- evidenced, evidencing
individual -- -ism, -ist, -ity, individualize
sacrifice -- sacrificing, sacrificed, sacrificial
coarse -- coarsely, coarseness
reference -- referenced, referencing
acre -- acreage (rule 7 overrides rule 16)

Ghost of Forgotten Sounds

Frank Irish in 1888 wrote a book called *The Fundamentals of the English Language*. In this classic work, he explains many silent letters as the "ghost of forgotten sounds." For example: *hymn* and *condemn* end with an N once pronounced but now silent. (For additional words like this see SWR p. 86.) Watch for other words in this lesson that have a silent N *(solemn, column)*.

mys te ri ous	Root = mystery	**Y's Ex Page**	[R4,5,24]
re lieve	[<L re- (back) + levitate (raise)]	**IE /EI Page**	[R4,9,6,7]
ad vise	[<OF advis (opinion)]		[R7]
sol emn	[<L sollemnis] Hear the N in derivatives *solemnize, solemnity*.		
ap pa rent	[<L apparere (to appear)] /a-r/ not /ar/.		[R29,4]
im age	G says /j/ before E.		[R3,7]
im ag ine	Drop the E. G may still say /j/ before I.		[R3,16,7]
col umn	[<L columna] Hear /n/ in derivative *columnist*. <u>Abbrev.</u>: col.		[R12]
in de pen dent	Root = depend		[R4]
ev i dence			[R5,2,7]
tes ti mo ny			[R5,4,6]
in di vid u al	[<L in- (not) + dividuus (divisible)]		[R5,4]
in no cence	[<L in- (not) + (nocere) harm]		[R29,4,2,7]
sac ri fice	[<L sacer (holy)] Root = sacred		[R5,2,7]
prej u dice	[<L prae (before) + judicium (judge)]		[R4,2,7]
coarse	<u>Homophone</u>: course		[R7]
lei sure	/z/ followed by U can say /zh/. EI exception word. **IE/EI Page**		[R9,7]
ref er ence	Root = refer Not rule 15; accent on 1st syllable.		[R2,7]
oc ca sion	Think /k/ twice for spelling but not normal speech. **SH/TI Page**		[R29,4,11]
a cre	A said /A/ at the end of a syllable.		[R4,7]

Spelling Enrichments

ANTONYMS.

guilt / *innocence*	work/ *leisure*	obscure/ *apparent*	jovial/ *solemn*
open mind/ *prejudice*	silky/ *coarse*	group/ *individual*	burden/ *relieve*
dependent/ *independent*	see/ *imagine*	predictable/ *mysterious*	

COMPOSITION. Dictate the following instructions:

Weave a *mysterious* tale about an *individual* who was *innocent* in spite of much *prejudice* against him. What was the *solemn occasion* that caused the problem? Who was brave enough to give a truthful *testimony* to help *relieve* him? What *sacrifice* was involved? How did the newly found *evidence* help?

Have students answer these questions in a news-type story that tells who, what, when, why, and how. Use as many of the current spelling words as can be logically included. If time permits, these stories will be fun to read in class.

DICTATION. Dictate this quote from Benjamin Franklin: *"Innocence* is its own defense." Discuss the meaning.

Preliminaries. Review especially <u>Spelling Rules</u>: 2, 3, 4, 5, 6, 7, 11, 12, 14, 15, 16, 17, 19, 20, 24, 28.
<u>Phonograms</u>: *ai, ci, ed, eigh, gn, ng, ou, si, ti,* as well as advanced phonogram *sc* (See page 188).
<u>Reference Pages</u>: Introduce or review **1-1-1** and **2-1-1 Pages**. See SWR Steps 32, 39.

Words for Section V-3

1801	weight	Music removes from the heart the *weight* of sorrow. --Martin Luther
1802	cam paign	While the army fought the *campaign,* the soldiers camped in tents.
1803	con scious ness	Suffering is the sole origin of *consciousness.* --Dostoevski
1804	con trol la ble	A child that obeys shows she has a *controllable* spirit.
1805	or gan ize	Please *organize* your school papers.
1806	or gan i za tion	We belong to a community *organization.*
1807	sense	Our *sense* of sin is in proportion to our nearness to God. --Thomas Bernard
1808	sen si ble	Only game fish swim upstream, but *sensible* fish swim down. --Ogden Nash
1809	com pres sion	*Compression* is the act of squeezing or pressing together.
1810	ex pe ri ence	*Experience* keeps a [costly] school. The fool will learn in no other. -- B. Franklin
1811	per mit ted	Smoking is not *permitted* in the airplane.
1812	prof it	Deny us for our good: so find we *profit* by losing of our prayers. --Shakespeare
1813	ar range ment	Mother could make a flower *arrangement* as lovely as a florist.
1814	dis cus sion	We had a deep *discussion* to dig out the truth of the subject.
1815	ses sion	Would the court *session* reach a desirable conclusion?
1816	wel fare	Work hard and earn your way rather than rely on the *welfare* of others.
1817	ty ing	Webster tried unsuccessfully to make "tye" the base word for "*tying.*"
1818	re sem ble	The opposite of *resemble* is to look different, dissimilar, or unlike.
1819	re sem blance	*Resemblance* reproduces the formal aspect of objects, but neglects their spirit.--Ching Hao
1820	mag nif i cent	*Magnificent* promises often end in paltry performances. --Aesop

Spelling Enrichments

PREFIXES. Most of these spelling words can be made into derivatives by adding prefixes. Students can use the prefix cards from page 116 or you can dictate the following: *counter-, dis-, in-, non-, ob-, over-, pre-, re-, sub-, un-, under-.* Have students list all the spelling words and as many derivatives as they can. They may use dictionaries.

weight	counterweight, overweight, underweight	*permitted*	unpermitted
campaign	precampaign, recampaign	*profit*	nonprofit
consciousness	subconsciousness, unconsciousness	*arrangement*	rearrangement, pre-, dis-
controllable	uncontrollable, noncontrollable, noncontrolled	*discussion*	prediscussion
organize	reorganize	*session*	obsession
organization	disorganization, reorganization, overorganization	*welfare*	prewelfare
sense	nonsense	*tying*	retying
sensible	insensible	*resemble*	--
compression	precompression, noncompression	*resemblance*	nonresemblance
experience	inexperience	*magnificent*	--

Suffix Endings May Change the Part of Speech

Mystery is a noun,	but adding the suffix -ous	makes it an adjective;	*mysterious.*
Depend is a verb,	but adding the suffix -ent	makes it an adjective;	*dependent.*
Prejudge is a verb,	but adding the suffix -ice	makes it a noun;	*prejudice.*
Refer is a verb,	but adding the suffix -ence	makes it a noun;	*reference.*

weight	Abbreviation: wt. Homophone: wait		[R12]
cam paign	[<F campagne (open country) <L campus (field)]		
con scious ness	sc + ci = /sh/. [<L con- (with) + scire (to know)]		[R11,17]
con trol la ble	[<OF contre (against) + rolle (roll)]	**2-1-1 Page**	[R15,19,4,7]
or gan ize	British spelling: organise		[R7]
or gan i za tion	Abbreviation: org.	**E's Drop Pg.**	[R5,4,11,12]
sense	Homophone: cents		[R7]
sen si ble	Root = sense		[R16,5,7]
com pres sion	Root = compress	**SH/TI Page**	[R11]
ex pe ri ence	[<L ex- (out) + peri- (try)]		[R20,4,5,2,7]
per mit ted	[<L per- (through) + mittere (let go)]	**2-1-1 Page**	[R15,28]
prof it	Not rule 15, accent is on 1st syllable		
ar range ment	2 consonants between vowels okay with silent E.		[R29,3,7,16]
dis cus sion	Root = discuss [<L dis- (apart) + quatere (to shake)].	**SH/TI Page**	[R11]
ses sion	[<L sessio <sedere (sit)]	**SH/TI Page**	[R11]
wel fare	*Fare* means paid, but welFARE means free handout.		[R7]
ty ing	Root = tie Drop E, change I to Y.		[R5,16,24]
re sem ble			[R4,7]
re sem blance	Root = resemble	**E's Drop Pg.**	[R4,16, 2,7]
mag nif i cent	Root = magnify [<L magnus (great) + facere (make)]	**Y's Ex Page**	[R5,2]

Spelling Enrichments

LATIN ROOTS. *Magnus* is a Latin root that we do not use alone as a word in English but we do see this word partly embedded in English words. *Magnus* means big, great, large. What do these words mean?

magnify --	to make larger	magnitude --	greatness
magnifier --	that which makes greater or larger	magnanimous --	great in spirit
magnificent --	great in character or deed	magnate --	person with rank or influence

DICTATION. We had a *magnificent discussion* about *reorganizing welfare*. People become lazy when *permitted* to loaf all day and still have plenty to eat. A better, more *sensible arrangement* would be to help them *profit* from a work *experience*. (Can you add to this using more spelling words?)

GRAMMAR. List the root words to as many spelling words as possible. The part of speech may change.

weigh -- *weight*	conscious -- *consciousness*	control -- *controllable*
organize -- *organization*	sense -- *sensible*	compress -- *compression*
permit -- *permitted*	profit -- profited	arrange -- *arrangement*
discuss -- *discussion*	resemble -- *resemblance*	tie -- *tying*
manify -- *magnificent*		

Preliminaries. Review especially Spelling Rules: 1, 2, 3, 4, 5, 6, 7, 9, 11, 16, 26.
Phonograms: *ar, ch, ea, ee, ei, er, th, ti, or, oy* plus French phonogram *eau* = /O/.   See SWR Step 38.
Reference Page: If you have not yet this year, teach the **IE/EI Page**. See SWR Step 40.

Words for Section W-1

1821	em ploy ee	Every *employee* tends to rise to his level of incompetence. --Laurence Peter
1822	ath lete	An *athlete* is a contender for victory. --A. Smith
1823	mul ti tude	The fool *multitude* choose by show. --Shakespeare
1824	bu reau	In French, *bureau* means office or desk and is the root of the word bureaucracy.
1825	heif er	A *heifer* is a young cow that has never had a baby calf.
1826	ve hi cle	Blood is the *vehicle* of life in the body. The life of the flesh is in the blood.
1827	li brar y	A *library* is thought in cold storage. --Herbert Samuel
1828	vi cin i ty	She had many friends in the *vicinity* of Portland.
1829	con fec tion er y	A store that specializes in candy confections can be called a *confectionery*.
1830	ath let ic	An *athletic* body is strong, robust, one fitted for vigorous exertions.
1831	an ni ver sa ry	An *anniversary* is an annual celebration of an event from a previous year.
1832	op por tu ni ty	A favorite disguise for *opportunity* is trouble.
1833	e mer gen cy	An *emergency* comes suddenly as an unexpected event.
1834	treach er y	Who was called a foe without hate, a friend without *treachery,* a soldier without cruelty?*
1835	dis ease	Louis Pasteur, a Christian, discovered that germs cause *disease*.
1836	cal cu la tor	You need to learn to work with numbers without a *calculator*.
1837	cal en dar	All time on the *calendar* is rendered as either before or after the time of Christ.
1838	isth mus	The *Isthmus* of Panama is a narrow ribbon of land with ocean on two sides.
1839	con se quence	Men never violate God's law without suffering the *consequences* sooner or later. --L. Child
1840	con tro ver sy	If there is no *controversy,* there is no truth.

Spelling Enrichments

APPOSITIVES. An appositive comes after another noun to explain who or what. Write the first sentence on the board; discuss. Dictate the rest of the sentences and have students use proper punctuation.

    a. *Our newest vehicle, **the jeep,** had a flat tire.* Set off the appositive, a jeep, by commas.
        Notice that the sentence would be complete without the appositive.
        Our newest vehicle had a flat tire.
    b. *The jeep, **our newest vehicle,** had a flat tire.*
        Where are commas needed? What is the appositive in this sentence?
    c. *The Isthmus of Panama, **the site of the famous Panama Canal,** connects which two oceans?*
    d. *Using a calculator, **an instrument for calculating numbers,** makes math easier.*
   *e. Robert E. Lee, **a general in the War between the States,** was called a friend without treachery.*
    f. *Daisy, **our heifer,** had milk disease.*
    g. *My parents' wedding anniversary, **July 1st,** is a very special day.*

LITERATURE. Explain Shakespeare's quote, "The fool *multitude* choose by show." (The majority of people are fooled by looks. Shakespeare was well-versed in the Geneva Bible. Could the story of King Saul's selection have inspired this observation? Man saw his handsomeness; God saw his heart.)

Root Words:

If you know the root word and its meaning, you can often figure out the meaning of the derivative form of the word. How would we spell *row* as in "row the boat?" The same sound is spelled differently in French. We have a word in this lesson that retains French spelling. As a result we have a new phonogram (eau = /O/). A French word can end with U.

em pl<u>oy</u> ee	[<L in- + plicare (fold)] Root = employ	
a<u>th</u> lē͡te	[<L <G athetes < athlon (prize)] This word has only 2 syllables.	[R7]
mul ti tu͡de	[<L multi- <mullus (much, many)]	[R5,7]
bu reau	[<F bureau (desk)] French: eau = /O/	[R4]
hĕif er	IE or EI? One of the exceptions? (Yes, use EI.) **IE/EI Page**	[R9]
ve hi cle	[<L vehere (to carry)]	[R4,5,7]
li bra ry	[<L librarium (chest for books) <liber (books)]	[R4,5,6]
vi cin i ty	Y stands in for I; English words do not end with I.	[R5,2,6]
con fec <u>tion</u> ĕr y	[<L com (up) + facere (make)] Root = confection **SH/TI Page**	[R11,5,6]
a<u>th</u> let ic	[<L <G athetes < athlon (prize)] Root = athlete	
an ni ver sa ry	[<L annus (year) + vertere (turn)]	[R29,4,5,6]
op por tu ni ty	Root = opportune	[R29,4,16,5,6]
e mer gen cy	Root = emerge	[R4,3,16,2,5]
trĕach er y	[<OF trichier (to cheat)--compares with trick]	[R5,6]
dis ease	[< dis- (no) + ease]	[R7]
cal cu la tor	Root = calculate	[R4,16]
cal en dar	[<L calendarium (account book) < calendae (day bills due)]	
is<u>th</u> mus	[<Gk. isthmos]	
con se quence		[R4,1,2,7]
con tro ver sy	[<L contro- (against) + vertere (turn)]	[R4,5,6]

GREEK AND LATIN ROOTS. Write roots on 3x5 cards. Have students match to the current spelling words.

annus	(year) -- *anniversary*	liber	(books) -- *library*
athlon	(prize) -- *athlete*	multi-	(many) -- *multitude*
facere	(make) -- *confectionery*	plicare	(fold) -- *employee*
com-	(up) -- *confectionery*	vehere	(carry) -- *vehicle*
contro-	(against) -- *controversy*	vertere	(turn) -- *controversy*
calendarium	(account book) -- *calendar*		

Words from *annus:* annals (events recorded by year), annuity (money paid yearly), biannual (every 2 years), centennial (every hundred years), millennial (every thousand years), perennial (through the years).

ART. Draw the Isthmus of Panama and label it neatly. You could also label surrounding places and oceans.

ORIGINAL SENTENCES. Write original sentences using the new spelling words. Include **at least:**
    a. three sentences with appositives
    b. three sentences with possessive nouns (i.e. *employee's anniversary, bureau's treachery*)
    c. five sentences with plural nouns.

Preliminaries. Review especially <u>Spelling Rules</u>: 1, 2, 4, 5, 6, 7, 11, 16, 20, 27.
<u>Phonograms</u>: *ar, ch, ci, ea, ee, er, ew, igh, or, ou, qu, ui*. Advanced: *q̊u, rh*.   See SWR Step 38.
<u>Reference Page</u>: Review or introduce **SH/TI Page**. See SWR Step 18.

Words for Section W-2

1841	ap pre ci ate	You can't *appreciate* home until you've left it. --O Henry
1842	cor dial	You may end a *cordial* letter with "cordially," followed by the author's signature.
1843	sin cere	You may end a *sincere* letter with "sincerely," followed by the author's signature.
1844	sep a rate	*Separate* the light and dark clothes before washing them.
1845	ex treme	*Extreme* fear can neither fight nor fly. --Shakespeare
1846	ac cu rate	Earn future trust by giving an *accurate* report of past events.
1847	pro ceed	Things which *proceed* out of the mouth come from the heart, and defile a man.
1848	in stan ta ne ous	The passage of electricity through space appears to be *instantaneous*. --Webster
1849	prac ti cal	Something that is *practical* has been proven to be valuable in PRACTICE.
1850	ar ti fi cial	Something *artificial* is made or contrived by human skill and labor.
1851	an tique	A precious, mouldering pleasure 'tis to meet an *antique* book. --Emily Dickinson
1852	char ac ter	*Character* will never be produced by money. --W. K. Kellogg
1853	ar chi tect	I call the work of an *architect* "petrified music." --Goethe
1854	grease	Don't *grease* the wheel if it doesn't squeak.
1855	as so ci ate	Be careful to *associate* only with the right kind of associate.
1856	re source	Great emergencies help us make wise use of every *resource*.
1857	per se vere	*Persevere* in prayer because God honors such faith.
1858	op por tune	It is an *opPORTune* time to visit the PORT.
1859	ad e quate	We have no *adequate* ideas of infinite power. --Noah Webster
1860	rhyme	We lack not *rhyme* and reason. --Tennyson

Spelling Enrichments

PUNCTUATION. Use commas to punctuate a series of three or more words. Dictate the following examples using W-1, W-2 spelling words. Make sure that commas are placed accurately.

NOUN SERIES: The *employees*, volunteer *associates*, and *architects* helped build the *library*.

VERB SERIES: The *multitudes* stir up *controversy*, cause *emergencies*, but fail to *calculate consequences*.

ADJECTIVE SERIES: I like a *practical, adequate, resourceful character*.
He was a *sincere, accurate, cordial architect*.
We have an *opportune, extreme, insincere associate*.
I bought a *greasy, impractical, antique bureau*.
The *athlete* was *practical, persevering*, and *accurate*.
Give me an *adequate, instantaneous, accurate calculator*.
He tried to sell the *inadequate, diseased heifer*.

Heteronym

A heteronym is a word with the same spelling but a different pronunciation. Examples: bow (weapon for shooting an arrow), bow (to bend); dove (a pigeon), dove (did a dive); object (to protest), object (a thing). This lesson has two heteronyms. See if you can you identify them.

ap pre ci ate	CI can say /c-i/ or /sh/. Here they overlap. ci = /shi/*	[R29,4,7]
cor di al	Think to spell /cor-di-al/. Say /cor-jal/. See SWR page 88.	
sin cere	Can S say /z/ here? Why not?	[R27,2,7]
sep a rate		[R4,7]
ex treme		[R20,7]
ac cu rate	[<L ac- (to) + cura (care)]	[R2,29,4,7]
pro ceed	[<L pro- (forward) + cedere (move)]	[R4,2]
in stan ta ne ous	Root = instant	[R4]
prac ti cal	Root word = practice	[R5,16]
ar ti fi cial	[<L artis (art) + facare (to make)]. **SH/TI Page**	[R5,11]
an tique	French I = /E/. qu = /k/.	[R1,6,7]
char ac ter	This ACT has my favorite charACTer.	
ar chi tect	[<Gk archi (chief) + tekton (builder)]	[R5]
grease	Heteronym: /grEs/ (soft animal fat); /grEz/ (smear with grease).	[R7]
as so ci ate	Heteronym: associate (verb); associate (noun). ci = /shi/ *	[R29,4,2,5,7]
re source		[R4,2,7]
per se vere	[<L per- (through) + severus (strict)]	[R4,7]
op por tune	[<L ob- (toward) portum (port)].	[R29,7]
ad e quate	[<L ad- (to) + aequus (equal)]	[R4,1,7]
rhyme	Greek rh = /r/ [<Gk rhythmos (rhyme)]	[R7]

CORRESPONDENCE. Dictate this assignment. Underline the spelling words from this section.

   Write a thank-you letter to a friend, an associate, or maybe an architect. State in a clear and accurate way what you appreciate. You may mention good character qualities or some practical way she has helped you. End the letter with either sincerely or cordially.

SUFFIXES. Add to spelling words: *-ance, -ed, -er, -ful, -ly, -ing, -ion, -ism, -ist, -istic, -ity, -ize, -ness, -or, -ure, -y.*

appreciate -- appreciation, appreciated, appreciating
cordial -- cordially
sincere -- sincerely, sincerity
separate -- separately, separating, separated, separation, separator
extreme -- extremely, extremeness, extremist, extremity
accurate -- accurately, accurateness
proceed -- proceeding, proceeded
instantaneous -- instantaneousness, instantaneously
practical -- practically, practicality
artificial -- artificially, artificiality

antique -- antiquity, antiqued, antiquing
grease -- greasy, greasiness, greased, greaser
architect -- architecture
character -- characteristic, characterize
associate -- associating, associated, association
resource -- resourceful
persevere -- persevered, persevering, perseverance
opportune - opportunity, opportunist, opportunism
adequate -- adequately, adequateness
rhyme -- rhyming, rhymed, rhymer

Preliminaries.

    Review especially <u>Spelling Rule Cards</u>: 2, 3, 4, 5, 6, 7, 9, 10, 11, 15, 16, 28.
    <u>Phonograms</u>: *ch, ci, ed, ei, er, gn, ng, sh, ti, oa, ou, wr.* Advanced: *ae, gi, sc* (SWR Step 38).
    <u>Reference Page</u>: Introduce or review **E's Dropping Page**. See SWR Step 29.

Words for Section W-3

1861	re proached	Even if I had done wrong you should not have *reproached* me in public. --Napoleon
1862	de struc tion	Young man know, most do unto *destruction* go. *--New England Primer*
1863	de vel op ment	We live in the new residential *development*.
1864	ben e fi cial	Your gift has been very *beneficial* to our ministry for the Lord.
1865	con ceive	How did you ever *conceive* such an idea?
1866	ap ply	Knowing is not enough; we must *apply* what we know.
1867	ae ro space	Many advancements are being made in *aerospace*.
1868	ae ro sol	My hair spray is in an *aerosol* can.
1869	con ta gious	Failure to quarantine *contagious* illness led to 60 million deaths in the Black Plague.
1870	con science	A guilty *conscience* needs no accuser.
1871	sov er eign	The true *Sovereign* molded the world like soft wax. --Carlyle
1872	as cend	If I *ascend* into heaven you are there. --Psalm 139:8
1873	mo not o nous	It is *monotonous* when one person does all the talking.
1874	bi cy cle	A *bicycle* is a vehicle with two wheels.
1875	tri an gle	Tri- means three; a *triangle* is a shape with three angles and three sides.
1876	con cen tra tion	Concentrate together in a common center, as in a *concentration* of troops.
1877	rins ing	Be careful not to spatter paint when *rinsing* the paint brushes.
1878	flu o res cent	She chose the paper with a *fluorescent* blue color.
1879	trans mit ter	A *transmitter* is a person or thing that transmits.
1880	ac com plish ment	Learning to play the piano is an important *accomplishment*.

Spelling Enrichments

PREFIXES Use the prefix cards from page 116 or dictate: *in-, mis-, non-, pre-, re-, un-*. Combine with current spelling to make as many new words as possible.

reproached --	unreproached	*conceive* --	misconceive, preconceive
destruction --	indestruction	*apply* --	misapply, reapply
development --	redevelopment	*contagious* --	noncontagious
beneficial --	nonbeneficial		

COMPOSITION. Brainstrom on ways to creatively connect spelling words. Write about a boring king (a *monotonous sovereign)* or an *accomplished aerospace* engineer who invents *beneficial* products like *aerosol transmitters* for the *destruction* of *contagious* diseases.

LITERATURE. See Aesop's *The Eagle and the Arrow*. The arrow that kills the bird is made with his own feathers. Dictate the moral: "We often give our enemies the means for our *destruction*."

The Development of the English Language

The Norman French invasion of England in 1066 added a French influence to English vocabulary, while Latin remained the principal language of religion and learning, and Anglo-Saxon-based English vernacular continued in common speech. The mingling of these three influences added new ways to express the same ideas, giving delicate shades of meaning. The Anglo-based word *kingly* gained three synonyms: *royal, regal,* and *sovereign.* The word *rise* gained the synonyms *mount* and *ascend.*

re proached			[R4,28]
de struc tion	[<L de (un-) struere (build)] Root = destruct	**SH/TI Page**	[R4,11]
de vel op ment	Root = develop		[R4]
ben e fi cial	[<L bene (good)]	**SH/TI Page**	[R4,11]
con ceive	[<L con- (together) + capere (take)]	**IE/EI Page**	[R2,9,6,7]
ap ply			[R29,5,6]
ae ro space	[<G aero (air, gas, atmosphere)] ae = /A/		[R4,2,7]
ae ro sol	[<G aero (air) + sol(ution)] ae = /A/		[R4]
con ta gious	[<L con- (with) + tangere (touch)] gi = /j/		[R4,3]
con science	[<L con- (together) + scire (know)] sc =/s/; ci = /sh/; sci = /sh/		[R7]
sov er eign	[< OF soverain < L super (over)] Root = reign	**IE/EI Page**	[R9]
as cend	[<L ad- (up) + scandere (climb)]		[R2]
mo not o nous	[<Gk mono- (one) + tonos (thing stretched)]		[R4]
bi cy cle	[<L bi- (two) + < G kyklos (circle, wheel)]		[R5,2,7]
tri an gle	[<L tri- (three) + angulus (corner)]		[R5,7]
con cen tra tion	[<L con- (together) + centrum (center)] Root = concentrate		[R2,4,11,16]
rins ing	Root = rinse	**E's Drop Pg.**	[R16]
flu o res cent	[<L fluor < fluere (to flow)] Think to spell silent O.		[R4,2]
trans mit ter	[<L trans- (across) + mit (send)] Root = transmit	**2-1-1 Page**	[R15]
ac com plish ment	[<L ad- (to) + complere (fill up)]	**SH/TI Page**	[R29,10]

Spelling Enrichments

GREEK AND LATIN ROOTS. Identify the spelling words that use the following Greek and Latin word parts: *aero-, bi-, con-,mono-, trans-, tri-, mit.*

aero -- (air) *aerospace, aerosol*   mono -- (one) *monotonous*   bi -- (two) *bicycle*
tri -- (three) *triangle*   trans -- (across) + mit (send)   *transmitter*
con -- (together, with) *conceive, contagious, conscience, concentration*

Using a dictionary, can you find other words with these roots? *Ex.: aero- -- aerodynamics, aeronautics, aeroplane* (British), *aerometer, aerogram, aeromechanics, aeromedicine, aerobatics, aerobics.*

ANTONYMS.   Identify the spelling word that has the opposite meaning.
   praised/ *reproached*   construction/ *destruction*   harmful/ *beneficial*
   remove/ *apply*   noncontagious/ *contagious*   servant/ *sovereign*
   descend/ *ascend*   exciting/ *monotonous*   dilution/ *concentration*
   dirtying/ *rinsing*   receiver/ *transmitter*   failure/ *accomplishment*

Preliminaries. Review especially Spelling Rules: 1, 2, 3, 4, 5, 6, 7, 9, 11, 14, 15, 16, 17, 18, 19, 20, 28. Phonograms: *ai, ci, ch, ee, ed, ei, er, si, or, ou, ough, th* as well as *q̊u* = /k/ and *gu* = /g/. SWR Step 38. Reference Pages: Review **ED, 1-1-1** and **2-1-1 Pages**. See SWR Steps 22 (especially p. 124), 32, 39.

Words for Section X-1

1881	fi nance	The word *finance* originally meant revenue collected from fines.
1882	thor ough	Do a *thorough* job of washing the dishes.
1883	seize	The opposite of *seize* is to release, relinquish, give up, free, or liberate.
1884	coun ter feit	Flattery is *counterfeit* money which we accept because of vanity.
1885	math e mat ics	God uses *mathematics* in everything he makes. --Asa Sparks
1886	vague	The opposite of *vague* is specific, explicit, clear, precise.
1887	per ceive	He could *perceive* that I was telling the truth.
1888	im mense	The opposite of *immense* is small, tiny, or minute.
1889	di gest	I like to read *Homeschool Digest* as I *digest* my lunch.
1890	ac com mo date	I will *accommodate* the guests.
1891	or ches tra	If you want to lead the *orchestra*, you must turn your back to the crowd.
1892	com mit tee	Commit thy way unto the Lord; He is the best *committee* chairman.
1893	pos sessed	He *possessed* liberty and did not want to lose it to tyranny.
1894	in tel li gent	God made man more *intelligent* than animals.
1895	ac cu ra cy	The value of testimony depends on its *accuracy*.
1896	ap prox i mate	The *approximate* sum of 55 and 43 is one hundred.
1897	im me di ate	Good name in man or woman is the *immediate* jewel of his soul. --Shakespeare
1898	a tro cious	The crime was *atrocious*.
1899	o paque	*Opaque* glass is milky or the opposite of clear.
1900	de ci sion	The opposites of *decision* are indecision and uncertainty.

Spelling Enrichments

PREFIXES & SUFFIXES. Make derivatives from the current spelling words using the following prefixes *(in-, re-, sub-, un-)* and/ or suffixes *(-al, -ally, -ation, -ence, -er, -ed, -eur, -ial, -ian, -ible, -ier, -ing, -ly, -tion, -ness, -ure)*.

finance -- financ**ier**, financ**ial**, financ**ed**

thorough -- thorough**ly**

seize -- seiz**ed**, seiz**ure**, seiz**ing**, **un**seized

counterfeit -- counterfeit**ing**, counterfeit**ed**, counterfeit**er**

mathematics -- mathematic**ian**, mathematic**al**, mathmatic**ally**

vague -- vague**ly**, vague**ness**

perceive -- perceiv**ing**, perceiv**ed**, **un**perceived

immense -- immense**ly**, immense**ness**

digest -- digest**ible**, **in**digest**ible**, digest**ed**, digest**ing**

accommodate -- accommodat**ing**, accommodat**ed**, accommodat**ion**

orchestra -- orchestr**al**, orchestra**tion**

committee -- **sub**committee

possessed -- **re**possessed

intelligent -- **un**intelligent, intelligent**ly**, intelli**gence**

accuracy -- **in**accuracy

approximate -- approximate**ly**, approximat**ed**, approxima**tion**

immediate -- immediate**ly**

atrocious -- atrocious**ness**, atrocious**ly**

opaque -- opaque**ness**

decision -- **in**decision

Adding Words to Reference Page Charts

A number of words in this list can be added to reference pages. We will not add them until after all twenty words have been taught. Then we will add all the words for any particular page at one time. For **IE/EI Page** add *seize, counterfeit, perceive.*   To **2-1-1 Page** add *committee.*   To **SH/TI Page** add *atrocious* and *decision.*

fi nançe₃	I usually says /i/ at the end ....C said /s/ because of the E.		[R5,2,7]
thor ough			
seize₅	EI Exception we learned.	**IE/EI Page**	[R9,7]
coun ter feit	EI Exception we learned.	**IE/EI Page**	[R9]
math e mat ics	[<Gk math (to learn)]		[R4]
vague	A said /A/ because of the E.	gu = /g/	[R3,7]
per ceive₂	[<L per- (fully) + capere (grasp)]	**IE/EI Page**	[R2,9,6,7]
im mense₅	[<L in- (not) + mensus (measure)]		[R29,7]
di gest			[R5,3]
ac com mo date			[R29,4,7]
or ches tra			[R18]
com mit tee	Root = commit	**2-1-1 Page**	[R29,15]
pos sessed	Root = possess		[R29,19,17,28]
in tel li gent			[R29,5,3]
ac cu ra cy	[<L ad- (to) + cura (care)]		[R29,2,4,5,6]
ap prox i mate			[R29,20,5,7]
im me di ate	Think to spell /Ate/; say /it/.		[R29,4,5,7]
a tro cious	[<L atrox (dark, black) + -ocis (fierce)]	**SH/TI Page**	[R4,11]
o paque	[<L opacus (dark, shady)]	qu = /k/	[R4,1,6,7]
de ci sion		**SH/TI Page**	[R4,2,5,11]

Spelling Enrichments

ANTONYMS.
genuine/ *counterfeit*	small/ *immense*	lacked/ *possessed*
incompletely/ *thoroughly*	release/ *seize*	overlook/ *perceive*
defectiveness/ *accuracy*	clear/ *vague*	indecision/ *decision*
exact/ *approximate*	stupid/ *intelligent*	transparent/ *opaque*

COMPOSITION. You can dictate the following paragraph in lieu of regular spelling test. You could also use this example as a sample of the way students could tie together spelling words by theme instead of just writing unconnected sentences using the words.

An immense problem seized the world of finance. Tellers lacked accuracy in their mathematics. Banks were flooded with counterfeit money. How could this atrocious situation be corrected? Bankers could not digest their food for fear of losing their jobs. An immediate decision had to be made. Orchestra music was piped in to calm nerves. An intelligent committee made a thorough search for approximately a week.   Their opaque findings were vague and unclear. They could not perceive what went wrong. What will happen to Wall Street if the situation is not corrected soon? Who can find the money leak?

Preliminaries. Do a fast-paced review of especially <u>Spelling Rules</u>: 2, 4, 5, 6, 9, 11, 16, 22, 24, 27, 28.
Phonograms: *ar, au, aw, ci, ed, ei, er, ew, kn, oi, ou, ow, si, ti, ui*. Advanced: *eu* (SWR Step 38).
<u>Reference</u>: Introduce or review **Number, ED,** and **Plural Pages**. See SWR Steps 15, 22, 27.

Words for Section X-2

1901	res tau rant	Take mom to a *restaurant* to give her a rest from cooking.
1902	su per in tend ent	The *superintendent* of the factory watched out for the welfare of his workers.
1903	pe di a tri cian	A doctor who specializes in the care of children is called a *pediatrician*.
1904	ec cen tric	Our *eccentric* neighbor did many strange things
1905	pre lim i nar y	*Preliminary* steps are ones taken BEFORE others.
1906	al lit er a tion	Always avoid awkward or affected *alliteration*.
1907	lab o ra to ry	We labored at experiments in a chemistry *laboratory*.
1908	am a teur	The *amateur* is a man of enthusiasm who has not settled down. --Atkinson
1909	es pe cial ly	Do good to all, *especially* to those who are of the household of faith. --Gal. 6:10
1910	an nu al	You have an *annual*, or yearly, birthday celebration.
1911	des sert	*Dessert* has two s's because we enjoy sweets more than a dry, hot desert.
1912	des ert	A *des-ert* is a de-sert-ed place.
1913	leop ard	A *leopard* is full of spots. The silent O is like one of the spots.
1914	mil len ni um	Were you born in the last *millennium?*
1915	re ceipt	Webster in 1828 tried to spell *receipt* without the P as in "conceit" or "deceit."
1916	dis ap point ed	Without counsel purposes are *disappointed*. --Proverbs 15:22
1917	pro tein	*Protein* is important for building muscle.
1918	sus pi cious	*Suspicious* thoughts always haunt the guilty mind. --Shakespeare paraphrased
1919	con ven ient	Trouble never comes at a *convenient* time.
1920	par lia ment	*Parliament* was formed as a way to restrain the king.

Spelling Enrichments

ALLITERATION. Match together the words that alliterate (have the same first sounds).
amateur, annual, alliteration   dessert, desert, disappointed
eccentric, especially   laboratory, leopard
restaurant, receipt   superintendent, suspicious
parliament, preliminary, protein, pediatrician

ORIGINAL SENTENCES. Make original sentences using spelling words. Include at least two words that alliterate in each sentence. Using alliteration can add a musical quality to writing if not used excessively. Avoid using too much alliteration with hissing sounds. Bad example: *Slothful Sally saw sleepy Sam slowly sip a sloppy slurpee.*

GRAMMAR. Can you change the ending and thereby change the part of speech to:
convenient	- adj.	convenience - n, conveniently - adv.
eccentric	- adj.	eccentrically - adv.
disappointed	- v.	disappointment - n.
suspicious	- adj.	suspicion - n. or v., suspiciously - adv., suspiciousness -n.

© 2003, Wanda Sanseri

Rhythm of Speech Affects Phonogram Sounds

Occasionally the **vowel I** sounds like the **consonant Y**. If we make the *I* in these words into a distinct syllable, we can hear how this happens. Think to spell the two-syllable word *mil -lion* as as a three syllable word: *mil-li-on.*   Other review words illustrating this include: *o-pin-i-on, on-i-on, un-i-on, fa-mil-i-ar, be-hav-i-or, com-pan-i-on, pe-cul-i-ar.* See SWR page 85.

res t<u>au</u> rant	Mark final A with a 3 if you say /ah/.		
s<u>u</u> p<u>er</u> in tend ent	Root = superintend		[R4]
p<u>e</u> di <u>a</u> tri <u>c</u>ian		**SH/TI Page**	[R4,5,11]
ec cen tric	[< GK ex- (out) + kentron (center)]		[R2]
pr<u>e</u> lim i n<u>a</u> ry			[R4,5,6]
al lit <u>er</u> <u>a</u> <u>ti</u>on	[< L al- (to) + litera (letter)] Root = alliterate		[R29,4,11,16]
lab <u>o</u> r<u>a</u> to ry	Markings are for thinking to spell.		[R4,5,6]
am <u>a</u> t<u>eu</u>r	[<L amator (lover) enjoy w/out pay] eu = /OO/		[R4]
es p<u>e</u>́ <u>c</u>ial ly	Root = special.	**SH/TI Page**	R11,29,5,6]
an n<u>u</u> al	[<L annus (year)]		[R29,4]
des̃² s̃²ert	Accent second syllable.		[R29]
des̃² ert	Accent first syllable.		
l<u>e</u> <u>o</u> p<u>ar</u>d	Think /LE-O-pard/; say /lep-ard/.		[R4]
mil len ni um	[<L mille (thousand) + annus (year)]	**Number Pg.**	[R29,5]
r<u>e</u> c<u>ei</u>̃²pt	**P** stands for *receiPt* of **P**ayment.	**IE/EI Page**	[R4,2,9]
dis ap p<u>oi</u>nt <u>e</u>d			[R29,28]
pr<u>o</u> t<u>ei</u>̃²n	Learned exception for EI.	**IE/EI Page**	[R4,9]
sus pi <u>ci</u>o̊⁴us	Root = suspect	**SH/TI Page**	[R5,11]
con v<u>e</u> ni ent	Think /con-vE-ni-ent; say /con-vEn-yent/.		[R4,5,16]
p<u>ar</u> li <u>a</u> ment	Add a syllable to think to spell. See SWR p. 88.		[R5]

WORD ETYMOLOGY.   What spelling words come from the following roots?

Latin: intendere (direct)   *superintendent*
     litera   (letter)   *alliteration*
     prae-   (before)   *preliminary*
     labor   (work)   *laboratory*
     amator   (lover)   *amateur*
     annus   (year)   *annual, millennium*
     specere   (look)   *suspicious*
     deserere   (abandon)   *desert*
     venire   (come)   *convenient*
     recepta   (receive)   *receipt*
     punctum   (point)   *disappoint*
     mille   (thousand)   *millennium*

French:
     desservir   (clear the table)   *dessert*
     parler   (to speak)   *parliament*
     restaurer   (to restore)   *restaurant*

Greek:
     pedi   (child)   *pediatrician*
     kentron   (center)   *eccentric*
     proteios   (of 1st quality)   *protein*
     leon   (lion)   *leopard*

PLURALS. List the spelling words that can be used as nouns and then make them plural:
     restaurants, superintendents, pediatricians, preliminaries, laboratories, amateurs, annuals, desserts, deserts, leopards, millenniums or millennia, receipts, proteins, parliaments.

Preliminaries. Review especially <u>Spelling Rules</u>: 1, 3, 4, 5, 6, 7, 9, 11, 20.
> <u>Phonograms:</u> Give a fast-paced review of at least *ar, ch, ci, ei, er, ie, oo, or, ou, ph, qu, tch, th, ti.*
> <u>Reference Pages:</u> Introduce or review **SH/TI** and **IE/EI Pages**. See SWR Steps 18, 40.

Words for Section Y-1

1921	ex qui site	The queen has *exquisite* taste and manners.
1922	par a ble	Jesus often used a *parable,* a special short story to illustrate a truth.
1923	pa ren the sis	Something in *parenthesis* is a statement beside the main point.
1924	par a med ic	A *paramedic* is one who works beside a doctor.
1925	par al lel	*Parallel* means to lie beside without touching, like the two L's in parallel.
1926	con junc tion	Can you name a *conjunction* in English?
1927	a the ist	An *atheist* does not believe in any god.
1928	heir loom	The quilt my grandmother made is my most precious *heirloom.*
1929	mis chief	That boy is the CHIEF source of *misCHIEF.*
1930	mis chie vous	Gossip is *mischievous* and easy, but grievous to bear and hard to get rid of. --Hesiod
1931	chan de lier	*Chandelier* is a French name for a fancy light fixture.
1932	bib li og ra phy	A *bibliography* is a listing of books.
1933	en thu si asm	Nothing great was ever achieved without *enthusiasm.* --Emerson
1934	per sis tence	Stick with it, because *persistence* often pays.
1935	kil o me ter	A *kilometer* is one thousand meters.
1936	ge og ra phy	*Geography* relates to God who created land and the world. --Haycock
1937	mor tal	The Christian need not fear what *mortal* man can do to him.
1938	mor ti cian	A physician examines the living and a *mortician* prepares the dead.
1939	mort gage	Like the silent T in *mortgage,* the bank is silent about the danger of debt.
1940	kin der gar ten	A *kindergarten* is a garden of children.

Spelling Enrichments

WORD ETYMOLOGY. Find the spelling word(s) built from the following foreign word parts.

<u>French</u>	meter	(measure)	*kilometer*
	mis-	(bad)	*mischief, mischievous*
	mort	(death)	*mortal, mortician, mortgage*
<u>German</u>	kinder	(children)	*kindergarten* (a garden of children)
<u>Greek</u>	biblio	(book)	*bibliography*
	graph	(draw, write)	*bibliography, geography*
	para-	(beside)	*parable, parenthesis, paramedic, parallel*
	theos	(god)	*atheist, enthusiasm*
<u>Latin</u>	candela	(candle)	*chandelier*
	geo	(earth)	*geography*
	junctum	(join)	*conjunction*
	per-	(to the end)	*persistence*
	quaerere	(seek)	*exquisite*

REFERENCE PAGE. Add as many words as possible from this list to the Reference Pages.
> **IE/ EI** -- *heirloom, mischief, mischievous, chandelier*   **TI/ CI/ SI** -- *conjunction, mortician*

Mr. Nobody A humorous poem, author unknown, contains one of this week's words. Can you guess which one?
>I know a funny little man as quiet as a mouse,
>Who does the *mischief* that is done in everybody's house!
>No one ever sees his face, and yet we all agree
>That every plate that breaks was cracked by Mr. Nobody.

ex qui site₅	[<L ex- (out) + quaerere (seek)]		[R20,1,5,7]
par a ble₄	[<Gk para- (beside) + bole (to throw)- throw a story beside an idea]		[R4,7]
pa ren the sis	[<Gk para (beside) + thesis (place)]		[R4]
par a med ic	[<Gk para- (beside) + medicus (physician)]		[R4]
par al lel	[<Gk para- (beside) + allos (other)]		[R29]
con junc tion	[< L con- (together) + junctum (join)]		[R11]
a the ist	[<Gk a- (without) + theos (god)]		[R4]
heir loom	[<heir (one who inherits) + loom (goods not real estate)]	**IE/EI Pg.**	[R9]
mis chief	[<OF mis (bad) + chief (head)]	**IE/EI Pg.**	[R9]
mis chie vous	Unvoiced F in chief changes to voiced V.	**IE/EI Pg.**	[R9]
chan de lier	[< F <L candela (candle) <candere (to shine)]	**IE/EI, SH Pgs.**	[R4,9]
bib li og ra phy	[< Gk biblio (book) + graph (write)]		[R5,4,6]
en thu si asm	[<Gk en- (in) + theos (God)]		[R4,5]
per sis tence₃	[<L per- (to the end) + sistere (stand)] Root = persist		[R2,7]
kil o me ter	[<F kilo (one thousand) + meter (measure)] British = kilometre		[R4]
ge og ra phy	[<L geo (earth) + graphein (describe, draw)]		[R3,4,5,6]
mor tal	[<F mort (death)]		
mor ti cian	[<F mort (death)]	**SH/TI Pg.**	[R5,11]
mort gage	[<F mort (death)] See SWR p. 86.		[R3,7]
kin der gar ten	[<G kinder (children) + garten (garden)]		

DERIVATIVES. Make new words using either the word parts on pages 98 and 116 or the plural endings (See SWR p. 143 for *parenthesis*). Prefixes: *overenthusiasm, overmortgaged, immortal, nonpersistence.* Suffixes: *exquisitely, exquisiteness, parentheses, paralleled, bibliographies, geographic, geographically, mortality, immortality, mortally, mortgaged, mortgaging, mortgagee, mortgages, atheistic.*

COMPOSITION. Dictate these questions and have the students write a response. What did the *mischievous kindergartner* do? How did it relate to the *geography* lesson and the *exquisite heirloom chandelier*? Why was the call for the *mortician* a false alarm? How did the *persistence* of the *paramedic* save the day?

DICTATION. In lieu of a spelling test, dictate this continuation of the Mr. Nobody poem.

The mischievous man's persistence travels far and wide. /Kindergarten student or mortician, none can hide. Anywhere that mortals live, throughout geography, /People with enthusiasm blame Mr. Nobody.

Exquisite heirloom salesman and many others do, /Paramedic, atheist, parable writer, too. Chandelier-maker, mortgage-giver, all alike proclaim, /People very different give a message much the same, The many sources form a kind of bibliography /To show all mischief problems come from Mr. Nobody.

Distance measured any way, kilometer or miles, / In conjunction with business or children's simple smiles, The parallel message remains the same, within parentheses, /Every group or nation has Mr. Nobodies.

Preliminaries

Review Spelling Rules: 1, 2, 3, 4, 5, 6, 7, 11, 16, 18, 20, 24.
Phonograms: *ai, ar, au, aw, ay, ci, ea, er, or, ou, ow, ph, qu.* Advanced: *yr, gu* (SWR Step 38).
Reference Pages: Introduce or review **Plus Endings Page**. See SWR Step 35.

Words for Section Y-2

1941	ex traor di nar y	Samson's *extraordinary* strength was taken from him.
1942	phy si cian	The Lord is sometimes called the Great *Physician*.
1943	en deav or	We must *endeavor* to live peacefully with one another.
1944	fail ure	A first *failure* may prepare the way to later success. --A Lobel
1945	en dur ance	Patient *endurance* attaineth to all things. --Longfellow
1946	rec i pe	If we can read, we can learn to cook by following a good *recipe*.
1947	por ce lain	The *porcelain* doll remained in the family as a priceless heirloom.
1948	cau li flow er	*Cauliflower* is nothing but cabbage with a college education. --Mark Twain
1949	mar tyr	The blood of *martyrs* is the seed of the church.
1950	cem e ter y	We go to the *cEmEtEry* with E's (ease).
1951	ac quaint ance	Any *acquaintance* is completely estranged from me. --Job
1952	tran quil	The opposite of *tranquil* is disturbed, unsettled, agitated, restless, or rattled.
1953	a pol o gy	The opposite of giving an *apology* is to accuse, defend, or blameshift.
1954	syl la ble	Tomorrow creeps in this petty pace from day to day to the last *syllable* of recorded time. -Shakespeare
1955	ap pro pri ate	It is not *appropriate* for Christian girls to dress immodestly.
1956	e lim i nate	The opposite of *eliminate* is to add or include.
1957	singe	Be careful not to *singe* your hair by the fire.
1958	suf fi cient	The opposite of *sufficient* is insufficient, inadequate, failing to meet the need.
1959	fa tigue	The opposite of *fatigue* is to be energized or stimulated.
1960	en vi ron ment	The word "*environment*" is not listed in Webster's 1828 dictionary.

Spelling Enrichments

LITERATURE. Read *Foxe's Book of Martyrs* or another book about a brave man or woman who died for a worthy cause. What can you learn from their examples? Write a paragraph describing one of the martyrs. Answer the questions: Who? What? When? How? Why?

ANTONYMS. Identify the spelling word that is the opposite of the following:

add	*eliminate*		unacceptable	*appropriate*
insult	*apology*		murderer	*martyr*
success	*failure*		stranger	*acquaintance*
ordinary	*extraordinary*			

SYNONYMS. Identify the spelling word that means the same as the following:

graveyard/ *cemetery*	perseverance/ *endurance*	exhaustion/ *fatigue*	try/ *endeavor*
doctor/ *physician*	adequate/ *sufficient*	calm/ *tranquil*	glass/ *procelain*

A New Spelling for /ER/

We have learned six spellings for /ER/. Name them: *er, ur, ir, wor, ear, our*. What letter is in all the examples? (R). What type of other letter is in every ER? (a vowel). The ERs are examples of R-influenced vowels. Can anyone guess the seventh spelling for ER? As a hint, what letter is used in Greek words in place of I? (Y). The Greek form of /ER/ is YR. This rare ER is used for only several words in our English dictionaries *(myrrh, myrtle, zephyr)*. Listen for one of the examples in this lesson.

ex tra or di na ry	Think 6 syllables for spelling.	[R20,5,4,6]
phy si cian	Greek-based words use PH for /f/ and Y for I. **SH/TI Page**	[R5,11]
en deav or	British spelling: en deav our (Use phonogram *our*.)	
fail ure	Root = fail	[R7]
en dur ance	Root = endure Drop silent E but retain sound of /U/.	[R16,7]
rec i pe	E is usually silent at the end of multi-syllable words.	[R2,5,4]
por ce lain	[<L porcus (hog) -- shell shaped like a pig's back]	[R2,4]
cau li flow er	[<L caulis (cabbage) + flores (flower)]	[R5]
mar tyr	[<Gk martyr (witness)] yr = ir = /er/ **ER Page**	
cem e ter y	Can you name all the rules used in this word?	[R2,4,5,6]
ac quaint ance	[<L ad- (to) + cognitus (know)] Root = acquaint	[R1,2,7]
tran quil	Q always need U. U is not a vowel here.	[R1]
a pol o gy		[R4,3,5,6]
syl la ble		[R29,4,7]
ap pro pri ate	Think verb form for spelling.	[R29,4,5,7]
e lim i nate		[R4,5,7]
singe	Reasons for E: g says /j/; clarifies word (not *sing*)	[R3,7]
suf fi cient	[<L sub- (up) + facere (make)] Root = suffice **SH/TI Page**	[R29,5,16,11]
fa tigue	French: i=/E/. gu=/g/. G says /g/ when followed by U.	[R4,3,6,7]
en vi ron ment	[<L in- (in) + viron (circle)] Root = environ	[R5]

DERIVATIVES. Build new words from the current spelling words by adding prefixes *(in-, mono-, poly-, re-)* and suffixes *(-al, -dom, -ed, -es, -ing, -ion, -ity, -ize, -izer, -ly)*.

martyr --	martyrdom	*singe* --	singeing**
cemetery --	cemeteries [R24]	*sufficient* --	sufficiently,
acquaintance --	reacquaintance		insufficient,
tranquil --	tranquility, tranquilize, tranquilizer *		insufficiently
apology --	apologies, apologize [R24]	*fatigue* --	fatiguing [R16]
syllable --	monosyllable, polysyllable	*environment* --	environmental
appropriate --	inappropriate, appropriation		
eliminate --	elimination, eliminated, eliminating		

*The accent is not on the last syllable, so these are not examples of the 2-1-1 Accent rule [R15].
The Oxford dictionary does not follow this rule. The British double the L in these words.
**Retain the E to keep meaning clear.

Preliminaries

Phonograms: *ai, au, ch, dge, ee, er, ir, oi, or, ou, si, ti, ur.*   Advanced *eu, gu, a̋u* (SWR Step 38).
Spelling Rule Cards: Review 2, 4, 5, 6, 7, 11, 12, 14, 15, 17, 20, 23, 26.

Words for Section Z-1

1961	dis cern	The word of God is living and powerful to *discern* thoughts and intents.
1962	hu mor ous	The humorist who told humor at the expense of another is not *humorous*.
1963	oc cur rence	Growth in maturity is not an overnight *occurrence*.
1964	guar an tee	Preparedness for war is the best *guarantee* of peace. --Aesop
1965	priv i lege	Driving a car is a *privilege*, not a right.
1966	tortoise	The slow and steady *tortoise* outraced the speedy but prideful rabbit.
1967	dis pense	A dispensary is a place from which a doctor or nurse may *dispense* medicine.
1968	com bus ti ble	Wood and coal are *combustible* elements used for campfires.
1969	in ces sant	I try to avoid her because she is an *incessant*, never-ceasing talker.
1970	rec om mend	The opposite of *recommend* is to disapprove, discourage, or slander.
1971	em bar rass ment	The boy caught in telling a lie dropped his head in *embarrassment*.
1972	pro cras ti na tion	*Procrastination* is the thief of time. --McGuffey
1973	mis cel la ne ous	The boy had a *miscellaneous* collection of bugs, stones, and other things.
1974	dis ci pline	A father will *discipline* the son he loves.
1975	chauf feur	*Chauffeur* is a French title for a paid automobile driver.
1976	vil lain	The *villain* was caught and put in prison.
1977	flam ma ble	*Flammable* and inflammable both mean "will burn!"
1978	ker o sene	During the power shortage, we needed a *kerosene* lamp.
1979	ex plo sion	People for miles around heard the *explosion*.
1980	pen i ten tia ry	Satan's friendship reaches to the *penitentiary*. --Turkish Proverb

Spelling Enrichments

DERIVATIVES. Nine of the words in the first column can be made into additional words by adding prefixes *(non-, re-, un-, under-)* and/or suffixes *(-able, -al, -ary, -ation, -ed, -ible, -ing, -ly, -ment, -ness).*

discern --	discernible, discerning, discerned, discernment
humorous --	humorously, humorousness
occurrence --	reoccurrence
guarantee --	guaranteed, guaranteeing
privilege --	privileged, privileging, unprivileged, underprivileged
dispense --	dispensary, dispensable, dispensation, dispensed
combustible --	noncombustible
incessant --	incessantly
recommend --	recommended, recommending, recommendation

ORIGINAL COMPOSITION. Relay a personal account of a *humorous* or *embarrassing occurrence* that caused an *explosion* of laughter. Use spelling words when possible, but don't force them.

Abbreviations

Abbreviations use a few letters to represent a larger word. What words do the following abbreviations represent? *(Dr., Mr., Ave.)* See SWR Step 25. Today's spelling words contain a word commonly abbreviated. Can you identify it? *(miscellaneous/ misc.)*

dis cern	C says /s/ because of the E.		[R2]
hu mor ous			[R4]
oc cur rence	Root = occur	**ER, 2-1-1 Pgs.**	[R29,2,15,7]
gua ran tee	[< OF guarant (warrant)]	gu = /g/	
priv i lege			[R5,3,7]
tor toise	[<L tortus (twisted)] Think /tor-tois/. Say /tor-tus/.		[R7]
dis pense	[<L dis- (out) + pend (weigh)]		[R7]
com bus ti ble	[<L com- (with) + urere (to burn)]		[R5,7]
in ces sant	[<L in (not) + cesser (stop)] Root = cease		[R2,29]
rec om mend	One C; spelling matches meaning (re- + commend)		[R29]
em bar rass ment			[R29,17]
pro cras ti na tion		**SH/TI Page**	[R4,5,11]
mis cel la ne ous	[<L miscellaneus (mixed)]	Abbrev.: misc.	[R2,29,4,12]
dis ci pline	Root = disciple		[R2,7]
chauf feur	French: ch = /sh/, au = /O/, eu = /oo/.	**SH/TI Page**	[R29]
vil lain	Think to spell /vil-lAn/; say /vil-an/.		[R29]
flam ma ble	[<L flamma (flame)] Unusual Synonym: inflammable		[R29,4,7]
ker o sene	[<Gk keros (wax)]		[R4,7]
ex plo sion	[<L ex- (out) + plosio (clap)]	**SH/TI Page**	[R20,4,11]
pen i ten tia ry		**SH/TI Page**	[R5,11,6]

DICTATION. Instead of giving a regular spelling test, have the students write the following selections from dictation. All of the spelling words (or derivatives of the words) are included at least once.

This *occurrence* of your carelessness was not *humorous*. I *discern* that *procrastination* is the cause of your *embarrassment*. If you keeping working as slowly as a *tortoise,* I *guarantee* you will need to be *disciplined.*

The *chauffeur* thought he had *guaranteed privileges* to do many *miscellaneous* things.

The *villain* who *dispensed flammable kerosene* near the car received punishment. The *combustible* material caused an *explosion.* The owner *recommended incessantly* that the *villain* go to the *penitentiary.*

ROOT WORDS. Identify the root.

embarrassment (embarrass)   *humorous* (humor)

occurrence (occur)   *procrastination* (procrastinate)   *penitentiary* (penitent)

discipline (disciple)   *recommend* (commend)   *incessant* (cease)

Preliminaries

Phonograms: Review all 70 and Advanced: *ah, eu, gi, pn, rh* (SWR Step 38).
Spelling Rule Cards: Give a final review of all rules espcially 1, 2, 3, 4, 5, 6, 7, 9, 11, 18, 27.

Words for Section Z-2

1981	hip po pot a mus	The *hippotamus* is a danger in the rivers of Africa. --M. Hungerford
1982	rhi noc er os	The *rhinoceros* walked near the elephant.
1983	a quar i um	The beautiful colors of the *aquarium* and the gentle movement of fish were calming.
1984	sou ve nir	A prized *souvenir* may have little value for anyone else.
1985	ma neu ver	A scheming woman knows how to *maneuver* people to do what she wants.
1986	an ti sep tic	The *antiseptic* kills germs.
1987	pro fi cien cy	Each person is unique and each should gain *proficiency* in something.
1988	sym pho ny	A *symphony* is music from many instruments that work together.
1989	syn o nym	A *synonym* is a word with the same meaning as another (little/small).
1990	syn chro nize	*Synchronize* means to do things at the same time.
1991	sur veil lance	The police kept careful *surveillance* over the released prisoner.
1992	dis sen sion	To a troublemaker, debate, *dissension,* and uproar are his joy.
1993	sta tion er y	Write a lettER to hER on your new *stationERy.*
1994	sov er eign ty	The Lord will REIGN with *soveREIGNty* over all the earth.
1995	lieu ten ant	Parents "to their children...are heaven's *lieutenants.*" --William Shakespeare
1996	pneu mo nia	*Pneumonia* is a disease of the lungs that makes it hard to breathe.
1997	ap pen di ci tis	*Appendicitis* kept Mitsuo Fuchida from dying in World War II.
1998	al le giance	I pledge *allegiance* to the flag of the United States of America.
1999	can ta loupe	*Cantaloupe* is his favorite kind of melon.
2000	hal le lu jah	We are finished with the spelling list, *hallelujah!*

Spelling Enrichments

MUSIC APPRECIATION. Play classical music as background while the student works with spelling words. Dictate the sentences: Music is important. Often a *sovereign* will search for composers with *proficiency* because the *allegiance* of people is stirred by national music. Listen to the *"Hallelujah* Chorus" by Handel. Hear how the *symphony* pleasantly *synchronizes* sounds.

HOMONYM. Write a sentence correctly using each of the spellings of stationary/ *stationery.*

CORRESPONDENCE. Dictate the assignment: Design *stationery* with a border containing a *hippopotamus, rhinoceros,* and marine life from an *aquarium.* Write a friendly letter on your *stationery.* Perhaps you can write a get-well message to someone recovering from *pneumonia, appendicitis,* or some other miscellaneous illness.

SYNONYMS. fish bowl/ *aquarium;* orchestra/ *symphony;* kingship/ *sovereignty;* strife/ *dissension;* writing paper/ *stationery;* praise the Lord/ *hallelujah;* loyalty/ *allegiance;* assistant/ *lieutenant;* watch/ *surveillance;* excellence/ *proficiency;* keepsake/ *souvenir;* disinfectant/ *antiseptic.*

Interjection

The final spelling word in the Wise List is an appropriate interjection. An *interjection* is a word which stands alone and expresses strong feeling: *Ouch! Fire! Help! Surprise!* (SWR Step 16). What word might express our sense of completion, happiness, and praise as we finish the list?

hip po pot a mus	[<Gk hippos (horse) + potamos (river)]		[R29,4]
rhi noc er os	[< Gk rhis (nose) + keras (horn)]	rh =/r/	[R5,2]
a qua ri um			[R4,1,5]
sou ve nir			[R4]
ma neu ver	British spelling: manoeuvre	eu = /OO/	[R4]
an ti sep tic	[<Gk anti- (against) + septikos (to rot)]		[R5]
pro fi cien cy		**SH/TI Page**	[R4,5,11,2,6]
sym pho ny	[<Gk syn- (together) + phone (sound)]		[R4,5,6]
syn o nym	[<Gk syn- (like, together) + onyma (name)]		[R4]
syn chro nize	[<Gk syn- (like, together) + chronos (time)]		[R4,7]
sur veil lance	Root = survey	**ER, IE/EI Pgs.**	[R9,29,2,7]
dis sen sion		**SH/TI Page**	[R29,11]
sta tion er y	Think to spell /er/. Homophone: stationary		[R4,11,5,6]
sov er eign ty		**IE/EI Page**	[R9,5,6]
li eu ten ant	[<F lieu (place) +<L tenere (hold)]	eu = /OO/	[R5]
pneu mo ni a	Add syllable for spelling. See SWR p. 85.	pn = /n/; eu = /U/	[R4,5,18]
ap pen di ci tis	Root = append		[R29,5,2]
al le giance	G may say /j/ when followed by I.	gi = /j/	[R29,4,3,2,7]
can ta loupe	Alternative spelling: cantaloup.		[R4,7]
hal le lu jah		ah = /a/	[R29,4]

ETYMOLOGY. Identify the words from the following foreign roots:

Greek	anti-	(against) --	*antiseptic*
	aqua	(water) --	*aquarium*
	chronos	(time) --	*synchronize*
	hippos	(horse) --	*hippopotamus*
	phone	(sound) --	*symphony*
	pneuma	(breathe) --	*pneumonia*
	potamos	(river) --	*hippotamus*
	rhino	(nose) --	*rhinoceros*
	syn-	(together, like) --	*symphony, synonym, synchronize*
Latin	facere	(make) --	*proficiency*
	manu	(hand) --	*maneuver*
	sensio	(think, feel) --	*dissension*
	tenere	(hold) --	*lieutenant*
	veiller	(watch) --	*surveillance*
	venire	(come to mind) --	*souvenir*

Explanation of Special Spelling Markings

1. <u>Syllabication</u>:
   Words are broken into syllables to illustrate relationships to rules more clearly.

2. <u>Single Underline</u>:
   a. Multi-letter phonograms that represent one unit of sound (**<u>eigh</u>t**)
   b. Single vowels at the end of a syllable if they say A-E-I-O-U (**m<u>e</u>, m<u>y</u>**)
   c. U, V, C, or G before a silent E to show why we need the E (**bl<u>ue</u>$_2$, ha<u>ve</u>$_2$, lan<u>ce</u>$_3$, lar<u>ge</u>$_3$**)

3. <u>Double Underline</u>:
   a. Silent letters, like a silent final E, or unexpected letters like the "b" in "**lam<u>b</u>**"
   b. To emphasize 1-1-1 rule (**hop p<u>i</u>ng**), or the 2-1-1 rule (**b<u>e</u> gin <u>n</u>ing**)

   A double underline is unnecessary in words like "**till**" [R17] or "**sud-den**" [R29].
   In these cases the verbal emphasis is adequate. In dictating the word "till" after the child
   sounds the first /l/ the teacher should interject the rule: "We often double F, L, and S..."   In
   dictating words like "sudden" the teacher should say, "We think to spell sud-den, we say "sud-en."

4. <u>A Bridge</u>:
   A bridge is drawn from a bold vowel, over the consonant, to the silent E (**tim͡e**).

5. <u>Numbers</u>:
   a. Above a phonogram to show which sound other than the first is used (**w$\overset{32}{a}$s, sl$\overset{2}{ow}$**),
   UNLESS the possibility of a second sound can be readily seen
      The number 2 is understood and not needed when:
      1. A single consonant follows Rules 2 (**cent**), 3 (**gym**)
      2. A single vowel follows Rules 4 (**m<u>e</u>**), 5, 6 (**m<u>y</u>**), 7 (**dim͡e**),   19 (**old**).
      Note: Occasionally a single vowel will make the second sound and not be covered by any
      of the vowel rules. In such a case, it will need a 2 (**$\overset{2}{a}$n <u>c</u>ient, con tr$\overset{2}{o}$l**).
   b. Beside the double underline for silent final E to show the reason for the E (**ap pl<u>e</u>$_4$,   com<u>e</u>$_5$**)
   c. Number 1 is placed above a phonogram to clarify that it is a single phonogram rather
   than a multi-letter one (**v$\overset{1}{e}$r y**) or where the pronunciation is an exception to a general
   rule (**n$\overset{1}{a}$ <u>tion</u> al**).

6. <u>An x</u>:
   An X is placed over a phonogram in place of a number when the phonogram makes a
   distinctly different sound from the sound(s) we taught with the phonograms (**$\overset{x}{o}$f, w$\overset{x}{ou}$ld**).

7. <u>A Bracket</u>: Shows relationships between words in the Wise List:
   a. Base word/ derivative   (day/daily)
   b. Same peculiarity in spelling   (any/many)
   c. Contrasts in sounds that might be easily confused   (picture/pitcher)
   d. Different tenses of the same verb   (run/ran)

SWR Spelling Rules

1. **Q** always needs a U. U is not a vowel here *(quit)*.

2. **C** usually says /k/ *(cat, cot, cut, clip, music)*. **C** says /s/ before E, I, or Y *(cent, city, cycle)*.
3. **G** usually says /g/ *(gap, got, guts, grip, bag)*, but **G** MAY say /j/ before E, I, or Y *(germ, giant, gym)*.

4. **A, E, O , U** usually say /A, E, O, U/ at the end of a syllable *(la-zy, me, go, u-nit)*.

5. **I and Y** usually say /i/ at the end of a syllable *(cli-nic, cy-nic)*, but may say /I/ *(li-on, cry)*.

6. English words do not end in **I, U, V, or J**. At the end of English words Y stands in for I.

7. **SILENT FINAL Es.** English has at least five reasons for a silent final E.
1st	dime	(The vowel sound changes because of the E.)
2nd	love, true	(English words do not end with V or U.)
3rd	dance, large	(The C says /s/ because of the E. The G says /j/ because of the E).
4th	ap ple	(Every syllable must have a vowel.)
5th	are	(The Odd Job E includes any miscellaneous reason not covered above.)

8. **O-R** usually says /er/ when W comes before O-R *(worship)*.

9. **IE or EI?** Use I before E *(chief)* except after C *(receive)*, if we say /A/ *(vein)*, and in some exceptions:
   Either weird foreign sovereign forfeited leisure. Neither heifer seized counterfeit protein or caffeine.

10. **SH** spells /sh/ at the beginning of a word *(she)*, at the end of a syllable *(fish)*, but not at the beginning of any syllable after the first one *(na-tion)* except for the ending -ship *(friend-ship)*.
11. **TI, CI, SI** can spell /sh/ at the beginning of any syllable after the first one *(nation, facial, tension)*.

12. **ABBREVIATIONS** use a few letters to represent a larger word (Mr. = Mister, m = meter, CA = California).
13. **CONTRACTIONS** replace a letter (or letters) with an apostrophe to contract (or shorten) a phrase (I am = I'm).

14. **1-1-1 RULE.** With a <u>one</u>-syllable word ending in <u>one</u> vowel then <u>one</u> consonant, double the last consonant before adding a vowel suffix *(get, getting)*.
15. **2-1-1-ACCENT RULE**. With a <u>two</u>-syllable word ending in <u>one</u> vowel then <u>one</u> consonant, double the last consonant before adding a vowel suffix IF the <u>accent</u> is on the last syllable *(for get', for get ting)*.

16. **SILENT FINAL E WORDS** commonly lose the need for the E when adding a vowel suffix *(hope/hoping/ hopeless)*. This is the **E's Dropping Rule.** In words like *noticeable* or *changeable* rules 2 and 3 override rule 16.

17. We often double **F,L,S** after a single vowel at the end of a base word *(off, all, confess)*. Occasionally other letters are doubled in this way *(ebb, odd, egg, inn, err, watt, jazz)*.

18. **A-Y** usually says /A/ at the end of a base word *(may, pay)*. When a word ends with A it says /ah/ *(ma)*.

19. **I and O** may say /I/ and /O/ before two consonants *(bind, gold)*.

20. **X** is never directly before S. *(boxes, excel)*. There is a /s/ sound in X.

21. **ALL** and **FULL** are written with one L when added to another syllable *(almost, fulfill)*. *All right* is two words just like *all wrong*. (TILL has been omitted from this rule since it only applies to *until*.) This is the **Dismiss L Rule.**

22. To make a word **PLURAL** just add an -s, UNLESS the word ending hisses (ch, s, sh, x, z), changes *(wife/ wives; fly/flies)*, or just stops with O *(tomato/tomatoes)*. In these cases add -es. Occasional words have no change *(sheep/sheep)*, an internal change *(man/men)*, or a foreign spelling *(alumnus/alumni; piano/pianos)*.

23. **DGE** is used only after a single vowel which says /a-e-i-o-u/ *(badge, edge, bridge, lodge, fudge)*.

24. **A SINGLE VOWEL Y** (not *oy, ey, ay*) changes to I when adding any ending *(try/tried)*, unless the ending starts with I *(trying, babyish, copyist)*. This is the **Y's Exchanging Rule.**

25. **CK** is used only after a single vowel which says /a-e-i-o-u/ *(back, peck, pick, pocket, truck)*.

26. **CAPITALIZE** words which are the individual names or titles of persons *(Jesus)*, places *(Ohio)*, or things *(Bible)*.

27. **Z, NEVER S**, spells /z/ at the beginning of a base word *(zoo, zero)*.

28. **E-D** past tense ending forms another syllable if the base word ends with /d/ or /t/ *(loaded, acted)*. If not, E-D sounds like /d/ or /t/ *(killed, picked)*.

29. **DOUBLE CONSONANTS** in multisyllable words should both be sounded for spelling but not in normal speech *(ap-ple)*. [Note: This rule is a guideline for teachers but not necessary for students to learn.]

phonogram	sound (s)	[For teacher only—Examples of words]			
a	/a/-/A/-/ah/	am	a-pron	wasp	
b	/b/	bat			
c	/k/- /s/	cat	cent		
d	/d/	dad			
e	/e/-/E/	elk	be		
f	/f/	fat			
g	/g/-/j/	big	gym		
h	/h/	hat			
i	/i/-/I/	it	i-vy		
j	/j/	job			
k	/k/	kit			
l	/l/	lap			
m	/m/	me			
n	/n/	nut			
o	/ah/-/O/-/OO/	on	go	to	
p	/p/	pan			
qu	/kw/—Q always needs a U.	queen			
r	/r/	ran			
s	/s/-/z/	sent	as		
t	/t/	tip			
u	/u/-/U/-/oo/	up	u-nit	put	
v	/v/	van			
w	/w/	wag			
x	/ks/	fox			
y	/y/-/i/-/I/	yard	gym	by	
z	/z/	zip			
ai	/A/ -- 2-letter /A/ that we may NOT use at the end of English words`	laid			
ar	/ar/	car			
au	/aw/ that we may NOT use at the end of English words	sau-cer			
aw	/aw/ that we may use at the end of English words	saw			
ay	/A/ -- 2-letter /A/ that we may use at the end of English words	play			
ch	/ch/-/k/-/sh/	child	Christ-mas	chef	
ci	/sh/-- short /sh/	fa-cial			
ck	/k/ -- 2-letter /k/	back			
dge	/j/ -- 3-letter /j/	edge			
ea	/E/-/e/-/A/	eat	bread	steak	
ear	/er/	ear-ly			
ed	/ed/-/d/-/t/ -- past tense ending	trad-ed	pulled	picked	
ee	/E/ -- double /E/ always says /E/	tree			
ei	/A/-/E/-/i/ that we may NOT use at the end of English words	heir	cei-ling	for-eign	
eigh	/A/ -- 4-letter /A/	eight			
er	/er/	her			
ew	/OO/-/U/ that we may use at the end of English words	flew	few		
ey	/A/-/E/-/i/ that we may use at the end of English words	they	key	val-ley	
gn	/n/-- 2-letter /n/ used both at the beginning and end of a base word	gnat	sign		
ie	/E/-/I/-/i/	piece	pie	col-lie	
igh	/I/-- 3 letter /I/	night			
ir	/er/	first			
kn	/n/ -- 2-letter /n/ used only at the beginning of a base word	know			
ng	/ng/	sing			
oa	/O/ -- 2-letter /O/ that we may NOT use at the end of English words.	coat			
oe	/O/ -- 2-letter /O/ that we may use at the end of English words.	toe			
oi	/oy/ that we may NOT use at the end of English words *	boil			
oo	/OO/-/oo-/O/	food	good	floor	
or	/or/	Lord			
ou	/ow/-/O/-/OO/-/u/	house	soul	group	coun-try
ough	/O/-/OO/-/uff/-/off/-/aw/-/ow/ though through	rough	trough	thought	bough
ow	/ow/-/O/	plow	snow		
oy	/oy/ that we may use at the end of English words	boy			
ph	/f/ -- 2-letter /f/	phone			
sh	/sh/	she	dish		
si	/sh/-/zh/	ses-sion	di-vi-sion		
tch	/ch/ -- 3-letter /ch/	butch-er			
th	/th/- /TH/ (motor off/ motor on)	thin	this		
ti	/sh/ -- tall /sh/	na-tion			
ui	/OO/	fruit			
ur	/er/	church			
wh	/hw/	whis-per			
wor	/er/	wor-ships			
wr	/r/ -- 2-letter /r/	wreck			